EVALUATING RESEARCH ARTICLES

EVALUATING RESEARCH ARTICLES

SECOND EDITION

From Start To Finish

Ellen R. Girden

Sage Publications
International Educational and Professional Publisher
Thousand Oaks ■ London ■ New Delhi

For information:

Sage Publications, Inc.
2455 Teller Road
Thousand Oaks, California 91320
E-mail: order@sagepub.com

Sage Publications Ltd.
6 Bonhill Street
London EC2A 4PU
United Kingdom

Sage Publications India Pvt. Ltd.
M-32 Market
Greater Kailash I
New Delhi 110 048 India

Printed in the United States of America

Library of Congress Cataloging-in-Publication Data

Girden, Ellen R.
    Evaluating research articles from start to finish /
by Ellen R. Girden.—2nd ed.
        p. cm.
    Includes bibliographical references and index.
    ISBN 0-7619-2213-X (cloth: acid-free paper)
    ISBN 0-7619-2214-8 (pbk.: acid-free paper)
    1. Research—Evaluation.   2. Research—Statistical methods.
3. Research design.   I. Title.
    Q180.55.E9 G57 2000
    001.4—dc21   00-011858

02   03   10 9 8 7 6 5 4 3

Acquisition Editor: C. Deborah Laughton
Editorial Assistant: Eileen Carr
Production Editor: Sanford Robinson
Editorial Assistant: Kathryn Journey
Typesetter: Marion Warren
Indexer: Molly Hall
Cover Designer: Jane Quaney

Contents

Preface

 This book was written to fulfill a need of potential consumers of research, as well as eventual researchers. Although research design courses emphasize designs and appropriate statistical analyses, the stress is on *constructing* good designs. As a result, students may be able to apply their knowledge to originating research. But most consumers of research read articles based on original research and may be unable to apply that same knowledge to evaluating the article in terms of soundness of the design and appropriateness of the statistical analyses. Such an evaluation is crucial for a practitioner who might consider adapting methods based on results to his or her practice, whether it be education, sociology, psychology, medicine, dentistry, or any other field. The goal of this book is to fill the void.

This is intended to be a supplement to more intensive textbooks, rather than a book that teaches design and statistics. As such, the intended audience is assumed to be familiar with elementary research design and to have a knowledge of at least intermediate-level statistics. This book is not concerned with the merits of a study in terms of its theoretical importance. It focuses on the evaluation of a study that was selected by a potential user of that study's outcome to help the individual decide whether the outcome, indeed, can be used. And, although the emphasis is on evaluation of a finished product, the principles apply equally to designing a study.

Whereas previous evaluation books have emphasized well-designed studies and presented statistical analyses in separate sections, this book includes flawed studies and introduces interpretation and evaluation of appropriateness of the statistical analyses as they appear in the article.

This is the second edition of the book and, as the result of excellent feedback and suggestions by reviewers of the first edition, has many added features:

- With one exception, all chapters contain two articles to evaluate.
- All articles are up-to-date research: All were published after 1990, and most were published in 1999 or 2000.

- All introductions have been expanded and include some materials suggested by reviewers.
- Assumptions of statistical tests have been added to all relevant chapters.
- Every chapter includes a list of "caution factors," details in a study that the reader should focus on.
- Every chapter now has an added additional suggested readings list.
- A glossary of all relevant terms has been added.

There is, however, a word to be said about variability of the subject matter of the articles. Although every effort was made to include studies from a variety of areas, diversity had to be compromised because of a lack of studies in some fields with statistical analyses at an appropriate level for this book. I had the choice of using articles in hard-core experimental areas with analyses that were beyond the scope of the book or resampling the same area (e.g., nursing and related fields), where statistical analyses were more appropriate for the widest audience. I chose the latter course.

Following a reasonably lengthy introduction to the design and statistical analysis, each article is accompanied by evaluative questions. These questions are grouped into four categories: the rationale and purpose of the study, design of the study, statistical analyses of the data, and the conclusions reached by the author(s). You read an article by sections, and so evaluations are presented in that order. If, after studying this book, you read your selected articles with skepticism, I will have accomplished my goal.

Acknowledgments

I am very grateful for the extremely helpful suggestions made by the reviewers of the first edition of this book.

Dr. Robert Kabacoff was always available to clear up some problems in those areas that are not my expertise; thank you. I also extend thanks to the staff at Sage for their cooperation and patience, especially Eileen Carr. And I continue to be grateful to the editor, C. Deborah Laughton, for her guidance, support, friendship, and, above all, confidence in me.

I would like to thank the following individuals for use of their articles:

Dr. C. Baker

Dr. A. T. Ben-Ari

Dr. B. J. Blanz

Dr. K. B. Colling

Dr. D. J. Cox

Dr. J. Coyle-Shapiro

Dr. B. F. Fuller

Dr. C. L. Hanson

Dr. R. M. Kowalksi

S. McBride, Ed.D., R.N.

Dr. Kim P. Moore

Dr. B. C. Murphy

Dr. M. A. Nies

Dr. G. Nobes

Dr. P. W. Paese

Dr. R. Pasnak

Dr. A. W. Place

Dr. J. L. Pressler

Dr. M. C. Ross

Dr. J. C. Ross-Kerr

Dr. M. D. Schwartz

Dr. YunHee Shin

Dr. E. E. A. Skoe

Dr. S. Upchurch

Chapter 1

Introduction

The purpose of this book is to train students—potential consumers of research and researchers—to critically read a research article from start to finish. You will grow to understand an introduction, which sets the stage by describing the rationale for the study (i.e., what led to it) as well as the purpose of it (i.e., what the study hoped to accomplish). You will learn how to "dissect" the method section so that you can decide whether precautions were taken to guard against threats to internal validity, in terms of assignment of participants to the various conditions of the study and use of control procedures and groups. You will become more familiar with interpreting results and even with performing additional calculations or checking a particular result. Finally, you will evaluate the experimenter's discussion of the results in terms of the extent to which the conclusion is justified, can be generalized, and has limitations.

Studies are presented in order of increasing complexity. Each is prefaced with an introduction that describes the basic design and sta-

tistical analysis. Every effort has been made to locate examples of good as well as flawed studies in each of the categories, ones that performed statistical analyses that are commonly taught at intermediate and advanced levels. When it is feasible, articles are presented verbatim (even their own table numbers have been preserved). For the most part, however, sections have been excerpted and/or revised for clarity. Ellipses and bracketed phrases are used to indicate some changes. More extensive **revisions or synopses** are indented from the margins, enclosed in brackets, and *always appear in bold italics*. All of the chapters except one contain two examples of studies that employed a particular design. In these instances, the first study is evaluated by you (with my help). Copious notes are added to alert you about potential flaws or good aspects of the design. These are indicated by an arrow in the margin; they are enclosed in parentheses and always appear in italics. When we evaluate articles together, questions and answers are shaded to make them distinct. The second article is excerpted, and it is followed by a series of critical guide questions. At the end of the questions, a page number directs you to the answers, which are found in a separate section at the end of the book.

The remainder of this chapter presents a review of the bases of empirical research (controlled observations that are reliable and valid) followed by a review of potential trouble spots that can invalidate a conclusion about the effectiveness of an independent variable.

EMPIRICAL RESEARCH

There are three key concepts associated with empirical research: controlled observation, reliability, and validity. *Controlled observation* refers to the precision of conditions under which data are collected. In essence, any "noise" that can affect the data is eliminated, minimized, or counteracted in such a way that any other observer can replicate the conditions. Superfluous factors in the environment are eliminated or minimized by gathering data under uniform conditions; environmental distractions (e.g., sights or sounds) are the same for all participants, surrounding temperature is the same, the data collector is the "same" (at the same level of expertise throughout testing), or if more than one is used, they are equally distributed throughout the various groups, and so forth. These features ensure that the collected data will be objective, precise, and verifiable.

Reliability refers to a broad range of phenomena. Reliability means repeatability or consistency. Empirical research should be reliable: Under the same experimental conditions, anyone else should be able to obtain the same results (i.e., the outcome of data collection should lead to the same conclusion). Reliabil-

ity also refers to precision of our measuring instruments. Precise instruments are more likely to yield consistent measures than cruder instruments. A determination of 4 oz of liquid will be more reliable if a calibrated measuring cup rather than a drinking glass is used. Reliability also refers to the extent to which a test measures consistently or yields a "true" or accurate measure of whatever it is the test measures. That accuracy shows up in two ways: the repeatability of the score on more than one occasion and the same relative standing of the individuals in their group on more than one occasion. Scores have two parts to them, although in practice it is hard to separate the parts. One is called systematic variance, the accurate measure of the characteristic, and the other is nonsystematic or error variance, a part of the score that is due to factors other than the characteristic: The instrument was crude, the person doing the measuring was erratic, the person's motivation changed, and so on. The less that error variance, the more reliable the test. Several procedures can be used to establish reliability. One is *test-retest*. The same group of people is given the test on two occasions. This measures stability of the scores. If the scores each time really measure the characteristic accurately, approximately the same scores should be achieved each time, and the individuals' relative standing in the group should be the same (the highest score should be achieved by the same person each time, etc.). This applies to tests that measure relatively stable characteristics (e.g., intelligence) as opposed to unstable characteristics (e.g., mood). Instead of using the same test on two occasions, one can use alternate forms of the test, if available, which yield alternate-form reliability or *equivalence*. Another procedure is to compare scores within one test administration to measure *internal consistency,* the extent to which items within the test measure consistently. One may compare scores on one half of the test with those of the other half. This is interitem or *split-half* reliability. You could literally look at the first half versus the second half, or even numbers versus odd items. The rationale is that if all items measure the same characteristic, there should be a relationship or correlation between scores achieved on each half of the test. The *Kuder-Richardson* formula 20 is used to measure reliability of a test whose items can be scored right or wrong, and it measures the extent to which all participants answered each item appropriately. To the extent that they did, the items are considered equivalent, and the test is considered reliable. Similarly, the *Cronbach's alpha* reflects the extent to which there is agreement among participant responders on a test whose items are scaled or weighted, as in a Likert-like test in which numerical response choices might reflect ranges from *strongly agree* to *strongly disagree*. In all instances, measures of reliability are in the form of a correlation coefficient that ranges from 0.00 to .99. There is one other form of reliability that has been determined. If participants have to be judged for the extent to which they display some behavior, it is desirable that more than one judge do the rating and that we have some basis for deciding how accurate are the judgments. This is a problem solved by measuring *interrater reliability,* if a correlation is determined, or *interrater agreement,* if you are looking for percentage agreement. And as a general rule of thumb, coefficients should be at least .65 for any measure to be considered reliable.

Validity is the final key concept of empirical research. It is synonymous with appropriateness, meaningfulness, and usefulness. With regard to research, we want to know whether conclusions are valid; are they appropriate, meaningful, and useful on the bases of the in-

tent of the investigator and the procedures used to fulfill that intent? Related to this, was the characteristic (anxiety, mood, caring, intelligence, etc.) the investigator intended to manipulate the one that was manipulated (varied)? This is part of construct validity. Validity also is an important issue in testing. Tests are valid if they measure the characteristics they were intended to measure. *Content validity* refers to the extent to which all items reflect the characteristic. Do items of a mood test sample only good moods, or do they sample good, bad, sad, and apprehensive moods? *Criterion validity* refers to the extent to which test scores correlate with a behavior (the criterion) the test supposedly measures (concurrent validity) or the extent to which test scores predict that behavior (predictive validity). Scores on an intelligence test should correlate with scores on an achievement test and should predict college performance. Finally, *construct validity* refers to the extent to which the test measures the characteristic it intends to measure, because the characteristic cannot be measured directly. Construct validity is most difficult to establish. If scores on the test correlate with other measures of that characteristic, this would yield convergent validity. For example, scores on a trait anxiety scale should correlate with behavioral measures in anxiety-provoking situations. If scores on a test do not correlate with measures of other characteristics, using the same test or other tests or measurements, this would be evidence of discriminant validity. For example, scores on an intelligence test should not reflect introversion or extroversion and should be unrelated to scores on a test of self-esteem or mood. To the extent that an experimental procedure varies the intended construct (characteristic), all other things being equal, statements about it will be valid, that is, appropriate, meaningful, and useful.

THREATS TO INTERNAL VALIDITY

To evaluate the soundness of each design, you need to keep in mind potential sources of *confounds* or other explanations of results. These are variables that may be operating in conjunction with the manipulated independent variable and make it impossible to determine whether observed changes or differences in the dependent variable are due to the manipulation, the confound, or a combination of the two. Because these potential confounds may threaten the extent to which the conclusion is valid or justified (i.e., internal validity of the study), they are called threats to internal validity. Briefly, the threats include those that operate when the study entails a pretest and posttest or any other situation with or without a pretest and posttest.

■ Studies With Pretests and Posttests

History. This refers to any event occurring in the interim that directly or indirectly could affect the behavior being measured and therefore also could account for the results.

Maturation. This refers to any change within the participant that occurs during the interim and can just as easily account for posttest performance.

Instrumentation. This refers to any change in the measuring instrument and/or assessor from pre- to posttest that can just as easily explain a change in scores.

Initial testing. This refers to a change in posttest performance that results from pretest experience.

Regression toward the mean. This is a predicted shift in posttest scores when participants were specifically selected because their pretest scores were extremely high or low. Posttest scores are predicted to be less extreme, regardless of treatment effects.

■ Other Research Situations With or Without Pre- and Posttests

Selection bias. This refers to the assignment of participants to the various test conditions on a nonrandom basis. Differences in performance may be associated with a participant characteristic instead of, or along with, the independent variable.

Selective loss (mortality, attrition). This is the loss of particular participants from a group (or groups) in such a way that remaining participants no longer can be considered to be initially equivalent with respect to the dependent variable.

Diffusion of treatment. This is the unintentional spread of treatment to a control group (or groups) when participants receive information withheld from them (e.g., through conversation with experimental participants) that results in a smaller difference among group performances at posttreatment assessment.

Compensatory equalization. This refers to the administration of some treatment to a control group to compensate for its lack of the beneficial treatment being received by an experimental group. This reduces differences between posttreatment means of the groups.

Compensatory rivalry. This refers to behavior of a control group such that participants attempt to exceed performance of an experimental group because they are not receiving equal treatment. This reduces posttreatment differences between groups.

Resentful demoralization. This is a lowered level of performance by a control group because participants resent the lack of experimental treatment. This increases the differences between posttreatment group means.

Interaction effects. These refer to threats that operate on a select group of individuals that also could account for observed results (e.g., a historic event that affects one particular group of participants).

Hawthorne effect. This refers to a change (usually positive) in participants' behavior because they were assigned to a treatment group rather than because of the treatment itself.

Experimenter expectancy. This refers to a characteristic of the individual who is collecting the data. When a researcher (e.g., author of the article) tests the participants, his or her expectations for certain results unintentionally may affect participants so that they behave in accordance with the hypotheses. Concomitantly, recording errors may be made, also in the direction of a hypothesis.

THREATS TO STATISTICAL CONCLUSION VALIDITY

In most instances of experimentation, the conclusions reached by the researcher are based on the outcomes of statistical analyses. Typically, this involves rejection or retention of a null hypothesis. When the null hypothesis is retained, the researcher concludes that there was insufficient evidence for a difference between group means (or whatever statistic was being evaluated). If treatment truly was ineffective, the conclusion is correct. However, if treatment effectiveness simply was not evident in the statistical analysis, the conclusion is erroneous, a Type II error. When the null hypothesis is rejected, the researcher concludes that there was evidence for a difference between group means, that the independent variable was effective. If this is so, the conclusion is correct. However, if treatment actually was ineffective, then the researcher's conclusion is erroneous. A Type I error has been committed. Box 1.1 summarizes the Type I and Type II errors.

Any factor that leads to a Type I or Type II error is a threat to validity of the statistical conclusion. Briefly, these threats include the following:

Insufficient power of statistical test. This is one of the most prevalent causes of a Type II error. Power refers to the likelihood of rejecting a null hypothesis that is false or correctly declaring a difference in some statistic significant. Assuming that a difference of a particular magnitude is anticipated, sample sizes have to be large enough to detect that difference. Often, because of research constraints, an insufficient number of participants are tested, not enough to reveal the effect of an independent variable,

---

BOX 1.1
Summary of Type I
and Type II Errors

| Type I | Rejecting the null hypothesis when it is true |
| Type II | Retaining the null hypothesis when it is not true |

---

particularly one whose effect is of small magnitude. Had the sample been large enough, had the significance level of the statistical test been less stringent, and/or had a more powerful statistical test been performed on the data, the effect would have been detected. Better studies include a prior analysis of the sample size required, when estimates of variance (variability in performance) are available, to obtain a difference or effect of given magnitude at a certain significance level. The flip side of the coin also should be mentioned. If samples are very, very large, almost any effect can be significant, and this could lead to a Type I error.

Unreliable instrument. If the measuring instrument is not reliable (does not measure consistently), performances will be variable, the error term of the statistical test will be inflated, and a true difference between means may not be evident.

Varied test conditions. If testing conditions are not uniform, within and between groups, performances will be variable and a true difference between means may not be evident.

Varied participant characteristics. If participants differ in age, gender, intelligence, or other characteristics that are related to the dependent variable measure, performances will be variable and a true difference between means may not be evident.

Violation of statistical assumptions. All statistical tests have underlying assumptions. If at least one is seriously violated, and the statistical test is not robust with respect to violation of certain assumptions, the analyses may fail to reveal a difference that truly exists (Type II error) or may reveal a difference that is really due to chance (Type I error).

Fishing. When an unreasonable number of statistical tests are conducted on the same data, by chance alone, one may reveal what appears to be a significant difference. This threat, which leads to a Type I error, can be reduced by statistical adjustments that effectively lower the probability level needed to declare any comparison significant.

Although there are also threats to construct and external validity, we can address the issues as they arise. These relate to the extent to which the intended construct (e.g., intelligence, stress, etc.) was manipulated and/or measured by a reliable and valid test and the extent to which obtained results can be generalized.

PLAN OF THE CRITIQUES

Questions within or after each article are designed to guide you step by step as you read. Questions will appear throughout the articles we are evaluating together. These are posed twice because they are questions that you should be asking yourself while you are reading an article. Two parts of an article are not addressed: the Abstract—a concise summary of the study—and References. You start with the **rationale** for the study. This lets you know what, in the past literature, aroused the investigator's interest in the subject matter to begin with: inconsistent or contradictory findings, a possible confound in earlier studies, curiosity, a logical deduction from a theory that could be tested, and so forth. Always ask yourself: What was the rationale for the study? Next, you move on to the **purpose** of the study. This lets you know exactly what the investigators intended to accomplish. Often, it is expressed in terms of testing particular hypotheses. Sometimes, it is expressed in terms of what the authors wanted to demonstrate or determine. Always ask yourself: What was the purpose or reason for conducting this study? The **method** section is next. You focus on participants first. You want to know who were tested, how they were recruited, whether participants were randomly selected or assigned, matched, lost because of attrition, and so on. Here is where you want to consider that groups may not have been initially equivalent. Next, you might want to look at tests that were used. If they are not well known, you want assurance that they are reliable and valid, and always consider the possibility that they might not be so. If more than one is included, you want assurance that they were presented in counterbalanced order. Finally, the rationales given for using the particular tests should indicate that they are appropriate for fulfilling the purpose of the study.

The procedure section focuses on what was done. A question about **general procedure** tests your basic understanding of what was done to the participants or what they were required to do. Specific questions alert you to possible sources of confounds (e.g., a shift in testing conditions, a failure to assess a manipulation, testing performed by the researcher rather than by a naive experimenter, etc.).

The questions relating to **results** of the study focus on appropriate analyses of the data. Readers always assume that no mistakes have been made and that assumptions underlying all tests have been met. This is not always true, and the outcome can be serious: A mistake in calculations can change the conclusion reached by the investigators. Hopefully, you will remember enough to check on the accuracy of degrees of freedom for independent and dependent t tests and analysis of variance, as well as appropriateness of the alpha levels used, especially for planned and post hoc comparisons. These points will be reviewed in the introduction to the article. Specific questions address these issues. Consider them as quick checks. If they are correct, hopefully, the calculations are accurate. Unfortunately, this will not tell you whether the statistical test is appropriate nor if basic assumptions have been met. But even here, quick checks are possible. If standard deviations are given, you can square the values to obtain variances and form simple ratios of the largest to the smallest to see whether there is homogeneity of variance. If the study involves repeated measures, you can check the significance of F ratios with $df = 1$ and $N - 1$ to see whether they are still significant. This checks the validity of statistical conclusions if lack of circularity—equality of variances of differences—has not been considered. If F ratios still are significant, results (at least statistical) are valid. If not, conclusions about means differences may not be warranted. Again, each will be reviewed with the relevant article.

BOX 1.2
**Essential Features
of a Critique**

Feature	Relevant Question(s)
Rationale	What is the reason for conducting the study?
Purpose	What does the researcher intend to accomplish?

Method

Participants	How were participants selected? Assigned? Which, if any, were lost?
Apparatus	Were measuring instruments reliable? Valid?
Procedure	What did participants do? How were they measured? With what? Who measured them? Were testing conditions uniform? Were factors other than the independent variable operating?
Results	How were data analyzed? Was analysis appropriate? Accurate?
Discussion	What were major conclusions? Are they justified (valid)? Can results be generalized? To which population(s)?

The final section of the report is the **discussion.** It is here that the researchers reach some conclusion regarding the outcome of their manipulation—for example, its effectiveness. It is here that questions deal with the validity of the conclusion. You will be asked to consider that threats to internal validity might not have been eliminated, rendering the conclusion unjustified. And because the intent of the study is to generalize the results, you may be asked to consider issues related to external validity (i.e., limitations in the extent to which results will generalize).

The relevant features of a critique are summarized in Box 1.2.

TWO SAMPLE STUDIES

Before beginning our detailed analyses, let's consider two studies in abbreviated form, both of which compare two group means but differ in the extent to which valid conclusions can be drawn. Both use two distinct groups of participants. In both cases, the groups are not formed by random assignment. Instead, they are based on differences that exist between the participants of each group. The first study does not attempt to match the participants on important variables that could account for group differences just as easily as the factor that makes each group unique. The second study does attempt such a matching procedure.

STUDY EXAMPLE 1.1

The present study compared reported health-promoting lifestyles among older African American women who lived below or above the poverty level of $7,360. Thus, poverty level is the basis for differentiating the two groups.

The Study

Brady, B., & Nies, M. A. (1999). A comparison of older African American women above and below poverty level. *Journal of Holistic Nursing, 17*(2), 197-207. Copyright 1999 by Sage.

[Poverty has been a major barrier to a healthy lifestyle among African American women in terms of their health status, use of health services, and mortality. The elderly have chronic health problems that are attributed to obesity because of lack of exercise, a sedentary lifestyle, and earlier age at first childbirth. Research suggests that exercise can reduce the risk of some of these chronic health problems by enhancing the quality of life of the elderly. Two thirds of African American women (vs. more than one half of all women) do not exercise. There are few studies of the health-promoting benefits for older African American women. Moreover, studies show that income level is correlated with health behavior, but this association in African Americans has not received much attention and has not been related to exercise. The purpose of this study was to compare the health-promoting lifestyles and exercise behaviors of African American women, above and below the poverty level, who lived in a community. The hypothesis was "that older African American women living above the poverty level will practice more health-promoting behaviors as measured by the Health-Promoting Lifestyle Profile (HPLP) than women living below the poverty level."]

Method

Design, Sample, and Setting

A descriptive study design was used for this pilot study. The convenience sample consisted of 58 African American women, 50 years of age and older, living in the community. The participants were recruited with the assistance of the pastor from a local Baptist church in the mid-South. All women 50 years of age and older attending the church were invited to participate in the study. A notice was placed in the church bulletin to encourage participation. The data collection took place on a Sunday after service in the Baptist church Bible study room. A brief description of the study was given to the women by the researcher and informed consent was obtained before completing the instruments.

▶ *(Note that all participants were volunteers who were asked to participate in the church after church services. Thus, some may have been more willing than others to take part. And all were Baptists.)*

Instruments

Instruments . . . included a demographic data sheet and the health-promoting lifestyle profile HPLP. . . . The demographic data sheet included information about (a) age, (b) income, (c) marital status, (d) education, and (e) assistance with income.

The HPLP is a 48-item measure with a Likert response format: *never, sometimes, often,* or *routinely.* . . . The six HPLP subscales and sample items are as follows: *self-actualization* ("am enthusiastic and optimistic about life"), *health responsibility* ("have my blood pressure checked and know what it is"), *exercise* ("engage in recreational physical activities"), *nutrition* ("eat breakfast"), *interpersonal support* ("discuss personal problems and concerns with person close to me"), and *stress management* ("take some time for relaxation each day").

On development, the HPLP was found to have high internal consistency, with an alpha coefficient of .92. The six subscales were also found to have a relatively high internal consistency. The correlations for the scales ranged from .90, for self-actualization, to .70 for stress management. . . . Test-retest reliability was $r = .93$ for the total scale and ranged from .81 to .91 for the subscales. . . . The instrument has been used with various ethnic groups, including . . . African Americans . . . and provided reliable and valid data.

The HPLP was scored by obtaining the mean of all 48 items on the total scale. The subscale of exercise was scored in a similar manner. Possible scores of the HPLP and exercise subscales ranged from 1.0 to 4.0. The alpha reliability coefficient of the HPLP in this study was .90. The exercise subscale of the HPLP consisted of five self-reported exercise behaviors. The alpha coefficient for the exercise subscale was .69.

▶ *(Note that the test was shown to be reliable, but validity measures are not reported. Furthermore, the sample question about nutrition asks about eating breakfast, which may or may not include a nutritious one. Likewise, the exercise subscale asks about "recreational physical activities," yet such activities as walking to a bus stop and housecleaning also are physical activities. Notice, too, that the reliability coefficient for this scale was lower than that for the group on which reliability first was established.)*

Procedure

. . . Women entered the room, and each was asked to sign a consent form before being handed the demographic sheet and HPLP instrument. . . . A brief description of the study and the importance of the study was given by the researcher. The importance of filling out the instruments and the availability of the researcher to assist if needed was discussed. An African American female facilitator assisted with data collection and encouraged women to participate in the study. On completion of the instruments, each was collected and examined by the researcher for completeness. . . . [Data were organized] for participants living above and below poverty levels.

▶ *(Note again that the women were encouraged to participate. Moreover, the researcher was available to assist anyone needing help in filling out the questionnaire and, if anyone did require assistance, inadvertently may have influenced the way some of the questions were answered. Most important, the two groups were formed on the basis of information provided in the demographic sheet. Although this was the only way to form the groups, poverty level is not the only factor that differentiates them. A more desirable procedure would be to match the two groups on other relevant variables, such as education and health status.)*

Results

. . . The mean age of the 58 African American women was 60.1 years, with a range of 51 to 88 years. Table 1 shows that of the 58 African American women, 26 (44.8%) had individual incomes below the poverty level and 32 (55.2%) had individual incomes above the poverty level of $7,360. Their education ranged from less than high school to college graduates. Frequency distribution of marital status and assistance with income (financial support provided by another person) are also shown in Table 1.

▶ *(Note that there is no way of telling from Table 1 what percentage of those above poverty level had been graduated from college and high school. Presumably, this would apply to a large percentage, but it is not necessarily so. Likewise, a large percentage were married or widowed, but we don't know their economic level. Married women, for example, would be more likely to*

TABLE 1 Demographic Characteristics ($N = 58$)

Characteristics	Group	n	%
Socioeconomic status	Above poverty	32	55.4
	Below poverty	26	44.8
Assistance with income	None	32	55.2
	Family	7	12.1
	Spouse	13	22.4
	Friend	2	3.4
	Missing	4	6.9
Education	Below high school	12	20.7
	High school	30	51.7
	Some college	10	17.2
	College graduate	5	8.6
	Missing	1	1.7
Marital status	Married	19	32.8
	Divorced	6	10.3
	Single	5	8.6
	Widowed	28	48.3

receive interpersonal support because their spouses are readily available. If they were mainly among the above-poverty group, this in part could explain their higher scores on the HPLP.)

The research hypothesis was supported. Participants living above the poverty level had higher overall scores on the HPLP ($M = 2.85$, $SD = .40$) than African American women living below the poverty level ($M = 2.51$, $SD = .51$), $t(56) = -2.79$, $p = .007$.

The range of scores of the total HPLP, along with the range of scores for the two income groups of African American women, [is] shown in Table 2. The total range of scores for the exercise subscale for African American women is shown in Table 3 along with the range of scores for the two income groups.

▶ *(Note that upper ranges of the total HPLP scores were very similar for both groups, whereas lower-range scores differed; those below the poverty level had a large range of scores, along with greater variability. Exercise scores, on the other hand, showed identical lower-range scores but differed on the upper range. And, although not reported, the two means are significantly different.)*

TABLE 2 Range of Scores for Total HPLP

Group	Range	M	SD
Total women (*n* = 58)	1.50-3.56	2.71	.48
Above poverty (*n* = 32)	1.90-3.56	2.85	.40
Below poverty (*n* = 26)	1.50-3.53	2.51	.51

NOTE: HPLP = Health Promoting Lifestyle Profile.

TABLE 3 Range of Scores for the Exercise Subscale

Group	Range	M	SD
Total women (*n* = 58)	1.00-3.60	2.05	.81
Above poverty (*n* = 32)	1.00-3.60	2.30	.77
Below poverty (*n* = 26)	1.00-3.40	1.72	.76

NOTE: HPLP = Health Promoting Lifestyle Profile.

Discussion

Findings from this study indicate that African American women living above poverty level engage in more health-promoting behaviors than do African American women living below poverty level. . . .

▶ *(Note that the conclusion is inappropriate. Health-promoting behaviors were not observed; they were reported. Because validity measures for the questionnaire were not offered, we don't know the extent to which test items accurately reflect behavior. Moreover, we don't know the accuracy of the self-reports.)*

The mean scores of African American women on the exercise subscale of this study were also low. . . . The five-item scale based on self-reported exercise behaviors was ranked as 1 (*never*), 2 (*sometimes*), 3 (*often*), and 4 (*always*). Thus, even if a woman never exercised, the mean score would be 1.0.

▶ *(Note that scores might have been higher if all forms of exercise, not just recreational, were reported.)*

Researchers for a previous study found that there was no significant difference in exercise behaviors between young, middle-aged, and older adults. In
fact, exercise had the lowest score of all six variables on the HPLP. . . .

Implications for holistic nursing, primary prevention, and primary care
practice include acknowledging and encouraging African American women
who do use health-promoting behaviors, especially exercise or some form of
physical activity in their daily life. . . .

For African American women living below poverty level, specific prescrip-
tions for exercise need to be developed that are culturally specific, practical,
and inexpensive. . . .

▶ *(This is misleading, because it implies that exercise is a main factor that
accounts for the difference in HPLP between the two groups. First, other
subscale differences were not considered, and they may have differed as well.
Second, factors that are not associated with one group being at below
poverty level and another group at above poverty level may account for the
differences in health-promoting behaviors [e.g., health status, intelligence,
childhood rearing, marital history, closeness with family members, etc.].
Third, we don't know the extent to which "encouraged" participation and
help in completing the questionnaire unintentionally affected responses and
did so for one group more than the other. Thus, if groups were matched on all
non-poverty level variables and were tested by a naive [with respect to the
purpose of the study] individual, it would be possible to reach a valid
conclusion.)*

STUDY EXAMPLE 1.2

This next study concerns developmental differences between two groups of newborn babies:
those born to insulin-dependent diabetic mothers and those born to mothers without diabetes.
Because measures were taken on two different days, the statistical analyses involved more than
just *t* tests. However, those results can be summarized without getting into these statistics, which
we'll cover in a later chapter.

The Study

Pressler, J. L., Hepworth, J. T., LaMontagne, L. L., Sevcik, R. H., &
Hesselink, L. F. (1999). Behavioral responses of newborns of insulin-
dependent and nondiabetic, healthy mothers. *Clinical Nursing Research, 8*(2), 103-118. Copyright 1999 by Sage.

[Mother-child interactions begin before and shortly after birth. The mother's reactions in part depend on the physical condition of the newborn. Of some concern is the newborn baby of a mother with insulin-dependent diabetes. Several studies have shown such babies to be slower to develop, as measured by the Neonatal Behavioral Assessment Scale. Other studies have found no differences between these babies and ones born to healthy mothers. These earlier studies focused on the mother's control of glucose during pregnancy. But there is a need to consider other aspects of pregnancy and delivery as well. The present study attempted to control for "type of delivery, labor and delivery medications, parity, race/ethnicity, and maternal education" to evaluate development of newborns of diabetic mothers (NDM) and to healthy mothers.]

Method

Participants

A convenience sample of 40 term newborns whose mothers had been cared for within the antenatal clinics of a metropolitan medical center and whose maternal diabetes had been closely monitored for glucose control and complications throughout pregnancy, was matched with 40 newborns of nondiabetic, healthy mothers (controls) for type of delivery, labor and delivery medications, parity, race/ethnicity, and maternal education. . . . Any pregnant diabetic mother who experienced complications related to diabetes or whose glucose levels were unable to be managed by her obstetrician was not considered eligible for this study.

▶ *(Note that nothing is said about how many clinics were involved nor whether both groups of participants were drawn from all or just one clinic. If prenatal care is more efficient in one clinic, then this might be a factor that further differentiates the groups.)*

Twenty-three of the NDMs and 18 of the controls were male, and 17 of the NDMs and 22 of the controls were female. Newborns' 5-minute Apgar scores were at least seven, admission physical examinations were assessed to be normal, no major congenital anomalies were evident, and none were placed under different from ordinary assessment protocols. Only newborns who were 37 to 42 weeks gestation . . . were studied, and there was no difference in gestational age between groups, $t(78) = .25$, $p = .80$. The NDMs had an average gestational age of 39.08 weeks ($SD = 1.47$) compared with controls' mean age of 39.15 weeks ($SD = 1.19$). Mean birth weights were 3,660 g ($SD = 542$) for the NDMs and 3,239 g ($SD = 298$) for the controls, $t(60.5) = 4.31$, $p < .01$.

▷ *(Note that the df for the weight t ratio is 60.5, but it should be 40 + 40 − 2 = 78. When the t is calculated using the means and standard deviations given and 40 in each group, the t is as presented, 4.31. Therefore, the reported df of 60.5 is a typographical error. It is equally important to note that not only do the two mean weights differ significantly, so does variability. This can be checked by forming a ratio between $542^2/298^2 = 3.308$. According to an F table [to be covered in a later chapter], the 3.308 is significant at p < .01. This indicates that there was a greater range of weight in the NDM group than in the healthy mothers group.)*

Of the 40 matched newborn pairs studied, 26 pairs were delivered vaginally and 14 were delivered by cesarean birth. Twelve mothers received either no medications before delivery or only a local anesthetic, 4 received analgesics and a local anesthetic, 19 received epidural anesthetics and analgesics, and 5 received general anesthesia and analgesics. Fifteen were firstborn and 25 were later-born pairs; 34 were Caucasian and 6 were African American.

▷ *(Note that these figures for type of delivery add up to 40. This indicates that both groups were perfectly matched on one critical potentially confounding factor, method of birth delivery.)*

The Neonatal Behavioral Assessment Scale (NBAS)

The Brazelton NBAS . . . was used to assess newborn behavior. At present, the NBAS is the more reliable measure of the neonate's interactive responses on a wide range of behavior in an interactional process. . . . The exam takes approximately 25 to 45 minutes to administer. In addition to the 20 reflex items, the NBAS exam contains 27 behavioral variables, scored for optimal performance, with 8 of the behavioral variables receiving a second score for modal performance, bringing the total number of items to 55.

. . . A modal response score can be created that represents the most frequently occurring orientation responses. . . . Higher scores on the reflex functioning dimension of the NBAS indicate poorer performance. Higher scores on the remaining behavioral dimensions and the modal response score indicate better performance. For the current study, the optimal score for the range of state dimension, which is an average score of those items contained within this dimension, was considered to be 3.

▷ *(Note that the test used to measure the infants is known to be reliable and valid.)*

Procedure and Data Analysis

The three NBAS examiners involved in this study received formal certification for NBAS administration and scoring. Interscorer reliability among these certified examiners was achieved when they were in at least 90% agreement on three tests. . . . Prior to data collection, interobserver agreement, allowing for a one-point discrepancy, was .93. All NBAS examiners maintained greater than a .90 level of reliability when intermittent reliability checks were completed during data collection.

All insulin-dependent diabetic mothers whose newborns met the selection criteria were approached for participation during early labor or during the first 12 hours postdelivery. After obtaining each NDM participant, control newborns were consecutively obtained when matched for the five maternal variables. All mothers gave informed consent for their newborns' participation in the study. All newborns were examined using the NBAS on the first and second days, at 12 to 24 hours and again at 36 to 48 hours of postnatal life. . . .

▶ *(Note that all examiners were well qualified and that data were included only when there was a high degree of interscorer agreement. This leads to reliable data. Note, too, that the healthy mothers had to be recruited after the diabetic mothers were recruited to ensure adequate matching. It would have been useful, however, to know how long after the diabetic mothers were recruited the healthy mothers were recruited, to estimate the time lapse between testing the NDM babies and the babies of healthy mothers.)*

Results

There were no differences between the groups on socioeconomic status (SES) as evaluated using Hollingshead's . . . four factor index of social status $t(78) = .98$, $p = .33$ . . . or on the first month seen by a physician during the pregnancy, $t(78) = 1.07$, $p = .29$. Diabetic mothers had an average SES score of 33.4 ($SD = 16.4$) and were first seen in the clinics at month 3.05 ($SD = 1.60$). The control mothers had an average SES score of 30.0 ($SD = 14.0$) and were first seen at month 3.42 ($SD = 1.53$).

As a reflection of the close monitoring of the diabetic mothers, differences were found between the groups on the number of prenatal visits, $t(61.6) = 3.92$, $p < .01$; the number of hospitalizations, $t(39.0) = 8.20$, $p < .01$; and the average number of prenatal visits, $t(62.4) = 3.85$, $p < .01$. The diabetic mothers had more prenatal visits ($M = 13.12$, $SD = 4.99$), more hospitalizations ($M = 1.52$, $SD = 1.18$), and more prenatal visits per month of prenatal care ($M = 1.92$, $SD = .64$) than control mothers ($M = 9.58$, $SD = 2.82$; $M = 0.00$, $SD = 0.00$; and $M = 1.47$, $SD = .37$, respectively).

▶ *(Note that the dfs reported for all three t tests are wrong and reflect typographical errors. Each should have 78 dfs, and when these t values were recalculated with the correct df, the same ts were obtained. Note, too, that the additional visits might put the diabetic group at an advantage. If the mothers-to-be were too sick, on the other hand, they would not have carried to term and would not have given birth to babies that weighed more than those born to healthy mothers.)*

The mean scores and standard deviations are presented in Table 2. . . . Only the significant results are presented here.

TABLE 2 Mean Scores and Standard Deviations, by Maternal Health Status and Time of Testing

		NDMs		Controls	
		Day 1	Day 2	Day 1	Day 2
Response decrement	M	6.58	6.38	7.20	5.85
	SD	1.43	.92	.97	.53
	n	6	6	6	6
Orientation	M	7.18	7.27	7.35	7.53
	SD	.83	.86	1.02	.83
	n	37	37	37	37
Range of state	M	1.95	1.76	1.93	1.93
	SD	.80	.91	.60	.90
	n	40	40	40	40
Motor processes	M	4.96	5.38	5.31	5.73
	SD	.76	.70	.73	.51
	n	40	40	40	40
Autonomic stability	M	6.07	6.37	6.18	6.41
	SD	1.07	1.00	.93	.77
	n	40	40	40	40
Regulation of state	M	3.98	4.16	4.78	4.51
	SD	2.12	2.04	2.19	2.04
	n	40	40	40	40
Reflex functioning	M	1.53	.93	.73	.13
	SD	1.26	1.54	1.11	.52
	n	40	40	40	40
Modal responses	M	6.57	6.89	6.84	7.20
	SD	1.13	.92	1.18	.91
	n	35	35	35	35

NOTE: NDM = Newborn of insulin-dependent diabetic mother.

Significant differences were found between NDMs and their matched controls on motor processes, $t(78) = 2.951$, $p < .01$; and reflex functioning, $t(78) = 5.551$, $p < .01$.

▶ *(Actually, F values were presented, but* F $= t^2$, *so the values presented are the square root of F. Also note that, because of sizes of the standard deviations, not all babies in the NDM group were slower. Some fit within the normal range.)*

The NDMs' motor performances were poorer than comparison newborns' motor performances and NDMs also had significantly more abnormal reflexes than their matched controls. . . .

Time of testing effects were found for response decrement, . . . autonomic stability, . . . reflex functioning, . . . and modal performance. . . . Except for the response decrement dimension, there was better performance on Day 2 than on Day 1 for motor processes, autonomic stability, reflex functioning, and modal performance. . . . None of the effects for orientation, range of state, or regulation of state were significant.

Discussion

Controlling for the maternal variables identified in this study, term NDMs evidenced a number of behaviors in motor processes and reflex functioning that would portray them as more lethargic and listless than their matched healthy controls. Also, the means for the NDMs on all behavioral dimensions were in the direction that one would expect for a tired and/or listless baby. The results also revealed that motor processes, autonomic stability, reflex functioning, and modal performance improved for both NDMs and control newborns after 24 hours, but the performance of NDMs on these dimensions was not as robust as that of healthy controls.

The poorer motor and reflex functioning of the NDMs might pose a challenge for parents. Mothers of NDMs need to be informed that their newborns might exhibit different behaviors from typical, healthy newborns and, consequently, present natural behavioral barriers toward effective parent-infant interaction. . . .

A limitation of the current study was that actual mother- infant interaction was not measured. Future investigations need to be conducted using both behavioral and interactive measures so that a knowledge base can be developed, with respect to any differences that might exist in newborn behavioral and early postnatal interactions of NDMs and their mothers compared with newborns of nondiabetic, healthy mothers. . . .

Finally, the findings of this study support the research of other investigators who found that even closely monitored and/or well-controlled diabetes during pregnancy can adversely affect NDMs' early behaviors. . . . It also emphasizes the importance of considering a number of maternal background variables in the design of the future studies, when the aim is to understand the influence of maternal diabetes on newborns' behavioral responses.

▷ *(This is the basic conclusion, that newborns of diabetic mothers can be slower in certain reflex and motor behaviors soon after birth. The implication is that the mother's physiology, particularly blood-sugar level, has an adverse effect on the prenatal baby. Diabetic women not only take insulin but also carefully monitor how much they eat from each food group. This is part of the treatment of diabetes. There is, however, a psychological side as well, a possible increase in stress as one tries to cope. To the extent that there is increased stress, there is an increase in stress hormones, which also might affect the fetus. What is important is that the effect on newborns to some part of having diabetes might be responses to slower development during the first 3 to 4 days that were the focus of the study. The samples were very well matched, ruling out as possible confounds a host of variables that might be associated with prenatal care and delivery. On these bases, the conclusion is justified. The only question is whether both groups of mothers were drawn from the same clinics. To the extent that they were, the conclusion holds up. To the extent that they were not, there might be differences in quality of prenatal care that might contribute to the observed differences in babies and that might even be unrelated to diabetes.)*

BIBLIOGRAPHY

Cook, T. D., & Campbell, D. T. (1979). *Quasi-experimentation: Design & analysis issues for field settings.* Chicago: Rand McNally.

Isaac, S., & Michael, W. B. (1995). *Handbook in research and evaluation* (3rd ed.). San Diego, CA: EdiTS.

Kasdin, A. E. (1992). *Research design in clinical psychology* (2nd ed.). Boston: Allyn & Bacon.

McMillan, J. H., & Schumacher, S. (1997). *Research in education: A conceptual introduction* (4th ed.). White Plains, NY: Longman.

Neale, J. M., & Liebert, R. M. (1986). *Science and behavior: An introduction to methods of research* (3rd ed.). Englewood Cliffs, NJ: Prentice Hall.

Additional Suggested Readings

Mason, E. G., & Bramble, W. J. (1997). *Handbook in research and evaluation* (3rd ed.). Dubuque, IA: Brown & Benchmark.

Pedhazur, E. J., & Schmelkin, L. P. (1991). *Measurement, design, and analysis: An integrated approach.* Hillsdale, NJ: Lawrence Erlbaum.

Vockell, E. L., & Asher, J. W. (1995). *Educational research* (2nd ed.). Englewood Cliffs, NJ: Prentice Hall.

Chapter 2

Case Studies

 This chapter is concerned with a descriptive method of assessing behavior. Case studies appear in all of the social sciences and are examples of *qualitative research,* studies conducted under conditions that are not controlled, in contrast to empirical research, which is conducted under controlled conditions (although it can be more rigorous than casual observation within a given setting, e.g., a therapist's office). The *case study* involves extensive observation of a single individual, several individuals, or a single group of individuals as a unit. In clinical psychology, observations generally are made before, during, and after some intervention. But what occurs goes beyond a mere observation of the individual or individuals because of the intervention. Despite the fact that intervention is neither systematic nor methodical, there is sufficient justification for studying a single individual. The study may suggest factors that precipitate a disorder, concern a rarely occurring disorder, involve a treatment that is in limited supply, lead to the development of a new treatment, provide the opportunity to use a common technique in a novel way, and/or provide evidence against a generally held principle. Because of the nature of the study, only descriptive statistics are possible as indicators of changes in the targeted behavior. Likewise, because of the laxity of such studies (e.g., nonsystematic introduction of treatment), only tentative cause-effect conclusions are possible. Potentially, many threats to internal validity plausibly can account for the obtained results, with the exception of instrumentation, initial testing, and regression toward the mean. The extent to which these threats play a role, however, depends on whether objective measures of behavior are made, when they are made, and whether more than one case is studied at a time.

Case studies range from those that are purely descriptive, with no measurements made, to those that include elementary descriptions of some behavior (e.g., frequencies, means, etc.). The latter extend from those that include pre- and posttreatment measures to those, better controlled, that include continuous monitoring.

Whereas clinical psychologists intend to attribute a behavioral change to an intervention (arrive at a cause-effect conclusion), other social scientists, such as ethnographists and anthropologists, strive to understand a single phenomenon: how the natural flow of events is perceived by the individual or group (unit); what it means to that individual or group in terms of feelings, ideals, thoughts, actions, and beliefs. Because these scientists believe that actions are affected by the context in which they occur, they collect lots of data over time in a specific setting, and generalizations about these actions are context-bound. Thus, *ethnographic analysis* is a description of some social event in which participants re-create their shared feelings, beliefs, actions, and knowledge about it. What is constructed by the group is reconstructed by researchers to give some understanding of what the event means to participants and how it is perceived by them. Some studies are exploratory, which may lead to the development of a concept or model (e.g., determining how a minority group feels about its treatment in a hospital); some studies attempt to describe and analyze a particular situation, event, or process (e.g., why neighbors didn't respond to the cries of a woman who was being raped); some studies focus on social beliefs, customs, and practices; some evaluate a program (e.g., how effective is the "One Florida" program, which eliminates racial quotas in college admissions, contract awards, etc.); some examine policy issues (e.g., how teachers feel about mandatory summer school); some studies are part of large-scale investigations (e.g., as part of an assessment of health practices in a hospital, the perceptions of one group of patients may be studied); and

some studies are precursors to quantitative studies (e.g., interview results may suggest research questions or hypotheses that can be explored in more controlled situations). In all cases, data can be gathered by observation, interviews, and examination of documents; individuals will be selected to participate; and someone will gather the information and interpret it. Internal validity is an issue when cause-effect relationships are concluded. Here, you are concerned with the participants who volunteered. Did any who were approached refuse to participate? Nonresponders might act (or answer) differently. How reliable are their statements? Do they remember accurately? Can they judge themselves accurately? And you are concerned about the data collector. Could his or her views bias the interaction with participants, the interpretation of data, or both?

The major points to consider and sources of confounds or threats to internal validity, which I'll call "caution factors," are summarized in Box 2.1.

In this chapter, we examine two case studies. We evaluate the first together; the second is evaluated only by you. The former is an example of ethnographic analysis, with some members of a minority group as the unit of study. It has no objective measures of the targeted behavior but instead analyzes narrative reports of their experiences. The latter case study, also an ethnographic analysis, includes an analysis of interviews of minority students for themes that reflect their experience as doctoral students in a program that includes mainly dominant-culture students. It does include one test to objectively measure attitudes. However, no statistics are reported.

BOX 2.1
Caution Factors
and What You
Should Look for
in Case Studies

- The reason the case was selected
- The nature of intervention, if any
- The objectivity of behavioral assessment
- The assessor of behavior
- The past and/or present factors, besides intervention, that could also change the behavior
- The method of selecting participants in a singe unit
- The reliability and validity of interview questions
- The extent to which investigator bias might color interpretation

STUDY EXAMPLE 2.1

This case study is of members of an Indian tribe in Canada who were treated in hospitals by care-givers who are part of the majority. The investigators were interested in the patients' perception of the care they received. Each was interviewed for 2 hours, and their narratives were analyzed for recurrent themes. The study includes no objective measures of behavior but relies on the memories of the patients and the interpretations of the narratives by investigators and, therefore, is potentially open to several threats to internal validity.

The Study

Baker, C., & Daigle, M. C. (2000). Cross-cultural hospital care as experienced by Mi'kmaq clients. *Western Journal of Nursing Research, 22*(1), 8-28. Copyright 2000 by Sage.

Members of cultural minority groups may find themselves surrounded by people whose values, beliefs, and interpretations differ significantly from their own during hospitalization. This often is the case for Canada's aboriginal population, as many live in culturally distinct communities. Few studies have examined their perceptions of being cared for in nonaboriginal settings, but the limited data available suggest this can be a problematic experience for them. . . . To promote healing among clients from minority cultural communities, it is important for nurses to understand the phenomenon of receiving care in an unfamiliar culture. This exploratory study examined how members of the Big Cove, Mi'kmaq First Nation Community in the province of New Brunswick, subjectively experienced being cared for in a nonaboriginal institution. It is part of a larger project investigating the hospital experiences of culturally diverse clients to understand cultural sensitivity from their perspectives. The ultimate goal is to increase the responsiveness of health care professionals to clients from minority cultural communities.

---

1. What was the rationale for the study?

Canadian aboriginal groups have their own cultural values, beliefs, and interpretations of events. When hospitalized in a nonaboriginal setting, they are surrounded by people of a different culture, and the experience can be problematic. Nurses need to understand the reception of care in such unfamiliar surroundings. This exploratory study attempted to determine the perceptions and experiences of some members of the Big Cove, Mi'kmaq First Nation Community in New Brunswick who had been patients in a nonaboriginal hospital. The study is part of a larger project that is investigating the perceptions of cultural sensitivity by diverse minority cultures in a hospital setting.

The Mi'kmaq

The Mi'kmaq have inhabited Eastern Canada for more than 2,000 years. . . . In 1992, there were 36,297 registered Mi'kmaq in Canada living in First Nation Communities. . . . The Big Cove reserve is located on the northeastern coast of New Brunswick and in 1992 had a population of 2,025.

. . . The decline of [the fur trade] industry and the British conquest in the 18th century set in motion a series of changes that culminated in reserve lands being set aside for them, a sedentary way of life, and a subordinate position in an expanding society of immigrants. When Canada formally became a nation, the federal government assumed administrative responsibility for the reserves. . . . Since 1995 communities have been negotiating self-government in such areas as health care, child welfare, education, and housing.

The Mi'kmaq language . . . is being replaced by English but continues to be the major language spoken on some reserves. In Big Cove, where this study was conducted, Mi'kmaq still is the dominant language used. . . .

Mi'kmaq have resisted assimilation and continue to have a distinct identity as a people. Their view of health is holistic and is linked to spirituality: Healing is associated with restoring harmony and connections. . . . Many members of Big Cove turn to healing rituals . . . and to traditional medicines from local plants to manage their health. . . . In the face of serious illness, however, they leave the reserve and use provincial hospital services. No previous studies have examined how Mi'kmaq perceive hospitalization.

▶ *(Note that participants recognize their subordinate position in the larger culture, that Mi'kmaq is the dominant language, and that they seek outside medical help only when illness is too serious to be treated by their traditional means.)*

Research Question

. . . How do Mi'kmaq from the Big Cove reserve in New Brunswick describe their experiences with caregivers during a recent hospitalization?

> **2. What was the purpose of the study?**
>
> To answer the question, How do Mi'kmaq natives from Big Cove describe their experiences with caregivers during recent hospitalization.

Method

The study was guided by interpretive interactionism developed . . . to investigate the relationship between personal troubles and the public institutions created to address these troubles. . . . Its aim is to provide authentic understanding of the problem being investigated. In this study, the need to access health care services was viewed as a personal trouble that brought members of Mi'kmaq communities into the public arena of the provincial health care system. The interpretive interactionist method involves collecting thick descriptions of personal experiences from people who have lived the phenomenon under investigation. . . . *Thick descriptions* are data that contextualize the phenomenon. . . . The investigator looks for . . . experiential moments that mark a person's life. They either may be major, shattering the person's life completely; cumulative, in which a transformational moment is the result of a series of events; illuminatory, when the person recognizes underlying elements of a situation; or, they may be relived in the sense that the illuminatory moment related to an event occurs at a later date.

Steps in an Interpretive Interaction Study

Deconstruction. The first step involves a critical analysis of how a phenomenon has been analyzed in the past. In the nursing literature, models for transcultural care encourage nurses to avoid cultural impositions, eliminate ethnocentric biases, and provide culturally appropriate care. . . . They [models] are . . . oriented toward identifying clients' cultural perspectives about health and caring. . . . Ironically, the models are themselves a product of culture. Although they encourage nurses to identify the meaning of caring *within* other cultures, they have not incorporated the perspectives of clients from other cultures about the constituents of effective caring *across* cultures.

Capture. In the second step, the investigator locates participants who have lived the personal trouble being examined, obtains narratives from them about it, and seeks out the epiphanies in their stories.

---

3. **What was the nature of the research method used to gather the data?**

Interpretive interactionism is a qualitative method of relating personal troubles and public institutions designed to address these troubles. In this study, the serious illness that brought clients to the hospital was viewed as personal trouble. The method involves obtaining data about all the actual and emotional experiences of the individual within the context, in this case, of being hospitalized. It involves, first, *deconstruction,* ways in which the experience has been analyzed. In the case of cross-cultural care, nurses were encouraged to be familiar with the client's perspective of health and caring. *Capture* involves obtaining a sample who lived the experience and eliciting narratives that include their illumination of the meaning of the experience.

. . . A nonprobabilistic purposive sampling strategy was used to select 10 participants from Big Cove who had been hospitalized in a New Brunswick hospital within the previous 3 years. Parents of dependent children requiring hospitalization also were accepted as participants. An effort was made to include participants of all ages.

The sample consisted of two mothers of young children who had been hospitalized, three participants older than 55 years of age, three participants in their late teens or 20s, and two participants in their 30s or 40s. Four participants were married, two were single, two were divorced, and two were widowed. Eight participants were women and two were men. They had been hospitalized at the Moncton Hospital [mainly English-speaking]; Dr. Georges-L. Dumont Regional Hospital [mainly French-speaking]; or Stella Maris Hospital, a satellite . . . of Dr. Georges-L. Dumont Hospital. . . . The first language

TABLE 1 Hospitalization

Hospital	Length of Stay	Diagnosis	Previous Hospitalization
Dr. Georges-L. Dumont	3 weeks	Pneumonia	Two visits to the Moncton Hospital emergency dept.
Dr. Georges-L. Dumont	2 months	Hip replacement	None
Dr. Georges-L. Dumont	2 weeks	Cerebral vascular accident	The Moncton Hospital (CVA, 24 years ago)
Stella Maris Hospital	1 week	Suicide attempt	None
The Moncton Hospital	4 days	Delivery	None
The Moncton Hospital	6 weeks	Bowel obstruction	The Moncton Hospital (multiple admissions)
The Moncton Hospital	5 weeks	Fractured pelvis	The Moncton Hospital (multiple admissions)
Dr. Georges-L. Dumont	2 weeks	Kidney infection	None
The Moncton Hospital	1 month	Fractured pelvis, arm, leg	Dr. Georges-L. Dumont (Surgery of a tumor 35 years ago)
The Moncton Hospital	6 weeks	Fractured hip	None

NOTE: CVA = cerebral vascular accident.

of all participants was Mi'kmaq, but they also spoke English. Table 1 summarizes data about diagnosis, length of stay, and previous hospitalizations. It excludes the data collected on comorbidity and details about respondents' health histories, as this information would identify them to other members of Big Cove.

▶ *(Note that nonprobabilistic purposive sampling is a method of selecting those individuals who are most likely to provide information-rich or fruitful data. This suggests that some potential clients may have been excluded, possibly because they did not remember their experiences in sufficient detail. Moreover, some may have refused to participate because they did not want to risk being identified. Furthermore, part of the experience may have been a function of the hospital the client stayed in. None of the clients understood French. Finally, the hospital experience occurred during the last 3 years, and memory of the experience may play a role in the narratives.)*

4. What was the nature of the sample?

Ten participants (two men and eight women) were selected. Two were mothers of young children who had been hospitalized, and the remaining eight ranged in age from the late teens to older than 55 years of age. Six were single, divorced, or widowed, and four were married. Half were hospitalized in a predominantly English-speaking hospital and half in a predominantly French-speaking hospital. All participants were able to speak English.

5. What are some troublesome aspects of the sampling technique and the sample itself?

A selective group of clients may have been excluded because they couldn't provide the informational data required; others may have refused to participate because they feared loss of anonymity. Responses may be a function of the hospital that admitted the client. And responses might be affected by ability to recall events that occurred as much as 3 years earlier.

6. Examine Table 1. Because the Stella Maris hospital is a satellite of Dr. Georges-L. Dumont, consider these patients as one group and those who were hospitalized in The Moncton Hospital as another group. What was the average length of stay for each group?

For the French-speaking hospital group, the mean length is 3.2 weeks, and the median is 2 weeks. For the English-speaking hospital group, the mean length of stay is 4.3 weeks, and the median is 5 weeks.

7. Now, look at prior hospitalizations for each group. Are there any differences?

Yes. For the French-speaking hospital group, three had no prior hospitalizations, and two had prior visits (one, 24 years earlier) to the English-speaking hospital. For the English-speaking hospital group, two had no prior hospitalizations, two had multiple prior admissions to the same hospital, and one had been in the French-speaking hospital 35 years earlier.

An open-ended interview schedule was used to obtain biographical data about the hospitalization experience. Questions were broad. . . . In what way was the hospital care what you expected; in what way was the hospital care different from what you expected? The interviewer, a Mi'kmaq nurse who works in Big Cove, conducted audiotaped interviews in Mi'kmaq. She translated and transcribed the interviews into English at a later date. Several words that had no English equivalent were transcribed in Mi'kmaq and a dictionary explaining their meaning was developed by the interviewer. Prior to collecting data, she was trained in interviewing techniques. Each interview took approximately 2 hours to complete.

Bracketing. Once narratives are collected, the analysis begins with bracketing. . . . Bracketing is the identification of the essential elements of the phenomenon being investigated. . . . The narratives are dissected. The investigator locates problematic experiences and epiphanies in the text. In this study, most epiphanies were of the illuminatory type. In some instances, they were cumulative. Key phrases then are identified and interpreted using first-order concepts. . . . Interpretations are reviewed and revised in a search for recurring themes. . . . Finally, essential themes or elements are identified. . . .

Construction. Construction builds on bracketing. The bracketed elements are reassembled into a coherent whole by identifying how they occur within the experience being investigated.

Contextualization. The last step involves relocating the constructed process back in the participants' world of lived experience. Narratives that either embody them or illuminate variations in stages are identified. The aim is to discover how specific lived experiences shape the phenomenon being studied.

▶ *(Notice that the interviewer was a nurse, who may have had certain expectations about client experiences that might affect the narratives or even follow-up questions. She also was a native, however, and conducted the interview in Mi'kmaq, which could motivate the clients to answer more openly. She interviewed male and female clients, and she might have elicited different responses from them. Finally, the analyses were performed by the authors, and interpretations might be influenced by their expectations.)*

8. What was the essential procedure?

Narratives were audiotaped during a 2-hour open-ended interview. The interviews were conducted by a trained Mi'kmaq interviewer who was a nurse. She elicited biographical information regarding each client's hospitalization history. The crux of the interview revolved around patient expectations and fulfillment of the expectations. Interviews were conducted in Mi'kmaq and later translated.

Narratives were subjected to the third step of interpretive interactionism, *bracketing.* This involved analyzing all until recurrent themes or elements could be identified. In the fourth step, *construction,* the themes or elements were studied to determine how they occur in the hospitalization experience, and in the final step, *contextualization,* they were related to the client's lived experience to discover how they affected the hospitalization experience.

9. What are potential sources of confounds or bias during the interview and analyses of the narratives?

The interviewer's expectations might have affected the way in which the clients responded. The interviewer's gender may have had a different effect on male and female clients. The analyses and subsequent interpretations may have been affected by expectations of the author.

Ethical Considerations

Participants and the interviewer signed a consent form explaining the study and guaranteeing anonymity and confidentiality. Participants were particularly concerned that the latter be respected. . . .

Rigor

From the postmodern, interpretive interactionist perspective, findings of any study are interpretations and, as such, always are provisional and incomplete. . . . Several strategies were used to enhance its creditability and dependability, two criteria of trustworthiness proposed. . . . To help establish creditability, the investigators presented the findings, first to the interviewer, second to a small sample of Mi'kmaq band council members and elders, and then to Mi'kmaq personnel of the Health Clinic at Big Cove. All confirmed that the interpretations fitted their understanding of the experience under investigation. . . . Participants were not consulted to validate findings, because they wanted their identity to be known only to the interviewer. Also, the interview translations were not validated, again to protect the confidentiality guaranteed to participants. An auditable decision trail was kept to enhance dependability. It included memos, all data-reduction products, data interpretations, and all data reconstruction products.

▶ *(Notice that clients were emphatic about maintaining anonymity. This fear (?) of having their identity revealed may have affected the extent to which they were open about their feelings during hospitalization. [The nature of the validation process, which could have been a potential weak spot, was discussed by a commentary about this article and addressed by the authors in their response to it. If you were reading this article in the journal, you would have seen both.])*

---

10. *What steps were taken to ensure anonymity and validity of translation of the narratives?*

All participants signed consent forms that guaranteed that identity would be kept confidential, and all translations were validated by showing them to superiors in the Mi'kmaq reservation in Big Cove. All reviewers agreed on the accuracy of the translation.

Results

The recurring themes in participants' narratives, regardless of where they had been hospitalized, revolved around issues of misunderstanding, being misunderstood, and feeling understood. They described leaving a familiar world to obtain necessary services from the "White man's" world and in the "White man's way." Participants found the latter world difficult to comprehend and experienced a sense of being a stranger while there. . . . They perceived caregivers to be equally liable to misunderstand them and, as a result, the Mi'kmaq felt lessened as persons. . . . All respondents also described valued moments of being understood during their hospitalization. Nurses who were kind to them, accepted their custom of family visiting, and treated them as social equals created these moments.

Our Ways/Their Ways

Participants differentiated between what they referred to as "our ways" and "their ways" and identified this dichotomy as the source of the misunderstandings experienced during their hospitalization. . . . Some described this dichotomy in fairly general terms, referring to the hospital and the reserve as two different worlds. . . . "We don't believe or think the same way as a White man." Others were more specific, giving concrete examples about behaviors to illustrate differences between the two worlds. One person described how a young nurse responded to an elderly (nonnative) patient: "Among our people, the young do not treat elders like that.". . . Another participant, whose child had been hospitalized, contrasted how children are treated in the two worlds: "White people . . . they're more strict with their children. We let our children run around and explore more freely because they learn best that way."

Being Misunderstood

. . . Participants perceived that having different ways and belonging to a different world created misunderstandings during their hospitalization. Relating through family and feeling lessened were common themes in their stories about situations in which they felt caregivers misunderstood them.

Relating through family. Participants expected to be, and were, visited by many family members while hospitalized. They also depended on family members to be with them when interacting with hospital personnel about treatment decisions to be made. . . . They also recognized that the presence of many family members was a custom that did not fit well with the "White man's way." They believed it engendered misunderstandings. For instance, a participant described an incident when family members arrived en masse to a meeting with the doctor saying, "That was the time he got mad and walked out. I don't know . . . maybe there were too many of us and we scared him." Another said, "My family was here every day, but I have such a big family I think we drove everybody crazy."

Participants described their custom of family visiting as a particularly important part of "their ways" even though it conflicted with the cultural expectations in the hospital.

Lessened as a person. All participants described one or two incidents in which they believed their needs were misunderstood by caregivers simply because they were natives. They felt that these misunderstandings reflected a perception of them as a category of people rather than as unique human beings. An adolescent related,

> Because one of the staff nurses found a louse on her, she accused me of having them. They [the nurses] really embarrassed me. They brought the doctor in. He prescribed medicine and they washed my hair. . . . They treated me like dirt. That is how I felt anyway. . . . I felt that it was done that way because I was a native person, and if it was anybody else it would have been done differently.

A second example concerns an older woman who . . . described being taken to the bathroom by a caregiver where she had a bowel movement. "She [the caregiver] was all excited for me and said 'Oh, you had a bowel movement: It's huge and black like you are.'"

Most (although not all) participants presented these negative experiences as exceptions to the type of care received. . . . Every participant had lived a misunderstanding of this nature. They left the hospital with a sense of having been demeaned while there.

Misunderstanding

. . . Participants . . . had difficulty understanding the ways encountered in the hospital world. . . . Although this sentiment probably is common among patients in general, respondents' bewilderment seemed to generate a sense of being a stranger. . . . A desire to avoid giving staff trouble contributed to their experience of misunderstanding, because they were reluctant to ask for information.

Being a stranger. The hospital milieu created feelings of aloneness and insecurity among participants. . . . Several described responding to this sense of being a stranger by withdrawing into themselves and, thus, increasing their sense of isolation. . . . Although participants' narratives specifically linked their sense of estrangement to difficulties in understanding the "White man's" world, Mi'kmaq personnel at the Big Cove Health Center believed it also reflected the historical relationship between the two worlds. They saw a link between respondents' estrangement and their own childhood experience of being expected to hide whenever there was a knock at the door. Apparently, this signaled a danger of being removed from their home.

Giving no trouble. Participants often felt insecure because they did not know what to expect, did not understand the hospital rules and regulations, and were confused about their treatment but did not ask questions about these things. . . . Participants explained their failure to seek information by saying they didn't want to give any trouble. . . . An informal rule of conduct among Mi'kmaq is that people should do things without being asked. One woman who believed her lack of understanding of hospital rules had created a good deal of inconvenience and distress observed, "I guess I didn't let them understand my needs, which led to their misunderstanding of my needs. I was assuming they would tell me without my asking."

Understanding

Participants also described encounters with caregivers marked by an understanding that crossed the divide between our ways and their ways. . . . They all singled out an individual staff member who made them feel understood. . . . Participants expressed a great deal of appreciation of these caregivers. The key themes in their descriptions of moments of understanding were that the caregiver treated them with kindness, accepted family visiting, and treated them as equals.

Given kindness. . . . Kindness appeared to involve responding to participants with empathy at a human level beyond cultural differences.

Visitors accepted. Participants acknowledged and appreciated caregivers who had conveyed a tolerance of family visiting, the native custom that seemed to be particularly problematic for staff but important to participants. In contrast to kindness, accepting family visitors concerned cultural differences between the caregiver and care receiver. Nevertheless, their descriptions of nurses who accepted family visitors emphasized their understanding of them as individuals, rather than their knowledge of Mi'kmaq customs.

Treated as equal. The theme of being treated as equal also concerned differences between participants and caregivers. . . . On one hand, participants felt that caregivers created understanding by acknowledging and accepting certain cultural differences; on the other, they felt that understanding was created when caregivers ignored social differences by treating them "the same as everyone else."

Participants . . . appeared to scan for evidence that they were being treated similarly or differently from other patients and valued situations in which caregivers ignored social differences between aboriginal and non-aboriginal patients.

▶ *(Notice that participants came into the hospital with the belief that the "two worlds" differ as well as a possible distrust of "White men" because of earlier childhood experiences. Therefore, feelings of being misunderstood may have been a fulfillment of expectations that affected how they perceived their experience. They may have felt that they were not understood because they expected to feel that way. Moreover, a sense of not knowing what is going on may be common to all patients who do not ask questions and may not be unique to Mi'kmaq patients.)*

11. *What were the essential results of the analyses?*

Recurring themes were related to misunderstandings, being misunderstood by caregivers, and feeling understood. Participants did not understand the "White man's world" and felt like strangers. They felt that caregivers did not understand them and made each feel like less of a person. But they also experienced being understood by caregivers, who accepted their family visits custom and treated them as social equals.

Misunderstanding stemmed from participants' views that the two worlds differed, for example, with respect to treatment of the elderly and of children. This made them feel like strangers. Participants are closely tied to their families and felt that caregivers did not understand the custom of visits by sometimes very large families, a practice that conflicted with hospital policy. Participants felt that they were perceived as "natives" rather than unique individuals, which was demeaning. All participants, however, described at least one caregiver who made them feel understood by treating them kindly, accepting their family custom, and treating them as equals.

Discussion

Broad conceptualizations of culture as the total way of life of a people have given way to definitions restricting the construct to the shared meanings individuals learn, create, re-create, and transmit as group members. . . . The dichotomy perceived by participants between "our ways" and "their ways" touches precisely this notion of culture as a symbolic system shared by members of a community. They were acutely conscious that their interpretations differed from those of the caregivers they encountered. This puts into relief the frequently made observation that cultural consciousness sharpens when people are out of their own culture and are surrounded by another. It is important . . . for nurses to differentiate two distinct contexts for intercultural transactions when examining issues related to cross-cultural caregiving. In one, the nurse provides care in a cultural community other than her or his own and must navigate within an unfamiliar cultural code. . . . In these situations, the nurse is more likely to have an experientially based sense of cultural differences than the people receiving care. In the second, . . . the context of this study, the care recipient is the person surrounded by another culture. Nurses need to be aware that the client may be more likely than the caregiver to have a heightened sense of culture.

Participants' increased awareness of shared meanings within their own culture and different meanings across cultures may explain why understanding was such a central theme in their narratives.

. . . An understanding of Mi'kmaq culture [cultural sensitivity], however, played little part in what participants described as good care. Instead, they focused on being responded to on a human level with compassion and as unique individuals. Even their appreciation of the acceptance of family visiting was framed in terms of the nurses' ability to recognize and accept a basic human need for security rather than an awareness of the cultural meanings involved.

. . . In contrast with nurses' knowledge of their culture, which was not discussed, a nondiscriminatory and accepting attitude figured prominently in participants' accounts. From their perspectives, this appeared to be a fundamental ingredient of effective cross-cultural caregiving.

> ### 12. What essential results were discussed?
>
> Given that culture reflects shared meanings, participants were aware that their interpretations differed from those in the hospital setting. Cultural consciousness sharpens when one is outside of one's culture and in another. Nurses who are cross-cultural caregivers have to differentiate between two situations: one in which they are in another culture and one in which patients are in another culture. Here, patients may have a heightened sense of cultural differences. This may be why understanding was so important to the participants. But, understanding was not considered important in the quality of care. Nurses did not have to understand the role of family visits or not asking questions to be compassionate and to accept each patient as a unique human being. An accepting attitude seemed most important in cross-cultured caregiving.

Conclusion

Findings of qualitative studies are inherently nongeneralizable. Nevertheless, participants' experiences may have implications for cross-cultural encounters. They suggest that members of cultural minority groups may be particularly aware of their own culture and of cultural differences when receiving care in mainstream institutions. They also illustrate how subtle norms may create misunderstandings despite this increased cultural awareness. The findings, however, underscore the importance of compassion and a nondiscriminatory attitude among caregivers. Such qualities may compensate for a caregiver's lack of knowledge about the client's culture in creating effective cross-cultural relationships. Their importance in this study, however, simply may reflect either the personal norms, values, and experiences of the particular participants interviewed or the norms, values, and collective experiences of one particular cultural community.

13. What were the major conclusions? Are they valid?

First, the study suggests that members of minority groups may be particularly aware of their culture and of differences when they receive care in mainstream institutions. But only 10 members of one minority group were questioned, and that awareness may be true of members of majority groups as well. Second, subtle norms may create misunderstanding despite this increased awareness. But participants may have entered the situation with preconceived expectations for misunderstanding. Third, the study underscores the importance of compassion and a nondiscriminatory attitude among caregivers. But the need for compassion was not shown to be unique to minority groups (even Mi'kmaq). Fourth, such compassion may compensate for caregivers' lack of knowledge about clients' culture. But caregivers' knowledge was not assessed and not compared with compassion for effectiveness.

Other drawbacks include the fact that basic concepts (themes) relied on interpretation of the author performing the analyses, which might be colored by expectancy; interviews and translation by a native, who may have had her own expectancy; memory of participants, all of whom did not want to be identified for some reason and half of whom were treated in a predominantly French-speaking hospital. The authors did respond to some of these issues by stating that their conclusions were offered as tentative explanations of the results. Again, you would have seen this had you read the article in the journal.

STUDY EXAMPLE 2.2

Although case studies are never free from threats to internal validity, some are better than others. If individuals are asked to participate and no one refuses, then there is no problem with characteristics of volunteers and nonvolunteers. If steps are taken to validate interpretations of interview responses, there is less of a problem regarding researcher interpretations. These features are present in the object of the present critique. The study examines the responses to interviews of minority students in a doctoral program to better understand their needs and determine the extent to which these needs are met.

The Study

Place, A. W., & Wood, G. S. (1999). A case study of traditionally underrepresented individuals' experiences in a doctoral program. *Journal for a Just and Caring Education, 5*(4), 442-455. Copyright 1999 by Sage.

There is a need to diversify university faculties as well as K-12 leadership positions. . . . Social conditions, as well as the entire educational system, are part of the milieu in which to consider diversity. . . . .

The complexity of the problem includes two major concepts. First, the almost ubiquitous evidence of the supply problem is the relatively small numbers of African Americans in academia. . . . Second, is the organizational climate at institutions of higher education, where there is

> evidence that indicates that racist perceptions, both in an individual and institutional sense, are still rather dominant, and subsequently have a tendency to not only restrict access for those who possess the requisite credentials but to also stifle the professional growth of those already in academia such that they become less visible signs of success. . . .

There is some evidence that university faculty believe they are committed to diversity. . . . However, the perception of one group is not always shared by others. For example . . . although a common perception in many universities is that faculty of color are highly sought after and can demand higher salaries . . . neither of those conditions [is] common. Therefore, in relation to the climate or commitment to diversity, the more salient question may be, What do students of color believe? To accomplish diversification, doctoral programs need to do a better job of recruiting, serving, graduating, and understanding persons of color.

. . . The present longitudinal qualitative study was designed to provide an addition to our understanding of students of color. It is an attempt to understand the complex problem faced by universities from the point of view of those most excluded from academia. . . . By attempting to hear and understand the voices of this traditionally underrepresented group of individuals, programs may be better able to attract and retain these valuable human resources.

Method

The informants in this study were 11 doctoral students in the Department of Educational Leadership. . . . 5 of the students were in the Adult and Community Education program and 6 were in the Educational Administration program. Seven were males and 4 were females. When the study began, 1 student was admitted to candidacy (all but dissertation—ABD) and 10 of the remaining individuals were engaged in course work. At the time that this article was submitted for publication consideration (April 1999), there were 6 students who had been graduated and 3 who were admitted to candidacy

(ABD). One individual considered himself delayed but was engaged in course work preparing for comprehensive exams and another individual moved with a spouse who accepted a position in another state. The last person was intending to complete the degree but has not been active for more than 2 years. The study informants included 7 African Americans, 1 Asian American, 1 Hispanic American, and . . . 1 from Jamaica and the other from China. . . .

In-depth, semi-structured interviews were conducted and recorded on three different occasions with each individual. The first interview was the least structured interview. The next two interviews came roughly at equal time spans during the following year and a half. . . . These interviews were slightly more structured, to explore very tentative themes or areas in which more than one student identified a related concept. The researchers worked separately and collaboratively. . . . Themes were determined when both researchers agreed that the data justified the existence of a theme. . . . To improve the fidelity of the themes, a fourth data collection, which served as a "member check," later was conducted (for some, this was after graduation thus increasing the potential for frank and honest reactions). This member check was done by having all informants read a rough draft of the themes, including selected quotes from individuals, and react to the themes in person as well as in written form if they chose. . . .

The researchers were two male European American faculty members— one in the Adult and Community Education program and one in the Educational Administration program. The latter left the institution after the initial interviews. . . . The former has since retired from the university. Having two researchers . . . allowed the interviews to be set up with persons the students felt comfortable with. . . . Because neither of the researchers is still connected with the university, it is hoped that we were able to use the insider's perspective as well as somewhat of an outsider's perspective and that our conclusions were less influenced by direct employment at the institutional setting in which this research took place.

Several areas or themes that emerged from the data provided a basis for the member check. . . . To validate themes, the researchers first independently identified themes that had supporting data in the three recorded interviews and in the related member checks. Then they met to decide which themes clearly emerged in the study.

Theme 1: Multicultural Perspectives

The first theme that emerged from the data, "multicultural perspectives," . . . was a general feeling among the informants that multicultural perspectives were not dealt with programmatically. The doctoral programs did not regularly or systematically provide multicultural perspectives. . . .

Theme 2: Issues of Gender

The second theme identified was "issues of gender." There was not a universal feeling that issues of gender were obvious, but there were comments that may indicate how gender is important in understanding the perspectives of traditionally underrepresented individuals, especially of women aspiring to leadership positions. . . . To some women in this study, gender was more important than race. . . .

One student noted the fact that there are not enough women in the department. . . .

Theme 3: General Impact of the Program on Self-Efficacy

The third major theme identified was impact of the program on individuals and self-efficacy. Many informants felt the program had a positive impact, but there were some who expressed differing perspectives. The hard work and sense of accomplishments when difficult tasks were accomplished were mentioned as very positive influences on self-efficacy. . . . Individuals in this study seemed to have strong self-efficacy prior to entrance in their program and were able, to vary[ing] degrees, to develop even more as they interacted with individuals and environmental influences in their program. For some, positive self-image was in part influenced by the fact that they were the first members in their families to be in a doctoral program, an accomplishment in itself. . . .

There were also comments about program situations that may have had adverse effects. One such situation was the fact that outside the university program they held, or had held, jobs of importance with an accompanying positive social status. As doctoral students, some found that their social status suffered. . . .

Theme 4: The Dissertation Experience and Its Impact on Self-Efficacy

A fourth theme centered on the dissertation experience. The dissertation was viewed as particularly challenging but in the end rewarding. . . .

Theme 5: Impact of Students on the Program(s)

A fifth theme that emerged was the impact of the students on the program. Most of the students felt that the two doctoral programs were not profoundly affected or changed by their participation but that they had a positive impact in certain ways. . . .

Other Themes

Several other themes emerged from the data and were determined to be worth considering, although their ramifications and commonality were somewhat less clear-cut than those already listed. Among them were the following themes:

Support From Family, Employers,
Social Friends, and University Faculty

The issue of support came up often, and there is little doubt that the informants valued all of the support they received. Virtually everyone cited some source of much-needed support. However, there were differences from student to student as to who supplied it. . . .

Special Situations That Support
Their Doctoral Work

At least three of the informants called attention to the fact that they had situations that provided special support for their academic work, such things as secretarial help in the workplace, friends with doctoral degrees who became advisors, and everyday access to special libraries or technologies.

Informants' Perspectives About Whether
They Are Typical of the Underrepresented
Group to Which They Belong

Participants were completely aware that they are members of underrepresented groups, but most saw themselves as not being typical of the people in the groups from which they come. Many saw themselves as overcoming, or ignoring, or rising above the attitudes, labels, and other self-perceived barriers that were accepted by some members of their groups. . . .

Timing of Decision to Begin Doctoral Work

Virtually all informants could cite particular conditions in their lives that influenced their decisions to begin doctoral work. For some, it had to do with financial support or encouragement by the employer. For others, family circumstances strongly influenced the decision. Three types of family situations were often cited as being related to the decision to begin the doctoral program: (a) The informants were not getting any younger; they had reached an age where they either had to make a move or forget the idea; (b) the children had reached an age where they were more self-sufficient than earlier, and returning to college would be less disruptive to the family; and (c) the relationship with a spouse or significant other had matured to the point that it would not likely be jeopardized by the distractions and pressures of getting a doctoral degree. . . .

Uniqueness of Having a Doctorate

Most informants acknowledged that having the doctorate made them unique in some way within their families, their employment situations, their social circles, and so forth. . . . Sometimes it became a source of criticism. . . .

Motivation to Get a Degree

Clearly there were identifiable motivators for all the informants, but the motivators varied a great deal across the group. Possibly the most common motivator in the group was self-efficacy. . . .

Difficulty of Academic Work

All informants acknowledged the difficulty of doctoral academic work. . . . However, they did not seem to feel that the work was unreasonable, nor did the difficulty exceed their expectations. It was something they expected and were prepared to face.

Cohort Groups and Cohort Issues

Some of the informants were part of larger cohort groups and some apparently had not had the experiences, except as temporary classroom groups were formed for particular courses. Those who had been in cohort groups were enthusiastic about them. Most thought that being in a cohort group was or would be very helpful to doctoral students, minority or not.

Mentoring

. . . Some of the informants had experienced help from a mentor of some kind; others had not. . . . But only in two cases was a mentor specifically mentioned as a special factor affecting success in the doctoral work.

Semantic Differential Data

During the process of analyzing the qualitative data, the researchers decided it would be helpful to develop a simple semantic differential instrument about feelings and attitudes. Informants were asked to complete the instruments by reacting to a short list of adjective pairs that related to their doctoral experience. Each pair represented the opposite ends of a continuum. The instrument then was also administered to a group of European American doctoral students at similar stages in the same two doctoral programs so that comparisons could be made.

Among the 20 pairs of adjectives, 7 showed differences in the responses of the two groups that were sufficiently pronounced that they might suggest attitudinal differences between underrepresented doctoral students and dominant culture doctoral students. On 6 of the 7, the differences were relatively modest. As a group, the study students felt slightly less successful than the European Americans. They also felt that the program was less equitable than did the European Americans, that the influence of their families was a little less positive, that the influence of their employers was a little less positive, and that the support of the university was slightly less positive. . . . The widest gap in the responses came on the question of whether the doctoral programs expressed multicultural or dominant cultural perspectives. Study informants saw the program as essentially having dominant cultural perspectives; their counterparts thought the program perspectives were considerably more multicultural. . . .

Conclusions and Implications

Six conclusions have been drawn from this study: One, doctoral program faculty need to have more than just sensitivity to multicultural situations. There need to be faculty from a variety of cultures, and all faculty, especially those from the majority culture, need to have read the important works of the authors from cultures other than their own. . . .

Two, the informants who were minority and female saw the gender issues as more important than the racial and ethnic issues, when those racial and ethnic issues were attempted to be separated or dealt with to the exclusion of gender issues. . . . The programmatic implication is that diversity is multifaceted and interactive. . . .

Three, the self-image of these students was positive before entering the program, allowing them to "take the plunge." They often went through a period of apprehension and self-doubt as they entered the program. As they began to succeed academically, they experienced an even stronger sense of self-confidence and self-efficacy, but they did not view the doctoral degree as their most important source of self-esteem.

Four, the male and female doctoral students of color in this study had more similarities with their European American peers than they had differences in their attitudes and perspectives concerning their doctoral work. The most profound difference . . . was their respective perceptions about the extent to which the university doctoral programs had a multicultural perspective, as opposed to a dominant culture perspective. . . .

Five, the informants believed that they influenced other students by their presence in the program, but they doubted that they had much lasting influence on the doctoral program or the academic department. . . .

Six, these study data and conclusions suggest that university administrators and faculty may need to take a harder look at higher education from the perspective of the members of the underrepresented groups whom higher education is trying to recruit. . . . Given findings of this study, the perspectives that matter to students from underrepresented groups seem far more complex and far less obvious than we might suspect.

CRITIQUE OF STUDY EXAMPLE 2.2

1. What was the rationale (i.e., background thinking) for the study?

2. What was the purpose of the study?

3. What are the major characteristics of the participants?

4. What are the major characteristics of the researchers?

5. What was the general procedure?

6. What control conditions were instituted to reduce experimenter bias?

7. What major themes were identified by the researchers?

8. What minor themes were identified?

9. How was the semantic differential developed?

10. What comparison group was used?

11. How was the group selected?

12. What were the major results of the semantic differential measure?

13. What conclusions were drawn from the study?

14. What are some possible weaknesses in these conclusions?

15. What factor(s) argue(s) against experimenter bias affecting the interpretations of the interviews?

16. What factors, aside from those mentioned in 14, might affect the validity of the conclusions?

17. Are the conclusions justified?

For answers to these questions, see page 327.

BIBLIOGRAPHY

Cook, T. D., & Campbell, D. T. (1979). *Quasi-experimentation: Design and analysis issues for field settings.* Chicago: Rand McNally.

Kasdin, A. E. (1992). *Research design in clinical psychology* (2nd ed.). Boston: Allyn & Bacon.

McMillan, J. H., & Schumacher, S. (1997). *Research in education: A conceptual introduction.* Reading MA: Addison-Wesley.

Neale, J. M., & Liebert, R. M. (1986). *Science and behavior: An introduction to methods of research* (3rd ed.). Englewood Cliffs, NJ: Prentice Hall.

Yin, R. K. (1994). *Case study research: Design and methods* (2nd ed.) Thousand Oaks, CA: Sage.

Additional Suggested Readings

Isaac, S., & Michael, W. B. (1995). *Handbook in research and evaluation: A collection of principles, methods, and strategies useful in the planing, design, and evaluation of studies in education and the behavioral sciences* (3rd ed.). San Diego, CA: EdITS.

Kazdin, A. E. (Ed.). (1992). *Methodological issues & strategies in clinical research.* Washington, DC: American Psychological Association.

Miller, D. C. (1991). *Handbook of research design and social measurement* (5th ed.). Newbury Park, CA: Sage.

Chapter 3

Narrative Analysis

 Many qualitative methods exist besides the case study. Participant observation, used by psychologists, sociologists, and other social scientists, involves observing group interactions by "joining" the group. Ethnographic analysis involves examination of cultural events or experiences. Originally, this entailed objective measures. As we saw in the case study (Chapter 2), the new ethnography also includes interviews with respondents, and the researcher looks for themes in answers to questions to better understand the event. A more prominent "newcomer" stems from methodology that originated in Europe, *narrative analysis.* This entails analysis of a life story (e.g., events while working, to explain why one was fired)— a segment of one's life that is of interest to the narrator and researcher—including experiences of the narrator perceived to be relevant to that life segment in terms of their impact, chronological sequence in the narration, and potential effect on the future course of actions by the narrator. The researcher is interested not only in content but in why the story was told *that* way: Why were certain experiences reported at certain times in their sequence, and why were some emphasized more than others? This describes what the components of the event meant to the narrator. Thus, a narrative includes a temporal sequence of experiences, some theme or themes running through them, and structural coherence. Explanations may be offered throughout as hypotheses, each tested by subsequent text. What is significant is the interaction between past, social, and present events in shaping the narrator's perception of these now and in the future. These narratives are assumed to provide more information on our perceptions about the effects of social variables than can be provided by traditional paper-and-pencil scales.

There are five aspects to a narrative report of one's experiences of an event. These are precipitated by the interview questions, which are generally open-ended. First, attention to certain phenomena make them meaningful. They are selected by the individual and become prominent. Second, narration is the telling of the event in the form of a story: the individual's understanding of what preceded the experiences, what happened during and after the experiences, in such a way that the individual's interpretation of the event (the point of the narrative) is clear and meaningful. Third, how the story is told depends on the listener. Narratives about the same event will differ when the listeners are friends, colleagues, or overseers. Fourth, transcribing is performed on an audiotaped narrative. It can be complete (with pauses, inflections, whispers, etc.) or partial, and it is selective. There is no one way to transcribe. It depends on the theory guiding the researcher, and different ways can lead to different interpretations of the narrative. People do not always begin a narrative at the beginning of a sequence of experiences. Transcribers typically order them sequentially. Fifth, analysis of the transcribed tape (or tapes) involves decisions about what will be included and excluded according to the researcher's anticipated responses. Causal sequences are identified to locate a turning point that represents a difference between the ideal and real self, something that shows a shift in the individual's perception of a phenomenon; for example, what led to a shift from a right-to-life to a pro-choice attitude. Other parts of the narrative may be summarized to present the gist of what the narrator was saying. Or the researcher may look at word choice, sentence structure, and clauses to determine their similarity in meaning. Still other parts are selected to be the focus of analysis, the bases for interpretation, and/or to support a particular view. Finally, different readers of the written analysis will attribute different meaning to the text depending on their personal experiences and expectations. A full understanding of how a phenomenon becomes meaningful, however, requires the full narrative (which would be available in print or from the author).

What is recognized, at the core of the analysis, is that the narration depends on the interaction between interviewer and narrator (not all theorists agree on this). Although researchers believe that this cannot be controlled, keep in mind that questions stem from a particular researcher, as do "all possible" hypotheses about why a report of Event A led to a report of Event B. In other words, tendered hypotheses are likely to be a function of the experiences and/or beliefs of the interviewer. Moreover, the data obtained in an interview are structured by the questions. The intent is to structure questions so that they encourage a narrative on the meaning of the life experience to the respondent rather than a mere report.

Evaluation of a narrative revolves around its validity. According to one view, the focus is not on accuracy of the narrator's statement but on trustworthiness of the interpretation. Interpretations are trustworthy if they are plausible and reasonable, they are supported by reports by the narrator, and alternative interpretations have been considered. Furthermore, there could be verification of interpretations by the narrator(s), but this is not practical if individuals are judging interpretations based on more than one narrative. Moreover, interpretations should be coherent in terms of the basic goals of the narrator, the ways in which the narratives are structured, and the themes that run throughout the narrative, all of which contribute to a meaningful picture. Finally, if a narrative becomes the basis for further investigations, it is considered trustworthy.

Because of the nature of narrative analysis, many of the threats to internal validity that exist for case studies apply here. The threats,

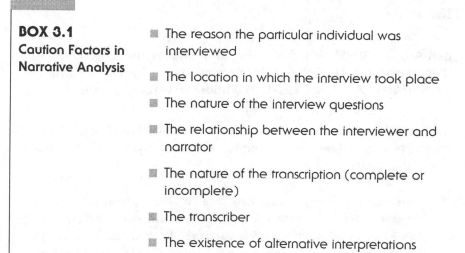

**BOX 3.1
Caution Factors in
Narrative Analysis**

■ The reason the particular individual was interviewed

■ The location in which the interview took place

■ The nature of the interview questions

■ The relationship between the interviewer and narrator

■ The nature of the transcription (complete or incomplete)

■ The transcriber

■ The existence of alternative interpretations

however, apply to identification of themes rather than cause-and-effect conclusions. The meanings and perceptions may be a function of the nature of the questions asked in the interview, the interviewer, and the place in which the interview occurred, rather than the actual experiences of the narrator. The narrative may be tainted by falsehoods, poor or distorted memory, or both. Although this is considered a characteristic of the individual's perception of an experience and its meaning to the narrator, the interpretation and analysis of the narrative are based on this description. The analysis may be a function of biases and/or expectations of the researcher or the ex-

tent to which the narrative is transcribed. Finally, a different type of analysis (e.g., ethnographic) may lead to a different interpretation. The major caution factors are summarized in Box 3.1.

The narrative analysis we will evaluate is concerned with how people change their worldview after a gay man discloses a previously held secret, his homosexuality. Some of my alerts and observations coincide with what the author subsequently reports. This is fine. Always think about possibilities and what strikes you as you read. That's what I did.

STUDY EXAMPLE 3.1

We will evaluate this study together. This example is from the field of social work. The investigator has conducted numerous interviews with homosexuals and their parents to understand the impact of "coming out."

The Study

Ben-Ari, A. (1995). It's the telling that makes the difference. In R. Josselson & A. Lieblich (Eds.), *Interpreting experience: The narrative study of lives* (Vol. 3, pp. 153-172). Thousand Oaks, CA: Sage.

Mark was 27 when we met at one of the small cafes in Berkeley, California. His intense blue eyes stared at an invisible spot as he began to put together the pieces that made up his story:

> It was during the holiday season. We had taken a friend of ours to the doctor and were waiting for her in the car. My mother raised the subject of the dance planned for the following night. She asked me why I had decided not to go. She waited a few seconds, sighed, and said, "Well, I keep hoping that some-time you are going to have a girlfriend that you will bring along," and I said, "That's never going to happen." She asked, "What?" and I said, "I am gay." She was silent for a few minutes, then whispered, "You must be kidding," and I quietly shook my head, "No, I am not." That is how I told my mother.

Mary, a soft woman in her late 50s, began her story:

> It was around Thanksgiving weekend. We were all staying at our friend's house. There was a big dance coming up the following night. I had bought tickets for everyone. The whole family planned on going, including my 87-year-old mother. A week before the party, Mark asked me to take his ticket back. . . .
>
> We had taken our hostess to her doctor's appointment and were waiting in the car. We were very quiet and didn't even look at each other. I have a very clear memory of that moment. I remember asking myself what was going through his mind and if this silence was significant. Then, breaking the silence, he asked, "Did you take back that ticket?" "Yes," I said, disappointed, "I'd really like you to go but there will be other times." But he shook his head and said, "Oh no, there won't." And I asked, "Why not?" and it was then he told me that he was gay. This is how I learned that I have a gay son.

▶ *(Notice that Mark did not look at the interviewer, a female, as he spoke. Also, Mark was more vague about the disclosure time, "during the holiday season," than his mother, who stated, "around Thanksgiving." Also, their recollections differ. Mark mentioned nothing about silence and not looking at each other and said that his mother raised the issue of the dance. His mother said that he raised the issue. Mark also said that she had hoped he would "have a girlfriend," whereas her account does not mention a girlfriend. Thus, Mark's account contains elements of what he probably assumed his mother wanted for him [a girlfriend], and his mother's account contained elements of initial avoidance, denial, or possibly repugnance [silence and not looking at each other].)*

Two personal and distinctly different accounts of the very same incident: a son's and a mother's attempts to arrange their lives within a meaningful context. At present, both Mark and Mary think of that weekend as a turning point in their lives.

The aim of this chapter is two-fold: It documents the attempts of two individuals to personally organize their life experiences around a particular turning point, using the narratives of Mary and Mark to illustrate what gay men, lesbians, and their parents may go through prior to, during, and following the discovery of a child's homosexuality. Researchers have argued that predictive and longitudinal research focuses mainly on demonstrating stability over time, which may result in neglect of a more interesting question, that of conditions accounting for change. . . . This chapter . . . examines a change in people's lives—a turning point—employing a narrative or interpretive approach.

▶ *(Note that the author is using the narratives of a mother and son to illustrate what gay men, lesbians, and their parents experience before, during, and after a homosexual child's disclosure.)*

. . . Little research has been devoted to understanding the reactions in the family to the discovery of a child's sexual orientation . . . and generally, the impact . . . on their parents' well-being has been overlooked. . . . I will confront these issues and look at coming out . . . by applying the concepts of privacy and intimacy and the dynamics between them to the process in which parents learn about their children's homosexuality. . . I will also examine the. . . process and its implications for the well-being of the parents.

---

1. **What is the rationale for the study?**

   Longitudinal studies have ignored factors accounting for changes in people's lives. Moreover, little research has looked at the family's reaction to learning of a child's sexual orientation and the impact on parents' well-being of a child's homosexuality.

2. What were the purposes of the study?

One was to examine how people attempt to organize their life experiences around a turning point in their lives, using the experiences of a gay man and his mother to illustrate what homosexuals and their parents go through before, during, and after the child's sexual orientation is disclosed. The second was to look at a change in a person's life, using a narrative approach.

One of the main arguments of the narrative approach is that constructing a "subjective truth" is at least as important as revealing "objective truth." . . . Eliciting the significance of the experience and its meaning to the individuals involved in it is the principal concern. To elicit first impressions and minimize the potential influence of a theoretical framework, open-ended and almost identical questions were presented to Mary and her son. When interviewing Mary, I asked her to describe her experiences as well as her perceptions of her son's experience throughout the process of coming out. . . . Mark was asked to describe his as well as his mother's experiences throughout the very same process.

▶ (Note that there is no report of where and when interviews took place and whether there were just two interviews—one for each of them—or whether there were more than two interviews over a period of time. Furthermore, instructions preliminary to the interview questions are not reported, and these could have affected the content of the narratives.)

Thus two first-person accounts and two descriptions of the other person's perceived experiences were available on completion of the interviews. The following is a presentation of these four perspectives of a single incident: a son revealing his sexual orientation to his mother. Obviously there are differences between the versions. Nonetheless, the purpose of discussing these differences is not to detect discrepancies among the stories, but to interpret and understand in terms of their respective contexts.

In their stories, Mary and Mark differentiate between predisclosure, disclosure, and postdisclosure thoughts, feelings, and experiences. A similar sequence underlies the organization of this chapter. It is important to point out, however, that the distinction between predisclosure, disclosure, and postdisclosure is predicated on adapting a retrospective outlook.

3. Who were the narrators?

A 27-year-old gay man and his mother, in her late 50s.

> **4. *What was the procedure? What is lacking?***
>
> Both were interviewed, individually, using identically phrased open-ended questions that were designed to elicit first impressions, significance, and meaning of the experiences. We don't, however, know anything about the circumstances of the interviews, except that at least one, Mark's, took place in a cafe. Nor do we know what instructions and background to the interview were given prior to the questions.

Predisclosure

All that can be said with any certainty about predisclosure is that it ends at disclosure. Yet significantly, both Mary and Mark felt the need to somehow define this period and seemed to want to consider how long this stage lasted, when it started, what it referred to, and what characterized it.

Mark talked about wanting to come out as well as his reservations about it.

I feel close to my mother. Her not knowing was an incredible barrier. I was hiding probably the most major facet of my life from her. I felt that I was living a lie by not telling her that I am gay.

▶ *(Note that he may be expressing a feeling of guilt.)*

Reflecting on his fears, he added,

I did not have any real ones, my mother is pretty liberal, I knew that there wouldn't be any major problems. And yet I knew that once I said it, I would never be able to take it back. The words would be out there and there would be no way to return. . . .

Mark characterizes predisclosure as a period of tension and conflict. He describes constant struggle: wanting to share and wanting to hide, on the one hand, longing to be open and honest about his homosexuality with his mother, and on the other hand wishing to remain secretive about the very same issue.

. . . Prior to disclosure, gay men and lesbians experience tension between the need to exercise control over the access to particular information (privacy) and the need to share that very same information (intimacy). . . . Disclosure occurs when the need to keep information private subsides and the wish to be open and share this information becomes more important.

▶ *(Notice that Mark clearly is in conflict about disclosing his homosexuality to his mother and that the author maintains that such conflict applies to gay men and lesbians, which is resolved when the "wish to be open and share this information" is more important. Yet, there are other possibilities: He was tired of being nagged about having a girlfriend; he suspected that his mother already knew; he was caught at a weak moment, and the disclosure was unintentional; he felt guilty about not telling her.)*

I asked Mary what she had thought were Mark's motives in coming out to her. She replied,

> I used to constantly ask myself the same question. At different times I came up with different answers. At first, still in the grip of pain, I asked myself why he did it, whether he was trying to hurt me, or to get back at me. I found myself constantly thinking about what it was that I had done. Later, I learned that he had been tired of hiding and pretending to be someone he was not. It took me several years to realize that Mark came out to me primarily because he valued our relationship. He felt that hiding that aspect of his life from me would cause our relationship to stagnate or even deteriorate. I really think he wanted to be honest and to share with me what he was going through back then.

▶ *(Note that Mary's initial reaction to Mark's disclosure, "he was trying to hurt me, or get back at me," could support a "tired of being nagged" explanation. Her final reaction absolves her of guilt and places the responsibility on Mark.)*

. . . Mary gives us a clear example of the developmental nature of interpretation. Her attempt to "make sense" of her son's behavior evolved through three major stages. Initially she focused mainly on herself, as if she or her behavior could possibly explain his behavior. She then moved to concentrating on him as the main locus of interpretation: He didn't want to live a lie, or he was tired of pretending to be someone he was not. Finally, she began to talk in terms of their relationship. It has been my observation that when parents . . . move away from seeking understanding in either themselves or their children, to thinking about the relationship between them, then they start adjusting to the discovery of their child's homosexuality.

Reflecting on Mark's then-anticipated fears, she said,

> Now, I can hardly think of Mark being afraid of telling me anything about his life. I don't think he was afraid that I would do something. But knowing that he did keep this information from me for a significant period of time is in and of itself indicative. Even now it is hard for me to admit that he did not tell me

because he was afraid to and yet, between the time he himself discovered his sexual orientation and until he told me, well it has been a fair number of years.
. . .

Studies . . . have suggested specific explanations for homosexuals' disclosure . . . to parents. . . . Hopes that disclosure will reduce the price exacted for "passing" (i.e., as heterosexual), permit greater honesty, open up channels of communication, strengthen family bonds, deepen love, and provide opportunities for mutual support and caring feature as reasons for disclosures.

However, self-disclosure is not always perceived as a positive experience. . . . Gay and lesbian children . . . avoid disclosures to their parents . . . because of fear of rejection, worry about parents' sense of guilt, guilt about parents' physical and mental pain, apprehension about being forced to seek treatment, desire to protect the family from crises, and uncertainty about their sexual identity. . . . Underlying all . . . is the realization that disclosure is irreversible. Mary describes being suspicious during the predisclosure stage. Suspecting that Mark was gay long before he told her, she recalls asking herself if it was normal that he didn't do the same things as his older brother . . . , that he never had a girlfriend, never expressed any interest in going out with girls? She also remembers, however, that as a teenager, he went through a period when he didn't want to be around anyone; days in which he stayed at home without leaving his room. She recalls that she often asked herself what the meaning of all this was and where it would all lead. Now she believes that it was during this period that he came to terms with his homosexuality. . . . Note, however, that Mark did not discuss this period of time in his story.

▶ *(It is interesting to note the discrepancy between Mary's claim that she and Mark had a close relationship and her assertion that she wondered about his behavior and never asked him about it. That she suspected his homosexuality suggests that she was avoiding the disclosure.)*

Mark admitted that he knew his mother suspected he might be gay before he actually came out. Both the mother and her son, in fact, were withholding information. Mark was secretive about his sexual orientation; Mary kept her suspicions to herself. Yet Mark knew about his mother's secret, much as Mary knew about her son's. Thus a complex of secrets and concealed awareness of the other party's secrets evolved throughout the predisclosure stage.

The first family member with whom Mark shared his secret was his sister. Mark knew that she had many friends in the gay community and that she would not have a problem accepting him as a gay brother. Our data . . . suggest that the majority of gay men and lesbians would first disclose their homosexuality to a family member other than a parent: a sibling or a member of the extended family. They think of the first disclosure to a family member as a trial, a "rehearsal" before the real performance. . . .

Mary and Mark think of predisclosure as a period of time during which they felt distant from one another, and their relationship deteriorated. "Not telling" enabled both of them to keep their secrets and protect their privacy. By the same token, withdrawing to the safety of their secrets left little space for exchange, sharing, and closeness.

---

5. How was the period of predisclosure described?

For the son, as a period of conflict between wanting to come out and not wanting to relinquish his privacy, which increased the boundary between himself and his mother. He also guessed that his mother knew. The motive was the need to be closer to her. For the mother, there were doubts about why he was different from his older brother and the suspicion that he might be gay.

6. Is any other interpretation of the motive plausible?

Yes. Mark may have felt guilty about his nondisclosure and/or his homosexuality and may have wanted to relieve the guilt. His mother may have nagged him about a girlfriend, and he wanted it to end.

Disclosure

Mary and Mark have different perceptions of what transpired during actual disclosure. . . . Mary is sure that Mark carefully planned the disclosure down to the very last detail. On the other hand, Mark casually implies that he intended to come out "sometime" during that weekend. Mary thought that Mark deliberately chose a time when she would be unable to make much fuss.

> Not only were we not at home; we were house guests. He made his disclosure when our friend was in the doctor's office, allowing only a very brief exchange between us. When the friend returned, we both tried to act as if it had never happened, hadn't been said. But I think he was very stiff at that point, and felt a little self-conscious. Later that day, I asked him when he first knew, and he told me that was too private and personal a question.

Mark's narrative focuses on a different aspect . . . :

> I was watching her through the rear mirror. She was in the back seat. I could see her. She could watch my eyes. We were both looking at each other

through the mirror. . . . At some point I think we both avoided looking at the mirror. Later that evening, I was sitting in front of these people's house and my mother came to talk to me. She asked me if I was sure that I was gay, if I wasn't just going through a phase. She also said that if it was true, she wouldn't know what to do about it. That was all we talked about.

▶ *(Notice that we have to rely on the author's summary of narratives to conclude that Mark planned the coming out "down to the very last detail" [according to Mary] or planned to come out "sometime" during the weekend. Also, there is no reason given for why Mark chose this particular time to come out.)*

Mark and Mary's perceptions of the disclosure reflect the differences in the meanings they attribute to it. . . . Generally, the initiating person is more likely to recognize the planning involved. . . . It is interesting to note, however, that in our case Mary is sensitive to the planning aspect of disclosure.

▶ *(Note that the author assumes that the time of disclosure in fact was planned because Mary emphasizes that it was. Mark [according to the summary] casually implied that he would disclose sometime during the weekend. Mary's perception does not mean that Mark planned to tell her while they were in the car. It simply may have happened then because of their discussion at the time [see opening narratives].)*

Neither Mary nor Mark includes details that might imply doubts pertaining to issues about which they currently feel certain. Yet the other person does. . . . Mark emphasizes his mother's questioning of his homosexuality, and Mary doesn't mention it in her account. These differences can be explained in light of how they currently perceive themselves. Mary views herself as a very accepting person. . . .

▶ *(This contradicts Mark's account. Look at the end of above quote. Or, Mary's perception of herself may have changed.)*

Mark, on the other hand, presents himself as never having doubted his homosexuality. . . .

On the basis of interviews with 27 parents and 32 gay men and lesbians, Ben-Ari . . . has developed the view that in most cases, gay and lesbian young adults disclose their homosexuality to their parents because they want to get closer to them. Indeed, telling parents about their homosexuality generally does improve the relationships between these children and their parents. Most of the interviews reflect a consensus during the time of the interviews, and in retrospect, the main motive for disclosure is "to be honest with parents; not to hide; not to live a lie."

Like their gay and lesbian children, an overwhelming majority of parents also prefer that their gay children disclose their sexual orientation to them. . . . They also prefer to receive "private" disclosure and that it be done in person. . . . Many parents expressed their regrets at not being told sooner. They feel that they missed an important part of their children's lives. Mary says,

> I really feel bad that I missed those years of his life, that I could not share with him when he was in high school, whatever he was going through. I think all mothers who have learned to accept this, feel this way. We miss. In my case, I missed 10 years of his life which he couldn't share with me, the questions and fears he had. Now, I wish I could replay those moments, hug him, and tell him how much I love him anyway.

---

7. How was the disclosure period interpreted?

The mother reported being convinced that Mark had carefully planned to tell her on a weekend when they were visiting friends and she could not make a fuss. Mark did not mention specific planning but said that he had intended to tell her sometime that weekend. Each omitted details that would imply doubt about issues at that time of which they were currently certain. In her narrative about disclosure, Mary said nothing that implied she questioned Mark's homosexuality, but at present, she is certain that she had accepted it. Mark spoke of her question. In his narrative, Mark said nothing that implied that he had doubts about coming to terms with his sexual orientation but at present felt that he had come to terms with it. Mary spoke of it.

8. How does the author interpret this discrepancy in reports?

In terms of how each perceives himself or herself today. For example, Mary perceives herself as accepting but may have had doubts about her acceptance then and omitted this from her account.

9. Are other interpretations plausible?

Yes. The omitted issue of past doubt might reflect denial. Psychoanalysts might attribute the omission to repression.

Postdisclosure

I met Mark and Mary more than 5 years after the initial disclosure. Mark remembers his mother right after disclosure:

> A little bit of surprise, quite a bit of disbelief, and unwillingness to deal with it. The hours and the days that followed, I think she kind of put it in the back of her mind and did not think about it because she had this social engagement she was going through, and she couldn't stop to process this knowledge. After that she talked a lot to my sister who has a lot of gay friends.

Mary remembers,

> I was pretty shocked, I think that when you are shocked like that you kind of have a dead feeling, you don't really know what to say next. I didn't cry, I was just shocked and thought what am I going to do now. I don't think I even reassured him that that's OK with me. . . . [Very quietly she added,] I don't think I even did that.

▶ *(Note that Mark was 22 years old at the time of disclosure and was telling his story as a 27-year-old adult. There is a big difference between perceptions of events by a 22- and a 27-year-old man.)*

Parental reactions to learning about their child's homosexuality are often seen in terms of typical grief responses, including shock, denial, guilt, anger, and acceptance. . . .

Mary's experience, however, does not reflect a typical process of grief following disclosure. Although describing herself as being shocked initially, she could not recall going through denial, anger, self-blame, or guilt. . . .

▶ *(Note that initially she reported thinking "what it was that I had done." In her narrative, she reported having a "dead feeling," which occurs with grief. And earlier, she reported being sure that Mark had planned his disclosure down to the last detail, which could reflect anger.)*

Our data did not confirm the traditional view and did not reveal significant differences between specified grief reactions . . . which may imply that parents do not necessarily go through a grief sequence after learning about their child's homosexuality. . . .

▶ *(Note that a mother's reaction may differ from a father's reaction.)*

Like many other parents, Mary thinks about her postdiscovery stage in terms of a chronological sequence. She differentiates, for example, between her thoughts and feelings right after she was disclosed to, during the first year, and at the time of the interview:

> Later on, maybe 6 months later, I think that I came to gradually accept more and more that this was really true. I felt very protective towards him and extremely concerned. I was more worried about him than I was about how I was feeling. After realizing that he could not change, I didn't even think about it anymore, I started to accept reality.

The search for an underlying theme that would characterize a period of time or a certain experience is indicative of the effort to organize and create meaning out of a particular experience. . . .

> When I think about it now, the emotion I found that I had within the first 6 months, or the first year, and still have to some extent is loneliness. I tend not to share this with anybody who I think will think less of him. Everybody in our family thinks very highly of him. I guess, I don't want anybody to think: Ha, he is not what we thought he was. Among my closest friends, there is no one with whom I could share the experience of having a gay son.

▶ *(It is almost impossible to know whether Mary is being protective or is too ashamed or embarrassed to tell her close friends.)*

Mark's recollection of his mother's postdisclosure experience is somewhat different. He remembers, for instance, that during the first 6 months, or even the first year, his mother didn't want to ask him about his personal life.

▶ *(Note that she reported earlier that when she asked him when he became aware of his homosexuality, he answered, "that was too private and personal a question.")*

> She was embarrassed to talk about it, or she thought it wasn't any of her business. I think she really didn't want to know what could be going on. She didn't want to know if I had a lover. She didn't know how to communicate about gayness with a gay child.

On completion of the interviews, I asked Mark and Mary, "What could the other person have done so it would be easier for you?"

Mark thought that if his mother had been able to communicate with him about his homosexuality earlier, it would have made the whole experience easier. He felt that his initiative to get closer to her was not reciprocated. Mary said that it would have helped if Mark were closer, physically and emotionally, so she would not have to be so alone.

▶ *(That was an interesting statement if she has a husband, and she does have two other children.)*

. . . One of this chapter's main concepts is that gay men and lesbians come out to their parents mainly because they want to get closer and be able to share their lives with them. Parents can ease their experiences following the discovery of their children's homosexuality by perceiving it as a quest for intimacy. By the same token, gay and lesbian individuals are not the only ones to keep information about their homosexuality private before disclosure. In most cases, the parents of these individuals also keep related thoughts and suspicions secret.

---

10. What were the accounts regarding the postdisclosure reactions?

Mark described his mother's reaction as surprise (shock) and disbelief, putting her coping at bay. Mary also described being shocked and wondering how she would cope. Both describe a period of loneliness.

11. How were Mary's reactions interpreted?

The author claims that there was no evidence of a typical grief reaction, which fit in with other data she obtained.

12. Is there question about the interpretation?

Yes. First, Mary earlier had questioned what it was she had done. On one hand, this may refer to "Why is he trying to get back at me?" On the other hand, it may refer to "How did I contribute to his being gay?" The latter suggests guilt. These are also signs that suggest grief and anger. Second, the conclusion that parents do not experience a typical grief reaction is based on a mother's account. The author does not report fathers' reactions to their sons' or daughters' homosexuality nor mothers' reactions to their daughters' lesbianism, and we are led to believe that all reactions are alike.

13. Does the narrative analysis fulfill its purpose?

Yes and no. It describes recollections of the impact of an event that was the turning point in the lives of a gay man and his parent. It shows that certain issues are emphasized and others casually mentioned or omitted—perhaps the major future effect of the event. If the intent is to describe the actual (not perceived) impact, the method did not fully succeed. It relied on retrospection of events that occurred 5 years earlier when the son was much younger; other factors, such as the participant's age then and now, can color objective and subjective reactions. Again, the author states that subjective truth is more important. The interview questions were loosely presented, and the place (aside from an outdoor cafe) was not specified, both of which could affect the nature of the narratives. Moreover, the interviewer was a female, and the male participant may have felt uneasy about reporting his homosexuality to a female. Most important, interpretations of this narrative report are influenced by the theoretical leanings of the interpreter. It may be that this particular case supported her views. And, because a complete transcript was not presented, the particular narratives might have been selected because they supported the author's views.

BIBLIOGRAPHY

Josselson, R., & Lieblich, A. (1993). *The narrative study of lives* (Vol. 1). Newbury Park, CA: Sage.

Josselson, R., & Lieblich, A. (1995). *Interpreting experience: The narrative study of lives* (Vol. 3). Newbury Park, CA: Sage.

McMillan, J. H., & Schumacher, S. (1997). *Research in education: A conceptual introduction* (4th ed.). White Plains, NY: Longman.

Riessman, C. K. (1993). *Narrative analysis.* Newbury Park, CA: Sage.

Additional Suggested Reading

Miles, M. B., & Huberman, A. M. (1994). *Qualitative data analysis* (2nd ed.). Thousand Oaks, CA: Sage.

Chapter 4

Surveys

The case study is the crudest of the descriptive methods for studying behavior. The focus is on a single individual or group of individuals studied as a unit. As such, if results can be considered internally valid, they can be generalized only to other similar individuals with like characteristics and backgrounds who would be measured under similar situations. In brief, case studies and most analytic studies lack external validity: Their results cannot be generalized to the population of which the participant is a sample. On the other hand, *surveys* are conducted with the specific intent of generalizing the results, almost always quantitative, to the population of interest. (Populations are always defined in terms of a target characteristic that is shared by all of its members.)

Surveys can be better controlled than case studies. They obtain information that is otherwise inaccessible. On occasion, surveys are conducted with the intent of obtaining a general sense of what people feel. Politicians, for example, may want to assess what people feel are important election issues. So, generalizations in terms of estimations of population means, stan-dard deviations, and the like are not considered. There are two broad types of surveys.

Attitude surveys measure likes, dislikes, and so on. *Research surveys* test hypotheses. With both, responses are related to demographic information.

Two crucial aspects of surveys are the development of a valid and reliable questionnaire and selection of the sample. Because the intent is to generalize the results to the population, the sample has to be representative. *Probability samples* are representative: There is a certain probability that every member can be included in the sample. The process of sample selection is the key to valid results. Sample selection depends on the *sample frame*, the population that has a chance to be selected. It can be an entire list of members, a list that is created as its members attend something (a clinic, a hospital, a meeting), or a list of members of units (such as houses). It should be comprehensive (all members have a chance of being selected) and exclude few; it should provide a determination of the probability of selecting each member; and it should be efficient (include only those members of interest). Researchers should note the criteria of inclusion and exclusion of members of the sample frame.

The sampling procedure can result in a random or a *stratified* sample. With the latter, the population is segmented on some basis (e.g., age, college level), and samples of each segment are in the same ratio as exists in the population. In either case of probability sampling, it is possible to calculate estimations of population values, usually means, standard deviations, and standard errors of the mean. Be leery of surveys that report these values for nonprobability samples.

Nonprobability samples are not representative because they unintentionally exclude members of the population. For example, telephone directories exclude people without telephones, with unlisted numbers, or with phones installed after the directory was published. *Quota* sampling obtains samples with certain characteristics in the same ratio that exists in the population but only from a particular location, and the participants are selected at the discretion of the interviewer. The most accessible may be selected and will have characteristics that differ from the population. Similarly, *convenience sampling* relies on participants who are accessible and available, for example, patients attending a particular clinic. They can provide useful information, but results are not likely to generalize.

The biggest potential drawback of surveys is that people are not always willing or able (because of illness or a language problem) to respond to the questionnaire. Therefore, what begins as a representative sample does not always end up that way, depending on the nature of the survey. There may be a difference between respondents and nonrespondents; that is, those responding may be a select group because nonresponders refused to respond, and this can place serious limitations on the extent to which results can be generalized. For nonthreatening surveys, a response rate of 70% or better should pose no threat of bias. If nonresponders have an important characteristic to the same extent as responders, bias is not a problem. But if it exists to a much lower or larger degree, bias is a problem regardless of response rate. For this reason, it is very important that, when reading results of a survey, you learn the initial size of the sample and the final percentage that responded. This is true regardless of whether the survey was conducted by means of a written questionnaire mailed to individuals or administered to a group, by telephone interview, or by face-to-face interview. Group administration, however, is likely to yield almost 100% returns. But all members of the group may not be present at administration time. It is equally important to know who gathered the data, how, and where.

Results of surveys are reported in terms of percentages. Tests of significance often involve chi-square. Other analyses, however, can be used (e.g., differences between proportions). *Chi-square tests* determine whether frequencies in certain categories differ from what would be expected on the basis of chance. When categories differ along a single dimension, the test is called *goodness of fit*. For example, all faces of an unbiased die should occur equally often when it is tossed many times. If you toss it 120 times, you would expect each face to appear 20 times ($120/6 = 20$). Suppose you obtain frequencies of 18, 20, 22, 30, 16, and 14 for Faces 1 through 6, respectively. Is there evidence to suggest a biased die? The $\chi^2 = 8.00$, and you enter the chi-square table with $6 - 1 = 5$ *df*. A chi-square of at least 11.07 can occur by chance 5 times out of 100 ($p = .05$). A value of 8.00 can be expected more often, and you conclude that the obtained frequencies do not differ reasonably from the expected frequencies of 20. There is not sufficient evidence to consider the die biased.

Contingency tests determine whether frequencies in one category depend on membership in another. For example, does preference for rare, medium, or well-done steak depend on gender? Males and females are surveyed about their preference. You end up with a 3 (Steak Preference) × 2 (Gender) table of frequencies. Expected frequencies are based on marginal totals across rows and columns for each cell ([row total × column total]/N). Then, chi-square is calculated and compared with a tabled value for $df = (\text{rows} - 1)(\text{columns} - 1)$. Here, $df = (3 - 1)(2 - 1) = 2$. If the obtained value is lower than the tabled χ^2, you conclude that steak preference does not depend on gender. If the obtained value is significant, then steak preference depends on gender. Then, further analysis is required to pinpoint the source of the significance of chi-square. There are, however, some requirements for using the chi-square test. The data are categorical, the basis for frequencies. The sample size should be sufficiently large that you end up with an *expected frequency* of at least 10 in a 2 × 2 table or 5 in a larger table. Most important, every entry is independent of every other entry. That means that frequencies refer to unique individuals (i.e., you can't have two entries for one individual in two categories).

To avoid threats to internal validity, the questionnaire should be reliable and valid for the target population; any measuring instrument or scale used also should be reliable and valid; testing should be conducted under uniform conditions; and administrators (for questionnaires that are not mailed and for interviews) should be naive with respect to any research hypothesis being tested, and they should be trained and supervised. To eliminate the possibility of a biased sample, some step should be taken to contact a sample of nonresponders to determine that they do not differ from the sample of responders. The caution factors associated with evaluation of a survey are in Box 4.1.

We begin our critical review by evaluating a survey together. Then you will evaluate another survey by yourself.

BOX 4.1
Caution Factors When Evaluating Surveys

- The sample frame
- The percentage of participants selected
- The criterion of exclusion
- The response return rate (is it less than 70%?)
- The method used to contact nonresponders
- The likelihood that characteristics of nonresponders introduced bias
- The nature of the questionnaire
- The reliability and validity of the questionnaire
- The number and characteristics of interviewers
- The training and supervision of interviewers
- The uniformity of the interview settings

STUDY EXAMPLE 4.1

This survey, conducted in England, determined whether mothers or fathers differed in the administration of punishment to their children.

The Study

Nobes, G., Smith, M., Upton, P., & Heverin, A. (1999). Physical punishment by mothers and fathers in British homes. *Journal of Interpersonal Violence, 14*(8), 887-902. Copyright 1999 by Sage.

Recent evidence indicates that harsh physical punishment of children leads to the development of emotional and behavioral problems. . . . Furthermore, it is likely that much abuse begins as physical punishment that goes too far. . . . To understand parental violence against children and to identify the characteristics of potential abusers, it is important to address the question of whether mothers or fathers administer most physical punishment. . . .

Two British studies have reported that mothers administer physical punishment considerably more frequently than fathers. According to the mothers interviewed . . . 11.1% of mothers and 3.3% of fathers smacked [spanked] their 3-year-old children daily or more frequently. Similarly . . . 15% of mothers of 11-year-olds reported smacking weekly or more often, compared with 5% who said their partners smacked this frequently. Furthermore, 79% of the mothers of 7-year-olds . . . reported that they smacked children more than did fathers, whereas only 10% of mothers said that fathers smacked most. . . .

▶ *(Note that greater frequency of spanking by mothers is consistent with the mothers spending more time with their children during the day, when children are most likely to misbehave.)*

However, mothers tend to underestimate fathers' use of physical punishment (and fathers underestimate mothers'). . . . Inasmuch as the . . . studies were based only on mothers' reports of their own and their partners' actions, it is likely that their findings are misleading. . . . In contrast, studies based on self-reports . . . and on people's reports of their own parents . . . all indicate little or no disparity between mothers' and fathers' rates of physical punishment.

▶ *(Note that self-reports are not always reliable, especially if the respondent does not want to be seen in a bad light.)*

Although this comparison of findings strongly suggests that because they have relied on mother reports, the British studies have underestimated the father's role in administering physical punishments, another explanation is that British families differ from those in countries in which most other studies have been conducted. . . . For these reasons, there is a need for information based on mothers' *and* fathers' self-reports. In addition, . . . it is important to assess how severely children are punished and to record parents' use of forms of physical punishment other than smacking.

Another issue that has rarely been addressed is the degree to which the extent of parents' physical punishments is a function of the amount of time they spend with children. Because most fathers have less contact with their children than do mothers, a finding of parity between mothers and fathers would mean that fathers are more physically punitive than mothers while with children.

In this article, we report a community self-report study of British mothers' and fathers' accounts of their use of physical punishments. Parents were asked about the frequency and severity of a number of forms of physical punishment. In addition, they reported who they considered to be responsible for most child care in their families and the activities they engaged in with their children. It was predicted that mothers and fathers would administer physical punishment to similar extents in terms of frequency and severity. In families in which parents were equally responsible for child care, however, fathers would use more physical punishments than mothers.

---

1. What was the rationale for conducting the survey?

Harsh punishment can lead to behavioral and emotional problems. Because abuse can start as punishment that goes too far, it is important to examine punishment of children by parents. Earlier British studies that relied on reports by mothers found that they punished their children more than did fathers. Other studies that relied on self-reports found that both parents punished their children equally. The disparity may be due to the method of gathering data or the origin of the studies. To clarify the discrepancies, it is important to obtain self-reports of both parents' use of punishment, its severity, and its form other than spanking. It is equally important to consider the amount of time each parent spends with the children. If fathers and mothers equally punish their children but fathers spend less time with the children, they are more punitive.

> ### 2. What was the specific purpose of this survey?
>
> Mothers and fathers were asked to report frequency and severity of different forms of punishment and to indicate which parent had primary care of the child. It was predicted that both parents would be similar in their reports, but when both parents had equal responsibility for child care, the father would be more punitive.

Method

Sample

The sample for this study was composed of 465 parents from 366 two-parent families. There were 362 mothers (all primary caretakers), 99 of their partners (secondary caretaking fathers), and 4 primary caretaking fathers.

These parents were from a larger original sample . . . of 434 families, each with a child aged 1.0, 4.0, 7.6, or 11.6 years. The original sample was randomly selected from health authority lists in an urban area outside London and an area of South London. The sampling was stratified so that, in the original and present sample, there were approximately equal numbers of children of each gender and each age group. All the primary caretakers in the original sample (425 mothers, 9 fathers) were interviewed, and in every fourth family the secondary caretaker was also invited to participate. If that family was headed by a lone parent, the secondary caretaker in the next eligible family was asked to take part.

▶ *(Note that the basis for stratification does not mean that the families had only one child. It means that a particular male or female child of the desired age was part of the family. Nonetheless, we do have an excellent example of stratified random sampling.)*

The 68 lone parents were excluded from the present sample because all but 5 were mothers, and their inclusion would have therefore risked confounding the actions of mothers with those of lone parents. . . . Also excluded were ineligible families (e.g., in which the respondents did not speak English) and 18 fathers who refused to participate.

▶ *(Note that the original sample included 434 families [425 primary-care mothers and 9 primary-care fathers]. The new sample excluded 68 of these, 63 mothers and 5 fathers, leaving 425 − 63 = 362 primary-care mothers and 9 − 5 = 4 primary-care fathers. The further exclusions [non-English-speaking and 18 fathers who refused to be interviewed] had to have occurred with the original sample. Keep in mind that the 18 refusers may have punished their children more than those who agreed to participate.)*

The response rate of primary caretakers from the original sample was 80.9%. Because no information about family structure or responsibility for refusal was available for most of the families who refused, we can only estimate the relative response rates of mothers and fathers. Exclusion of families in which both parents were approached, and of those in which the father was the primary caretaker, leads to an estimated response rate of 85.3% in families in which only the mother was asked to participate. Among confirmed two-parent families in which both were invited to take part, the figure fell to 65.8%. These figures indicate that approximately 15% of primary caretaking mothers and 23% of secondary caretaking fathers refused to be interviewed.

▶ *(Keep in mind that 65.8% acceptance is low but not unreasonably so, considering that the study involved families. But the 15% of primary-care mothers and 23% of secondary-care fathers who refused to participate may represent harsher punishers than those who participated. It is also possible, however, that refusers did not have time to participate.)*

All but 20 mothers and 9 fathers were White. Thirty-two mothers and 10 fathers were born outside the United Kingdom. There were 8 stepfathers and 2 stepmothers, and five children were adopted. Of the fathers, 8 were unemployed and 2 worked part-time, whereas 166 (45.5%) mothers were not employed and 101 (27.7%) worked part-time. The remaining parents worked at least 25 hours per week. For the purpose of this research, "fathers" are defined as men who had a cohabiting relationship of at least a year's duration with the mother.

▶ *(It is worth keeping in mind that we don't know how many "fathers" were birth fathers, were always involved in the lives of their children, and had cohabited with the mother as a stepfather for at least 1 year.)*

---

3. How was the sample of parents obtained?

Through stratified random sampling, families were selected from health authority lists to ensure equal numbers of male and female children at ages 1.0, 4.0, 7.6, or 11.6 years. From the 434 parents, 68 lone parents were excluded, leaving 366 two-parent families. Non-English-speaking individuals also were excluded, and 18 fathers refused to participate.

4. What was the response rate of confirmed two-parent families in which both parents were asked to participate?

It is estimated to be 65.8%, with about 15% of primary-care mothers and 23% of secondary-care fathers refusing to participate.

5. What can be said about the refusers?

They may have been parents who severely punish their children. Because there were more fathers than mothers who refused, a finding of no differences in this survey may be misleading. On the other hand, the refusers may have been unable to participate.

6. Describe the final sample.

There are 362 primary-care mothers, 99 secondary-care partners, and 4 primary-care fathers. Most were White, most of the "fathers" (men who had lived with the mother for at least 1 year) were employed full-time, whereas only 45.5% of the mothers stayed at home full-time.

Procedure

Parents . . . were sent a letter about the study. Unless they declined at this stage, parents then were visited to explain the research and, if they were willing, to arrange the interviews. Interviews took place in the family home. When both parents participated, mothers and fathers were interviewed separately and, in all but eight families, simultaneously, by different members of the research team. Interviews lasted approximately 3 hours.

▶ *(Note that interviews were not taped, for practical reasons. Therefore, all subsequent measures relied on interviewer notes as well as their accuracy.)*

7. What was the general procedure?

Letters initially were mailed to potential participants. Positive responders were visited, and those who agreed later were interviewed for about 3 hours. Most parents who were both included were interviewed separately at the same time by different interviewers. (A footnote thanks three individuals for their assistance. It is difficult to know whether they or the authors conducted the interviews.)

Measures

The interviews were interview-led and semistructured. Mothers' and fathers' interviews were directly comparable within an age group. There were some small differences between the interview schedules for different child-age groups, so that the content was appropriate to the child's age. Parents were asked about the nature and frequency of their own use of physical punishments of children. The interview also covered a number of other topics relating to parental control, family members, and relationships.

Types of punishment. Physical punishments were grouped into one of four categories, these being,

> "smacking/hitting," including spanking, slapping, and beating. "Smacking" usually involves use of the open hand. . . .
> "physical restraint," including pushing, shoving, shaking, throwing, and holding. . . .
> "punishment by example," consisting of punishments such as squeezing, hair pulling, biting, and pinching, usually administered with the intention of demonstrating to children the consequences of their actions. . . .
> "ingestion," including washing the child's mouth out with soap and water and forced feeding. . . .

▶ *(Note that each category is clearly defined.)*

For each category, parents were asked whether they had administered to the child any of the different punishment types included in the category. . . .

Frequency of punishment. Unless parents replied that they had never used a punishment of a particular type, frequency of use of that type was established by asking such questions as, "When was the last time? And the time before?" and so forth, until the interviewer was confident [he or she] could make an estimate of the frequency of use in the last year (3 months for 1-year-old children). . . . Frequencies of use of the four physical punishment categories were coded on a seven-category ordinal scale, from *never* to *daily or more often.* Reliability of these measures, assessed by two researchers interviewing and coding 12 mothers 2 weeks apart, was high ($\alpha = .98$ for smacking/hitting).

▶ *(Note that reliability of scoring was established, but a similar procedure was not reported for the remaining categories of punishment, nor are there reports of validity measures.)*

A derived measure of the frequency of use of physical punishment, of any kind, was also calculated. This measure ("any physical punishment") takes into account the frequency of all four categories of physical punishment. It is based on the frequency of the category of punishment that the parent uses most often: If a parent smacks once or twice a week, pushes a few times a year, and does not use other physical punishments, the frequency of use of any punishment will effectively equal that of smacking ("weekly or more often"). . . .

Severity of punishment. To assess severity of punishments, parents were asked to describe actual events. . . . The intensity and consequences of the most recent incident in each category were recorded from parents' replies to such questions as, "[on the last occasion,] how many times did you smack? Where on her body? Did it leave a mark? Did you use your hand (which part?)? Or something else?" Information about the most severe punishments ever administered by the parent was sought. . . .

On the basis of all the information available, interviewers judged the severity of the most serious punishment in each category. . . . "Mild" punishments were nonprolonged and nonrepeated actions that did not involve the use of implements, had no prolonged effect, and were not intended to harm. "Moderate" punishments were intermediate between mild and severe. "Severe" punishments were those that were intended to, had the potential to, or actually did cause harm to the child, and included actions that were repeated, prolonged, or involved the use of implements.

▶ *(Note clear definitions of severity.)*

All incidents that were rated either moderate or severe were cross-validated on completion of fieldwork, at which point it was possible to collate and directly compare descriptions of all these events. . . .

Parental involvement. . . . The frequency during the previous week of joint engagement in six activities (e.g., reading, playing indoors and out, and household tasks) was measured on a scale of 0 (no joint activities) to 18 (all six activities daily or more often). . . . Parents were also questioned about who took most responsibility for looking after the children, and fathers were asked about the amount of time that they spent alone with their children. This was rated on a 6-point scale, from *none* to *more than 2 whole days a week* (or equivalent).

Punishment roles. Parents were asked who they considered to be the main punisher. . . . The possibility that, in some families, fathers administer punishments on behalf of the mother was investigated by asking both parents whether one would sometimes execute a punishment that was initiated by the other.

---

8. What general measures of punishment were made?

Four types of punishment, their frequency (including all forms of punishment as a single score) and severity, as well as parental involvement with the child and parental roles in administering punishment. In most instances, responses were converted to category scales.

Results

Frequency of Physical Punishments Reported by Mothers and Fathers

The great majority of parents had physically punished their children at some time in some way. . . . Approximately equal proportions of fathers and mothers reported having never done so (24 mothers [6.6%] vs. 9 fathers [8.7%], ns). . . . No overall difference was found between mothers' and fathers' frequencies of administration of physical punishments. A total of 26.8% of mothers, compared with 26.2% of fathers, reported using some sort of physical punishment at least as often as weekly.

Almost all parents had smacked, slapped, spanked, or hit their child (see Table 1). Mothers and fathers were almost equally likely to report never having punished in any of these ways (8.8% mothers, 9.7% fathers, ns). There was no overall difference between mothers' and fathers' frequency . . . in this smacking/hitting category. However, a somewhat greater proportion of mothers than fathers smacked weekly or more often (25.1% mothers, 17.5% fathers . . .).

In the category of physical restraints as means of punishment or control . . . fathers' frequency of use was significantly higher than mothers' ($p < .005$). Almost four times the proportion of fathers as mothers reported using such methods with a frequency that was rated as at least monthly (4.7% mothers, 18.6% fathers). . . . Fathers who frequently used physical restraints were also more likely than other fathers to smack frequently ($r = .35$, $p < .001$).

Approximately equal proportions of mothers and fathers reported ever having used punishments in the "punishment by example" category . . . and no difference was apparent between mothers' and fathers' rates.

TABLE 1 Percentage of Parents Using Physical Punishments						
Punishment Category	N	Ever	In Last Year	Monthly or More Often	z	p
Smacking/hitting						
By mothers	362	91.2	76.8	39.8		
By fathers	103	90.3	76.7	35.9	1.07	.29
Physical restraint						
By mothers	362	39.5	25.4	4.7		
By fathers	102	50.0	42.2	18.6	3.00	.003
Punishment by example						
By mothers	361	38.8	12.7	1.1		
By fathers	103	30.1	14.6	2.9	1.20	.23
Ingestion						
By mothers	267	9.7	5.2	0.0		
By fathers	77	3.9	3.9	0.0	1.57	.12
Any physical punishment						
By mothers	362	93.4	80.4	42.5		
By fathers	103	91.3	80.6	45.6	.17	.87

The small number of parents who had used some form of ingestion as a punishment were mostly mothers, although this difference was not significant (9.7% mothers, 3.9% fathers. . . .). . . .

There were no significant differences between mothers' and fathers' rates of punishment either of boys or of girls: 46.4% mothers and 40.7% fathers smacked their sons at least monthly, whereas 33.1% mothers and 30.6% fathers smacked their daughters at least monthly.

There were few differences between mothers and fathers relating to children's ages. Among parents of 1-year-olds, fathers reported significantly higher rates of use of any punishment than did mothers ($z = 2.35$, $p = .02$). This difference was largely accounted for by fathers' markedly more frequent use of physical restraints at this age ($z = 3.32$, $p < .001$). . . . Mothers of 4-year-olds smacked more than did fathers of 4-year-olds ($z = 2.00$, $p = .05$). . . . There were no apparent differences between mothers and fathers of 7- or 11-year-olds in their frequency of use of punishment.

TABLE 2 Most Severe Punishment Administered by Parent

Most Severe	Mother		Father	
	n	%	n	%
None/not applicable	24	6.7	9	9.1
Mild	163	45.5	52	52.5
Moderate	115	32.1	17	17.2
One or more severe incidents	56	15.6	21	21.2
Total	358	100.0	99	100.0

---

9. What were the basic results regarding frequency of punishment by mothers and fathers?

More mothers than fathers smacked their children on a weekly basis, but more fathers used physical constraint as punishment. There were no differences in the use of punishment by example between mothers and fathers, nor were there differences in the frequency of punishment of all kinds of male or female children. But fathers punished 1-year-old children most frequently, and more often than did mothers, with physical restraint, and mothers smacked 4-year-old children more frequently than did fathers.

Severity of Fathers' and Mothers' Physical Punishments

The proportions of mothers and fathers who reported ever having used punishment rated as severe (Table 2) were 15.6% and 21.2%, respectively ($\chi^2(1) = 1.72$, $p = .19$).

The proportion of mothers who reported having used an implement in punishing their children was also less than that of fathers (35 mothers [10.7%] vs. 14 fathers [15.2%], $\chi^2(1) = 1.56$, $p = .21$). The majority of implements used were either slippers or wooden spoons . . . sticks or belts . . . hairbrushes, folded newspapers, or a flyswat. . . .

Fathers had inflicted significantly more punishments rated as severe on sons than daughters (30.8% vs. 10.6%, $\chi^2(1) = 5.98$, $p = .01$). . . . The difference between mothers' and fathers' use of severe punishments on boys was marginally significant ($\chi^2(1) = 3.40$, $p = .07$) but not on girls ($\chi^2(1) = .07$, $p = .78$). There were no significant differences between mothers' and fathers' use of severe punishments at any of the four age groups.

10. What were the basic results regarding severity of punishment by mothers and fathers?

There was a tendency, although it was not significant, for more fathers than mothers to have reported using severe punishment at some time. There also was a tendency for more fathers than mothers to use implements other than a hand to punish their children. Fathers used severe punishment more often on sons than on daughters and did so more often than did mothers. There were no differences in frequencies of severe punishment by fathers and mothers as a function of age of the child.

▶ *(Here is an opportunity to check some statistics. We have a 4(Severity) by 2 (Parent) contingency table and can perform a chi-square test to determine whether the degree of severity of punishment depends on whether the parent was a mother or father. I performed a straightforward test and obtained $\chi^2(3) = 8.851$, p < .05. Therefore, the degree of severity of punishment depends on whether the punisher is a mother or a father. Now, to isolate the source of the contingency, we can look at the individual cells and compare the extent of difference between observed and expected frequencies by z = observed frequency − expected frequency/$\sqrt{expected\ frequency}$. There is only one outstanding difference: Fewer fathers administered moderate punishment (17) than would be expected (28)—derived from the performance of the test—if both parents were equally likely to administer this degree of punishment. This also means that more mothers than fathers administered moderate punishment. [An excellent discussion of isolating the source of a significant chi-square is in Hayes, 1988, pp. 775-779.])*

Involvement with child. In the families in which mothers reported themselves to be the main caretakers (81.4%), there were no significant differences either between mothers' and fathers' frequency of smacking/hitting or in the proportion of mothers and fathers who reported having used severe punishments. . . . In the remaining families in which fathers were described by mothers as taking at least as much responsibility as the mother for the children, all 67 mothers and 25 of the fathers were interviewed. There was no evidence . . . of differences either in self-reported rates of smacking/hitting or in the use of severe punishments by mothers and fathers. . . . Furthermore, the parents' role as either main caretaker or secondary/equal caretaker was not associated with mothers' or fathers' frequency of punishment or with mothers' or fathers' use of severe punishment.

The extent of mothers' and fathers' involvement in activities with their children was positively correlated with their frequency of use of smacking/hitting ($r = .25$, $p < .001$ and $r = .24$, $p = .04$, respectively) but was associated with neither mothers' nor fathers' use of severe physical punishments. According to self-reports, there was no significant difference between mothers' and fathers' involvement in activities with their children. . . . Within the group of parents . . . who were described as relatively highly active . . . with their children, mothers and fathers smacked or hit their children equally frequently. . . . Similar proportions had used a severe physical punishment. . . . Mothers . . . and fathers . . . who engaged in relatively few activities with their children also smacked or hit at similar rates and were almost equally likely to have used a severe physical punishment. . . .

Fathers' frequency of smacking/hitting was not correlated with the amount of time they were alone with their children during each week. . . . Comparisons of fathers who had and had not used one or more severe physical punishments showed no difference in the amounts of time they spent alone with their children, and they reported being responsible for similar proportions of the caretaking of their children.

> **11. What were the results regarding role of caregivers?**
>
> Although frequency of punishment was related to amount of time spent with a child, there were no reported differences in that frequency between mothers and fathers, even when mothers were the primary caretakers. Moreover, mothers and fathers reported being equally involved with their children, and regardless of whether this involvement was high or low, mothers and fathers reported punishing their children equally often. Punishment by fathers was not related to time spent alone with their children nor to severity of punishment.

Punishment Roles

According to mothers and fathers, fathers' punishments were at least as effective as mothers'. About half of the mothers (48.0%) and a third of the fathers (36.8%) reported that children responded best to punishments by fathers, compared with about one in six parents (18.7% mothers and 16.2% fathers) who thought that mothers' punishments were more effective.

Most of the mothers (76.3%) and fathers (61.0%) said that parents did not administer punishments for each other in their families. . . .

Discussion

The data indicate near-parity between mothers' and fathers' frequencies of use of physical punishment of their children. Very similar proportions of mothers and fathers reported ever having administered a physical punishment, and almost identical proportions did so weekly or more often. An exception . . . is that fathers more often physically restrained (pushed or force-fully held) their children than did mothers. This was most evident in parents of 1-year-olds. . . .

. . . Those fathers who frequently physically restrained their children were also more likely to smack/hit more frequently than other fathers. This sug-gests that fathers typically sometimes choose to smack or hit and at other times choose to restrain. In contrast, when mothers physically punish their children, they almost always resort to smacking/hitting.

We can speculate that the greater tendency for fathers than mothers sometimes to restrain their children occurs because . . . fathers are better equipped successfully to restrain the child and are less willing to hit, fearing that they might hurt or injure the child . . . supported by the fact that this dif-ference between mothers' and fathers' rates of use of physical restraint was particularly evident among parents of 1-year-old children.

Although nonsignificant, the finding that higher proportions of mothers reported smacking/hitting their children weekly or more often than did fa-thers concurs with those reported by other researchers who recorded rates of smacking/hitting. . . .

No difference in incidence was evident in the present study when all physical punishments were considered. . . .

Regarding the severity of punishments, although mothers' and fathers' use of severe punishment showed no statistically significant differences . . . the present data suggest that fathers were more severely punitive. Greater proportions of fathers than of mothers reported having used implements and were judged to have administered a punishment rated as severe. These differ-ences solely reflect fathers' greater tendency than mothers to punish sons severely. . . .

These data concur with those of studies of official and clinical reports of abuse that adjusted for father absence. . . . They also are consistent with the findings of studies of victims' reports of their own parents. . . . All indicate that fathers are more often the perpetrators of violence to, and abuse of, children. However, . . . according to other community self-report studies, greater pro-portions of mothers than fathers have severely punished their children. . . .

The present study, then, is alone among self-report studies in indicating that fathers are no less, and may be *more,* severely punitive than mothers. . . . An explanation is that the fathers in the present study were willing to report their administration of severe punishments, because the relevant questions were asked in the context of a long interview concerning many aspects of family life. . . .

. . . Mothers were the main caretakers in the large majority of families. The finding that, in the families in which this was the case, mothers and fathers ad-ministered approximately equal amounts of physical punishment, suggests that fathers are more punitive relative to the amount of time spent with children. However, in the small number of families in which the father was as responsible for caretaking as the mother, again no difference was found. . . .

A possible explanation of these findings is that fathers who take equal responsibility in caretaking, and spend as much time with their children as do mothers, are an exceptional group who are also similar to their partners in their use of physical punishment. The large majority of fathers, though, have a more traditional father's role that involves less caretaking and more physical punishment relative to the amount of time they spend with their children. . . .

In summary . . . British mothers and fathers reported using physical punishment with approximately equal frequency. No significant difference in the proportion of mothers and fathers who had used physical punishments was found. A slightly higher proportion of fathers than of mothers reported having inflicted severe punishment. Because most mothers spend more time with their children than do fathers, these findings are consistent with the view that, relative to the amount of time they spend with their children, most fathers are somewhat more physically punitive than mothers. However, in families in which mothers' and fathers' caretaking roles are similar, so too are their roles as disciplinarians.

12. What were the major conclusions?

British fathers and mothers administer punishment with about equal frequency, although there are some differences in type of punishment administered. Notably, mothers used smacking and hitting; fathers used smacking and hitting as well as physical restraint. And although the difference was not significant, there was a greater tendency for fathers than mothers to use more severe punishment, especially with their sons. Because fathers and mothers were found to be equal in frequency of punishment, and because fathers spend less time with their children, fathers are relatively more punitive than mothers.

13. Are the conclusions justified?

Tentatively, if the self-reports are accurate and if nonresponders would have responded in the same way. Even here, the conclusions would apply only to parents of similar socioeconomic status, with similar families and work histories of each parent. Self-reports, however, are not always accurate. Parents had to rely on their memory of how frequently they administered punishment to a particular child (if there was more than one child in the family) during the last week, month, and year. There is room for error in memory the longer the time span. Moreover, parents would not want to present themselves in a bad light, and this, too, could result in underestimation of frequency, severity, or both. Indeed, no parent would want to be accused of child abuse. Finally, all figures were based on rating scales, some of whose reliability were not reported, and interpretations were based on notes by the researchers, who may or may not have been the authors. There is a possibility of error here, too.

A more important problem is with nonresponders. A relatively large percentage of fathers from two-parent families refused to participate, and one has to wonder why. If they were too busy to participate, then they probably would have responded as did the participants. But if they did not want to discuss their punishment behavior, they may have been more frequent (and possibly more severe) punishers, and study results may have been very different. Related to this, we don't know how many of the "fathers" who cohabited with the mothers actually fathered the children. Behavior of these two groups may well have differed.

STUDY EXAMPLE 4.2

The following article reports the results of a survey conducted on female college seniors regarding experiences of being forcibly raped or being subjected to nonconsensual sex while intoxicated.

The Study

Schwartz, M. D., & Leggett, M. S. (1999). Bad dates or emotional trauma? The aftermath of campus sexual assault. *Violence Against Women,* 5(3), 251-271. Copyright 1999 by Sage.

The public image of campus sexual assault has come full circle, at least in the viewpoints expressed in the mass media. . . . It was not until the 1980s that the media generally became aware that sexual assault on the college campus was more than a problem of stranger rape. . . . Study after study began to document that men the women knew and with whom they were often friends or even lovers were the most common sexual aggressors on campus. . . .

In the 1990s, however, there has been an extensive movement to minimize the problem. . . . The "backlash" has been a strong tactical offensive by men and a few women who argue that campus rape either does not occur or else what we have been calling campus rape is not particularly important. . . . What researchers call acquaintance rape is often simply the result of a woman regretting her consensual sexual encounters and consequently overreacting. . . .

Roiphe's most popular claim is that the women who say that they are victims of acquaintance rape are commonly not affected by the sexual encounter. . . . Roiphe believes that . . . women [who were drunk when supposedly raped] know that they could have had less to drink and maintained some more control, but they did not, so the morning after they have to face up to the fact that they were too drunk and went a little too far with a man. Because the women were in control of their own drinking, they have no reason to blame the man for the sexual activity. . . .

. . . What is important is that the backlash message has gotten into the general discourse. Do women who have had too much to drink and then find that a man has engaged in sexual intercourse with them without their permission become emotionally upset by this incident? Or, is Roiphe right that most of them just see this as a bad date? Who do these women blame for such incidents? Do they indeed see themselves as rape victims? The data in this article will speak at least preliminarily to these three concerns.

Sexual Assault on Campus

. . . Because these women often did not define their experiences as *rape,* rape must not be what happened. Researchers are making an issue out of sexual experiences that women simply engaged in but then regretted. . . . These women would have at least talked to a rape crisis center had they remotely thought they had been raped. . . . Because rape crisis centers do not automatically report rapes to the authorities, any woman would feel safe about reporting the rape and discussing her experiences.

. . . Because these women did not report that they had been raped, then . . . researchers are using a different definition than the one in the criminal law—they are using the radical feminist critique. . . . Because the women questioned were in college, they were too educated not to realize they had been raped. . . .

Another controversial area deals with the problem of sexual intercourse while the woman is too drunk or high to give consent. . . . The issue is whether a woman who has had too much to drink and is physically incapable of giving her consent has been raped or if she has simply not refused. . . . But the law is clear . . . that the crime of rape consists of sexual acts without a woman's consent, and that the act is rape if the woman is incapable of giving consent (unconscious, of low mental capacity, too intoxicated to give consent). . . .

. . . In our study we tried to make the connection [between drinking and consent] more clear by asking if the woman had sexual intercourse when she did not want to because she was unable to give her consent or stop the man because of being intoxicated or on drugs. This is an act that is without doubt a felony crime. . . .

Self-Blame

The importance of these questions is that many women believe that if they are too intoxicated or drugged to say no, then they are to blame for the sexual assault. . . . There has not been much study of this question, but the few studies that have compared stranger rape victims with acquaintance rape victims have found more self-blame among the latter group. . . .

As critics have noted, some respondents . . . do not claim that they are rape victims. It is not uncommon for women who have been attacked to be unable to fully understand that the incident that is bothering them is actually an event defined by criminal law as felony rape. . . .

Emotional Effects

An area closely related to self-blame is how affected emotionally and psychologically the woman is after a sexual assault. . . . The reaction of her friends and the amount of self-blame she takes upon herself can be relevant to this distress. There is a reasonably large literature in psychology that divides the victims of sexual assault into two groups: stranger rape and acquaintance rape. . . . Very little work had been done comparing acknowledged versus unacknowledged rape victims. . . . Women who do not admit to themselves that they are rape victims are just as likely to suffer from psychological distress as those who name their experiences as *rape.*

. . . Critics have claimed that women who engaged in unwanted sexual intercourse or other sexual acts while too intoxicated to give consent or protest were not as psychologically distressed as women who were victims of rape by force. . . .

Thus, a goal of this research was to investigate the claims of critics that women are not as affected by acquaintance rape as feminists claim, by looking directly at the differences between those women who were assaulted while drunk or high and those women who were forced into sexual intercourse or acts.

Hypotheses

It is an important part of backlash arguments that women who experience unwanted sexual intercourse because of intoxication are relatively unaffected by the sexual experience. . . . Women physically forced to have sex are the victims of "real rape" . . . and . . . "real rape" victims are more emotionally distressed by what happened. Thus, the first hypothesis is:

1. The women who were raped due to intoxication are significantly less affected by the event than the women who were raped due to physical force.

Second, there is no question that an important psychological factor in rape is self-blame, and that a large number of rape victims blame themselves after being raped. . . . Thus, the second hypothesis:

2. The women raped because of alcohol or drugs blame themselves for the event more than do the women raped by physical force.

. . . Women whose experiences meet the legal definition of rape generally do not believe that they were raped. . . . Here, . . . we further specify that even fewer women who were raped because of intoxication will report that their experience was a rape.

3. The women who have been raped because of force will be more likely to label their experiences as rape than will women who had unwanted sex because they were too intoxicated to resist.

Methods

. . . We created a questionnaire using previously used surveys, but mainly Koss's Sexual Experience Survey (SES). . . . We added open-ended questions at the end discussing the aftermath of the experience. . . . We decided to limit our sample entirely to seniors. In this way, we thought, we might be maximizing the amount of time available for sexual experiences while at college.

▶ *(Regarding the selection of seniors, the authors have noted that the opposite effect could have occurred, i.e., that fewer victims were available because some victims might have quit college or transferred to another college.)*

The university used requires senior-year integrative classes. By sampling these classes [on the first day of classes], we obtained usable questionnaires from 388 females in 25 classes.

▶ *(Data collectors were female.)*

Although data were simultaneously collected from men, in this study we used data only from the female respondents.

▶ *(The authors approached all 36 instructors, but 11 refused because they could not afford the class time. The 11 did not seem to be associated with a particular area of study.)*

The students were given a human subjects research consent form, which was read verbatim by the administrator, then signed, dated, and collected from each participating student. Each anonymous survey was completed voluntarily and students were informed verbally and in writing that they were free to stop answering questions at any time with no questions asked and no penalties. Only five females did not complete usable questionnaires.

Given the criticisms that SES questions were loosely worded, we tightened up several questions to remove any misunderstanding. For example, . . . we asked, "Have you engaged in sexual intercourse when you didn't want to but were so intoxicated or under the influence of alcohol or drugs that you could not stop it or object?". . . It is clear that the reason the woman had sex with the man was because she was physically or mentally unable to resist. It is clear the act was rape under virtually all state statutes. . . .

. . . To see if the two types of victims under discussion here were different on our questions, we created a variable called *rapetype.* This variable divided attempted and completed rape into two categories: (a) rape (and attempted rape) while unable to give consent because of alcohol or drug intoxication, and (b) rape (or attempted rape) because the male used or threatened physical force. . . . Of course . . . we did not use the word *rape* with the respondents; they were asked about their behavior as described in the statute.

Self-blame was measured by a simple variable. Women who reported that they were the victims of events measured by rapetype were asked to report for the most serious event whether they blamed themselves for what happened, whether they blamed the man for what happened, or whether they blamed both themselves and the man. . . .

Finally, the women in this survey who reported that they were the victims of unwanted sexual experience were asked to self-report on how much they were psychologically and emotionally affected by that experience. We asked the women to categorize their response using the following choices:

1. It was not very important to me; I was not much affected.
2. It did not bother me for very long; I bounced back fairly quickly.
3. It affected me. I changed as a person (e.g., not as trusting, depressed, unhappy, or some other reaction).
4. It deeply affected me and caused emotional pain.

TABLE 1 Whether Women Were Affected by the Type of Assault

| | Type of Rape | | |
How Affected	Alcohol	Physical Force	Total
Unaffected	5.7	16.7	10.8
Somewhat affected	51.4	26.7	40.0
Affected	31.4	36.7	33.8
Deeply affected	11.4	20.0	15.4
Total	53.8	46.2	100.0

Chi-square = 5.18
df = 3
Significance = 0.159

NOTE: Total affected: alcohol = 94.2%; physical force = 83.4%.

Findings

Of the 388 women who filled out the questionnaires in this survey, 65 reported that they were victims of an event that would under Ohio law be considered a felony rape. Thirty-five reported that they had been the victims of unwanted sexual intercourse when they were helpless to resist or stop the man, whereas 30 reported that they were overcome with force or a threat of force.

In Table 1, we see that of the women raped due to physical force, there were 16.7% who claimed to be unaffected versus only 5.7% of women victimized because of alcohol or drugs. . . . Of the women raped because they were unable to give consent due to intoxication, 94.2% claimed to be affected by the event versus 83.4% of the physically forced women. . . . There were similar numbers of women affected or deeply affected by the experiences in each category. . . . There is no statistically significant difference in the reported emotional outcome between the two groups of women. . . . These data do not support the first hypothesis prediction that women who were raped by intoxication were less likely to report psychological or emotional distress.

Table 2 shows rapetype by whom the women blame for the event. Once again, it is the lack of statistical significance in this table that is interesting. . . . 79.3% of the women who were raped while intoxicated put all or part of the blame on themselves. All of these women were the victims of a felony crime, and all said specifically that the only reason that they had unwanted sexual

TABLE 2 Whom the Women Blame, by the Type of Assault

| | Type of Rape | | |
Who to Blame	Alcohol	Physical Force	Total
Myself	27.6	22.7	25.5
Man	20.7	50.0	33.3
Both	51.7	27.3	41.2
Total	56.9	43.1	100.0

Chi-square = 5.16
$df = 2$
Significance = 0.076

intercourse was that they were unable to resist or fight back. What might be surprising to many is that 50% of the women raped by force or threat of force also took on some degree of self-blame. . . . Slightly more than one fourth of all of the women raped while intoxicated completely blamed themselves for what happened. However, virtually one quarter of the women raped by force took on all of the blame also.

At the end of the questionnaire, removed from the other questions, we asked the simple question of whether the woman answering the survey had been raped since coming to college. . . . All of the 51 women who chose to answer this question had already stated in response to the questions used to develop Tables 1 and 2 that they had in fact been victims of rape since coming to college. However, Table 3, for the first time, introduces the use of the word *rape*. . . . All of the women being asked if they had been raped had in fact been raped. Yet, in response to the question that specifically asked "Have you ever been raped?" only 1 victim (3.3%) raped while too intoxicated to give consent answered affirmatively, and only 5 victims (23.8%) raped because of physical force said that they had. The latter figure generally agrees with . . . researchers who have found that about 25% or so of rape victims label the event as rape.

What is important in Table 3 is that what Koss called the problem of the "hidden rape victim" is much worse in the case of the woman raped while intoxicated. Hidden rape victims who do not define what happened to them as rape do not seek out the services of rape counselors, do not attend to various mental health services, and often do not understand why they are suffering from various symptoms of emotional pain. . . . These hidden rape victims do not seek care because they do not see that they are victims. They do not make this recognition because they live in a society that makes women responsible as gate-keepers for sexual relations, rewards men for sexual aggressiveness,

TABLE 3 Whether Woman Says She Was Raped, by Type of Assault			
	Type of Rape		
Have Ever Been Raped	*Alcohol*	*Physical Force*	*Total*
Yes	3.3	23.8	11.8
No	96.7	76.2	88.2
Total	58.8	41.2	100.0

Chi-square = 4.99
df = 1
Significance = 0.026
Phi = .31

and blames women for their own victimization. What we have found in this society is that a tremendous number of women engage in self-blame for being victimized by predatory rapists.

Discussion and Conclusions

The first decision made in this study was to reject Hypothesis 1; there is no evidence that women raped due to intoxication were less affected emotionally than women who were raped by force. The numbers show that virtually all victims of rape are affected, regardless of the circumstances surrounding the act. . . . Virtually everyone who has done research in this field argues that the methodology we used is likely to be conservative in terms of eliciting admissions from women that they were victims of rape. . . . Many women report on anonymous questionnaires that they have never told anyone of their experience, and it is at least logical to assume (if we cannot prove it) that some of these women would continue to keep their secret, even in an anonymous questionnaire.

The second hypothesis specifies that the women who were raped while intoxicated would blame themselves more than would women who were raped by force. This hypothesis was also rejected. Still, although the table did not reach statistical significance, it is instructive to look at the percentages in the table. As mentioned earlier, about one quarter of all rape victims blame themselves entirely. . . . Women continue to blame themselves even when they are the victims of a rape accomplished through the use of force. . . .

. . . So many women are affected emotionally and psychologically by it, but still blame themselves and do not report it to the police. . . . Here, we found . . . of 43 women who answered this question, only 2 (4.7% had reported their sexual assault to the police. Women generally do not report their victimization, in part because of self-blame and embarrassment. . . .

Technically, our third hypothesis was confirmed. There is a statistically significant difference in that women who were raped by force or threat of force are more likely to classify their experience as rape than are women raped while intoxicated. The problem with this interpretation, however, is that it is only technically correct. . . . Although the hypothesis is correct, actually very few women of *any* experience labeled their experience as rape.

The results of this study are simple enough. . . . The percentage of women who report being victimized by sexual assaults remains high. At the same time, the strong tendency shown here is for women to commonly take the blame upon themselves, either fully or partially, for the behavior of male rapists and sexual aggressors. This continues to create hidden victims and to keep women from seeking the help they need. . . .

The implications of this study are clear. . . . Rape programming [on] college campuses needs to center clearly on blame and self-blame. . . . Clearly, those women who have been victimized by acquaintances in a situation without force but where they were too drunk to resist also are in need of various forms of support. Furthermore, another form of rape programming must be to educate people on how to react to friends who have survived an unwanted sexual experience. . . .

Universities and colleges need to actively work to search out hidden victims. . . .

CRITIQUE OF STUDY EXAMPLE 4.2

1. What was the rationale for the survey?

2. What was the purpose of the survey?

3. What was the general procedure?

4. What are some sources of selective losses?

5. How valid and reliable is the questionnaire?

6. What are some potential weaknesses in using this self-report questionnaire?

7. What were the reported effects of being raped and "rape type?"

8. In Table 1, are degrees of freedom for the chi-square test accurate?

9. What is the source of 53.8%? 46.2%?

10. What were the major results regarding self-blame and type of rape?

11. Look at the total percentages reported in Table 2. They differ from those (53.8% and 46.2%) of Table 1. What does this tell you?

12. What were the results regarding the question that specifically asked if the women had been raped since entering college?

13. Only 51 out of 65 women answered the rape question. What might you suppose about the 14 women (5 in the alcohol group and 9 in the physical force group) who did not answer it?

14. Examine Table 3, whose statistical analysis reveals a significant $\chi^2(1) = 4.99$ and an interpretation that a yes or no response depends on the group to which the rape victim belonged. Frequencies are easy to obtain: Each percentage is multiplied by its total N, to yield $51 \times .588 = 30$ and $51 \times .412 = 21$. Then $.033 \times 30 = 1$ and $.238 \times 21 = 5$ for the yes responses and the remaining frequencies are 29 and 16 for the no responses. You now have enough information to verify that if chi-square is computed in the usual fashion, it is indeed 4.99. However, two of the frequencies (1 and 5) are very small and require that a correction (of continuity) be applied to all cell values in calculating chi-square. A value of .50 must be subtracted from each absolute difference between obtained and expected frequencies before that difference is squared. For the first cell (yes, alcohol), this is $(|1 - 3.53| - .50)^2 = (2.53 - .5)^2 = 4.1209$. Then 4.1209 is divided by 3.53, and so forth for each cell. Recalculate the chi-square with the correction. What is the result? What do you conclude?

15. What was the conclusion regarding the first hypothesis? Is it justified?

16. What was the conclusion regarding the second hypothesis? Is it justified?

17. What was the conclusion regarding the third hypothesis? Is it justified?

For answers to these questions, see page 329.

BIBLIOGRAPHY

Fowler, F. J., Jr. (1993). *Survey research methods* (3rd ed., Applied Social Research Methods Series, Vol. 1). Newbury Park, CA: Sage.

Hayes, W. L. (1988). *Statistics* (4th ed.). New York: Holt, Rinehart & Winston.

Isaac, S., & Michael, W. B. (1995). *Handbook in research and evaluation: A collection of principles, methods, and strategies useful in the planning, design, and evaluation of studies in education and the behavioral sciences* (3rd ed.). San Diego, CA: EdITS.

McMillan, J. H., & Schumacher, S. (1997). *Research in education: A conceptual approach*. White Plains, NY: Longman.

Selltiz, C., Wrightsman, L. S., & Cook, S. W. (1976). *Research methods in social relations.* New York: Holt, Rinehart & Winston.

Weisberg, H. F., Krosnick, J. A., & Bowen, B. D. (1989). *An introduction to survey research and data analysis* (2nd ed.). Glenview, IL: Scott, Foresman.

Additional Suggested Readings

Ary, D., Jacobs, L. C., & Razavieh, A. (1996). *Introduction to research in education* (5th ed.). Orlando, FL: Harcourt Brace.

Frey, J. H. (1989). *Survey research by telephone* (2nd ed.). Newbury Park, CA: Sage.

Rea, L. M., & Parker, R. A. (1992). *Designing and conducting survey research.* San Francisco, CA: Jossey-Bass.

Chapter 5

Correlation Studies

Correlation studies attempt to establish relationships between two or more variables. Generally, one of the variables is some continuous quantitative measure and is designated the dependent variable, Y. The other variable can be any sort of quantitative measurement and is designated the independent variable, X. Participants with the characteristics of interest are selected and measured. Because individuals have other characteristics as well, cause-and-effect conclusions about a relationship that might be established are not possible; the relationship may be due to an unmeasured variable, to the mutual effects they have on each other (e.g., achievement and intelligence), or to chance. If only two variables are involved, we can end up with a *correlation coefficient*. The best known is *Pearson's product moment correlation coefficient, r.* It is a considered a *zero-order* correlation because it does not control for any other variable. The coefficient describes the strength and positive or negative direction of the relationship. *Positive relationships* indicate that both characteristics covary

in the same direction (e.g., amount of exercise and fatigue). *Negative relationships* indicate that both characteristics covary in opposite directions; an increase in one is accompanied by a decrease in the other (e.g., hours of sleep and fatigue). The correlation coefficient also describes the strength of the relationship. This is a value ranging from 0 to ±1.00. The closer the value is to 1.00, the stronger the linear relationship or degree of covariation. In fact, one of the most important assumptions made when r is computed is that the relationship between the two variables is a straight line (as opposed to being curvilinear). It is further assumed that the to-be-related variables were accurately measured. Now a straight line that best fits the data can be drawn. The final assumption, known as *homoscedasticity*, is that the amount of scatter of the plotted points around that line is the same for the entire range of X scores. It would show that the relationship between the two variables (X and Y) is equally strong for all values of X. Should the amount of scatter differ, it would indicate that the units of measurement in X, Y, or both have to be transformed or that if a relationship between X and Y exists, the relationship is not linear. This much would be clear when looking at a scatter plot of the two sets of data. A calculation of the Pearson r would be inappropriate. Note that no assumptions are necessary if the intent is just to describe the relationship between two sets of variables. Some but not all statistical assumptions are necessary if the coefficient is the basis for predicting a correlation for the population.

Any two sets of values can yield a correlation coefficient. A value may be obtained, however, and effectively still be equal to zero. Thus, once the value is calculated, it is then tested statistically to determine whether it is significantly greater than zero. It is here that we would worry about violating statistical assumptions underlying r. The statistical test, however, is robust with respect to violations. The degrees of freedom associated with the test are $N - 2$, where N = number of pairs of scores. If the obtained value can occur by chance 5 or fewer times in 100, it is considered to represent a real correlation.

Note that failure to obtain a significant coefficient may be due to a range of X values that is too restricted. The correlation between IQ scores and job proficiency among a group of computer programmers likely will be low, because computer programmers have relatively high IQ scores, leaving no room for variation in the X scores, even though proficiency scores may vary. Another factor that can lower the value of an existing correlation is the use of measuring instruments that are unreliable. The effect is called *attenuation,* and both situations of underestimated correlations are said to result in *spurious correlations.* On the other hand, a spurious correlation can be an overestimation if a third variable is common to the two

being measured. Body height and intelligence might be "highly" related because of age: Height increases with age, as does intelligence. Finally, if the sample is more heterogeneous or homogeneous than the population from which it was drawn, a spurious correlation is possible (if the intent is to generalize rather than to describe).

Whenever a correlation coefficient is declared significantly greater than zero, we run a risk that we've made an error in the decision we've reached: The coefficient may, in fact, be a chance occurrence. Such a value, on rare occasions, may occur even when two events are not correlated. When working at the .05 level of significance, we risk making this (Type I) error 5 times out of 100. If two coefficients are computed, each tested at the .05 level of significance, the risk of a Type I error with either decision is greater than .05. And the more coefficients we compute, the greater the risk of a Type I error when reaching a decision (i.e., declaring any coefficient significant when it is not) about a coefficient in the entire set. Behavioral and social scientists prefer to keep that overall risk of a Type I error at about .05. This can be accomplished in several ways. One way is to test each coefficient at a significance level that equals .05/C, with C = number of coefficients computed. If five coefficients are computed, each would be tested for significance at alpha = .05/5 = .01. Therefore, any coefficient that can occur by chance (when variables really are not related) more than one time in 100 (e.g., .02 or even .05) would be declared "not significantly greater than zero." Because such a procedure may be too conservative, an alternate remedy was suggested by Larzelere and Mulaik. Coefficients are arranged in order of magnitude. The highest coefficient is tested at .05/C (e.g., .05/5 = .01). The next one is tested

BOX 5.1
Obtaining Exact
Probabilities for
Correlation
Coefficients

In many cases, in the absence of the exact *p* value actually reported for each coefficient, that value can be approximated. If *N* is sufficiently large (at least 50), then we can determine the *Z* score for each *r* and read off the associated *p* value from the normal curve table. Here, $Z = r/[1/\sqrt{N}]$. If the actual *p* value (depending on *Z*) is equal to or lower than the critical *p*, then the *r* is significant.

at .05/C − 1 (e.g., .05/4 = .0125). The next is tested at .05/C − 2 (e.g., .05/3 = .0167), and so forth, with the lowest coefficient tested at .05/1 = .05. This is extremely important because many authors have not made the adjustment. Therefore, some of the coefficients they declare significant, especially at the .05 level, may not be significantly greater than zero. For those wanting to be more precise, Box 5.1 presents a way of calculating an exact probability value for a reported correlation coefficient.

The most common type of covariation is linear. And the most common linear correlation coefficient is the Pearson *r*. It measures the degree to which the two variables are linearly related. A more precise description of degree of linear relation is r^2, the *coefficient of determination*. This describes the percentage of shared variance or percentage of variability in one characteristic that is accounted for by the other variable. It is an extremely useful statistic, which allows you to judge the usefulness of a coefficient declared to be significant. Thus, if *r* between IQ and grade point average (GPA) equals .45, then $r^2 = (.45)^2 = 20.25\%$ of variability in GPA is associated with IQ. Those with higher GPAs are likely to have the higher IQs. The remaining variability is due to time spent studying, other activities, and so forth. And if a coefficient of .25 is significant, you know that it

only accounts for $(.25)^2 = .0625 = 6.25\%$ of variability.

Although cause-and-effect relationships are not likely to result from correlation studies, the effects of some obvious "third variables" can be removed statistically, by means of a *partial correlation*. The simplest removes the effect of one variable from the ones of interest and answers the question: If participants are equal on variable X, what is the true correlation between A and B? Such a correlation that controls for the effect of one variable also is called a *first-order correlation*. One that controls for two variables would be a second-order correlation, and so on.

Pearson's *r* describes the linear relationship between a dependent and independent variable, but other sorts of data can be gathered and related to each other. Commonly, ordinal data, in the form of actual or imposed ranks, are assessed for their degree of relationship. *Spearman's rank correlation coefficient* is based on actual ranks or on data that have been ranked; it shows the amount of agreement between pairs of ranks. Because the degree of association between the ranks can be calculated by Pearson's method (provided that no ranks are tied), it is a correlation. However, the correlation cannot be used as a predictor (regression analysis) and generally is computed for descriptions of extent of agreement between

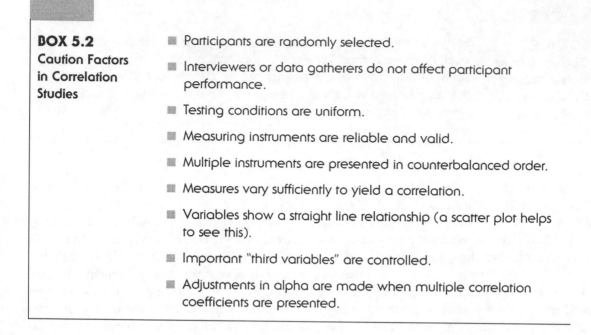

BOX 5.2
Caution Factors in Correlation Studies

■ Participants are randomly selected.

■ Interviewers or data gatherers do not affect participant performance.

■ Testing conditions are uniform.

■ Measuring instruments are reliable and valid.

■ Multiple instruments are presented in counterbalanced order.

■ Measures vary sufficiently to yield a correlation.

■ Variables show a straight line relationship (a scatter plot helps to see this).

■ Important "third variables" are controlled.

■ Adjustments in alpha are made when multiple correlation coefficients are presented.

ranks. The other popular method of determining a relationship between ranked or ordinal data is *Kendall's tau,* which is not a correlation. It measures the number of times pairs of ranks agree and disagree, relative to the number of pairs of ranks, a coefficient of agreement.

Before we look at a correlation study, it is worth noting that we have to consider more than just the correlation coefficients in evaluating a correlation study. If individuals are selected to participate, they should be randomly selected. If tests are used to obtain the measurements, they should be valid and reliable. If more than one test is used, the order of presenting the tests should be counterbalanced (e.g., AB to half and BA to the other half). If other methods are used (e.g., ratings of some behavior), they should be valid and reliable. The data gatherers also have to be considered (sex, experience, training, etc.), as well as the location in which the data are gathered. All of these factors can differentially affect the performance of participants, leaving the correlation coefficients suspect. The major caution factors are summarized in Box 5.2.

The studies to be reviewed are concerned with establishing relationships between two variables at a time. We'll look at the first study together, and you'll evaluate the second one.

STUDY EXAMPLE 5.1

In this study, the focus was on relating characteristics of young adolescents that measure a disposition to feeling sympathy with prosocial behavior. It was part of a longitudinal study that began when the participants were 4 through 6 years old, who were measured again when they 6 through 8 years old, and again when they were 8 through 10 years old. Although longitudinal studies are favored for studying developmental characteristics, they risk losing participants and possibly ending up with a selective loss. The other popular technique, a cross-sectional study, has its own risks: personality differences, because different individuals are measured at each level, and differential exposures to social factors, because the older individuals have lived longer.

The Study

Murphy, B. C., Shepard, S. A., Eisenberg, N., Fabes, R. A., & Guthrie, I. K. (1999). Contemporaneous and longitudinal relations of dispositional sympathy to emotionality, regulation, and social functioning. *Journal of Early Adolescence, 19*(1), 66-97. Copyright 1999 by Sage.

In recent years, there has been increasing interest in children's vicariously induced emotional responses in relation to their social functioning. . . . *Empathy* often is defined as an emotional reaction resulting from the comprehension of another's emotional state. . . . A possible consequence of empathizing with another individual is sympathy. . . . *Sympathy* is an other-oriented reaction that involves feelings of sorrow or concern for another based on the other's perceived emotional state. However . . . another possible consequence of empathizing with another is a self-focused, aversive reaction, which has been referred to as personal distress. . . .

Empathy and sympathy theoretically have been linked to the quality of social functioning, particularly to positive social behaviors. . . . Theorists have posited that empathy and sympathy contribute to positive behavior because individuals who experience others' negative emotional states are motivated to reduce others' distress and to inhibit aggression toward others. . . . Unlike sympathy, personal distress reactions have been linked conceptually to low levels of prosocial behavior because the focus is on the self rather than on others. . . .

. . . Because empathy can result in sympathy as well as personal distress, there is a clearer conceptual link between sympathy and positive behaviors than between empathy and positive behavior. However, researchers generally have focused on empathy rather than distinguishing between sympathy and personal distress. Therefore, it might be beneficial for researchers to focus specifically on sympathy rather than on empathy in general.

Although research exists on the relations of empathy and sympathy to prosocial behavior . . . there has been little research regarding the relation between sympathy and the quality of children's social functioning. . . . Sympathetic people would be expected to be relatively socially appropriate and sensitive. Therefore, one purpose for the present study was to examine young adolescents' dispositional sympathetic tendencies . . . in relation to a variety of aspects of their social functioning and adjustment.

Despite the conceptual importance of sympathy in children's social functioning . . . little is known about the characteristics of children who dispositionally are sympathetic. Thus, another purpose for the present study was to examine personal characteristics that are associated with individual differences in dispositional sympathy during early adolescence. . . . Sympathetic tendencies are likely to be associated with the abilities to manage vicariously induced emotions. Specifically, individuals who are able to maintain their emotional reactions within a tolerable range (i.e., not so arousing as to be highly aversive) would be expected to experience sympathy in empathy-inducing situations. . . . In contrast, individuals who experience high emotional arousal in empathy-inducing contexts would be likely to experience vicariously induced emotions as aversive. Thus, they would be expected to be self-focused and to experience personal distress rather than sympathy. . . .

The primary purpose for the present study was to examine further the relations of dispositional sympathy to emotional intensity, regulation, and social functioning during early adolescence. Much of the research to date has focused on younger children or adults, not on adolescents. . . . A variety of measures pertaining to 10- through 12-year-olds' dispositional sympathy, emotionality, regulation, and social functioning were obtained from teachers (school setting) and parents (home setting). Moreover, because participants were part of a longitudinal study . . . reports of emotionality, regulation, and social functioning were obtained 2, 4, and 6 years prior to the current assessment when participants ranged in age from 8 though 10 years, 6 through 8 years, and 4 through 6 years, respectively.

. . . Relatively high levels of regulation were expected to be associated with sympathetic tendencies, whereas negative emotional tendencies were expected to be associated with relatively low levels of dispositional sympathy. Emotionality and regulation are considered aspects of temperament and are relatively stable across time. . . . Thus, contemporaneous reports of young adolescents' emotionality and regulation as well as reports obtained 2, 4, and 6 years earlier were expected to be associated with dispositional sympathy at 10 through 12 years of age. . . . Young adolescents' sympathetic tendencies were expected to be related to the quality of their social functioning. Specifically, young adolescents viewed by parents or by teachers as possessing relatively high sympathetic tendencies were expected to be relatively high on constructive social behaviors as well as popularity and relatively low on problem behaviors. . . .

Gender also was considered in the present study to obtain a better understanding of young adolescents' sympathetic tendencies. . . . Boys and girls are exposed to differing socialization pressures . . . and these differences affect the ways in which boys and girls negotiate their social worlds. . . . There might be a stronger association between sympathy and regulation, emotionality, and social functioning for girls than for boys.

1. What is the rationale of the study?

Recent research has focused on relating children's emotional responses to their level of social functioning. Empathy can lead to sympathy or to personal distress. Empathy and sympathy are related to positive behaviors, whereas personal distress is related to low levels of prosocial behavior. Because empathy can lead to sympathy and personal distress, there is a clearer link between sympathy and positive behaviors than between empathy and positive behaviors. Whereas stress has been placed on empathy, it seems wiser to focus on sympathy.

Although empathy and sympathy have been related to prosocial behavior, little is known about sympathy and the quality of social behavior in children. Moreover, little is known about the characteristics of children who are sympathetic. One such characteristic is ability to manage vicariously aroused emotions in an empathy-producing situation. Those who manage their emotions would be sympathetic; those whose emotional arousal is aversive would experience personal distress. Research has related sympathy to emotional intensity, emotional regulation, and social functioning of young children and adults but not of adolescents.

2. What were the purposes of the study?

One purpose was to examine young adolescents' tendencies toward sympathy. A second purpose was to examine the characteristics of young adolescents that are associated with different tendencies toward sympathy. The main purpose was to relate sympathy in young adolescents to intensity and regulation of emotion and to social functioning. Participants were 10 through 12 years old but had been studied at ages 4 through 6, 6 through 8, and 8 through 10 years.

High regulation of emotions was predicted to be associated with sympathy and low regulation (negative emotion) with low levels of sympathy, and the relationship was predicted to be stable over time. Sympathy was expected to correlate with positive social behavior at home and at school. Girls were expected to show stronger relationships than boys.

Method

Participants

Participants were 33 girls and 31 boys who were part of an original group of 94 children studied approximately 6 years previously. For this group of 64 children, data were collected from 62 parents and 59 teachers. Participants were in the fourth, fifth, or sixth grade ($\overline{X}$ = 10.96 years, SD = .60, range = 10.08 through 12.17), and 93% were non-Hispanic Caucasian (2% were Asian, 3% were Black, and 2% Hispanic). Of the children, 89% lived in two-parent households, and annual household income ranged from $12,000 through $200,000 ($\overline{X}$ = $81,170, SD = $30,710). Of the parents who participated, mothers' and fathers' years of education averaged 17.06 (SD = 2.40, range 12 [high school] through 20 [graduate school]) and 17.53 years (SD = 2.11, range 12 through 20), respectively. Of the 13 children who did not participate in the current follow-up (henceforth called T5) but had participated at the previous assessment, 1 refused participation, 5 could not be contacted, and 7 agreed to participate but did not return the questionnaires.

▶ *(Note that the bulk of children came from two-parent homes and were in high middle-income brackets. All parents had finished high school, and about one third of both mothers and fathers had completed graduate school.)*

The original group of participants was studied during two consecutive academic semesters approximately 6 years prior to the current assessment (henceforth called T1 and T2) when they were attending university kindergarten or preschools (45 girls and 49 boys; $\overline{X}$ age = 5.37 years, SD = .56, range = 4.42 through 6.58). . . . Two years later (henceforth called T3), data were collected for 82 of the original participants (38 girls and 44 boys; $\overline{X}$ age = 7.25 years, SD = .59, range = 6.42 through 8.50). Data at T3 were collected in the laboratory for 74 children and through the mail for 8 children. Seventy-seven children (36 girls, 41 boys; $\overline{X}$ age = 8.84 years, SD = .58, range = 8.08 through 10.17) participated in the 4-year follow-up (henceforth called T4). Of the participants, 65 came in to the laboratory, and data were obtained through the mail for an additional 12 children.

▶ *(Note that there were considerable losses of male and female participants from the original group. A large percentage was lost 2 years after the first testing: 7/45 = 15% of the girls and 5/49 = 11.36% of the boys. Relatively fewer were lost at the second testing: 2/38 = 5.3% of the girls and 3/44 = 6.8% of the boys. But by the final testing, 6 years after the longitudinal study began, 3/36 = 8.3% of the girls and 10/41 = 24.4% of the boys were lost. In total, 12/45 = 26.6% of the girls and 18/49 = 36.7% of the boys from the original sample were lost. Because almost one third of the parents [at least in the final sample] were professionals [and 6% of the children were from single-parent homes], part of the loss could be attributed to a change in residence. But, if any of the children were among extreme scorers [although not outliers], this might have the effect of reducing the magnitude of a correlation. Note, too, that original testing was done at the school, and later testings were done in a laboratory and by mail. The final testing was done by mail.)*

---

3. Who were the participants?

The original sample (T1 and T2) consisted of 45 girls and 49 boys from university kindergarten or preschool. The second testing (T3) included 38 girls and 44 boys from the original sample, who were tested in the laboratory (74/82 = 90.25%) or via mail (8/82 = 9.75%). The third testing (T4) included 36 girls and 41 boys of the original sample, who were tested in the laboratory (65/77 = 84.42%) or via mail (12/77 = 15.58%). The final sample included 33 girls and 31 boys of the original sample. They were in Grade 4, 5, or 6. Most were Caucasian, from high-middle-income and two-parent homes. All were tested by mailed questionnaires.

4. Are there any potential sore spots to keep in mind?

A large percentage of participants were lost, which may or may not be a selective loss of high or low scorers. And testing conditions varied, which may or may not affect responses on the questionnaires.

Procedure

Unlike in previous studies involving this sample, all measures at T5 were collected through the mail. Primary care-giving parents were sent the same packet of questionnaires that they had completed in the laboratory 2 years previously. Many of the same or similar measures had been completed in the laboratory 4 and 6 years prior to this data collection. . . . Typically packets were completed by mothers ($N = 57$ at T5); however, five fathers at T5, one father at T4, and two fathers at T3 also completed the primary parent packet. All fathers were sent the problem behavior checklist to complete and return ($N = 55$ at T5). Toward the end of the data collection at all assessments, participants' current teachers completed some of the same questionnaires as were completed by parents ($N = 59$ at T5). As in previous time periods involving this sample, parents and teachers responded to questionnaires in random order.

▶ *(This is a good feature of the design. Carryover effects from one questionnaire to the next are not a problem.)*

---

5. What was the general procedure?

Questionnaires were mailed to the primary care parent (mainly mothers), who were the same as or similar to those of prior testings. Current teachers also completed some of the same questionnaires. Orders of questionnaires were randomized.

Measures

. . . A summary of measures of emotionality, regulation, and social functioning is presented in Table 1.

Measures of Sympathy

At T5, teachers and parents reported on young adolescents' sympathetic tendencies with six items. Teachers and parents responded to five sympathy items . . . using the . . . 4-point response scale. Teachers and parents were instructed to select one of the two statements (e.g., "This [my] child often feels sorry for others who are less fortunate" or "This [my] child does not feel sorry for those who are less fortunate") and indicate whether the chosen statement was *really true* or *sort of true* of each child. An additional sympathy item ("in general, to what degree does this [your] child feel sympathetic?") was rated using a 5-point scale (1 = *very slightly or not at all*, 5 = *extremely*). Items were standardized and averaged for teachers and parents (alpha = .92 and .84, respectively).

[Tests, based on items that were rated on a Likert scale, were administered to measure emotionality (negative emotional intensity, dispositional negative affectivity, and autonomic reactivity) and regulation (attention control; impulsivity, inhibition control, and global self-control). There were standardized scales, so it is assumed that reliability and validity are established, and in all cases, alpha coefficients for the present samples are presented.]

Measures of Social Functioning

Socially appropriate behavior. At T1 and T2, teachers and teacher aides completed seven items adapted from the Perceived Social Competence Scale for Children . . . to assess children's socially appropriate behavior. The Harter

TABLE 1 Composite Scores for Emotionality, Regulation, and Social Competence

Group	Parent	Teacher
Negative emotionality		
T1/T2	Emotional intensity (averaged across T1/T2) and autonomic arousal (T2 only)	Emotional intensity (averaged across T1/T2) and autonomic arousal (T2 only)
T3, T4	Negative affectivity, negative emotional intensity, anger/frustration, attention shifting (reversed), reactivity/soothability (reversed)	Negative affectivity, negative emotional intensity
T5	Negative affectivity, negativity emotional intensity, anger/frustration, falling reactivity/soothability (reversed)	Same as T3 and T4
Regulation		
T1/T2	Attention control (attention shifting and attention focusing averaged at T2)	Attention control (attention shifting and attention focusing averaged at T2)
T3	Attention focusing, inhibition control, self-control, impulsivity (reversed)	Attention focusing, attention shifting, self-control
T4	Same as T3	Attention focusing, attention shifting, inhibition control, impulsivity (reversed)
T5	Attention focusing, inhibition control, self-control, impulsivity (reversed), attention shifting	Same as T4
Social competence		
T1/T2		Same-gender and other-gender sociometric ratings
T3, T4	Mother and father ratings of problem behavior	Social skills, prosocial behavior, disruptive behavior (reversed), popularity, aggression (reversed), puppet responses (friendliness minus aggression)
T5	Same as T3 and T4	Social skills, prosocial behavior, disruptive behavior (reversed), popularity, aggression (reversed)

4-point response scale was used to evaluate statements such as "This child is usually well behaved" or "This child is not well behaved." Teachers and aides selected one of the two statements and indicated whether it was *really true* or *sort of true* of each child. . . . At T3, T4, and T5, teachers completed four items from the original scale. . . .

Popularity. At T3, T4, and T5, as part of the measure of socially appropriate behavior, teachers rated children's popularity with three items (e.g., "This child has a lot of friends" or "This child doesn't have a lot of friends") using the same 4-point scale used for the socially appropriate behavior scale. Items were adapted from the Perceived Social Competence Scale for Children. . . .

Social behavior. At T3, T4, and T5, teachers rated disruptive behavior (e.g., "This child bothers kids when they are trying to work"; 8 items . . .), aggression (e.g., "This child says mean things to peers, such as teasing or name calling"; 8 items . . .), and prosocial behavior (e.g., "This child is good to have in a group, shares things, and it helpful"; 4 items . . .) with items from the Coie, Terry, Dodge, and Underwood . . . Teacher Checklist using a 7-point scale (1 = *never* through 7 = *almost always*). . . .

Problem behavior. Mothers and fathers completed the Lochman and Conduct Problems Prevention Research Group . . . Child Problem Behavior Checklist. Twenty-three items (e.g., "breaks things on purpose," "defiant toward adults") were rated on a 1 = *never* through 4 = *often* point scale. . . .

Children's ratings of sociometric status. At T1 and T2, procedures adapted from Asher, Singleton, Tinsley, and Hymel . . . were used to assess children's sociometric status. . . . Children sorted pictures of their classmates into three piles marked with smiling faces. The smiles ranged from a lot to virtually not at all to represent distinctions between peers that the target child "really likes to play with," "likes to play with some," and "likes to play with only a little bit." Children were assigned a score of 3 every time their peers placed them in the "really like" pile, a 2 for the middle pile, and a 1 for the least positive pile. Scores were summed and standardized within class and gender and then were averaged across T1 and T2 to create same-gender and other-gender sociometric status composites.

Enacted puppet procedure. At T3 and T4 children used puppets to act out how they would behave in five peer interaction situations. . . . Experimenters presented the following five stories in random order to the child (with props): (a) a peer criticizes and marks on the child's picture, (b) the child is excluded from a game, (c) the child is pushed into a water fountain, (d) the child is called "a baby" for playing with "baby toys," and (e) a peer grabs a toy away from the child. After each story, children used their puppet to show their response.

Children's responses to the puppet vignettes were coded using criteria adapted from Mize and Ladd. . . . Responses to each story were rated on a scale of 1 (*hostility;* i.e., negative outcome likely for the peer) through 5 (*friendliness;* i.e., prosocial outcome likely for the peer). A 5 included polite suggestions and consideration of positive outcomes for both parties, whereas a rating of 1 included responses such as name calling and destruction of the peer's property. Presence or absence of physical aggression also was coded. . . .

▷ *(Note that the enacted puppet test at T3 and T4 was a live procedure that had to be performed in person; hence, it was performed in the laboratory. Recall, however, that 8 children at T3 and 12 children at T4 were contacted through the mail and presumably did not take part in this procedure. Note, too, that there were many items to complete at each time period, and had the questionnaires not been randomized, there would have been a serious question about fatigue effects.)*

---

6. What was the general nature of the measures used in this study?

Standardized tests or some adaptations of them, all valid and reliable, were used to measure sympathy, emotionality, regulation of emotions, and social functioning. These scales were used to rate the children by the parents, primary care parent, and/or the children's teachers and teacher aides. Composite scores that reflected distinct characteristics measured by all similar tests were used in the final analyses.

Results

Initial analyses were conducted to examine participant attrition and relations of T5 variables with age and gender. In addition, across-reporter (parents and teachers) relations of sympathy, emotionality, regulation, and social functioning were examined. Subsequent analyses tested the predictions that in early adolescence, dispositional sympathy would be associated positively with regulation and constructive social behavior and associated negatively with negative emotionality and problem behavior, both contemporaneously and over time. . . . Results are presented for teachers' as well as for parents' rating of sympathy, negative emotionality, regulation, and social functioning. . . .

Participant Attrition

Of the original 94 children at T1/T2, 64 remained at T5. To examine whether T5 participants differed from those who discontinued participation throughout the longitudinal study, a series of t tests was computed to compare the ratings (i.e., sympathy, emotionality, regulation, and social functioning) that T5 participants received at T1/T2, T3, and T4 to the ratings of all of the children who subsequently dropped out of the study after T1/T2, T3, and T4.

Young adolescents (T5) did not differ on sympathetic tendencies (as rated by parents and teachers) from the children who discontinued participation throughout the longitudinal study. However, at T4, the T5 participants were rated by teachers as lower in negative emotionality than were the 13 children who did not participate subsequently at T5, $t(73) = -1.97, p < .05$. In addition, at T3 and T4, T5 participants were rated by teachers as higher on school social competence than were the 17 and 13 children, respectively, who did not participate at T5, $ts(80 \text{ and } 73) = 2.12$ and 2.96, $p < .04$ and $.004$, respectively. Finally, at T1/T2, parents rated the 30 children who did not participate at T5 as lower on regulation than they did the children who participated subsequently at T5, $t(77) = 1.97, p < .05$.

▶ *(This check for selective loss is a very good feature of the study. It showed that no extreme scorers were lost with respect to sympathy, but some may have been lost regarding other measures.)*

> **7. What did the check for selective loss reveal? What does it suggest?**
>
> Compared to the current participants, participants lost at T4 were more emotional and showed less regulation of their emotions (the same was true of those lost from T1/T2). This suggests that correlations between sympathy and emotionality and sympathy and regulation may be lower than anticipated. Furthermore, participants lost at T3 were less socially competent than the present participants. This may affect the correlation between sympathy and social functioning.

Relations With Age and Gender

In general, gender differences obtained in the present study were similar to gender differences found at previous time periods . . . . Specifically at T5, teachers and parents rated girls higher than they rated boys on regulation, $ts(57 \text{ and } 59) = 3.41$ and 2.92, $p < .001$ and $.01$, respectively. However, teachers and parents did not rate boys and girls differently on negative emotionality. In addition, mothers rated boys higher than they rated girls on problem behaviors, $t(55) = -2.14$, $p < .05$. Finally, teachers and parents viewed girls as more sympathetic than they viewed boys at T5, $ts(55$ and $60) = 2.91$ and 3.48, $p < .01$ and $.001$.

Because of the gender differences on numerous measures, results are presented by gender as well as for the total sample, and gender-related differences in findings also are noted.

---

8. *What were the general findings regarding gender differences in ratings by teachers and parents?*

At T5, girls were found to be more capable of regulating their emotions, in ratings from teachers and parents. Boys and girls did not differ in teacher or parent ratings on negative emotions. Mothers rated boys higher than girls on problem behaviors. Girls were rated as more sympathetic than boys by teachers and parents.

Correlations of Analogous Teacher and Parent Measures of Sympathy, Emotionality, Regulation, and Social Functioning at T5

Sympathy. Teacher and parent reports of sympathy were not related significantly at T5, $r(53) = .14$, ns. Findings across reporter did not differ markedly for boys and for girls.

▶ *(Note that expression of sympathy may have differed at home and in school. Moreover, lack of correlation means that correlations have to be calculated separately for parents and teachers.)*

Regulation and emotionality. Although regulation was related significantly across reporter (teacher and parent) at T5, negative emotionality was not related significantly across reporter at T5, $rs(55) = .44$ and $.12$, $p < .001$ and ns. Correlations were similar for boys and for girls.

Social functioning. Mothers' reports of young adolescents' problem behaviors were associated positively with analogous fathers' reports, $r(49) = .65$, $p < .001$. However, mothers' and fathers' reports of young adolescents' problem behaviors were not related significantly to teachers' reports of young adolescents' school social competence, $rs(48, 47) = -.15$ and $.01$, respectively, ns. None of the correlations differed significantly by gender.

> **9. What were initial results regarding parent and teacher ratings of sympathy, regulation and emotionality, and social functioning?**
>
> There was no relationship between parent and teacher ratings of sympathy, negative emotionality, nor social functioning. Ratings of regulation of emotionality by parents and teachers were correlated. And ratings of problem behaviors by mothers and fathers were correlated.

Relations of Dispositional Sympathy to Measures of Regulation and Emotionality

Reports of dispositional sympathy during early adolescence (at T5) were examined in relation to contemporaneous reports of their regulation and negative emotionality, as well as in relation to reports of regulation and emotionality obtained at previous time periods. . . . Zero-order correlations were computed separately for teachers' and parents' ratings to examine predictions within the different contexts of home and school.

Teachers' reports of sympathy, regulation, and emotionality. Contemporaneous and longitudinal zero-order correlations of teachers' ratings of early adolescents' dispositional sympathy with negative emotionality and regulation are presented in Table 3. Predictions pertaining to negative emotionality and regulation generally were supported. . . .

As expected, contemporaneous ratings of young adolescents' sympathy and regulation at T5 were associated positively. In addition, children viewed as relatively high in regulatory abilities at ages 8 through 10 (T4) were viewed as relatively sympathetic 2 years later (T5). Furthermore, at T5, girls' but not boys' dispositional sympathy was associated with low negative emotionality. . . . Regarding longitudinal relations, teacher-reported sympathy during early adolescence generally was predicted by negative emotionality at younger ages. Specifically, for the total sample, young adolescents who were rated by their teachers as relatively high in sympathy at T5 were viewed by their teachers as relatively low in negative emotionality 2 ($p < .10$), 4, and 6 years earlier. Relations were somewhat stronger for girls than for boys (see Table 3).

Parents' reports of sympathy, regulation, and emotionality. . . . Hypotheses regarding contemporaneous ratings of parent-rated sympathy in relation to negative emotionality and regulation were supported, especially for boys. Moreover, regulation . . . during younger years was associated with sympathetic tendencies during early adolescence.

TABLE 3 Correlations of Time 5 Teacher and Parent Ratings of Sympathy With Analogous Reporter Ratings of Regulation and Emotionality Contemporaneously and Across Time

Measure	Young Adolescents' Dispositional Sympathy as Rated by Analogous Reporter		
	Overall	Girls	Boys
Teacher ratings			
Negative emotionality			
Time 5	−.26*	−.38**	−.06
Time 4	−.23*	−.42**	.08[a]
Time 3	−.31**	−.28	−.25
Time 1/Time 2	−.27**	−.46***	−.01[b]
Regulation			
Time 5	.46****	.48***	.27
Time 4	.38***	.55***	.12[c]
Time 3	.26*	.21	.12
Time 1/Time 2	.19	−.03	.23
Parent ratings			
Negative emotionality			
Time 5	−.28**	.02	−.35*
Time 4	−.11	.18	−.18
Time 3	−.13	.08	−.21
Time 1/Time 2	−.17	−.01	−.18
Regulation			
Time 5	.42***	.08	.48***
Time 4	.40***	.08	.47***
Time 3	.23*	.00	.26
Time 1/Time 2	−.12	−.24	.01

a. The correlations for girls and for boys were marginally significantly different, $z = 1.85$, $p < .10$.
b. The correlations for girls and for boys were marginally significantly different, $z = 1.73$, $p < .10$.
c. The correlations for girls and for boys were marginally significantly different, $z = 1.74$, $p < .10$.
**p < .05; ***p < .01; ****p < .001 (*p < .10, trend).

Specifically, young adolescents (especially boys) who were viewed by their parents as relatively high in sympathy tended to be relatively high in regulation and relatively low in negative emotionality. Furthermore, parents who viewed their children as relatively high in regulatory abilities 2 years earlier (T4) rated their young adolescents as sympathetic at T5. . . .

▶ *(Look at Table 3. Because raters were the same at any given time period [e.g., T5] and because N differed for the overall group, girls, and boys, we can look at three groups of four correlation coefficients, one for overall ratings at T5, one for ratings of girls at T5, and one for ratings of boys at T5. The first group [overall] consists of the following ordered coefficients: .46, .42, −.28, and −.26. The .46 should be tested at alpha = .05/4 = .0125, .42, at alpha = .05/3 = .0167; −.28, at alpha = .05/2 = .025; and −.26, at alpha = .05. On this basis, the two highest coefficients are significant but not −.28 nor −.26.)*

10. **What were the authors' results for the T5 correlations between sympathy and regulation and between sympathy and negative emotions for the group as a whole? What changes when alpha levels are adjusted for multiple correlations?**

     The coefficients were as predicted: There were positive correlations between sympathy and regulation of emotions as rated by parents and teachers and negative correlations between sympathy and display of negative emotions. When alphas are adjusted, the correlations between sympathy and negative emotions no longer are significant.

11. **Correct the alpha levels for those coefficients reported to be marginally significant or significant at the .05 level. Do any conclusions change?**

     For T4 ratings by teachers, −.23 is not significant: Sympathy is not related to negative emotions shown 2 years earlier. Likewise, ratings of regulation for the group by teachers and parents at T3 (.26 and .23) are not significant. And −.27 at T1/T2 (ratings of negative emotions by teachers) is not significant. Regarding ratings of girls, the correlation between teacher ratings of negative emotions at T4 and sympathy at T5 (−.42) is not significant. And regarding the boys, the correlation between parent ratings of negative emotionality and sympathy (−.35) is not significant.

12. How do these reevaluations change the reported results?

With one exception, none of the reported results regarding negative emotionality was significant. Sympathy shown in adolescent girls, as rated by teachers, was negatively correlated with negative emotionality shown at the earliest age (T1/T5).

13. Consider the r = .46 (teacher-rated regularity and sympathy for overall group) and r = −.46 (teacher-rated negative emotionality at T1/T2 and sympathy). Interpret them in terms of r^2.

$(.46)^2 = .2116$ indicates that 21.16% of variability in teacher-rated sympathy in adolescents is associated with ratings of their current ability to control their emotions. Likewise, 21.16% of variability in teacher-rated sympathy of adolescent girls is associated with ratings of negative emotions displayed 6 years earlier; the higher the rating of emotional behavior, the lower the rating of sympathy by these girls.

Relations of Dispositional Sympathy to Measures of Social Functioning

Young adolescents' dispositional sympathy was examined in relation to contemporaneous ratings of their social functioning as well as social functioning measured 2, 4, and 6 years earlier. Zero-order correlations were computed to examine relations within the school setting (as rated by teacher or by peers) as well as the home setting (as rated by mothers and by fathers). Overall, the findings supported predictions.

Teachers' reports of sympathy and school functioning. In general, teachers' ratings of young adolescents' sympathy at T5 were associated positively with their school functioning contemporaneously as well as across time (see Table 5). Specifically, young adolescents who were rated as sympathetic tended to be viewed as socially competent by their present teachers as well as by teachers 2, 4, and 6 years earlier. Furthermore, young children who were well liked by their same-gender peers at T1/T2 were viewed by their teachers as sympathetic young adolescents. The pattern of findings generally was stronger for girls than for boys.

TABLE 5 Correlations of Time 5 Teacher Ratings of Sympathy With Social Competence and Sociometric Status Contemporaneously and Across Time

	Teacher Reports of Sympathy		
Measure	*Overall*	*Girls*	*Boys*
School social competence			
Time 5	.59****	.64****	.45**
Time 4	.33**	.63****	−.08[a]
Time 3	.26*	.25	.10
Time 1/Time 2	.36***	.55***	.06[b]
Same-gender sociometric status			
Time 1/Time 2	.31*	.22	.42**
Other-gender sociometric status			
Time 1/Time 2	−.02	.11	−.03

a. The correlations for girls and boys were significantly different, $z = 2.88$, $p < .01$.
b. The correlations for girls and boys were significantly different, $z = 1.98$, $p < .05$.
**$p < .05$; ***$p < .01$; ****$p < .001$ (*$p < .10$, trend).

14. *What were the reported results regarding the correlation between social functioning, as measured or rated by teachers, and sympathy?*

There was a positive correlation between the two variables at T5 for the overall group and for girls and boys. There was a positive correlation, overall, for ratings at the different times and current sympathy. The relationship between the two variables was stronger for girls than for boys.

15. *Because teachers differed at the different times, consider the three coefficients (Table 5) at a single time as one group. The adjusted alpha levels at T5 should be the following: for .64, alpha = .05/3 = .016; for .59, alpha = .05/2 = .025; and for .45, alpha = .05. By these criteria, all three coefficients are significant. Perform similar adjustments for the rest of the table. What do you conclude?*

At T4, the correlation between social functioning for the whole group and sympathy (.33) is not significant. At T3, the correlation between social functioning of the group and sympathy (.26) is not significant. And measures using sociometric scales at T1/T2 yielded no significant correlations with adolescents' sympathy.

TABLE 6 Correlations of Time 5 Parent Ratings of Sympathy With Mother and Father Ratings of Problem Behaviors Contemporaneously and Across Time

Measure	Parent Reports of Sympathy		
	Overall	Girls	Boys
Mothers' reports of problem behavior			
Time 5	−.46****	−.24	−.52***
Time 4	−.42***	−.17	−.43**
Time 3	−.42***	−.18	−.38**
Fathers' reports of problem behavior			
Time 5	−.46***	−.40*	−.47**
Time 4	−.17	−.11	−.32
Time 3	−.31**	−.14	−.39*

**p < .05; ***p < .01; ****p < .001 (*p < .10, trend).

Parents' reports of sympathy and problem behavior. As can be seen in Table 6, parents' reports of young adolescents' sympathy at T5 were associated negatively with mothers' contemporaneous reports of problem behavior as well as reports obtained 2 and 4 years earlier. . . . Parents (mothers') reports of young adolescents' sympathy at T5 were associated negatively with fathers' reports of young adolescents' problem behavior contemporaneously and 4 years earlier but not 2 years earlier.

16. What did the authors report regarding parental ratings of sympathy and their reports of problem behavior?

Mothers' problem behavior reports correlated with adolescents' sympathy at T5, T4, and T3. Fathers' problem behavior reports correlated with adolescents' sympathy only at T5 and T3.

17. Adjust the alpha levels across each time interval. What do you conclude?

The correlations were significant for mothers' reports for the whole group, but for boys, this was true only at T5. The correlation was significant for fathers' reports only for the group at T5. All significant correlations indicate that the fewer the problem behaviors, the greater the rating of sympathy in the adolescents.

Discussion

Findings from the present study provide further support for the view that dispositional sympathy is associated with high regulation, low negative emotionality, and constructive social functioning across development. . . . Young adolescents' dispositional sympathy was examined in relation to their regulation, emotionality, and social functioning contemporaneously and as much as 6 years earlier. Individual differences in emotionality and regulation continued to affect sympathetic tendencies into early adolescence despite the numerous biological, psychological, and social changes individuals experience during the transition into adolescence. . . .

In interpreting the findings, it is important to note that relations might have been difficult to detect during early adolescence because there was less variability in emotionality, regulation, and social functioning at T5 than at previous assessments due to the loss of participants throughout the years . . . . It should be noted that the majority of the findings at school were for girls, whereas the pattern of findings at home was somewhat stronger for boys than for girls.

. . . Young adolescents who were viewed by adult raters (teachers or parents) as relatively high in sympathetic tendencies were viewed by the same raters as relatively high in regulatory abilities during early adolescence. . . . Across development, regulatory abilities likely prevent individuals from becoming overwhelmed when they experience another's distress, allowing them to focus on the other's distress rather than their own distress. . . .

In the school context, sympathy was associated particularly with high regulation for girls. . . . Teachers are likely to expect higher levels of regulatory abilities with age and increasingly might evaluate adolescents on the basis of the regulation of their vicarious emotional responding. This might be especially true for girls who might be expected to be more regulated than are boys in interpersonal contexts. Perhaps highly regulated girls increasingly are viewed as sympathetic because regulation and sympathy both are consistent with the adult stereotypic feminine role. In contrast, boys who are emotionally responsive to others might not be viewed as regulated because displays of emotion and caring are inconsistent with the adult masculine role. . . .

It is of interest that teachers' current reports of sympathy and previous reports of negative emotionality tended to be related, whereas this was not the case for parents' reports. . . . Teachers' ratings of young children's negative emotionality appeared to reflect displays of overt negative emotion such as anger and frustration, whereas mothers' ratings reflected those types of emotions to a lesser degree. Perhaps teachers continue to attend primarily to disruptive externalizing negative emotions; if so, it is not surprising that sympathy at school would be negatively related to displays of anger. In contrast, parents might attend to a greater range of children's negative emotions, making the relation of negative emotionality to sympathy somewhat complicated. . . .

. . . . In the present study, young adolescent girls' dispositional sympathy was associated negatively with contemporaneous and longitudinal reports of their negative emotionality. . . .

Given that the pattern of findings at school between sympathy and emotionality/regulation was more consistent for girls than for boys, it is surprising that the pattern in the home context was somewhat more consistent for boys than for girls. However, parents rated girls higher than they rated boys in sympathy. To examine whether the different pattern of findings for boys and for girls could be due, in part, to differences in the distributions of parents' ratings of boys' and girls' sympathetic tendencies, a test of variances was conducted. Indeed, there was less variability in parents' ratings of sympathy for girls than for boys. . . . Thus, the restricted range of parent-reported sympathy scores could explain why findings in the home context were primarily for the total sample and boys rather than for girls.

As expected, both in the contemporaneous and longitudinal data, young adolescents' sympathetic tendencies were associated positively with appropriate social behavior, social competence, and peer sociometric status (T1/T2 only) in the school context (primarily for girls), and negatively associated with problem behaviors in the home context (primarily for boys). In the home context, the relation of sympathy to low levels of problem behavior held across reporter (i.e., when mothers reported on sympathy and fathers on problem behavior). . . .

In summary, the present findings are consistent with the view that dispositional sympathy is associated with individual differences in regulation, emotionality, and social functioning across development. . . .

---

18. *What did the authors conclude? Are the conclusions justified?*

Dispositional sympathy in adolescents is associated with high regulation of emotions, low negative emotionality, and constructive social functioning. But the relationships between sympathy and the other variables may have been difficult to detect because of the loss of participants over the years, which would reduce variability in ratings. Relationships at school were stronger for girls (especially between sympathy and regulation), whereas relationships at home tended to be stronger for boys.

Teachers' but not parents' current rating of sympathy tended to be related to present and past ratings of negative emotions. This was particularly true of adolescent girls. More consistent relationships for girls at school and for boys at home is attributed to a more restricted range of ratings, at home, for girls than for boys.

Adolescent sympathy was positively associated with present and past social competence and sociometric ratings and negatively associated with problem behavior at home. Positive relationships were stronger for girls, and negative relationships were stronger for boys.

Conclusions basically are justified. Associations involving negative emotions mainly were not significant, although they were in the predicted direction, when alpha levels were adjusted. And correlations involving sociometric ratings and adolescent sympathy were not significant, although they were in the expected direction, when alpha levels were adjusted.

---

19. What probably accounts for lack of stronger, predicted relationships? What might be done to overcome the problem?

As noted by the authors, the loss of high (particularly in negative emotions) and low (particularly in social competence) scores could have the effect of reducing variability in the remaining scores, leaving a more restricted range and lower correlation coefficients. Because this was part of a longitudinal study, not much could be done to restore participant scores that have been lost. But a new, larger group of adolescents might be selected and rated on the same variables. Larger groups make it more likely that a range of scores will be obtained, and if the correlations do exist, as this study suggests, they would be evident with the new sample.

STUDY EXAMPLE 5.2

This study, which you will evaluate, concerns the effects of course community service projects on various attitudes toward learning and academic performance. The statistical analyses included correlations and more advanced techniques. You'll only have to focus on the correlations.

The Study

Moore, K. P., & Sandholtz, J. H. (1999). Designing successful service learning projects for urban schools. *Urban Education, 34*(4), 480-498. Copyright 1999 by Sage.

Few people will argue against the value of community service but not all see the connection to the public school system. . . . In the past decade, hundreds of schools across the country implemented service learning programs or required community service for graduation. . . . Service learning is part of a widespread movement aimed at rebuilding communities and reforming public education.

As the name implies, service learning is different from community service in that it has two inseparable components: service and learning. Service learning is typically defined as a "pedagogical technique for combining authentic community service with integrated academic outcomes." . . . The premise is that students' involvement in community service can also contribute to their learning and growth. . . . Some supporters suggest that the balance between service learning and academic learning in schools needs to shift, with service learning becoming an integral part of the school curriculum rather than an extracurricular activity. . . .

As part of the curriculum, service opportunities . . . [are] employed as a curricular tool to help students bridge the gap between theory and reality. . . .

A primary advantage of using service learning as a teaching methodology is that . . . learning stems from direct experience . . . . However, data from the National Service-Learning Clearinghouse indicate that the primary focus of most programs is personal and interpersonal knowledge with the least focus on academic or subject matter learning. . . .

Those directly involved in service learning programs report a variety of benefits for participating students, including enhanced self-esteem, . . . clarification of values, . . . social and personal development, . . . and enhanced academic performance. . . . Service learning can be an effective way to increase the connection of youth with their society and to develop good habits of citizenship. . . . However, to achieve these purposes, service learning programs must . . . encourage and require student reflection on the dynamics of volunteerism, the responsibilities of citizenship, and an understanding of multicultural societies and the larger meaning of community. Through this process, students' attitudes about themselves (academically and socially) and their neighborhoods may change over the course of their participation in such a program.

Despite their potential, not all service learning programs achieve positive changes in students' attitudes or performance. . . . If service learning programs are to achieve their promising potential, researchers need to continue examining the experiences of students involved in these projects and to expand the knowledge of the key features needed for successful programs.

In this article, the authors draw on data from a 3-year evaluation to compare the strengths and weaknesses of 10 different service learning programs. The authors provide a brief background about the program, describe the research design, examine critical elements in designing effective service programs, and discuss the connections among them.

Background

The service learning programs included in this research took place in a large urban school district in southern California. The district is located in an economically depressed community with high rates of unemployment and crime. Approximately one third of the county's population is younger than the age of 18 years. School and community leaders are concerned with trends in the youth population such as gang violence, drive-by shootings, teenage parenting, and failure to graduate from high school. One primary objective of the service learning programs was to help change these trends by involving the youth in citizenship training through service.

The district began its venture into service learning by piloting the concept at a single high school during the first year. In the second year, the program expanded to three high schools. During the third and final year of the evaluation, the district implemented service learning at all six high schools in the district. The 172 participants included approximately an equal number of male and female students, but the majority were either freshmen or sophomores. The ethnic composition of the program participants was 60% Hispanic, 20% Caucasian, 9% African American, 9% Asian American, and 2% other.

At the beginning of each year, interested teachers at each high school attended a training session on service learning where they were encouraged to adopt service learning as a part of their regular curriculum. Service learning was broadly defined to give teachers the maximum amount of flexibility and to encourage creative projects that would fit both the service and learning aspects of the definition. Because service was strongly recommended but not mandated, participation by teachers was voluntary.

The 10 projects included in this study . . . is contained in Table 1.

Methodology

For this study, the authors used both quantitative and qualitative data from the third year of the program to examine the greatest number of service learning projects. The 172 students participating in service learning completed a 35-question attitudinal survey at the end of their projects. The survey addressed five main categories of student attitudes: academic success, school socialization, future planning, self-perception, and community pride. Academic success encompassed issues of individual academic achievement, grades, participation in class discussions, and students' perception of the efficacy of instruction. This category referred to all classes, not just the specific course that included service learning. School socialization included students' relationships with other students, attitudes toward multiculturalism in the

---

TABLE 1 Description of Projects

Project	Description
World History Awareness (world history class)	This project involved high school students in making presentations to elementary students on the importance of world history.
Head Start (interdisciplinary English and social studies class)	This project placed students with Head Start preschoolers for a limited time. Students worked with the preschoolers as program volunteers.
Miles of Smiles (English-as-second-language class)	This project trained limited-English-proficient students as guides for non-English-speaking guests at the high school.
Peace Coaching (English class)	This project involved high school students acting as coaches and mentors for kindergarten student-designed children's books to help elementary students learn various subjects.
Quilt Blocks (mathematics class)	This project required students to design a 12-inch-square quilt block using at least one geometric transformation. The students were each given a packet of materials and a brief lesson on sewing. Each student was responsible for cutting out pattern pieces for his or her design. Most of the students tried to sew their own square with the help of family and friends. The blocks were sewn together into unified quilts that were donated to local organizations.
School Guides (English-as second-language class)	Duplicate of Miles of Smiles at a different school.
Snagology (integrated science class)	A short-term project that encouraged environmentalism through recycling.
Spanish Song Books (Spanish class)	This project involved a Spanish honors class. The class divided into groups of four students and created song boards and audiocassettes that were sent to elementary schools in the area. This project lasted 1 week and was completed in class.
Stereotypes Presentation (English class)	This project focused on the negative power and energy of stereotyping. Students were trained to present a workshop on tolerance to their peers.
Teachers for the Dream (English class and after-school club)	This project gave future teachers an opportunity to practice their skills with younger students (middle school and elementary). Student teachers addressed the whole child during the project, helping with academic and social problems. The project lasted the entire year.

---

school setting, participation in school activities, and general perceptions about the high school experience. In the area of future plans, students responded to inquiries regarding their postsecondary educational plans and the part altruism might play in their life goals. The self-perception category included students' perceptions regarding their appearance, achievements, happiness, and respect for themselves and others. Finally, questions regarding community pride asked students about their perceptions of their neighborhoods with regard to safety, desirability, and pride.

▶ *(Please keep in mind that influence cannot be determined in a correlational study.)*

To determine the extent to which program features influenced student attitudes in each of the five areas, the authors rated each of the 10 projects according to four design elements: duration, location, personal contact, and focus of the project. The design elements were identified based on 3 years of studying and evaluating both successful (as judged by teacher and student input) and less-than-successful service learning programs. However, there may be a number of other possible factors that might have influenced the attitudes of the students involved in the service learning projects studied: teacher quality, student interest in the subject matter, socioeconomic status, teacher interest, and so on. Although this study does not determine definitely all of the design elements for successful service learning programs, it does begin to identify key characteristics of programs and provide a position for future research.

The authors' experience suggests that duration, location, personal contact, and focus of the project are elements that may contribute to the success (or failure) of service learning endeavors. The authors developed a rating scale of 1 to 5 (low to high) to delineate the range in program components found in the projects studied. Table 2 details the rating scale. . . .

The ratings for each project on duration, location, personal contact, and focus are given in Table 3.

. . . The authors . . . looked at the correlations between the five attitudinal categories and the four criteria. . . .

Quantitative data provided corroborating information regarding student gains and program effectiveness. Students wrote an essay prior to participation in service learning addressing the following query: "Give a brief description of what you hope to gain from this service learning project." Following participation in a service learning project, the students responded to a similar essay: "Give a brief description of what you gained from this service learning project. How does what you gained compare to what you thought you might gain before starting this project?" Qualitative data were analyzed in conjunc-

TABLE 2	Scoring of Four Critical Elements			
Scale	*Duration*	*Location*	*Personal Contact*	*Focus of Project*
1	Project lasts less than 4 weeks	Project done at home and then brought to school	No direct contact with beneficiaries of project	Includes little or no service
2	Project lasts from 4 weeks to 9 weeks	Project done in the classroom	A representative makes contact ((i.e., contact by another student or the teacher) with the beneficiaries of the project	Some focus on service
3	Project lasts from 9 weeks to 18 weeks	Project done at the high school campus	Students have a single contact with the project's beneficiaries	Moderate amount of service
4	Project lasts from 1 semester to 1 year	Project done at another school's campus (often an elementary or middle school)	Students have sporadic contact with the project's beneficiaries	Significant amount of service
5	Project lasts longer than 1 year	Project conducted in the community	Students have repeated and sustained contact with the beneficiaries of the service learning project	Extensive focus on service

tion with the quantitative data to assist in determining the extent of each project's effectiveness, based on the four design elements. . . .

Results

There was broad variation in the 10 service learning projects evaluated, resulting in a wide range of attitudinal outcomes in the five areas measured (i.e., attitudes toward academic achievement, school socialization, self-esteem, future plans, and one's community). The results of the . . . correlational analysis (Table 5) . . . indicate that the higher the four criteria (duration, location, personal contact, and focus), the higher the students' attitudes toward academic achievement, plans for the future, self-esteem, school socialization, and their communities.

TABLE 3 Rating of Each Project						
Project	Duration Rating	Location Rating	Personal Contact Rating	Focus of the Project Rating	Total Points	Rank of Project
World History Awareness	2	4	3	3	12	4
Head Start	2	4	4	4	14	3
Miles of Smiles	1	1	1	1	4	9
Peace Coaching	3	4	5	4	16	2
Quilt Blocks	3	2	2	1	8	5
School Guides	1	1	1	1	4	9
Snagology	1	3	1	3	8	5
Spanish Song Books	1	2	1	3	7	7
Stereotypes Presentation	1	2	1	1	5	8
Teachers for the Dream	5	4	5	5	19	1

Duration

Results indicate that the longer the service learning project, the greater the positive attitudinal scores regarding future plans and school socialization. Students participating in projects that lasted less than 1 month showed the smallest attitudinal scores in these areas. Projects that lasted continuously over the student's entire high school experience corresponded with the higher scores. . . .

Students who spent the longest time working with people in their communities who needed their help reported getting along better with the students at their own schools and were better able to solidify their goals for the future. The data in this study support what proponents of service learning have long maintained: Longer is better.

Location

Service learning projects took place in three locations: at the student's home high school, at a school district other than the home school of the student, and in the community at large. Those projects that involved the student working with others away from his or her home campus corresponded with higher student attitudinal scores in the areas of future plans, self-esteem, and school socialization. Projects that took place on the home campus yielded low scores in these areas. Those projects that involved students in the neighbor-

TABLE 5 Correlations of Attitudes With Criteria

	Academic Achievement	Plans for the Future	Self-Esteem	School Socialization	Attitudes Toward the Community
Duration of project	$r = .09$	$r = .34$	$r = .14$	$r = .25$	$r = .06$
	$p < .24$	$p < .0001$	$p < .06$	$p < .001$	$p < .45$
Location of service learning	$r = .14$	$r = .32$	$r = .32$	$r = .38$	$r = .14$
	$p < .07$	$p < .0001$	$p < .0001$	$p < .0001$	$p < .07$
Extent of personal contact	$r = .16$	$r = .39$	$r = .21$	$r = .29$	$r = .08$
	$p < .03$	$p < .0001$	$p < .005$	$p < .0001$	$p < .27$
Focus of the project	$r = .08$	$r = .16$	$r = .27$	$r = .24$	$r = .11$
	$p < .33$	$p < .04$	$p < .0004$	$p < .002$	$p < .15$

hood, such as those run in conjunction with the local volunteer center, produced the greatest overall scores.

Personal Contact With Recipients

Although some projects involved an interaction with residents of the community, they did not involve personal interaction. Projects of this type usually consisted of producing a product in class that was then distributed to community recipients. . . . The data indicate students had higher attitudinal scores when they had direct personal contact with the beneficiaries of their efforts. . . .

Of the four criteria, personal contact was the most significant. Although face-to-face contact was not the norm among the service learning projects studied, those projects that included this aspect showed higher student attitudinal scores in four of the five areas: academic achievement, plans for the future, self-esteem, and school socialization. . . .

Focus of the Project

Greater positive attitudinal scores occurred in students who participated in projects that had an emphasis on service with learning as a necessary by-product rather than in projects that had an emphasis on learning with service as an added component. Projects that were designed to provide a service to others generally contained a learning component. . . . Projects that concentrated most extensively on service showed significant results in three of the five areas (plans for the future, self-esteem, and school socialization).

. . . Comments from student essays point out the differences in students' perspectives. Projects with an academic focus alone elicited responses such as "I am doing this project because it is a part of my grade" and "I am participating because my teacher made me." In describing what was gained from participating, students emphasized academic learning. . . . In contrast, students who participated in more service-oriented projects focused on personal values. For example, one student wrote, "When I first started the project I thought it was stupid. But later after I did the assignment I realized that I was doing a good deed by taking a little time out to make other people's days brighter." . . .

Discussion

The two key components of service learning, service and learning, directly correspond with the two most common goals of service learning projects in public schools: an increase in academic achievement and the inculcation of citizenship. This analysis supports the proposition that service learning projects of longer duration that place students in direct contact with service beneficiaries away from the school campus result in higher student attitudinal scores. However, the critical question is: Do higher attitudinal scores indicate or lead to increases in academic achievement and citizenship? The authors argue that they can.

With regard to citizenship, students who participated in service learning projects that scored high on the four criteria (duration, location, personal contact, and focus) reported that they were more involved in school activities, got along better with their peers, enjoyed being in school, and cared more about what their teachers thought of them than students who participated in service learning projects with low ratings. At the same time, these students reported that they knew what career paths they would follow after high school and that they believed helping other people was important to their futures. . . .

The challenge for service learning has not been in demonstrating its effect on citizenship but in establishing its connection to increased academic achievement. The data in this study indicate that: An increase in personal contact with the beneficiaries of service correlates with an increase in attitudes toward academic achievement, and students who travel away from the school site to perform service show an increase in self-esteem. . . .

. . . Researchers examining motivational issues argue that students who feel that they control their learning perform at higher academic levels than those who do not. One suggested method for maximizing control is to increase project-based learning. . . . Students who were engaged in a project over a longer period of time and who controlled the project by engaging directly with the beneficiaries reported higher levels of self-esteem and more positive attitudes toward academic achievement.

Although these data do not provide direct evidence of improved academic achievement, they do demonstrate increases in the motivational elements that lead to achievement.

Conclusions

The results of this research lead to three main conclusions regarding the implementation of service learning programs into the public school curriculum. First, to have a meaningful influence on students, service learning projects must achieve a delicate balance between the service and learning components. . . . The process of combining both service and learning component into a viable program is complex. . . . The results of this study suggest that projects with a clear emphasis on service fare better than those with service as an adjunct feature. . . . The learning component must be meaningfully incorporated into the service component. . . .

Second, many of the critical features of successful service learning projects are challenging to implement within the current school structure. This research suggests that personal contact with the beneficiaries, locating the project away from the school site, and conducting the project over a long period of time are crucial if both service and learning goals are to be achieved. . . . Once back in the classroom, the integration of service and learning must be completed and solidified. . . .

Third, the benefits of service learning may not be readily apparent over the short term. Although service learning may not result in immediate, short-term increases in academic achievement (as measured by standardized tests), it can more immediately affect student attitudes. . . . These results indicate that the longer the service learning project, the greater the positive attitudinal scores for students. Service learning programs that begin early and are continuous throughout schooling appear to achieve the greatest gains with respect to both citizenship and academic performance. . . .

CRITIQUE OF STUDY EXAMPLE 5.2

1. What was the rationale for the study?
2. What was the purpose of this study?

3. Where did the programs take place over the course of 3 years? Why were they introduced?

4. What are the general characteristics of the participating students? What information is missing? Of what consequence might it be?

5. Only teachers who volunteered to participate introduced programs in their curriculum. What problem may this present when evaluating the conclusions?

6. What was the general nature of the programs?

7. What five attitude-related variables did students rate after the project was finished?

8. What can be said about reliability and validity of the questionnaire?

9. What were critical aspects of the projects? How were they determined?

10. Are there any weaknesses of this rating procedure?

11. Are there any questionable ratings in the rating scale, found in Table 2?

12. Are there any questionable ratings of the projects, found in Table 3?

13. What was the time relationship between administration of the questionnaire and the essay written at the end of a project?

14. Did all students fill in the questionnaire at the same time? At the same place?

15. Look at the correlation coefficients in Table 5. There are 20 reported, presumably without adjusted alpha levels. Arrange them from highest to lowest and adjust each alpha, starting with $\alpha = .05/20 = .0025$ for $r = .39$. What do you conclude?

16. Interpret $r = .39$ and $r = .24$ in terms of r^2.

17. Is the statement regarding the relationship between duration of the project and attitudinal scores consistent with the results of the correlation analysis?

18. Is the statement regarding the relationship between location of the project and attitudinal scores consistent with the results of the correlation analysis?

19. Is the statement regarding the relationship between degree of personal contact and attitudinal scores consistent with the results of the correlation analysis?

20. Is the statement regarding the relationship between focus of the project and attitudinal scores consistent with the results of the correlational analysis?

21. What did the authors maintain the results showed?

22. Are these statements justified?

23. What did the authors conclude?

24. Are the conclusions justified?

25. What might account for the low correlation coefficients that were obtained?

26. What factors, other than the projects, might have resulted in positive attitudes?

For answers to these questions, see page 331.

BIBLIOGRAPHY

Cohen, J., & Cohen, P. (1983). *Applied multiple regression/correlation analysis for the behavioral sciences* (2nd ed.). Hillsdale, NJ: Lawrence Erlbaum.

Hays, W. L. (1988). *Statistics* (4th ed.). New York: Holt, Rinehart & Winston.

Howell, D. D. (1992). *Statistical methods for psychology* (3rd ed.). Boston: PWS-Kent.

McMillan, J. H., & Schumacher, S. (1997). *Research in education: A conceptual introduction* (4th ed.). White Plains, NY: Longman.

Additional Suggested Readings

Achdeacon, T. J. (1994). *Correlation and regression analysis*. Madison: University of Wisconsin Press.

Ary, D., Jacobs, L. C., & Razavieh, A. (1996). *Introduction to research in education* (5th ed.). Orlando, FL: Harcourt Brace.

Keppel, G., & Zedicki, S. (1989). *Data analysis for research designs: Analysis of variance and multiple regression/correlation approaches*. New York: Freeman.

Chapter 6

Regression Analysis Studies

When two variables are found to be correlated, one may be used to predict the other. If extroversion is shown to be correlated with salesmanship (both measured at the same time), extroversion now may be used to predict salesmanship (which will be measured at a later time) of prospective salespersons. *Regression analysis* deals with predicting certain continuous, behavioral variables on the basis of knowledge about other, independent, variables, some of which may be *dummy-coded* categorical variables. Or it describes the role played by certain independent variables in a particular dependent variable. Thus, it may describe how well graduate record exam (GRE) scores predict performance in graduate school, or it may describe the average amount of change in blood glucose for each unit change in stress. The variable that is being predicted ($\hat{Y}$: salesmanship, graduate school success, blood glucose) is called the *criterion variable*. The variable from which the prediction is made (X: extroversion, GRE, stress) is called the *predictor variable*. When we are concerned with a single dependent variable but more than one independent (or predictor) variable, the problem is called *multiple regression analysis*. In this instance the regression equation is

$$\hat{Y} = b_0 + b_1X_1 + b_2X_2 + \ldots + b_pX_p$$

Here, the *predicted* criterion variable is designated $\hat{Y}$. Assuming a straight line relationship between Y (the *actual* criterion variable) and Xs, b_0 is the Y intercept, the average value of Y when each X equals 0, and the remaining bs are regression coefficients or, more accurately, partial regression coefficients. Each reflects the average amount of change predicted in Y for each unit change in the corresponding X *when all other independent variables are held constant*. That is, each b is a partial regression coefficient. For example, b_2 is the coefficient for the regression of Y on X_2 with the effects of $X_1, \ldots, X_p$ partialed out, removed, or statistically controlled.

Because we often want to directly compare the contributions of each variable in predicting Y, βs (*beta weights*) or standardized regression coefficients, based on Z scores, are computed instead of bs, based on raw scores. Because beta weights are based on Z scores rather than units of measurements that may differ, they can be compared directly. Now we can say that a predictor variable with a larger β is associated with a larger unit change in the criterion than one with a smaller β. Each β reflects the average amount of change predicted in Y in terms of standard deviation units for each unit change in X. Each of the βs is tested for significance. If one is not significant, then its corresponding independent variable does not significantly contribute to the predicted $\hat{Y}$, once the other variables are included, even though it may correlate highly with the criterion variable. If βs are tested for significance, df for an F test (analysis of variance test, covered in Chapter 11) are 1 and N (number of sets of scores) $- p$ (number of predictor variables) $- 1$.

Another bit of information that emerges from multiple regression analysis is *multiple R:* the correlation between the dependent variable and the predictor variables. Its square is interpreted as any r^2 as percentage variance in the dependent variable that is associated with the predictor variables. This is so because R actually is the correlation between Y and $\hat{Y}$. It is calculated by $R = \sqrt{\beta_1 \, r_{1y} + \beta_2 \, r_{2y} + \ldots + \beta_p \, r_{py}}$ (or by $r = \sqrt{r^2_{y1} + r^2_{y(2.1)} + \ldots + r^2_{y(p.12 \, \ldots \, p-1)}}$, where each r^2 is the squared semipartial correlation between each variable and the criterion with the effects of remaining variables removed only from the variable). Its significance is tested by an F test with p (number of predictor variables) and $N - p - 1$ df. This is an important test. If R is not significantly greater than zero, $\hat{Y}$ cannot be predicted from the predictor variables taken together.

If the intent of the analysis is to determine whether certain predictor variables *explain or account* for an outcome measure, all variables are entered into the equation simultaneously. However, if the intent is *to predict* the outcome (criterion) variable, alternate multiple regression procedures are available. In *hierarchical analysis,* the investigator decides ahead of time on the order in which each variable will be added. As each one is added, it is followed by a multiple regression analysis. Therefore, the unique effect of each independent variable can be determined (the effects of earlier variables are partialled out). But the predetermined order (usually based on "causal" priority to the criterion) is important, because partial regression coefficients—and, consequently, any increment in R^2—will change when effects of different variables are partialled out. The best-known procedure, which is used when investigators have no a priori basis for ordering the variables in terms of their probable "causal" priority to the criterion variable, is *stepwise multiple regression.* After the significance of all predictor variables has been determined, the most significant predictor, in terms of having the highest correlation with the dependent variable, is entered into the equation, and R^2 is determined. Then, semipartial correlations (with the effect of the first variable removed) are determined between remaining independent variables and the criterion variable. The second most significant predictor, the one with next highest semipartial correlation (i.e., the effect of the first variable is partialled out from the effects of the second variable) with the dependent variable, is added, Y is regressed on these two variables, and R^2 is redetermined. This represents the percentage variability in Y that is attributed to the first variable and to the second variable that is over and above that attributed to the first. If the change in R^2 from the first to this second one is significant, the effect of the first variable (originally chosen only because of its correlation with the criterion) is reexamined to see whether it still makes a significant contribution. If it is still significant (i.e., still accounts for a reasonable amount of variance), the next variable, based on the same criterion, is entered and the process is repeated until the change in R^2 no longer is significant. That last variable is removed. In this instance we are moving in a forward direction. (In *forward selection*, the re-evaluation steps are eliminated.) In *backward elimination*, all predictor variables first are added to the equation. Those predictors with nonsignificant partial regression coefficients or nonsignificant semipartial correlations (again, between the criterion and variable, with the effect of remaining variables removed only from the predictor) are eliminated, and the analysis is repeated with the remaining predictors, which will now yield new semipartial correlation coefficients because of the removal of one (or some) independent variable from the equation. Again, predictors with nonsignificant partial regression coefficients or semipartial correlation are eliminated, and the process is repeated until the equation includes only those predictors whose partial regression coefficients are significant. This difference in procedure also means that variables that might be considered important when analysis in a forward direction is conducted might not correspond to variables that are considered important when a backward elimination analysis is performed.

Use of multiple regression analysis is not without cautions. Sloppy data yield misleading results of the analyses. In addition, if extreme scores (outliers) are included, these can distort results. Any serious analysis should be preceded by diagnostic tests. *Stem and leaf plots* (a form of frequency distribution) of each predic-

tor variable should reveal relatively symmetrical distributions with few, if any, outliers. A preliminary regression analysis will yield measures of *distance* (the deviations of Y scores from the regression line), *leverage* (the deviation of X scores from their means), and *influence* (outliers that deviate on both variables). Outliers may or may not affect predictability. Preliminary analysis compares errors in predictions (called *residuals*) with and without these potentially influential cases. If there is a difference, these cases are examined to determine whether there is justification for eliminating them from the final analysis. Otherwise, both regression equations could be presented, the data can be transformed (e.g., log transformation) to reduce variability, or more data might be gathered. If no mention is made about tests for outliers, an examination of means and standard deviations can give you some idea about the shape of the distribution of scores.

Other problems can occur with stepwise regression analysis. Some variables declared to be significant predictors may be significant by chance because so many tests are conducted (especially with a large number of predictors). No adjustments are made in the successive alpha levels when each new R^2 is generated, nor is it considered when the variable is selected from the pool on the basis of intercorrelations between the criterion and independent (predictor) variables. Variables that are significant when one sample is measured may not be so for another sample and vice versa. This would be evident in a cross-validation study in which the regression equation is tested on an independent sample of data. For these and other reasons, the results of stepwise regression analyses should be interpreted cautiously.

Another problem can arise if one independent variable is highly correlated with another independent variable or with a linear combination of some or all of the remaining independent variables. The phenomenon is called *multicollinearity*. It might be suspected if R^2 is high, an outcome of high correlations between independent variables, but the partial regression coefficients are not (or one may be unusually larger or smaller than anticipated). Therefore, the net effect is to increase the degree of error in estimating each partial regression coefficient. The estimations of partial regression coefficients for the population will be very unstable (i.e., change from one sample to the next) and will not provide reliable predictions. An examination of intercorrelations between independent variables will be of little help in detecting multicollinearity, because it misses possible correlations between one and some *combination of other variables*. One procedure that is favorable is to regress each variable on the remaining ones. If the resulting R^2s are low, there is no problem. If one or more is high, then the problem exists. If an investigator recognizes the problem, he or she can combine the correlated variables if they can be logically combined. Here, the researcher may first conduct a factor analysis (see Chapter 7), which results in uncorrelated sets of variables, and then select representative variables from each set as the predictors. Or, if the variables are of interest, they can be entered first in a hierarchical analysis, before the critical variables are entered. Of course, a reader is not likely to be able to carry out the procedure but can at least suspect that high multicollinearity is a possibility when expected partial regression coefficients are not significant.

Regarding design issues, multiple regression studies should be as rigorously conducted as an experiment. Given that some of the predictors are scores on psychological tests, the tests should be reliable and valid and be administered in counterbalanced order; that is, each test should appear in each position an equal number of times. Moreover, the individuals administering the tests should be naive with respect to crucial bits of information so as not to influence those who are tested. Finally, testing conditions should be uniform to reduce variability, and volunteer participants should not differ radically from those who refused to take part in the study; that is, there should be no selective loss of participants. In addition to these factors, which can affect accuracy of the prediction, two others should be mentioned. The time intervening between measurement of the criterion and predictor variables is important. The longer the interval, the greater the opportunity for other variables to affect the criterion variable besides the predictors. Finally, some criterion variables are more difficult to predict than others because they are affected by so many variables, all of which may not be included in the multiple regression equation. Caution factors associated with multiple regression analyses are presented in Box 6.1.

Now we are prepared to review two articles that involved multiple regression. We'll evaluate the first one together, and you'll evaluate the second one alone.

BOX 6.1
Caution Factors Associated With Multiple Regression

- Tests used are reliable and valid.

- Sample is not biased (no undue number of nonresponders).

- Multiple tests were presented in counterbalanced order.

- Test administrator was naive with respect to study's purpose.

- Testing conditions were uniform.

- Time between tests and criterion measurement is reasonable.

- Intercorrelations between independent and criterion variables are significant at adjusted alpha level.

- Hierarchical analysis is performed if a priori basis exists for ordering variables.

- Stepwise procedure is used in absence of rationale for ordering variables.

- Data were examined for outliers and multicollinearity.

STUDY EXAMPLE 6.1

This study evaluates the impact of a total quality management program introduced into an organization that supplies engineering and electrical components multinationally. Total quality management is a concept and process that has been used in the United States for at least 20 years. The goal is to view production as a process that involves participants at all levels of an organization, from management to workers, to improve quality of a product so that it meets customer requirements. In this study, employees were surveyed before and after the program was introduced to determine the extent to which participation in the program affected their perception of its benefits and commitment to the organization.

The Study

Coyle-Shapiro, J. A.-M. (1999). Employee participation and assessment of an organizational change intervention: Three-wave study of total quality management. *Journal of Applied Behavioral Science, 35*(4), 439-456. Copyright 1999 by Sage.

As a management innovation, total quality management (TQM) has come under scrutiny from a number of fronts. First, the diversity of practices being implemented under the rubric of TQM has created ambiguity as to what TQM is and what it is not. . . . TQM, as set out by its founders, is a coherent philosophy with a distinctive set of interventions, but the reality of organizational practices does not mirror that philosophy.

. . . The conceptual mapping of the impediments to achieving successful TQM change is not matched by empirical studies investigating the introduction and development of the TQM process. Toward this latter end, this article examines the process of change involved in implementing TQM, as well as employees' experiences of participation, and evaluates the impact of employee participation in TQM on their commitment to the organization using a longitudinal research design.

Process of Change

The type of change associated with TQM is subject to debate, with some commentators viewing TQM as a distinct management paradigm associated with transformational change. . . . Others challenge this view, adopting a more cautious interpretation of TQM as tectonic change. . . . In contrast, there is broad consensus regarding the process by which TQM is implemented. An underlying assumption of TQM is that . . . top management commitment and support is a precondition for the success of TQM. . . . Change is assumed to occur in a straightforward manner throughout the managerial hierarchy, culminating with first-line supervisors involving employees in TQM. Second, the primary levers for change include training, education, and recognition. . . . The underlying assumption is that change occurs as a consequence of education and training, not only in terms of individual attitudes and behaviors but also as a stimulus for changes in organizational practices to support a TQM philosophy. . . .

. . . . The support of first-line supervisors is crucial to effecting change at the level of employees. As TQM requires greater involvement from employees regarding quality and improvement issues, supervisors who operate along participative lines may be more likely to involve employees in a TQM intervention. . . .

Participation in TQM

. . . Although the consequences of TQM for employees are keenly debated, what is clearly absent is a more dispassionate empirical test of employees' assessments of their participation in TQM. Therefore, it is important to empirically test the link between participation in TQM and evaluation of the benefits accruing from that participation.

Outcomes of TQM

. . . Although TQM does not set out to enhance organizational commitment directly, the implementation of TQM elicits greater involvement in organizational activities. . . . Therefore, through increased communication and consultation, employees may feel a greater identification with, involvement in, and loyalty to the organization. Based on the above discussion, the following hypotheses are proposed:

Hypothesis 1: There will be a positive relationship between employees' perceptions of the participative style of their supervisors prior to TQM and their participation in TQM.

Hypothesis 2a: There will be a positive relationship between employees' participation in TQM and their assessments of the benefits of TQM.

Hypothesis 2b: Employee assessment of the benefits of TQM will be more important in predicting subsequent participation in TQM than is employees' initial participation.

Hypothesis 3: There will be a positive relationship between employees' participation in TQM and their commitment to the organization.

▶ *(Note that all hypotheses involve concepts that will have to be measured: employee perception of supervisor's style of participation, assessment of benefits, importance of assessment of benefits, participation, and commitment.)*

1. What was the rationale for the study?

Because of diverse practices in implementing total quality management (TQM), there is controversy about what it is and is not. Although obstacles to achieving successful TQM have been studied, few have looked at its introduction and development. The present study examines the introduction and development of the process, employees' experiences of participating in it, and the impact of their participation on their commitment to the organization.

There is debate about the type of change involved in TQM, managerial or constructive. There is more agreement about its implementation, which requires support and commitment by top managers. Change is assumed to occur in a downward fashion from managers to supervisors to employees through education and training. Supervisor attitude seems to be more important in the effect of TQM on employees because supervisors come into direct contact with them. But little is known about employee participation in TQM and their benefits gained from participation. And an outcome of TQM could be greater commitment of participators to their organization.

2. What was the purpose of the study?

The study tested the following hypotheses: Employees' perception of supervisor's style of participating in the organization before TQM and employees' participation in it will be positively correlated; employees' participation in TQM will be positively related to their perceived benefits of TQM; subsequent participation in TQM will be better predicted by perceived benefits than by initial participation; employees' participation in TQM will be positively correlated with their commitment to the organization.

Method

Institutional Setting

This study was conducted at one site of a U.K.-based multinational supplier of engineering and electrical components that employs approximately 600 people. . . . In the late 1980s . . . changes were introduced to the terms and conditions of employment, the pay-grading structure was amplified, and harmonization of methods of the payment and pension scheme occurred. . . . In 1990 the site launched continuous improvement groups . . . for employees to contribute to . . . on a voluntary basis. Overall, employee participation in these groups was sporadic, with some groups disbanding while others started. Against what was perceived by management as the failure of the grassroots approach to improvements, the site embarked upon TQM. . . .

The TQM Intervention

. . . The objective was to change the culture of the site toward continuous improvement, and this was to be achieved by the "participative involvement" of everyone.

With the assistance of a TQM proponent from within the organization and a group of outside consultants, a change program focusing on education and training was designed. . . . The initial targets for change were those in the management hierarchy. . . . It was assumed that as a consequence of the training and education program, a series of changes would occur throughout the site. . . .

The starting point was the training and education program, which the outside consultants ran off-site for the executive team. Subsequently, a group of internally selected facilitators were taken off-site and undertook the program as well as a facilitation workshop. . . . Supervisors and managers, having completed the program, were held responsible for training their subordinates. It was assumed that after completing the program, managers and supervisors would actively cascade the training to their employees and set up improvement teams. In practice, this approach to change led to an uneven involvement of employees in TQM activities as a consequence of the recalcitrance of some supervisors.

. . . In autumn of 1993, in view of the pockets of continued resistance, it was decided that progress in the intervention was to become an integral part of each manager's annual performance objectives and thus part of their performance appraisals. . . . After some debate, the steering committee decided against compulsory participation at employee levels. However, all new employees would be required as part of their jobs to participate in the intervention. During 1994, the site took over the manufacturing of a new product from a different site and consequently hired a new group of employees who were informed that their participation in TQM was integral to their employment at the site.

---

3. *What is the general background of the testing site?*

The site employed 600 people in distributing engineering and electrical components. Changes, which began in the late 1980s and included continuous improvement groups, were not successful and led to the introduction of TQM. Attempted gains in improvement were implemented by education and training, starting at the managerial level. Some supervisors, however, resisted change, and this resulted in uneven involvement of employees. Participation was not compulsory, except for new employees.

Research Design

The research method employed consisted of a before-and-after study of the TQM intervention with three measurement occasions: 6 months prior to the commencement of the intervention and 9 months and 32 months after the start of the intervention. . . . Prior to the administration of the first-round questionnaire, trade union representatives were informed of the research, given the opportunity to raise questions and/or concerns, and asked to support the research. Subsequently, as part of a quarterly communications day whereby all employees in groups are given a 40-minute presentation on relevant issues for the site, I introduced myself to the entire workforce and stated my independence from management at the site and the overall organization. In addition, employees were informed that the results of the survey would be communicated to them. All these steps were taken to facilitate continued cooperation.

▶ *(Note that the author [far from being uninvolved] introduced herself to the entire workforce and informed them that they were taking part in the study. This might open the door for the Hawthorne effect.)*

A random sample of 40% of employees stratified by work area was asked to participate in the research. Participants were informed that they would be allocated a code number so that they could be identified and tracked over time. Most of the employees completed the questionnaire on a one-to-one basis away from their work areas during work time. The first phase of data collection took place . . . 6 months prior to the commencement of the TQM intervention, at which stage none of the respondents were aware of the pending initiative. Therefore, the baseline questionnaire was not influenced by individuals' knowledge of the forthcoming intervention. The same administration procedure was adopted for the postintervention measurements.

▶ *(Note that the 40% who were selected might have felt "special" even though they didn't know about the forthcoming intervention. But the author presumably knew, and most questionnaires were filled out on a one-to-one basis. Moreover, they were completed while employees were on the job but away from their work area.)*

At Time 1, 186 of the 200 employees asked to complete the questionnaire did so, yielding a response rate of 93%. The employee participant sample was reduced to 166 at Time 2 and 118 at Time 3, due primarily to employees leaving the site in the intervening period. Consequently, the sample used in the analysis was confined to employees who completed questionnaires on all three measurement occasions. At Time 3, the participant group was 95%

male, with a mean age of 48.0 years, a mean organizational tenure of 18.0 years, and a mean job tenure of 8.85 years. The sample consisted of machine operators (33.3%), craftsmen (26.4%), engineers (14.5%), and material/purchase controllers (7.9%), with the remainder of the sample in administrative positions.

▶ *(Note that there were virtually no nonresponders in the pre-TQM phase, but by Time 3 [32 months after the introduction of TQM], there was a loss of 36.6% [186 – 118/186] of the employees. Because these were people who had left the organization, we have to consider that they may have been dissatisfied with the program. Moreover, even though information was available, there is no mention of a comparison made between those who left and those who remained.)*

4. What was the general design of the study?

This was a before-and-after study, with questionnaires filled out (mainly on a one-to-one basis with the experimenter) 6 months before and 9 and 32 months after TQM was introduced.

5. What were the initial and final samples?

A random sample of 40% of the workforce (200) was approached, and 186 consented to take part in the survey. Six months later, the sample size was reduced to 166 employees, and 32 months later, it was reduced to 118. Most were males and about 48 years old; they had been with the organization for about 18 years and at their present job for almost 9 years. The majority were machine operators and craftsmen. The remainder were engineers, machine/purchase controllers, and administrators (almost 18%).

6. What are some weak spots in the design?

First, the experimenter approached and tested the participants. They knew they were part of a survey and might have felt special or may have been unintentionally influenced by the experimenter. Second, there may have been a selective loss of employees who were most dissatisfied with the new program. Third, we know nothing about those who left nor how they compare with those who remained at the site.

Measures and Analysis Procedures

. . . Employees were asked to indicate the extent to which they were participating in the activities of the intervention along a 5-point Likert-type scale ranging from *not at all* to *a very great extent* (coded from 1 to 5). . . . As a checking measure, when employees responded to this question they were subsequently asked to elaborate on why they responded in a particular manner. . . . The following classification was used: Employees whose response was either *not at all* or *not much* (coded as 1 and 2, respectively) were aware of the intervention and had received communication about the intervention when it was launched. These employees had not received training and effectively were not (as yet) participating in the intervention. . . . Individuals who responded in the *to a great extent* and *to a very great extent* (coded 4 and 5, respectively) categories had received training by their supervisors and were participating in teams with the aim of making improvements in their work areas. The remaining employees who responded in the *to some extent* (coded 3) category were not participating in teams. However, they were trained in the principles of TQM by their supervisors and participating at a more informal (unstructured) level, such as monitoring internal customer requirements or instigating corrective action based on problems identified by another improvement team.

A sample of the remaining scale items, the number of items in the scale, and Cronbach's alpha coefficient for the scales are shown in Table 1. . . .

▶ *(It is noted that most scale items were adapted from published scales.)*

Finally, respondents were asked to give details on their age, gender, organizational tenure, and job tenure. Respondents were asked at Time 2 and Time 3 whether they had experienced a change in supervisor. The hypotheses were tested using hierarchical regressions. In each equation, the control variables were entered in Step 1, as these variables could potentially affect both the independent variables and the dependent variables. For example, perceived management commitment to quality may have an effect on employee participation in TQM and organizational commitment. Subsequently, the independent variable of interest is entered into the equation.

> **7. Are there any questionable aspects of the scales used to measure participation, perceived participation and commitment of supervisors, or perceived benefits of TQM?**
>
> No. Most items were adapted from other scales, and Cronbach's alphas are reasonable. But no mention is made about the order in which the scales were presented. If they were not counterbalanced, it is possible that a carry-over effect might affect the responses on some of the scales.

TABLE 1 Measurement of Variables

Variable Name and Sample Survey Items	Number of Items	Alpha
Supervisory participative style	7	.84
The person I normally report to:		
Encourages people to participate in important decisions		
Encourages people to speak up when they disagree with a decision		
Allows people to use their own judgment in solving problems		
Is successful in getting people to work together		
Supports me in getting my job done		
Organizational commitment	6	.78
I am quite proud to tell people I work for [name of organization]		
I feel myself to be part of [name of organization]		
To know that my own work had made a contribution to the good of [name of organization] would please me		
Even if [name of organization] was not doing too well financially, I would be reluctant to change to another employer		
Perceived management commitment to quality	5	.84
Management is genuinely committed to improving quality		
Management sets examples of quality performance in their daily activities		
Management has attempted to involve everyone in continuous improvement		
Management provides support for quality improvement throughout the organization		
Improved support for total quality management (TQM)	5	.79
Compared to a year ago:		
Top management is more committed to Total Quality		
Visible progress has been made in improving things at this site		
Top management is more supportive of suggestions to improve the way things are done around here		
Total Quality is a greater priority at this site		
People are encouraged more to say how they think things could be done better		
Perceived benefit of TQM	4	.75
There is no benefit for me in [name of TQM intervention]		
[Name of intervention] is a management initiative to get people to do more work[a]		

a. Reverse scored.

Results

Descriptive statistics and correlation coefficients of the main variables are reported in Table 2.

▶ *(Note that 36 correlation coefficients have been presented with no corrected alpha level. The adjusted alpha level for the highest coefficient, .71, is .05/36 = .001. Because the author only states that significance for coefficients greater than .23 is p < .01, it is difficult to know which coefficients are significant. Therefore, I did t tests for several of the coefficients to determine which are significant at the adjusted level. For r = .32, the adjusted alpha level is .05/20 = .0025 and $t = r\sqrt{N-2} / \sqrt{1-r^2} = .32\sqrt{118-2} / \sqrt{1-.32^2} = 3.638$, p < .001. None of the lower coefficients are significant at the adjusted level.)*

---

8. ***Examine the coefficients and interpret the ones relevant to the hypotheses.***

The first hypothesis predicts a positive correlation between supervisor's participative style before TQM and employees' participation in the program. That coefficient is .24 and is not significant. The second hypothesis predicts a positive correlation between employees' participation in TQM and their perceived benefits of it. The correlation for measurements taken at Times 1 and 2 is .40 and is significant. The correlation for measurements taken later (for participation only) is .28 and is not significant. The third hypothesis predicts a positive correlation between employees' participation in TQM and their commitment to the organization. Measurements of these variables at Times 1 and 2 yielded a coefficient of .22, which is not significant, and a coefficient of .37 at the later time, which is significant.

9. ***Why is it inappropriate to use the coefficients to retain or reject the hypotheses?***

These are zero-order coefficients and include the effects of some of the other independent variables. The regression analyses partial out the unwanted effects.

Hypothesis 1 predicted that perceived supervisory participative style would be positively related to employee participation in TQM. Table 3 presents the results. In the first step, participation in TQM (Time 2) was regressed on several control variables: age, gender, job tenure, organizational tenure, change of supervisor, organizational commitment, and perceived management commitment to quality. When supervisory participative style (Time1)

TABLE 2 Descriptive Statistics and Correlations for Main Study Variables

	M	SD	1	2	3	4	5	6	7	8
Organizational commitment (Time 1)	5.39	0.90								
Supervisory participative style (Time 1)	4.98	1.12	.16							
Management commitment to quality (Time 1)	5.07	1.09	.48	.48						
Improved support for TQM[a] (Time 2)	5.03	1.06	.32	.41	.40					
Participation in TQM (Time 1-Time 2)	2.56	1.10	.08	.26	.14	.36				
Perceived benefit of intervention (Time 2)	4.16	1.26	.22	.19	.23	.35	.40			
Organizational commitment (Time 2)	5.50	0.94	.69	.33	.47	.51	.22	.28		
Organizational commitment (Time 3)	5.46	0.97	.56	.27	.29	.38	.14	.20	.71	
Participation in TQM (Time 1-Time 2)	2.74	1.25	.27	.24	.18	.26	.24	.28	.35	.37

NOTE: Correlations greater than .17 are significant at $p < .05$. Correlations greater than .23 are significant at $p < .01$.
a. TQM = total quality management.

was entered in the equation, it produced a significant beta coefficient ($\beta = .24$, $p < .01$), indicating that it explained unique variance of participation that was not accounted for by the other variables, which supports Hypothesis 1.

▶ *(You should be looking at the values listed in the first column.)*

When improved support for TQM (Time 2) was entered in a subsequent step,

▶ *(Now examine the second column, all representing new values when that variable is added to the equation.)*

it produced a significant beta coefficient ($\beta = .34$, $p < .01$) and reduced the effect of supervisory participative style (Time 1). However, the effect of improved support is likely to be inflated, as it was measured at Time 2, in contrast to the measurement of supervisory participative style at Time 1. An additional regression equation (not reported here) establishes a significant positive relationship between supervisory participative style (Time 1) ($\beta = .31$, $p < .01$) and improved support for TQM (Time 2). This suggests that the participative style of the supervisor is important in shaping employee perceptions of the degree of support for TQM in the organization. Taken together, these results indicate that the behavior of the first-line supervisor plays an important yet overlooked role in eliciting employee participation in TQM.

---

10. In Table 3, what is the difference between the first two columns of numbers, with participation in TQM as the dependent variable?

The first column represents standardized regression coefficients after supervisory participative style had been added as a predictor variable in Step 2. The second column represents standardized regression coefficients after improved support for TQM then was added as another predictor variable in Step 3.

11. Interpret $\beta = .24$ and $.34$.

$\beta = .24$ indicates that every .24 unit increase in perceived supervisory participative style is accompanied by a unit increase in employees' participation in TQM. $\beta = .34$ indicates that every .34 unit increase in perceived management's improved support for TQM 6 months after it was introduced is accompanied by a unit increase in participation by employees.

12. Interpret $R^2 = .12$, taking into account results of Step 3 and the regression equation reported in the text.

Twelve percent of variability in employee participation in TQM is associated with perceived supervisory participative style and perceived management's improved support for TQM.

Hypothesis 2a posited that participation in TQM would be positively related to perceived benefit of TQM. To test this hypothesis, the control variables and supervisory participative style were entered in the equation initially and participation in TQM entered in a subsequent step. The results shown in Table 3 reveal that participation in TQM produced a significant beta coefficient ($\beta = .40$, $p < .01$), explaining an additional 15% variance in perceived benefit of TQM, supporting Hypothesis 2a.

TABLE 3 Hierarchical Regressions Predicting Participation in and Perceived Benefit of Total Quality Management (TQM) at Time 2 ($N = 116$)

Independent Variables	Participation in TQM (Time 2)		Perceived Benefit of TQM (Time 2)
Step 1			
Age	–.02 ns	.00 ns	.00 ns
Gender	.00 ns	–.03 ns	.03 ns
Job tenure	.08 ns	.11 ns	–.14 ns
Organizational tenure	–.09 ns	–.12 ns	.06 ns
Change of supervisor	–.14 ns	–.11 ns	.10 ns
Organizational commitment	.02 ns	–.05 ns	.18 ns
Perceived management commitment to quality	.02 ns	–.05 ns	.10 ns
Supervisory participative style	—	—	.02 ns
Change in R^2 for Step 1	.00 ns	.06 ns / $F\Delta$ 0.99	.09 ns / $F\Delta$ 1.36
Step 2			
Supervisory participative style	.24**	.13 ns	—
Participation in TQM (Time 2)	—	—	.40**
Change in R^2 for Step 2	.04* / $F\Delta$ 5.08	—	.15** / $F\Delta$ 20.72
Step 3			
Improved support for TQM (Time 2)	—	.34**	—
Change in R^2 for Step 3	—	.08** / $F\Delta$ 10.84	—
Overall adjusted R^2	.04	.12	.18

NOTE: Entries beside main variables are standardized regression coefficients.
Significant F and beta coefficient *$p < .05$; **$p < .01$ level.

---

13. What finding is taken as support for Hypothesis 2a?

The significant $\beta = .40$ indicates that employees' participation in TQM 6 months after its introduction predicts their perceived benefit of it.

Hypothesis 2b predicted that employees' assessments of the benefits accruing from TQM (Time 2) would be more important than employees' initial participation (Time 2) in explaining subsequent participation in TQM (Time 3). To test this hypothesis, two regressions were conducted. The control variables were entered in Step 1, participation in TQM (Time 2) was entered in Step 2, and perceived benefit of TQM (Time 2) in Step 3. The second regression reversed the entry of the variables, with perceived benefit of TQM entered in Step 2 and participation in TQM in Step 3. Reversing the order in which the variables are entered into the equation permits an examination of the relative importance of each of the predictors. [In either case, the] beta coefficient $\beta = .23$, $p < .05$. These results suggest that perceived benefit of TQM (Time 2) is more important than participation in TQM (Time 2) in explaining subsequent participation in TQM (Time 3), thus supporting Hypothesis 2b.

---

14. When testing Hypothesis 2b, what was the logic of entering perceived benefit of TQM after employees' participation in TQM at Time 2 and, in a separate regression, adding it after participation to predict participation in TQM 32 months after its introduction?

If perceived benefit is a significant predictor in both instances, relative to participation, it is a more important predictor of continued, later participation in the program.

Hypothesis 3 posited that participation in TQM would be positively related to organizational commitment. As the effects of employee participation in TQM may take time to materialize, this hypothesis was tested twice using different measurement occasions. In the first regression, organizational commitment (Time 2) was regressed on the control variables (including organizational commitment at Time 1) in Step 1 and participation in TQM (Time 2). The same procedure was followed regressing organizational commitment (Time 3) on the control variables (including organizational commitment at Time 2) in Step 1 and participation in TQM (Time 3) in Step 2. . . . Irrespective of the time period examined, participation in TQM does not explain unique variance in organizational commitment and does not produce a significant beta coefficient at either time period. Thus, Hypothesis 3 is not supported.

---

15. Why was it concluded that the last hypothesis was not supported?

The beta coefficients for employees' participation in TQM at Times 2 and 3 were not significant; that is, participation did not predict commitment to the organization 6 or 32 months after TQM was introduced.

Discussion

. . . The data suggest that supervisors have a positive role to play in getting employees involved in TQM. The extent of employee involvement is positively related to the assessment of benefits of TQM. Furthermore, how employees assess the beneficial impact of TQM is more important in predicting subsequent participation in TQM than is their initial participation. However, employee participation was not found to enhance commitment toward the organization.

The finding that supervisory behavior is positively related to employee participation in TQM is not surprising and is consistent with the more general research on employee participation and empowerment . . . yet, within the TQM literature, the role of first-line supervisors receives scant attention. . . . In this study, employee involvement in TQM was unproblematic where supervisors were participative prior to the introduction of TQM. However, the training and education as part of the TQM change process did little to change the behavior of supervisors operating in a traditional "direct and control" manner.

The effect of participation on perceived benefit of the intervention is broadly consistent with prior research . . . and supports the view that TQM can provide benefit to employees. . . . In this study, the findings . . . suggest that the greater employee participation in TQM, the more likely the intervention will be judged to be beneficial. . . . It would be naive to conclude that the consequences of TQM for employees are entirely beneficial. Clearly, there are trade-offs and . . . TQM may simultaneously lead to greater work effort and enhanced job satisfaction.

A commonly held assumption in empirical studies of voluntary employee participation programs is that employees are likely to withdraw their participation if they become disillusioned with the program as a result of unmet expectations. This study finds empirical support for the assumption that employees who do not see a change intervention as beneficial in the early stages of implementation are unlikely to participate subsequently. Therefore, when employees exercise choice in participating in a change intervention, the degree to which they assess it as beneficial may be pivotal to their decision to participate.

▶ *(Note that the author does recognize the probability of a selective loss of those employees who were dissatisfied with the introduction of TQM. This recognition, however, still does not tell us who they were or how they might have completed the questionnaires had they remained.)*

The enhancement of organizational commitment did not occur as a consequence of employee participation in TQM. In view of the specific limits of employee involvement under TQM, this type of narrowly focused participation may limit the extent to which enhanced commitment could be reasonably expected to occur. . . .

As with the majority of studies, the design of the current study is subject to limitations. The issue of generalizability of the findings is one limitation, particularly in view of the potentially different practices implemented as part of TQM. A second issue is the small sample size, due to the mortality effects inherent in conducting longitudinal studies. . . .

16. What were the author's major conclusions?

Supervisors play a major role in getting employees to participate in TQM. Employees' perception of the benefits of TQM predicts their participation in it. But commitment to the organization is not enhanced by participation.

17. To what extent were the conclusions justified?

The use of hierarchical analyses was appropriate for testing the hypotheses. The effects of independent variables that might have masked the critical effects were entered first and were therefore controlled by having their effects partialled out. Although zero-order coefficients relating supervisors' participatory style and participation in TQM by employees were not significant, the significant beta coefficient for supervisory style showed that it predicts participation. Likewise, the zero-order correlation between participation and perceived benefits of TQM was not significant, but the significant beta coefficient for participation showed that it predicts perceived benefits. Further regressions showed early perceived benefits to be a more important predictor of later participation than early participation in TQM. Finally, regression analysis revealed that participation in TQM does not predict early or later commitment to the organization, even though zero-order correlations between these two variables were significant.

18. What factors weaken the tenability of the conclusions?

First, there is the probability of a selective loss of employees who were nonparticipators in TQM. Inclusion of their data might have had positive or negative effects on the outcomes. If they would not have been affected by their supervisor's participative style, Hypothesis 1 may not have been supported. Too, they might not be likely to perceive benefits of TQM. Ironically, this would strengthen support for Hypothesis 2a. But, if they did not want to participate yet perceived the benefits of it, this would weaken support. Furthermore, their data may have had the same beneficial or detrimental effects on Hypothesis 2b. Finally, it is difficult to hypothesize what effect their data may have had on Hypothesis 3. Second, responses on some of the scales may have been affected by a knowledge that these employees had been selected for the surveys, by unintentional effects of the author, or by the sequence of the scales, given that counterbalancing was not mentioned.

> **19. To what population may the results generalize?**
>
> These results would generalize to employees in the United Kingdom working on similar jobs in similar organizations and who are willing to participate in TQM.

STUDY EXAMPLE 6.2

This study, to be evaluated by you, is concerned with the relationship between independence of older adults and factors associated with it. The association was determined by multiple regression.

The Study

Upchurch, S. (1999). Self-transcendence and activities of daily living: The woman with the pink slippers. *Journal of Holistic Nursing, 17*(3), 251-266. Copyright 1999 by Sage.

Understanding factors that influence older adults' ability to remain active and independent will become increasingly important in the next 20 to 30 years as the United States experiences a major demographic change. Persons older than 65 now represent nearly 12% of the population. The elderly are predicted to comprise 20% of the population by 2030. . . .

As people age, chronic health problems become a major concern. Of persons 65 years and older, 85% have at least one chronic problem; 69% have more than one. . . . Chronic health problems influence the well-being of older adults and may lead to dependency. Dependency influences functional well-being. . . . For many older individuals, the loss of independence is their primary worry. . . . The degree to which a person remains independent in activities of daily living (ADL) is affected by personal and environmental factors. . . . Even in the face of chronic health problems and potential dependency, differences between older adults' ability to perform ADL remain varied. . . . Why do some older adults continue to remain independent, regardless of their health status, whereas others become dependent?

. . . In each phase of life, various resources emerge that allow people to cope with life's challenges. In this context, aging is perceived as a developmental, not a decremental, experience. . . . A major resource of developmental maturity is self-transcendence (ST). Reed . . . defines self-transcendence as the capacity to extend personal boundaries multidimensionally and to be oriented toward perspectives, activities, and purposes beyond the self without negating the value of the self. Self-transcendence is the expansion of self-boundaries, inwardly in introspective experiences; outwardly through concerns for others' welfare; and temporally, whereby the past and future are integrated into the present. . . . This study builds on the work of Reed to explore the relationship of a developmental resource, that is, self-transcendence, to the physical domain. . . . Self- transcendence is a resource of successful aging by which a person has the capacity to extend self-boundaries and become oriented toward activities greater than self and to make decisions and choices as life changes. . . . The purpose of this study was to explore the relationships among self-transcendence (ST), health status (SHS), and activities of daily living (ADL) in older adults.

. . . Self-transcendence, a resource of successful aging, affords a person the potential to extend self-boundaries and become oriented toward activities, such as ADL, despite changes in health status. The following research question directed this study: Is there a relationship between self-transcendence, health status, and activities of daily living in noninstitutionalized older adults?

. . . Only one study could be found that directly related self-transcendence to physical health and functioning. . . . In a group of 46 HIV-positive individuals with the mean age of 37.8, . . . self-transcendence and health and functioning are significantly related. Higher self-transcendence scores were related to better health and functioning. To further explore the relationship between physical and self-transcendence the following research question was posed for this study: Is there a relationship between self-transcendence, health status, and ADL in older community-dwelling adults?

Method

Samples and Procedure

Eighty-eight men and women, 65 years of age or older, who were participants in senior-citizen and community-center organizations completed the study. Nonprobability, purposive sampling was used. To be included in the study, participants had to be older adults living in the community, who were oriented to person, place, and time, and who could read and write English. The sample was selected because it exemplified older adults who were successful in remaining independent. The study was in compliance with the rules and regulations of the Human Research Review Committee. Agency permission was obtained. Older adults were asked to complete questionnaires about their ability to stay active and take care of themselves. At center meetings, the investigator described the study and distributed consent forms and the questionnaires, in packets, to those who agreed to participate. The participants completed the forms and returned them to the investigator at the end of the meetings. One hundred and ten packets were distributed, and 88 usable packets were returned. Participants took an average of 15 minutes to complete the forms.

Instruments

. . . Self-transcendence was measured with Reed's . . . Self-Transcendence Scale (STS). The Self-Rated Health Subindex (SHS) was used to assess health status. . . . The instrument for measuring ADL was Lawton's Instrumental Activities of Daily Living Scale (IADL). . . . Demographic data also were collected.

Self-Transcendence Scale. The Self-Transcendence Scale (STS) is a 15-item summated scale. . . . The STS was constructed to measure the developmental resource, self-transcendence. . . . The purpose of the scale is to evaluate self-transcendence. Self-transcendence refers to the capacity to expand personal boundaries and be oriented toward perspectives, activities, and purposes beyond the self without negating the self. The scale has been used mainly with older adults. Responses to the 15-item instrument are based on a 4-point scale ranging from 1 for *not at all* to 4 for *very much.* The responses are then summed for a total score. . . .

Reliability as estimated by Cronbach's alpha ranges from .80 . . . to .93. . . . Support for construct validity is confirmed with scores from other related measures. . . .

Self-Rated Health Subindex. The SHS is a Likert-type scale that is a subindex of the Multilevel Assessment Instrument (MAI). . . . The MAI was constructed with concepts related to the well-being of the older person. . . . The SHS is a part of the physical health domain. . . . The SHS has a total of four items. The items are composed of a checklist format of three to four alternative responses to each question. The score for each item ranges from a 4 for *excellent* to a 1 for *poor.* The scores from each item are added for a total score for the subscale. The authors reported an internal consistency of .76 for the four-item self-rated scale and a 3-week test-retest reliability of .92. . . .

Activities of Daily Living. The Instrumental Activities of Daily Living Scale (IADL) offers a cumulative score of ability to perform a set of ADL. The purpose of the scale is to evaluate the functional abilities of older persons on different levels of competence, in particular, physical and instrumental autonomy of activities of daily living. . . . [which] include housekeeping, shopping, food preparation, telephoning, laundry, use of transportation, and financial behaviors. . . .

The IADL is a nine-item Guttman scale. Individual items are scored from 1 to 3. The item scores are then added together for a total score. The higher the total score, the more independent the individual. . . . Reliability as estimated by Cronbach's alpha was .91. Construct validity was established by existing knowledge about the concept and the domains of ADL. . . . Validity also was tested by comparing results with three other instruments. . . .

Demographics. A demographic sheet was used to collect information on age, gender, ethnicity, marital status, income, and education. All data were collected by the author.

Results

Characteristics of the Sample

The sample of 88 older adults ranged in age from 65 to 93 years. More than 50% were younger than 75 years of age. Women outnumbered men by a ratio of 3:1. All but 2 of the participants were non-Hispanic White; 2 were Hispanic. The majority were widowed, and 48% reported incomes of less than $2,000 per month. Sixteen of the participants did not respond to the monthly income question. The group was fairly well educated ($M = 13.2$ years); the most frequently occurring number of years of education was 12. In short, a typical participant was 73 years of age, female, non-Hispanic White, widowed, with 13 years of education and a monthly income less than $2,000.

Research Question

This research was conducted to determine the relationships among self-transcendence, health status, and ADL. As can be seen in Table 1, the mean score for the STS scale was 52 ($SD = 5.1$), indicating the group possessed a fairly high degree of self-transcendence. Health status, SHS, had an average score of 9.9 ($SD = 1.8$), suggesting that the participants viewed their health more positively than negatively. The composite score for the IADL scale ranged from 19 to 27, with a mean score of 25.7 ($SD = 1.7$). Forty-seven percent produced a score of 27, the highest possible score. The overall scores indicated a very capable group in terms of IADL.

TABLE 1 Mean Scores, Standard Deviations, and Cronbach's Alpha of the Self-Transcendence Scale (STS), the Self-Rated Health Subindex (SHS), and the Instrumental Activities of Daily Living Scale (IADL)

	Range	M	SD	Alpha
STS	30-60	52.0	5.1	.72
SHS	4-13	9.9	1.8	.69
IADL	19-27	25.7	1.7	.69

The relationship between variables was explored by means of Pearson correlations. The results revealed that health status, SHS ($r = 47, p < .001$) and self-transcendence, STS ($r = .39, p < .001$) were significantly correlated with the Instrumental Activities of Daily Living Scale, IADL.

Multiple regression analysis was employed to predict variance on activities of daily living associated with SHS and STS. Inasmuch as SHS had the highest correlation with ADL, it was entered into the regression equation first and accounted for 22.6% of the explained variance. Self-transcendence, STS, was entered into the analysis next; its unique contribution in explaining ADL was approximately 6% and was statistically significant (F change = 6.65, $p < .05$). The multiple correlation coefficient was .53, $F(2, 85) = 16.66, p < .001$; that is, the percentage of variance accounted for by the two predictors was approximately 28%. High multicollinearity was not observed, due to a moderate, though significant, correlation between the two predictors ($r = .36, p < .01$). . . . Results are summarized in Table 2.

TABLE 2 Multiple Regression Analysis of IADL on SHS and STS

Step Variable Entered	R	R^2	F	R Change	F Change
SHS	.475	.226	25.02**	—	—
STS	.531	.282	16.66**	.056	6.65*

NOTE: IADL = Instrumental Activities of Daily Living Scale; SHS = Self-Rated Health Subindex; STS = Self-Transcendence Scale.
*$p < .05$; **$p < .001$.

Discussion

Discussion is directed toward two perspectives, theoretical and practical. Theoretically, this study contributed to an understanding of the theory of self-transcendence. Reed . . . proposed that health and human functioning are integrally related to developmental resources. The study operationalized and lent support to Reed's . . . proposition. . . . The results showed that health (SHS) and a developmental resource, self-transcendence (ST), correlated with and contributed to functioning (IADL).

From a clinical perspective, some older persons may continue to remain independent despite their health status because of their ability to engage in or experience self-transcendence. Results showed that IADL and SHS were significantly correlated, with SHS explaining 22.6% of the variation. These findings are not surprising, because logically one would expect health status to account for some of the ability to perform ADL. . . . The results of this study showed that self-transcendence contributed another 6% toward explaining the ability to perform IADL. The idea that self-transcendence contributes to ADL in the older adult had not been explored previously. Self-transcendence has been shown to contribute to the well-being of the older adult and to mediate illness distress in persons with serious illnesses. . . . Self-transcendence has been shown to negatively correlate with depressive symptoms. . . . Depressive symptoms have been associated with a greater risk of the onset of disability in activities of daily living, even when taking into consideration health and social status. . . . Consequently, self-transcendence may assist older adults to remain able to perform activities of daily living through the mediating effects of well-being.

. . . Exploring resources within the older adult, like self-transcendence, is most important work. The population is aging; the potential for improving the emotional well-being and the ability to perform activities of daily living in older adults [would] improve the quality of life for a large number of people. However, this study has several limitations. The very exploratory nature of the study limits interpretation. Only a small number of variables were explored for a very complex problem, older adults and independence. The homogeneity of the sample and the limited variability of the dependent variables places restrictions on the testing of the relationship and the generalizability of the findings.

CRITIQUE OF STUDY EXAMPLE 6.2

1. What is the rationale for the study?

2. What was the purpose of the study?

3. Who took part in the study?

4. Is the sample representative of noninstitutionalized adults?

5. What was the general procedure?

6. What information is missing?

7. What can you say about the 20% nonusable questionnaires?

8. Is there any concern about the three scales?

9. What are the general characteristics of the sample?

10. How does Table 1 show the select nature of the sample?

11. Interpret the correlation coefficients between SHS and IADL and STS and IADL.

12. What kind of multiple regression was performed? How can you tell?

13. Because interest was in only the relationship between IADL and the two predictor variables, was it necessary to conduct a multiple regression analysis?

14. What did the author conclude?

15. Is the conclusion justified?

16. To what population do these results generalize?

For answers to these questions, see page 335.

BIBLIOGRAPHY

Cohen, J., & Cohen, P. (1983). *Applied multiple regression/correlation analysis for the behavioral sciences* (2nd ed.). Hillsdale, NJ: Lawrence Erlbaum.
Hays, W. L. (1988). *Statistics* (4th ed.). New York: Holt, Rinehart & Winston.
Howell, D. C. (1992). *Statistical methods for psychology* (3rd ed.). Boston: PWS-Kent.
Keppel, G., & Zedeck, S. (1989). *Data analysis for research designs: Analysis of variance and multiple regression/correlation approaches.* New York: Freeman.

Additional Suggested Readings

Archdeacon, T. J. (1994). *Correlation and regression analysis.* Madison: University of Wisconsin Press.
Crown, W. H. (1998). *Statistical models for the social and behavioral sciences: Multiple regression and limited-dependent variable models.* New York: Praeger.

Pedhazur, E. J., & Schmelkin, L. P. (1991). *Measurements, design, and analysis: An integrated approach.* Hillsdale, NJ: Lawrence Erlbaum.

Chapter 7

Factor-Analytic Studies

 Factor analysis is a set of procedures that attempts to reduce a large set of correlated variables to a smaller set of derived variables, hypothetical characteristics, traits, or factors that underlie the correlations. Sometimes, the purpose of factor analysis is to determine the minimum number of factors accounting for the correlations. This is exploratory factor analysis. What may start out as 45 correlations between 10 variables with redundant information may result in three factors that contain the information in the original variables. Sometimes, the purpose of the analysis is to determine the underlying factor structure of the original variables (i.e., their underlying traits), which gives meaning to the factors. And at other times, the intent is to test a hypothesis that certain factors account for the observed variables. This is confirmatory factor analysis.

Of the various methods for simplifying data, the most popular is *principal components*: an attempt to determine the main factors (components) accounting for the largest proportion of variability in the scores of all of the variables. The method is designed to summarize the data in such a way that the first factor accounts for the bulk of variability in all of the scores of all variables. The remaining factors account for progressively less of the variability. But you end up with as many factors as there were variables, although all will not be used in the final interpretation. An important assumption, here, is that all of the factors are orthogonal, uncorrelated, or independent. Each factor measures something that is measured by (i.e., common to) the variables but also measures something unique. The advantage is parsimony or the simplest explanation of the observed data. The disadvantage is that the factors, in reality, may be correlated.

A brief review of the various steps involved in the principal component analysis should clarify terms you are likely to encounter when reading a factor-analytic report. Consider that five variables, in the form of five different tests, are routinely administered to new admissions to an institution. Because some of the tests may be measuring the same basic underlying factor or may have something in common—a common factor—a factor analysis is conducted. The net result of the analysis is that all of the tests may not have to be administered.

A correlation matrix will, by eyeballing, reveal how many factors are likely to account for the data. You are looking for high correlations between variables within a subset and low correlations between variables of different subsets. If, for example, A and E within a subset are correlated with each other, B, C, and D within another subset are correlated with each other, and A and E are not correlated with B, C, or D, one factor may account for the A and E subset and a second for the B, C, and D subset. One variable from each subset then could be used in another statistical procedure, such as multiple regression, without a potential multicollinearity problem. In practice, however, eyeballing a correlation matrix won't help if the matrix contains a large number of correlation coefficients.

To extract the first factor, a mathematical procedure is used to arrive at a weight (w, derived from the original correlation matrix) for each of the five variables such that the factor will account for the largest proportion of variance for all of the data. Imagine a table consisting of the standardized (Z) scores of all participants on all of the variables (the five tests). This yields five columns of Z-scores with each participant providing five scores. A *factor score* can be determined, or derived from the five variables, for each participant. This is the sum of the Z-scores weighted by the appropriate weights for each variable, or $F_i = w_A Z_A + w_B Z_B + \ldots + w_E Z_E$. This yields an additional (sixth) column of scores for each participant, namely factor scores. Now, we proceed to determine the correlation between Z-scores of variable A and the factor scores, Z-scores of variable B and the factor scores, Z-scores of

variable C and the factor scores, and so forth. Each of the five correlations between the variable and the factor is known as *factor loading*. The higher the correlation (i.e., factor loading), the more that Factor 1 underlies that variable.

We have five factor loadings, or correlation coefficients. If each is squared and the sum obtained, that sum is called the *eigenvalue;* that is, Σ(factor loadings)^2 = eigenvalue and equals the total variance *for this factor.* It is this sum of squared correlation coefficients that has been maximized. When the eigenvalue is divided by the total variance *for all data* (which is 1.00 for each variable because scores are standardized and, therefore, is the same as the number of variables), we have the *proportion of variance* accounted for by Factor 1. For example, given .8A, .2B, .7C, .65D, and .9E, eigenvalue = 2.4025 and 2.4025/5 = .48. Thus, Factor 1 accounts for 48% of total variability of all the scores. Conceptually, eigenvalue represents the average number of variables accounted for by a factor. Here, we can say that Factor 1 accounts for an average of 2.4 variables or accounts for as much variability as does 2.4 variables. We can consider that, on average, each of the five variables should account for 100%/5 = 20% of the total variability, and 2.4 × 20 = 48%. Generally, when factors have eigenvalues of at least 1.00, the factors are considered to be stable and replicable. They account for as much variability as does a single variable. Those with eigenvalues less than 1.00 are not considered to be stable. They account for less variability than does a single variable and are not retained in the analysis. In this sense, you end up with fewer factors than the original number of variables. (Eigenvalues are also properties of correlation matrices that indicate the number of factors that can be extracted.)

The retention of factors whose eigenvalues are at least 1.00 is the *Kaiser criterion*. It works best with a small or moderate number of variables (between 10 and 30), a sample size of more than 250, and a mean communality of about .60 (discussed later, the amount of variance in a variable that is accounted for by a set of factors). Another method, the *scree test,* is graphic and works best for situations in which the sample size is greater than 200. The test involves a plot of eigenvalues on the vertical axis and their ordinal number (the first, second, third, etc.) on the horizontal axis. The plot reveals a sharp decrease in eigenvalues as ordinal position increases (and explained variance rapidly decreases), followed by a leveling off thereafter. The first eigenvalue at the leveling-off point may be taken as the cutoff for retaining the corresponding factor. With this method, however, some useful factors may be eliminated. In practice, both criteria often are employed.

The second factor is extracted in exactly the same way with new weights applied to the *Z*-scores of each of the five variables and with the stipulation that these weights are orthogonal to the first set. The factor loadings will, of course, differ from those for the first factor, the eigenvalue will be smaller, as will the proportion of variance accounted for by Factor 2. But this second factor also is extracted in such a way, as all subsequent factors will be, that the explained variance is maximized. Each of the factors measures something that is measured by each of the variables, but they measure something unique because they are orthogonal. Now, we can also obtain an additional bit of information. If the Factor 1 and Factor 2 loadings on variable A are squared and summed, we have a measure of the proportion of variability in variable A accounted for by Factors 1 and 2. This can be done for each of the variables, and each sum is called a *communality*. This is an important feature. If communality is a low value, it means that variance of that variable is not explained by the extracted factors, that the variability may be explained by other factors yet to be extracted. On the other hand, if all factors have been extracted and communality is low for a variable, it may not be meaningful.

Whereas some statisticians consider principal components analysis to be a factor-analytic procedure, others differentiate it from factor analysis. In "true" factor analysis, the focus is not on *total variance* but on total *common* (or shared) variance. In *principal axis* factor analysis, each factor is extracted so that it accounts for the maximum amount of this common variance (which does not contain unique variance contributed by that variable). Whereas total variance of each factor still is its eigenvalue/p, common variance of a factor equals its total variance/Σ(communalities)^2 or the percent common variability associated with that factor.

The final step of this first phase involves setting up a table of the Factor 1 loadings and Factor 2 loadings (or more if additional useful factors are extracted) for each variable. Such a table is a factor structure matrix, and it would be considered to have a simple structure if each variable loads heavily on one factor and very lightly on the remaining factors. This would indicate a sharp distinction in the meaning of the factors, but it seldom occurs. Too many variables may load heavily or moderately heavily on the first factor, making it difficult to describe the underlying characteristic. This leads to the second phase, rotation. Most commonly, *varimax rotation* is performed. The purpose is to redefine the factors, by redistributing the loadings of their variables, so that there is a sharper distinction between them. Imagine a rectangular coordinating system with Factor 1 loadings on the vertical axis and Factor 2 loadings on the horizontal axis. Now, plot each variable to correspond with its Factor 1 and Factor 2 loadings. Correlated variables will tend to cluster together in one quadrant. The aim of the factor rotation (performed mathematically) is to bring one of the axes (e.g., Factor 1 loadings) closer to the variables so that they are simultaneously farther from the other axis (e.g., Factor 2 loadings). Because the plotted variables remain in the same original physical location in the quadrant, their *factor loadings* will change so that they load heavily on one factor and lightly on the others. Whereas initially they may have a high loading on one factor and medium or low loadings on the other factor(s), after rotation, they have a high loading on one and mainly low loadings on the other factor(s). This reduces the number of variables that underlie any given factor and sharpens its meaning. Therefore, explained variance is redistributed so that the first factor does not *necessarily* account for maximum variance of all scores, in contrast to the lopsided distribution in which the first factor accounts for most variability because so many variables had high or moderately high loadings on it. Varimax rotation, by redistributing factor loadings so that they are high on one factor and low on another, maximizes *variance for each factor* by maximizing the variance of the squared factor loadings. Note the differences in Factor 1 before and after rotation. Factor 1 was derived in such a way that the *sum of the squared factor loadings* accounts for most of the variability in the scores. After varimax rotation, the *variance of the squared factor loadings* is maximized because some of the loadings are high and the rest are low. Thus, the rotation also redistributes explained variance and tends to equalize it among the factors. This reduces the number of variables associated with each factor and makes it easier to interpret each factor. If both

axes are rotated together as a unit, we have orthogonal rotation, and the factors are considered to be uncorrelated. This is the varimax rotation I just described. (There are other methods, but varimax is the most popular.) If each axis is rotated separately, we have *oblique rotation,* and the factors are considered to be correlated. This is performed when the researcher believes that the underlying constructs in reality are correlated. In contrast to varimax rotation, oblique rotation maximizes the correlation between the variable and factor (factor loading) but at the same time shows that the factors are correlated, not independent. The disadvantage is that variables are more difficult to interpret because factor loadings are high on one factor and moderately high on another or others. If the purpose of the study is to discover the factor structure, this may be appropriate, or both may be performed to see which does a better job. Thus, investigators often do both to see which results in a factor structure matrix that has simple structure.

There are certain statistical precautions that researchers need to be aware of when performing an exploratory factor analysis. If the sample size is small and the correlation matrix reveals mainly low intercorrelations, Bartlett's sphericity test should be conducted. It tests whether the variables in the population are uncorrelated. If the null hypothesis cannot be rejected (i.e., the variables *are* uncorrelated), the component analysis would be unwarranted because the variables already are orthogonal. (Remember, this is precisely what component analysis accomplishes.) A second precaution involves magnitude of factor loadings when sample size is small. These are, after all, correlation coefficients. If particular loadings (say, below .40) are being interpreted and sample size is small ($N = 100$ or less), they should be tested for significance. A third pre-

BOX 7.1
Caution Factors for Factor-Analytic Studies

■ Tests, scales, or items are relevant to purpose of the study.

■ Tests, scales, or items are reliable and valid.

■ Tests or scales are presented in counterbalanced order.

■ No tests, scales, or items are virtually identical.

■ Sample is randomly selected.

■ No selective loss of participants for extended study.

■ Sample size is at least 100 for fewer than 10 variables or greater than 150 if at least 10 factor loadings are .40 or lower.

■ Tests, scales, or items are administered under uniform conditions by a naive tester.

■ Factor loadings that are below .40, with $N < 100$, are tested for significance.

caution concerns sample size. There is much debate here. Certainly with fewer than 10 variables, there should be no less than 100 participants. The concern is with reliability of the factors. One authority proposed that any factor with at least three loadings above .80 is reliable. Another maintained any factor with 10 or more loadings of .40 or less would be reliable if sample size is greater than 150.

From a design point of view, threats to internal validity are the same as those for any correlation study. The administration of several tests requires that they be reliable and valid and that the orders be counterbalanced to rule out that performance on one test is a function of what came before. The scales used, the

input variables, should be meaningful with respect to the purpose of the study or else the interpretation of results will be meaningless. Too, none of the variables should be virtually identical (e.g., two intelligence tests), or else explained variability will be inflated. The sample is expected to be large enough to yield reliable results and to be representative, and participants should be tested under uniform conditions. Finally, the administrator should be naive regarding the purpose of the study. The cautions factors for factor-analytic studies are in Box 7.1.

Two factor-analytic studies are presented. We will evaluate the first one together, and you will evaluate the second.

STUDY EXAMPLE 7.1

This factor-analytic study relates to teenagers with diabetes and the strategies they use to cope with life stress—the focus of the factor analysis—and factors that predict the coping strategies. Thus, it is an example of an exploratory study to isolate potential, uncorrelated predictors that will be applied in a multiple regression problem.

The Study

Hanson, C. L., Cigrang, J. A., Harris, M. A., Carle, D. L., Relyea, G., & Burghen, G. A. Coping styles in youths with insulin-dependent diabetes mellitus. *Journal of Consulting and Clinical Psychology, 57*(5), 644-651. Copyright © 1989 by the American Psychological Association. Adapted with permission.

Coping styles may be viewed as the cognitive and behavioral efforts used in response to stressful conditions. . . . Compas . . . emphasized the importance of understanding the contextual framework of coping behaviors in youths. The youths' individual characteristics and resources interact with environmental characteristics (e.g., family strengths, community resources, the nature of the stressor) to produce certain coping responses. . . . Although several areas of child research would suggest that this type of contextual model best explains coping styles, empirical investigations of these models are limited. . . . Moreover, Compas . . . suggests that an examination of the role of the family in predicting coping styles in children and adolescents is an empirical priority.

Coping adaptively with the demands and stressors of insulin-dependent diabetes mellitus (IDDM) can be a formidable task for adolescents. . . . The daily treatment demands of the illness require vigilance and perseverance with several onerous tasks. . . . Moreover, normal alterations in day-to-day activities . . . require compensatory adjustments in dietary intake and/or insulin dosages in order for the youth to maintain good metabolic control. In addition to the daily treatment demands, the youth is faced with emotional stressors related to the illness. . . . Additional stressors that the youth faces include feeling different from peers during a developmental stage in which identification with the peer group is extremely important, and striving to emancipate from parents while simultaneously feeling dependent and vulnerable to the illness. Thus, the demands of IDDM and its treatment require continual adaptation to stressful events.

Little is known about the associations among coping strategies, psychosocial functioning, and health outcomes (e.g., adherence, metabolic control) in youths with IDDM. . . . To our knowledge, only two studies have evaluated the relations among coping styles and health outcomes. . . . In a sample of 39 adults with IDDM, Frenzel et al . . . found that coping styles were not associated with adherence behaviors. . . . The researchers suggested that there is a greater use of coping strategies by individuals who are experiencing the stress of being in poor metabolic control. . . . In a sample of 27 adolescents, Delamater and colleagues . . . found that adolescents in poor control used coping strategies more frequently than those in good metabolic control. . . .

The purposes of this study are twofold. First, we examine the relationships between coping styles and health outcomes (i.e., adherence and metabolic control) in a large sample of youths with IDDM. Second, we examine the family environment and its interaction with individual characteristics to predict coping styles in these youths. We evaluate how the age of the youth and the duration of IDDM are related to coping styles. . . . Because family relations and chronic stress are associated with health outcomes in youths with IDDM . . . these variables were chosen as important contextual factors. Thus, we assess whether individual characteristics (i.e., age, duration of illness), the environmental context (i.e., family relations, stress), and/or the interactions between the individual characteristics and the environment predict the youths' coping styles.

---

1. What is the rationale for the study?

Coping styles refer to cognitive and behavioral responses to stress. Compas believes that coping style is an interaction (i.e., joint function) between characteristics of the individual and his/her resources and environmental features. This model of understanding coping styles, however, has not been tested.

Adolescents with insulin-dependent diabetes constantly have to cope with stressors associated with their disease and peer pressure. Despite this, little is known about the interrelationship between their coping strategies, psychological functioning, and health outcome (adherence and metabolic control). The few studies reviewed found little association between coping strategies and psychological functioning and between coping strategies and health outcome, although one study suggested that more coping strategies are used by adolescents who are experiencing the stress of poor metabolic control. Another found a more frequent use of coping strategies by adolescents in poor rather than in good control. All studies, however, used small *N*s.

> ### 2. What was the purpose of the study?
>
> First, to evaluate the relationship between coping styles and health outcome in a large sample of teens with insulin-dependent diabetes. Second, to study the interaction between family environment and characteristics of the teen to predict coping styles. This includes the characteristics of age of the teen and years with the disease.

Method

Subjects

Subjects were 135 adolescents with IDDM and their parent or parents. Twenty-nine families were father-absent; the remainder were two-parent families. The adolescents' mean age was 14.5 years ($SD = 2.4$, range = 10.4 to 20.0), the average duration of IDDM was 66.3 months ($SD = 46.2$), the average age at diagnosis was 8.9 years ($SD = 3.8$), and 53% were female. Twenty percent of the families participating were Black (the remainder were White), and the sample was predominantly middle class. . . .

> ### 3. Who served as participants in the study?
>
> One hundred and thirty-five teens and their parents. Twenty-nine of the families had no father present. Average age of the teens was 14.5; they had had diabetes for an average of 5.5 years and were first diagnosed at about 9 years of age. About half were females, and 80% were White; participants were mainly middle class.

Procedure

The parents of all adolescents who were scheduled for a clinic appointment at a large children's hospital during a 7-month period were contacted and asked to participate in a study examining how adolescents and their families learn to live with diabetes. Only 8% of the families declined to participate. Families who lived in the immediate area were interviewed in their homes, and out-of-town families were interviewed at the hospital.

▶ *(Note that [135 × .08] only 11 families refused to take part, so selective loss is not likely to be a problem. But testing conditions varied [at different homes or at the hospital], which may or may not have affected responses.)*

Written consent was obtained, and the confidentiality of all information was assured. The questionnaires were administered in a counterbalanced order, and interviews were conducted to accommodate the eating and glucose-testing schedule of the adolescent. . . .

▶ *(Note that counterbalancing the questionnaires is a good feature of this study.)*

The interviewers included three doctoral students and two advanced undergraduates who received extensive training (100 to 120 hr. with approximately 70% of the time spent in group training sessions and 30% in individual training) regarding the nature of IDDM, testing and observational instruments, and interviewing techniques. Interviewers were uninformed as to the subjects' level of metabolic control.

▶ *(Here is another good feature of the study. Interviewers did not know the metabolic control status of interviewees, and earlier studies had linked coping strategies to metabolic control.)*

---

4. What was the general procedure?

Families of teens attending a clinic were contacted and requested to take part. Only 8% refused. Those living near the clinic were interviewed at home; out-of-towners were interviewed at the clinic. All gave written consent, tests were counterbalanced, and interviewers were intensively trained, although naive about the level of metabolic control of the teens.

5. Were there any potentially troublesome parts of the procedure?

Testing did not occur under uniform conditions, which could affect the responses in the home and clinic situations.

6. What were the good features of the design?

Questionnaires were administered in counterbalanced order; independent interviewers were used; interviewers were naive with respect to health status of the teen.

Measures

Adherence. The youths' adherence to the IDDM treatment regimen was assessed with an instrument originally developed by Hart and colleagues. . . . Self-report and observational methods were used to measure adherence across five areas designated as important by the American Diabetes Association and researchers of adherence behaviors. . . . The 5 areas were diet, insulin adjustment, hypoglycemia, glucose testing, and foot care. Scores from each area were summed to provide an overall index of adherence. . . . Three-month test-retest reliability of the composite index is . . . $r(17) = .70$, $p < .001$. . . .

[Validity measures also are reported.]

Metabolic control. The metabolic control of the adolescents was determined by averaging the hemoglobin A_{1c} (HbA_{1c}) levels taken at the time of the clinic visit and during the year prior to the interview. . . . In our laboratory, the range of HbA_{1c} values for children and adolescents without diabetes is 3.0% to 7.4%, with a mean of 5.2%. The HbA_{1c} values in the present sample ranged from 4.6% to 14.4%, with a mean of 9.4% ($SD = 2.02$). High HbA_{1c} values reflect poor metabolic control. Ideally, the HbA_{1c} values for children with diabetes should be as close as possible to the range of values for children without diabetes.

Coping. The coping styles of the adolescents were assessed using the 54-item Adolescent-Coping Orientation for Problem experiences (A-COPE). . . . Youths rated how often they engaged in each coping behavior when faced with difficulties or when feeling tense from 1 (*never*) to 5 (*most of the time*). The A-COPE was originally factor-analyzed into 12 factors. . . . The 12 factors included Ventilating Feelings . . . Seeking Diversions . . . Developing Self-Reliance and Optimism . . . Developing Social Support . . . Solving Family Problems . . . Avoiding Problems . . . Seeking Spiritual Help . . . Investing in Close friends . . . Seeking Professional Support . . . Engaging in Demanding Activity . . . Being Humorous . . . and Relaxing. . . .

Family relations. The 30-item Family Adaptability and Cohesion Evaluation Scales (FACES-II . . .) was used to assess family cohesion and family adaptability. FACES-II has discriminated between functional and dysfunctional families in several samples . . . and is considered to be one of the best instruments to assess families on a system level. . . .
. . . The scores of the adolescent and the parent or parents were summed to provide a global assessment of the family's perception of family cohesion and adaptability. . . .

Stress. Chronic life stress was determined by the adolescents' responses on the 50-item Adolescent-Family Inventory of Life Events and Change (A-FILE . . .) . . . test-retest reliability is .80 over a 4- to 5-week period. . . . The A-FILE also possesses strong convergent validity. . . .

> 7. **What general measures were made?**
>
> Adherence by the teen to the diabetic regimen, metabolic control by glycosylated hemoglobin averaged over two measures made a year apart, coping styles to stress, family functioning, and chronic life stress.
>
> 8. **Are there any concerns about reliability, validity, or both of any of the measures?**
>
> No, all are well-established tests.

Results

Coping Scales

Correlational analyses of the 12 scales from the A-COPE indicate a high degree of intercorrelation among the scales. To obtain a smaller number of more unique coping indices, the 12 coping scales were subjected to a principal component factor analysis using the varimax method of factor rotation.

> ▶ *(The authors have a footnote to indicate that the Bartlett test was performed on the correlation matrix. The results indicated that the variables are correlated. This is a good feature of the analysis.)*

The factor analysis derived a two-factor solution accounting for 51.6% of the variance in the scales. One of the scales, professional support, had relatively high loadings on both factors (i.e., .50 and .58). In order to obtain as much orthogonality between the factors as possible, this scale was dropped from further analyses. A second scale, relaxation, was also removed because it had a very low communality value (.23). The remaining 10 scales were subsequently reanalyzed, and a similar two-factor solution was obtained, accounting for 55.4% of the variance in the scales. Factor loadings for each of the scales are presented in Table 2.

> 9. **Scores on the coping scale were factor analyzed. How many factors accounted for variability in the scales? What are their eigenvalues?**
>
> Two factors, with eigenvalues of 3.9287 and 1.6104.
>
> 10. **Verify that, in the final solution, 55.4% of variance is attributed to the two factors.**
>
> $(3.9287 + 1.6104)/10 = .55391 = 55.4\%$.

TABLE 2 Factor Loadings From the Two-Factor Rotation of the A-COPE

Coping Scale	Factor 1	Factor 2
Ventilating feelings	−.075	.767
Seeking diversions	.648	−.007
Developing self-reliance	.813	.083
Developing social support	.794	.111
Solving family problems	.657	−.370
Avoiding problems	.093	.831
Seeking spiritual help	.666	−.215
Investing in close friends	.675	.215
Engaging in demanding activity	.694	−.288
Being humorous	.625	.001

> **11. What two variables did not load heavily on Factor 1?**
>
> Ventilating feelings and avoiding problems.

Eight scales loaded on Factor 1. . . . This factor represents behaviors that involve the acquisition of emotional support and assistance from family members, participation in social relationships and activities, the diversion of attention from problems to positive interests, a reliance on personal skills to manage problems, attending church activities, and maintaining a sense of humor. Two of the 10 coping scales (i.e., ventilating feelings and avoiding problems) loaded strongly on the second factor. These coping responses involve getting angry and blaming others for problems, avoiding the problem by minimization, and engaging in negative activities such as drinking, smoking, and using drugs. Based on the grouping of the scales, Factor 1 is labeled Utilizing Personal and Interpersonal Resources and Factor 2 is labeled Ventilation and Avoidance.

> **12. Which variable had the lowest communality? What does it mean?**
>
> Being humorous (.391). This means that 39% of variance of these scores, which reflect a humorous strategy of coping with stress, is accounted for by Factors 1 and 2.

TABLE 3 Correlations Between Coping Factors, Health Outcomes, and Individual Characteristics

| | Coping | |
| | Utilizing Personal and | |
Variable	Interpersonal Resources	Ventilation and Avoidance
Adherence	−.055	−.367**
HbA$_{1c}$	−.025	−.045
Age	.042	.347**
Duration of IDDM	−.146*	−.144*
Gender	.078	.021
SES	−.111	.083

NOTE: Because of the number of correlations, correlations that are significant at the .05 level should be considered only of marginal statistical significance.
*$p < .05$; **$p < .0001$.

---

13. Which variable had the highest communality? What does it mean?

Avoiding problems (.699). This means that 69.9% of variance of these scores, which reflect an avoidance strategy of coping with stress, is accounted for by Factors 1 and 2.

Coping and Health Outcomes

Pearson product-moment correlations were conducted to assess the zero-order associations between the two coping factors, the health outcome variables, and the pertinent demographic characteristics (see Table 3).

Adherence to treatment and metabolic control. The ventilation and avoidance coping style was negatively related to adherence behaviors, whereas utilizing personal and interpersonal resources was not associated with adherence to the IDDM regimen. Neither coping factor significantly correlated with HbA$_{1c}$.

Individual characteristics. The ventilation and avoidance coping style positively related to the age of the adolescent and was marginally related ($p < .05$) to the duration of IDDM. In contrast, utilizing personal and interpersonal resources was negatively associated with duration of IDDM ($p < .05$). Neither coping style related significantly to gender or SES.

. . . We tested whether ventilation and avoidance coping contributed a significant amount of the variance to adherence after the effects of disease duration and adolescent age had been taken into account. In the first step, disease duration and adolescent age were entered, and only adolescent age marginally predicted adherence, . . . $p < .059$. In the next step, ventilation and avoidance coping significantly accounted for an additional 10% of the variance, . . . $p < .0001$.

---

14. *When demographic variables were correlated to Factors 1 and 2, two of them highly correlated with Factor 2. Interpret the coefficients.*

   Adherence is one variable. The more the teen adhered to the regimen, the less he/she used ventilation and avoidance as ways of coping with stress. $-.367^2 = .1347$, so 13.47% of variability in adherence is associated with use of ventilation and avoidance to cope with stress. Age is the second variable. The older the teen, the more he/she uses ventilation and avoidance as means of coping with stress. $.347^2 = .1204$, so 12.04% of variability in use of ventilation and avoidance to cope with stress is associated with age.

15. *Does coping style have any relationship to metabolic control?*

   No. The correlations between HbA_{1c} and Factors 1 and 2 were nonsignificant.

16. *Examine Table 3 and determine the rationale for attempting to predict only ventilation and avoidance (Factor 2) coping styles.*

   Adherence was the only behavioral variable associated with this factor. This variable was not related to Factor 1. And only duration of IDMM was (marginally) related to Factor 1.

Predictors of Coping

Because the ventilation and avoidance coping style was associated with adherence, a simultaneous MRA [multiple regression analysis] was conducted only on this coping style. . . . Table 4 presents the standardized beta and the associated *F* values for the final regression equation. Beta indicates the strength and direction of the association between the predictor variable and the coping style and the *F* tests whether the predictor variable is statistically significant.

High ventilation and avoidance coping was predicted by high life stress, low family cohesion, and older adolescent age (i.e., youths in late adoles-

TABLE 4 Summary of Findings From Multiple Regression Analysis of Predictors of Ventilation and Avoidance Coping

Variable	F	β	$F_{(df = 1, 128)}$	p
Main effects				
Age	.207	7.16	.008	
Stress	.189		6.27	.014
Family cohesion	−.298		13.97	.000
Family Adaptability × Duration	−.196		6.95	.009

NOTE: Beta is the standardized regression coefficient. Percentage of variance in the coping factor accounted for by the regression equation (R^2) is .32.

cence). In addition, ventilation and avoidance coping was predicted by the interaction of Family Adaptability × Duration of IDDM. The R^2 for the five significant predictors was .32. . . .

▶ *(An interaction here means that association between ventilation and avoidance and duration of IDDM varies with level of family adaptability.)*

. . . . Low family adaptability (i.e., rigidity) was strongly related to high levels of ventilation and avoidance coping in adolescents with long duration of IDDM. In contrast, when families demonstrated high adaptability (i.e., flexible relations), the adolescents with long disease duration used low levels of ventilation and avoidance coping.

17. What did the multiple regression analysis reveal?

The use of ventilation and avoidance is predicted by older age of the teen, greater life stress, less cohesion in the family, and the interactive effects of the family's adaptability and length of time the teen had diabetes.

18. Interpret the R^2 *of .32.*

Approximately 32.00% of variability in (these) coping scores is associated with the predictor variables.

> **19. *What did the interaction indicate?***
>
> Teens from rigid (low adaptability) families tended to use more ventilation and avoidance to cope with stress, especially when they had had diabetes a long time. Teens from highly adaptable families tended to use less ventilation and avoidance to cope with stress, especially when they had had diabetes a long time.

Discussion

The first goal of this study was to examine the relationships between coping styles and health outcomes in youths with IDDM. Two factor-analytically derived coping styles were identified in these youths: utilizing personal and interpersonal resources and ventilation and avoidance. The frequent use of avoidance and ventilation coping related to nonadherence to IDDM treatment, whereas the use of personal and interpersonal resources was not related to health outcomes. . . . The frequent use of avoidance and ventilation coping seems to reflect a poor fit between the child's style of coping and effective management of the diabetes. Although older adolescent age has been associated with poor adherence to treatment . . . our results also indicate that it is ventilation and avoidance coping, not adolescent age, that predicts poor adherence.

Secondly, we examined whether individual characteristics (i.e., adolescent age, the duration of IDDM), the environmental context (i.e., family relations, life stress), and/or the interaction between individual and environmental factors predicted the use of ventilation and avoidance coping. Independent of family relations and life stress, older adolescent age was related to the more frequent use of ventilation and avoidance coping. . . .

Longitudinal research, however, is necessary to determine (a) what developmental changes occur in the type and use of emotion-focused coping strategies (e.g., avoidance and ventilation) and (b) whether these changes result in differential outcomes. . . . Perhaps ventilation behaviors (e.g., yelling, blaming others) do not change substantially over time, nor do the negative outcomes; but the alternatives chosen for avoiding stressful situations develop with age and become more adaptive. The sequence of using such strategies over the course of a stressor may also differ for adults compared with youths. . . .

Low family cohesion was also related to the frequent use of ventilation and avoidance coping, independent of other individual and environmental conditions. Low family cohesion has been associated with a variety of problems during adolescence. . . . The youths' coping style could as likely contribute to low cohesion among family members, as low family cohesion contributes to the more frequent use of ventilation and avoidance coping in the youths. The relatively strong contribution of family cohesion in predicting ventilation and avoidance coping seems consistent throughout the entire span of adolescence. . . . These results are similar to other recent research that indicates the influence of family relations on psychosocial functioning does not decrease in magnitude during later adolescence, as once thought. As Harter . . . speculates, it is the nature of family relationships that changes with development . . . not necessarily the relative importance of family relations.

One reason for the absence of relationships between the coping styles and metabolic control might be that the stressors were not diabetes specific, nor were the coping behaviors related to diabetes management. The relationships may have been stronger if, for example, the youth was asked how he or she copes with the fear of experiencing hypoglycemia when going to a social event, and if the coping responses were diabetes specific. . . .

---

20. To what extent was the first purpose of the study fulfilled?

The authors related coping style (but only one basic strategy) and health outcome but only in terms of adherence. They concluded that ventilation and avoidance (both related to denial and projection) predicted adherence: High use of this style of coping is associated with poorer adherence to the diabetic regimen.

21. To what extent was the second purpose of the study fulfilled?

The second purpose was to determine predictors of coping style. The authors focused on ventilation and avoidance and found that it is predicted by age (more venting and avoidance with older teens), life stress (more venting and avoidance with increased life stress), family cohesion (more venting and avoidance associated with families of low cohesion), and family adaptability × duration of IDMM. However, the predictors account for only 32% of variability in these coping behaviors.

22. Are the conclusions justified?

Yes. This was a well-controlled study.

23. To what extent do the results generalize?

To similar teens with IDDM, who come from similar homes and who experience similar life stresses (specifically measured by the stress scale). As the authors note, if a different stress scale had been used—one directly related to diabetes management—results might have differed.

STUDY EXAMPLE 7.2

The following article reports a psychometric evaluation of an established test used in the United States, which then was used on a group of elderly Koreans. A common factor analysis is conducted on items of the original scale to determine whether the seven factors found earlier will be found with this population.

The Study

Shin, Y. H., & Colling, K. B. (2000). Cultural verification and application of the Profile of Mood States (POMS) with Korean elders. *Western Journal of Nursing Research, 22*(1), 68-83. Copyright 2000 by Sage.

In Korea, the elderly population is growing rapidly, due to socioeconomic development and better medical services, thus leading to the extension of the average life expectancy. Elders, older than the age of 60 years, constituted 9% of the population in 1995, and they are anticipated to reach 10.7% by the year 2000. An elder's average life span was 72.9 years in 1995, and it is anticipated to increase to 74.3 years by 2000. . . . This increase in the elderly population gives rise to the need for a stronger focus on issues that affect the health and well-being of this special population group.

Physiological, psychological, emotional, environmental, and behavioral changes constantly interact within the elder person. . . . The relationship of aging, depression, and related affective disorders has been increasingly studied in recent years. . . . Most of the research has focused specifically on the elderly and their adjustment to aging. The most frequently researched question regarding the affective status of older persons is whether they are happy and satisfied with life, especially when compared to younger adults. . . . Studies of life satisfaction, morale, happiness, and subjective well-being . . . consistently have found significant correlations between well-being and health, socioeconomic status, and social activity for persons 60 and older. . . .

Currently, little is known about the relationship between normal variations in mood and affect in older populations. . . . Mood state has been identified as a crucial factor in the psychological health of elders. . . . Health professionals should understand how elderly people perceive their moods in later life, to help them achieve psychological health independent of the aging process.

Many theorists in the area of emotion seem to find no special purpose for the term *mood,* using it interchangeably with other terms, such as *affect* or *emotion.* In summary, moods can be defined as affective states that are capable of influencing a broad array of potential responses, many of which seem quite unrelated to the mood-precipitating event. Compared to emotions, moods typically are less intense affective states. . . .

The accurate measurement of the mood state is especially thought to be of considerable importance when assessing the health of older persons. . . . The majority of the currently available self-report psychometric questionnaires have been developed in young adult populations and simply applied to the elderly without formally establishing the reliability and validity of the instrument within this group. . . . There are a number of multidimensional mood state inventories currently available. . . . Of the more comprehensive inventories, the Profile of Mood States (POMS) questionnaire has become one of the most popular and widely used. . . .

Although it has many strengths, this 65-item scale tends to be too long for many elders, and it commonly can be experienced as repetitive and unnecessarily burdensome to those who have some cognitive limitations. In addition, several studies have suggested that the elderly may be more conservative in their expression of emotion. . . . This tendency is more notable culturally in the Korean elderly, because Korean elders usually are not willing to express their mood, especially negative mood. . . . Studies specifically demonstrating reliability and validity of state measures in older populations are a logical prerequisite to the use of such scales in gerontological research. Therefore, psychometric evaluation is necessary when an instrument such as the POMS, which was developed in another country, is used to examine the mood states of the Korean elderly. . . .

. . . The purpose of this study was to evaluate the cultural verification of the POMS . . . for the Korean elderly, based on Shin's study . . . which assessed psychometric properties of the POMS, and to examine their mood states, using the revised instrument specific to Korean elders.

Method

Sample

The participants in this study were 370 persons older than 60 years of age, who were recruited from personal contact or senior centers in apartment complexes at Seoul, Pusan, Daejeon, ChongJu, and Kunpo in Korea, through convenience sampling. They verbally consented to participate in this study and could communicate in the Korean language. A total of 370 questionnaires were completed, however, 51 were excluded due to missing data, leaving 319 for analysis. . . . According to Comrey, . . . a sample size of 200 is adequate, and 319 is considered to be more than adequate for factor analysis.

Of the 319 elders, females constituted 59.2% of the sample, whereas males made up 40.8%. The majority of the sample, 192 participants (60.3%), were between the ages of 60 and 69. Participants between the ages of 70 and 79 numbered 92 (28.8%), whereas those older than the age of 80 years constituted 10.9% ($n = 35$) of the sample. . . . The vast majority of elders (78.7%), 251 participants, did not hold a job. Most participants currently were married (67.7%), followed by 30.5% who had been widowed. . . . Sixty-six participants (20.7%) had no prior education. Even though these elders did not have a formal education, they could read and write Korean because they had been informally schooled at home. . . . Eighty participants (25.1%) had an elementary level education, 43 (13.5%) had a middle school education, 57 (17.9%) had attended high school, and 72 (22.6%) had more than a level of university education. . . . More than half the sample, 167 (52.4%), indicated their economic status as middle income, 63 (19.7%) were in the high-middle range and eight elders (2.5%) stated they held high economic status. Eighty-one participants (25.4%) were middle-low to low in terms of economic status. A little less than a majority (44.5%), 142 participants, depended on themselves for their source of income, and 35.1% ($n = 112$) were dependent on their children for money. Forty-five participants (14.1%) depended on spouses for income and 20 participants (6.3%) did not respond.

Research Instrument

The instrument used in this study was the Profile of Mood States (POMS), which had been translated by Yun [in 1993] into the Korean language. . . . A number of factor-analytic studies performed during the development of the questionnaire had suggested six primary dimensions of mood: Depression-Dejection, Tension-Anxiety, Anger-Hostility, Vigor-Activity, Fatigue-Inertia, and Confusion-Bewilderment. . . . There also was some evidence for a seventh factor, Friendliness. Although the profile included items to measure all seven dimensions, in most studies only the first six are scored. . . . For purposes of this study, the seven-factor POMS was used. There were a total of 65 items with 5-point adjective rating scales (1 = *not at all*, 2 = *a little*, 3 = *moderately*, 4 = *quite a bit*, 5 = *extremely*). Positive-mood items were interposed with negative-mood items and were reverse scored so that the lower score on the POMS indicated the more optimal emotional state. Participants filled in one space under the answer that best described how they had been feeling during the past week, including today. Before the instrument was used in this study, the face validity was assessed by a selected Korean expert panel. . . . Experts were asked to review each item and assess it in relation to facilitating its comprehension by Korean elders. . . . [This resulted in some changes in words to make understanding easier for the Korean elders.]

Data Collection and Analysis

. . . During data collection, the researcher and four research assistants were available to assist the elders when they required explanations or meanings of the questions.

Results

Cultural Verification and Psychometric Evaluation of the POMS

Cultural verification and psychometric evaluation of the POMS were conducted in the following manner. First, for the item analysis of the POMS, analysis of each item to the total correlation and the item's contribution to Cronbach's alpha coefficient were performed. . . . A rule of thumb is that items that correlate below .30 are not sufficiently related and therefore do not contribute to measurement of the core factor. . . . The higher the corrected correlation between the item and the total, generally the better the item. Therefore, in this study, the items also were analyzed for item to total correlation (> 0.30) and an increased alpha coefficient if the item was deleted. Through this procedure, 10 items whose item-to-item correlations were below 0.30 were deleted.

Second, face validity was ascertained by the expert panel that evaluated the instrument to review its cultural appropriateness for Korean elders. Twenty-four items with overlapped, broad, or ambiguous meanings were deleted. The deleted 31 items included five items in the Tense-Anxiety factor, seven items in the Depression-Dejection factor, three items in the Vigor-Activity factor, three items in the Fatigue-Inertia factor, two items in the Confusion-Bewilderment factor, five items in the Friendliness factor, and six items in the Anger-Hostility factor. . . . The final instrument yielded 34 items that were determined to be appropriate and necessary to assess the mood states of Korean elders. The final 34 items are in Table 1.

Third, common factor analysis with squared multiple correlation (SMC) was performed to confirm construct validity of the revised POMS. To find the simple structure of the factors, the principal axis factoring method was performed with varimax rotation. The number of factors [was] assigned to seven factors because the POMS already was constructed in seven factors.

TABLE 1 Revised POMS and Factor Analysis

Variable	Items	F1	F2	F3	F4	F5	F6	F7
V1	Angry	0.15	−0.04	0.41	0.08	0.55	−0.06	−0.10
V2	Clear-headed	0.31	0.48	−0.01	0.39	0.10	0.18	0.10
V3	Lively	0.31	0.63	0.01	0.31	0.08	0.07	0.01
V4	Confused	0.49	0.06	0.25	0.11	0.36	−0.10	−0.07
V5	Sorry	0.49	0.00	0.27	0.12	0.36	−0.12	0.14
V6	Shaky	0.66	0.16	0.20	−0.07	0.25	0.01	0.02
V7	Listless	0.69	0.22	0.03	0.05	0.21	−0.18	−0.06
V8	Peeved	0.40	0.12	0.35	0.05	0.46	0.05	−0.12
V9	Sad	0.60	0.11	0.24	−0.04	0.23	0.25	0.24
V10	Active	0.16	0.56	−0.03	0.20	−0.13	−0.03	−0.17
V11	Blue	0.71	0.16	0.15	0.01	0.17	0.19	0.06
V12	Hopeless	0.74	0.14	0.06	0.09	0.00	−0.11	0.22
V13	Spiteful	0.17	−0.03	0.58	0.09	0.04	−0.09	−0.12
V14	Uneasy	0.73	0.16	0.12	−0.08	0.28	0.15	−0.04
V15	Unable to concentrate	0.68	0.29	0.06	−0.09	0.04	0.01	−0.07
V16	Fatigued	0.59	0.10	0.02	−0.08	0.03	0.10	−0.35
V17	Helpful	0.24	0.52	−0.06	0.32	−0.07	0.06	0.06
V18	Nervous	0.49	0.05	0.38	−0.09	0.23	0.09	0.07
V19	Lonely	0.72	0.13	0.12	0.04	0.01	0.05	0.15
V20	Cheerful	0.29	0.45	0.03	0.37	0.07	0.15	0.09
V21	Bitter	0.76	0.05	0.11	0.06	0.03	0.00	0.06
V22	Exhausted	0.79	0.18	0.18	0.05	0.06	−0.04	−0.09
V23	Anxious	0.73	0.15	0.19	−0.07	0.21	0.28	0.03
V24	Ready to fight	0.21	−0.13	0.62	0.01	0.09	0.09	0.11
V25	Sluggish	0.56	0.36	0.08	−0.09	0.02	−0.16	−0.15
V26	Helpless	0.75	0.28	0.07	0.08	0.09	−0.05	−0.18
V27	Alert	0.14	0.58	−0.21	0.26	−0.15	−0.02	−0.02
V28	Deceived	0.27	0.04	0.60	−0.05	0.02	0.10	0.26
V29	Efficient	0.27	0.56	−0.05	0.44	0.07	0.02	−0.06
V30	Worthless	0.73	0.14	0.27	0.06	−0.12	−0.06	0.19
V31	Forgetful	0.55	0.12	−0.01	0.01	−0.07	−0.04	−0.21
V32	Terrified	0.57	0.07	0.35	−0.06	−0.06	0.00	−0.01
V33	Vigorous	0.27	0.69	−0.13	−0.06	0.02	0.11	0.08
V34	Uncertain about things	0.71	0.17	0.10	0.08	−0.06	−0.09	0.04

F1 = Anxiety-Depression (21 items); F2 = Vigor (8 items); F3 = Anger (5 items).

TABLE 2 Mean Score of Korean Elders' Mood States

Factor	Mean	SD	Minimum	Maximum
Anxiety-Depression	1.36	0.94	0	3.71
Vigor	2.42	0.85	0	4.00
Anger	0.72	0.69	0	4.00
Total mood	1.51	0.75	0.06	3.53

Table 1 shows the factor loadings and factor structure through the analysis. As can be seen in Table 1, almost all items, with the exception of V1 and V8 of the remaining 34 items that were retained from face validity, belonged to Factors 1, 2, and 3. Because the loading of item 1, *angry,* and item 8, *peeved,* in Factor 3 were greater than 0.30 and the meanings were closer to other items of Factor 3, the two items also were included in Factor 3. The loadings of most items ranged from 0.40 to 0.79. . . . Through this analysis, three dominant factors accounting for 73.2% of the variance were revealed.

Therefore, the 65-item original POMS was revised and reduced to a three-factor, 34-item instrument specific to Korean elders. The Cronbach coefficient alpha of the revised instrument was 0.95 and is considered to be excellent. . . .

The Mood States of Korean Elders

The results of the analysis of mood states of Korean elders using the revised POMS are shown in Table 2. . . . Results showed that the mean score of Vigor factor was the highest, the next was Anxiety-Depression factor, and the lowest mean score was Anger factor. Inasmuch as higher scores indicate lower levels of that factor, Korean elders assessed the vigor factor of their mood state to be low.

The analysis of the mood states of Korean elders according to their demographic characteristics . . . showed significant differences according to gender ($p = 0.0010$), as well as age, job, marital status, education, economic status, and source of income (all with $p = 0.0001$). The mood state of elderly men was better than that of elderly women. Generally the younger elders had more positive mood states than the older elders. The elders who were employed perceived their mood more positively than the elders who were unemployed. The married elders had better mood states than widowed and divorced elders. Elders with more education had better mood states than those who were less educated. The elders who had higher economic status and who were providing their own source of income perceived their mood states to be better than the elders who had poorer economic status and who depended on their children for their source of income. [A detailed table of results is presented with scores on the three factors as a function of demographic variables. No differences were found for Factor 3, Anger.]

Discussion

The revised POMS for Korean elders appears to be an internally consistent, multidimensional instrument with a relatively stable factor structure that accounted for a high percentage of the total variance in this sample. The sample in the original factor-analytic studies of the POMS included very few adults older than the age of 60 years, and no participants were older than 80 years of age. . . . One study has provided some preliminary evidence for the construct validity of the POMS when used in elderly adults . . . a sample of American elderly nursing home residents. . . . The results showed reasonable agreement with the factor structure first isolated in the original factor-analytic studies. Although the study . . . provided preliminary evidence for the validity of the POMS when used with elderly populations, a number of aspects warranted further examination, especially for culturally different populations. On the basis of this need for further examination, the seven-factor, 65-item original POMS was revised and reduced to a three-factor, 34-item instrument specific to Korean elders.

As a result of this analysis, almost all items that had belonged to the Tension-Anxiety, Depression-Dejection, Fatigue-Inertia, and Confusion-Bewilderment were classified into the first factor, and it was named the Anxiety-Depression factor. The remaining negative mood states implying different meaning to the first factor were classified into the third factor and it was named the Anger factor. All items implying the positive mood states were classified into the second factor and it was named the Vigor factor.

The demonstration of age-related differences in self-reported levels of mood raises the issue of whether older persons are less emotionally labile or whether they simply underreport psychological symptoms. . . . This . . . is thought to reflect a developmental process or cohort effect in which older adults are said to have greater management and control of affect, thereby reducing the intensity of emotional reactions. . . . An alternative view has emphasized that older adults may be less willing to report emotional states or else exhibit a greater tendency to portray themselves in a good light by endorsing only socially desirable responses. . . . These views may be consistent with results shown in this study. Korean people traditionally make much of moderation, which is defined as a state of no lack and no excess. . . . They generally are taught that one is considered to be of excellent virtue if one restrains disclosure of mood and expresses less emotion. As Koreans age, this tendency of moderation in expressing feelings has been remarkably strengthened. . . . Therefore, because Korean elders perceived many items of the original POMS to overlap and to imply similar mood or emotion, the original 65 items were reduced. . . . Scales of the original POMS tend to be long for many elders. . . .

As revealed in the results of this study, the reduced 34 items had an excellent internal consistency and had been divided into three clear factor structures. Kaye et al. . . . and Norcross, Guadagnoli, and Prochaska . . . emphasized that because three scales (Depression-Dejection, Tension-Anxiety, Confusion-Bewilderment) of the POMS did not emerge consistently as major independent components, and they were highly correlated, caution was recommended in the separate scoring and interpretation of these scales. . . . The measurement of general distress, rather than some specific dimension (e.g., anxiety or depression) was decided on because of accumulating evidence that psychological distress is hierarchical, with the most information coming from one powerful underlying factor. Furthermore, the psychometric separation of constructs, such as anxiety and depression, is difficult if not impossible in psychologically healthy samples. . . .

. . . Results showed that Korean elders perceived their overall mood states to be good. Several explanations may account for this finding. Participants in the study were relatively healthy elders living in the community. In addition, Korean elders often are not willing to overtly express their emotional states. Even though this perception of being in generally good mood states was evident, Korean elders perceived the second factor, Vigor, as being the lowest mood factor. . . . Frailty and general lack of vigor are common problems in persons of advanced age.

In addition, the mood states of Korean older people showed significant differences according to their demographic characteristics, such as gender, age, job, marital status, education, economic status, and source of income. . . . In . . . studies of American elders, mood states are closely affected by their sociodemographic characteristics and this also was evident in this study. . . .

CRITIQUE OF STUDY EXAMPLE 7.2

1. What was the rationale for the study?
2. What was the purpose of the study?
3. What were the general characteristics of the sample?
4. Is there any concern about a biased sample?

5. What is the general nature of the test?

6. Why was only face validity established?

7. Were testing conditions uniform?

8. What were the results of item analysis and face validity procedures?

9. Why was common factor analysis performed rather than principle components analysis?

10. What might account for finding only three factors as opposed to the six or seven found in previous research?

11. Is there a sound basis for eliminating Factor 5 and adding its two items (angry and peeved) to Factor 3?

12. Examine the 21 items under Factor 1. Are there any that do not fit in with Anxiety-Depression? What does this suggest?

13. What were the major findings regarding mood states of the elderly Koreans?

14. In the results listed in Table 2, what suggests that probable differences in testing conditions were of little consequence?

15. Is there any indication of a possible problem with Factor 3 in relation to demographic characteristics and mood states? What else might account for the finding?

16. What did the authors conclude? Are the conclusions justified?

For answers to these questions, see page 336.

BIBLIOGRAPHY

Diekhoff, G. (1992). *Statistics for the social and behavioral sciences: Univariate, bivariate, multivariate*. Dubuque, IA: William C. Brown.

Dillon, W. R., & Goldstein, M. (1984). *Mutivariate analysis: Methods and applications*. New York: John Wiley.

Duntman, G. H. (1984). *Multivariate analysis*. Beverly Hills, CA: Sage.

Kim, J. O., & Mueller, C. W. (1978). *Factor analysis: Statistical methods and practical issues* (Quantitative Applications in the Social Sciences, No. 14). Beverly Hills, CA: Sage.

Kim, J. O., & Mueller, C. W. (1978). *Introduction to factor analysis: What it is and how to do it* (Quantitative Applications in the Social Sciences, No. 13). Beverly Hills, CA: Sage.

Kleinbaum, D. G., Kupper, L. L., & Muller, K. E. (1988). *Applied regression analysis and other mutivariable methods* (2nd ed.). Boston: PWS-Kent.

Stevens, J. (1992). *Applied multivariate statistics for the social sciences* (2nd ed.). Hillsdale, NJ: Lawrence Erlbaum.

Additional Suggested Readings

Grimm, L. G., & Yarnold, P. R. (1995). *Reading and understanding multivariate statistics*. Washington, DC: American Psychological Association.

Kline, P. (1994). *An easy guide to factor analysis*. Boston: Routledge Kegan Paul.

Pedhazur, E. J., & Schmelkin, L. P. (1991). *Measurement, design, and analysis: An integrated approach*. Hillsdale, NJ: Lawrence Erlbaum.

Chapter 8

Discriminant Analysis Studies

Discriminant analysis is a technique that bears some similarity to multiple regression, analysis of variance (discussed in Chapter 11), and factor analysis. Multiple regression attempts to establish a linear combination of independent variables that results in the most accurate prediction of some *quantitative* criterion (dependent) variable. Analysis of variance establishes whether group differences, *qualitative* variables, are evident in a dependent variable as the result of some manipulation of an independent variable. Factor analysis reduces data to establish which independent variables contribute to an underlying characteristic or trait (factor). And *discriminant analysis* also reduces data by arriving at a linear combination or combinations of *quantitative* discriminant (predictor) variables that result in the largest separation of groups of individuals or objects, which are *qualitative* (criterion) variables. In addition, it establishes patterns among the discriminant variables that discriminate or differentiate the groups (i.e., how the groups differ). Whereas multiple regression yields a

dependent variable score (e.g., grade point average) based on several predictors (e.g., SAT, GRE, high school average), discriminant analysis yields most likely group membership (e.g., barely succeeds, clearly succeeds, succeeds with honors). Whereas analysis of variance yields group differences based on a single independent variable (or combination of single levels) per case, discriminant analysis usually is based on several different discriminant variables per case. And whereas factor analysis determines correlations between factors and independent variables (loading), discriminant analysis determines correlations between discriminant function scores and original discriminant variable scores (also called loading) to see just which variables differentiate the groups. Thus, we learn which predictor variables are related to the criterion variable, and we would be able to predict values on the criterion variable (group membership) on the basis of the predictor variables. For example, given certain data on credit history, we could determine which data differentiate those likely to pay off a loan from those whose reliability is questionable and those who are most likely to default. And on the basis of the predictor variables, a bank could predict the potential risk of an applicant defaulting. Thus, discriminant analysis achieves with qualitative criterion variables what multiple regression analysis achieves with quantitative criterion variables. Note, however, that multiple regression is a more powerful analysis and should not be replaced by discriminant analysis if the criterion is a continuous variable; you would not want to impose a dichotomy on a continuous variable (e.g., "divide" hours of school attendance into truants and non-truants) and perform a less powerful, inappropriate analysis of the data.

Discriminant analyses are conducted for one of two reasons. First, groups may differ, and the researcher wants to determine those characteristics that differentiate them. For example, which variables differentiate college majors in clinical, industrial, and physiological psychology? Second, given that established groups have been differentiated, to which group does an unknown data case belong? For example, is a given case to be classified as autistic, learning disabled, or mentally challenged?

The *discriminant function* is at the heart of each goal. Its correlate in multiple regression is the weighted sum of predictor variables to arrive at a quantitative criterion value. Discriminant function is the weighted sum of certain discriminant (independent) variables, sometimes referred to as predictors, to arrive at a classification, or qualitative criterion value, of an object in a group. These may be a number of different scores obtained from the members of each of the groups to be differentiated. If the intent is to discriminate among groups, a number of discriminant functions may be derived. Generally, the maximum number of functions

depends on the number of criterion groups being measured and the number of discriminant (predictor) variables. This number is one less than the number of criterion groups or the number of discriminant (predictor) variables, whichever is smaller. If there are three groups and four discriminant variables, there can be two discriminant functions. The first function will provide the best (i.e., largest) separation among groups and may discriminate one group from the others. The second may differentiate between the remaining two. These functions are derived simultaneously by determining the weights of the discriminant variables in such a way that they maximize group differences and minimize errors in classifying data cases. The first function will have the greatest discriminating power. This means that if the mean discriminant function scores for each group are determined, the average difference among the group means will be largest for the first function and smaller for those mean differences for the remaining functions.

As is true of multiple regression, a number of procedures can be used to arrive at the discriminant functions. If there aren't too many discriminant variables, all can be entered simultaneously. Alternatively, a stepwise procedure can be used. In forward analysis, each variable is included if it contributes to maximum separation of the groups. In backward analysis, each variable is removed if its removal results in the smallest loss of maximum separation. A weakness of either procedure is that the included variables may be most useful for the particular sample but not for an untested sample. But each provides a way of reducing the number of variables that are highly correlated and provide redundant information or simply are not relevant. Finally, in hierarchical analysis, the researcher establishes the criterion for including a variable at each step.

It may be in terms of expense of the variable if the intent is to keep cost down by establishing functions with the least expensive variables. Or the researcher might want to know whether group separation (e.g., purchasers of family cars, vans, convertibles) is enhanced by a set of related variables (e.g., age of driver, marital status, hobbies, occupation) after another set (e.g., cost of car, cost of maintenance, safety rating) has been removed.

Whatever the procedure used to arrive at the discrimination functions, these functions can be tested for significance by a multivariate statistic called Wilks's lambda, which is often converted to an F ratio: a ratio of between-group variability to within-group variability. The more the groups have been differentiated by a discriminant function, the greater the between-group variability and the larger the F ratio. (Or it may be converted to chi-square, as is done in the second article you will read). If the ratio for the first overall test is significant, it is concluded that at least the first discriminant function differentiates among groups. The next step removes discrimination provided by the first function and repeats the test of significance to determine whether groups still can be separated by the remaining functions, each of which is orthogonal or independent of the others. If the first F ratio is not significant, none of the functions are significant, and it would be concluded that the discriminant variables do not differentiate the groups.

Values equivalent to R^2 can be determined to indicate percentage variability in the discriminant function scores for a particular function that is associated with the different groups. Therefore, these values indicate discriminating power of the function. The values may be reported as squared canonical correlations (correlations between discriminant scores and independent variables) or in terms of eigenvalues. Eigenvalues indicate discriminating power of a function. The higher the eigenvalue, the more the groups will be separated. And the ratio of an eigenvalue for a function to the sum of eigenvalues for all functions yields discriminating power of that function. Because the first function always indicates greatest differentiation, its value always will be largest, with remaining functions accounting for less of the variability. The interpretation is on the order of "X% of variability in discriminant function scores is associated with group membership." To better understand *how* the groups differ, we can examine the correlations between each set of discriminant function scores and scores on each discriminant variable. If we have two discriminant functions, we know that the groups differ in two ways (e.g., with respect to two of the discriminant variables). For example, with discriminant variables A, B, and C, we may find a high correlation between the first function and A and high correlations between the second function and B and between the second function and C. This tells us that A is the critical discriminating factor for the first function, and B and C (probably correlated) account for the second function. This information, plus a scattergram of group membership as a function of discriminant function1 scores (X axis) and function2 scores (Y axis)—especially where the groups cluster—will make a more complete interpretation of the analysis.

Once significance of discriminant functions has been demonstrated, it is useful to determine the relative importance of each predictor variable in the discrimination. One approach has been to test for mean differences for each variable. This method is not considered appropriate, however, if some of the variables are correlated. Tests of mean differences assume uncorrelated means. Another method is to convert scores on the predictor variables to standardized scores so that the function is expressed in terms of standardized scores weighted by beta weights, which have the effects of the other variables removed. The squared value of each beta weight would indicate the relative contribution of each variable. Relative contributions, however, depend on which predictor variables are included in or excluded from the function and can very well change with deletions and/or additions of other variables—just as is true in multiple regression. Another method is discrimination loading, the correlations between discriminant function scores and discriminant variable scores. Each squared value will indicate the percent variability in that function that is attributed to that variable.

To get the flavor of discriminant analysis, imagine that we want to know what variables differentiate clinical psychologists, general practitioner MDs, and psychiatrists. We choose 20 of each profession and administer a battery of three tests. Say they measure empathy, locus of control (the extent to which one attributes experiences to one's own control as opposed to fate), and self-esteem. This yields a column of 60 group identification scores, 60 empathy scores, 60 locus of control scores, and 60 self-esteem scores. Because there are three groups and three discriminant variables, two discriminant functions are possible. Each function is derived mathematically so that the weights assigned to each predictor variable (the three tests) score for the first function will maximally separate the groups, and the weights assigned to those variables for the second function will be such that the second set of discriminant scores is orthogonal to the first. When the weights are applied to the scores of each participant, we have two additional columns: discriminant function1 scores and discriminant function2 scores, uncorrelated with each other.

One of the first analyses on these discriminant function scores lets us know if they are significant. If so, all that this indicates is that the groups differ. We can determine how much of variability in each of the two sets of scores is associated with group membership, but these tests do not indicate which of the three variables separates the groups. One useful step would be to determine the intercorrelations between the scores on the three predictor variables. It might reveal that empathy is uncorrelated with the remaining two, but that locus of control and self-esteem are correlated and might be measuring, say, self-confidence.

Now we can determine the correlations between discriminant function scores and scores on each of the three variables (i.e., the discriminant loadings). These will yield three correlation coefficients for discriminant function1 and three for discriminant function2 and will indicate which variable(s) is(are) the differentiator(s) in the first and second function. For example, the highest correlations for the first function may be for locus of control and self-esteem. The second function may yield the highest correlation for empathy. These analyses plus a scattergram of each group member's first and second discriminant function scores might reveal that psychologists are relatively more empathic than the remaining two groups (seen by a spread of clusters along the X axis, with psychologists forming a cluster around high empathy and the remaining two groups clustering away from them), whereas general practitioners and psychiatrists are relatively higher in self-confidence (seen by a spread of clusters along the Y axis, with general practitioners and psychiatrists clustered near the higher end of self-confidence). Or the latter two groups might be differentiated in the degree to which each feels self-confident. These findings, however, apply to the sample used to arrive at the discriminant functions. To determine their accuracy, they should be validated with another sample. Whereas errors in predictions should be low in the original sample, we expect them to be higher with a new sample but still relatively low if the functions are efficient. These errors in prediction can be established with the original sample by comparing actual group membership with membership predicted on the basis of discriminative scores to yield a degree (percentage) of accuracy.

The bulk of published research focuses on group differentiation. Classification of unknown cases, the second purpose of the discriminant analysis, is achieved by setting certain discriminant scores as "cutoff scores." One now sets standards on the order of the following: If the discriminant score of the unknown case is greater than the cutoff, that case is classified one way; otherwise, the case is classified another way. Concern here is with errors in classification and relative cost of the errors.

There are several statistical assumptions underlying the analysis. First, discriminant function scores are assumed to be normally distributed in each group. Second, the analysis assumes that the variances of the predictor variables are the same in each criterion group as the variances in the population from which they were drawn. Third, correlation matrices for predictor variables are assumed to be the same for each criterion group (e.g., positive correlations for each criterion group). Fourth,

because the analysis includes several predictors, multicollinearity is just as much of a problem here as it is in multiple regression. If it exists, the variable (or variables) causing it should be identified and eliminated. Recall that multicollinearity refers to instances in which one variable is a linear combination of other variables. Finally, outliers can create problems. Identification of these is more difficult than eliminating them because a case may have test scores that are within bounds but produce extreme discriminant function scores. If groups are large and of equal size, discriminant analysis is fairly robust with respect to violations. What is "large"? A rule of thumb is to have a number of cases that is 20 times the number of variables. So, a three-variable study should have a total sample size of at least 60 cases. Nonetheless, statistical packages usually include tests of the assumptions.

Our other concern is with the bases for obtaining the data for the analysis. We want some assurance that the samples within each group are not biased (i.e., there was no selective loss of participants within a particular group), testing conditions were about the same for all groups, a naive data collector was employed, the tests are reliable and valid, and the tests were not presented in the same order for all data cases. A list of caution factors for studies using discriminant analysis of the data is in Box 8.1.

Two research articles that included discriminant analysis now will be evaluated, the first together and the second only by you. Neither one provides eigenvalues. There is no rule on just what statistics should be presented in an article; much depends on editorial policy of the journal.

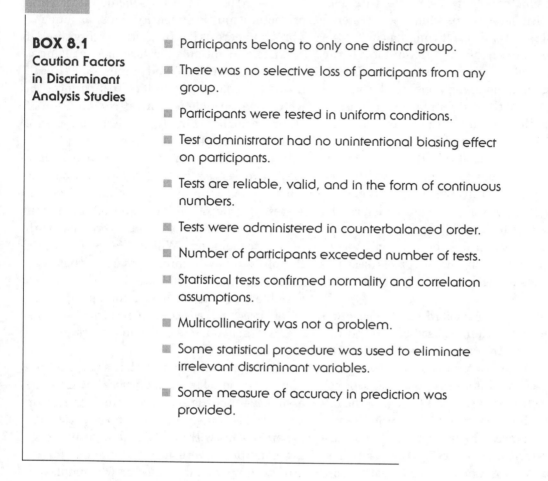

BOX 8.1
Caution Factors in Discriminant Analysis Studies

- Participants belong to only one distinct group.

- There was no selective loss of participants from any group.

- Participants were tested in uniform conditions.

- Test administrator had no unintentional biasing effect on participants.

- Tests are reliable, valid, and in the form of continuous numbers.

- Tests were administered in counterbalanced order.

- Number of participants exceeded number of tests.

- Statistical tests confirmed normality and correlation assumptions.

- Multicollinearity was not a problem.

- Some statistical procedure was used to eliminate irrelevant discriminant variables.

- Some measure of accuracy in prediction was provided.

STUDY EXAMPLE 8.1

This study is taken from the medical field and involves the identification of variables that differentiate adolescents with Type I diabetes who are at risk for a psychiatric disorder from somatically normal adolescents. It makes use of several statistical tests, including discriminant analysis. The particular kind is stepwise and, like regression analysis, involves first entering the most powerful discriminator, pairing it with each of the remaining variables to find the most potent pair, then pairing that pair with each of the remaining variables, and so forth, each time testing whether the addition increases the discriminating power of the function.

The Study

Blanz, B. J., Rensch-Riemann, B. S., Fritz-Sigmund, D. I., & Schmidt, M. H. (1993). IDDM is a risk factor for adolescent psychiatric disorders. *Diabetes Care, 16*(12), 1579-1587. Reprinted with permission by the American Diabetes Association.

Psychiatric disorders and social problems are now recognized as common in children and adolescents with chronic medical disorders. . . . This should also be true for IDDM [insulin-dependent diabetes mellitus], because IDDM differs from most other conditions in two respects that should increase the risk for psychiatric disorders and social problems. . . . First, despite the fact that IDDM affects virtually all aspects of everyday life, IDDM children and adolescents are encouraged to lead a normal life, without many of the concessions usually made to chronically ill patients. Second, IDDM children and adolescents are expected to bear much of the responsibility for treatment decisions that will affect their immediate and long-term health.

However, the results of studies dealing with the question of whether the rate of psychiatric disorders in IDDM children and adolescents has increased or not compared with healthy control subjects are equivocal. . . .

Four reasons arise for variability among findings in previous studies. First, reliability and validity of the instruments were mostly doubtful. . . . Second, different instruments (ratings, questionnaires, interviews) and different methods for case definition (a case is a psychiatric disorder of a moderate or severe degree) were used. . . . Third, most studies investigated broad age-groups. . . . This led to problems with the instruments used for the whole age range, as certain symptoms like enuresis have a totally different meaning for children 6 yr of age than those 15 yr of age. . . . Fourth, in 6 of 17 studies . . . a control group was not used. Therefore, the methodological uncertainties and the heterogeneity of these study results do not allow a final answer to the question of whether the rate of psychiatric disorders in children and adolescents increases or not.

---

1. What was the rationale for the study?

Psychiatric disorders often occur in adolescents with chronic disorders and should be prevalent in those with IDDM because of demands placed on them. However, studies concerned with the issue have produced equivocal results due to methodological weaknesses and the use of certain tests across a broad range of ages when some problems are age-specific.

This study, which was designed to overcome the limitations of previous research, involved the use of a reliable and valid interview, used a narrow age range (17-19 yrs of age), and compared the diabetic group with a (somatically healthy) control group.

▶ *(Note that a healthy group is not an adequate control for chronic disorder per se nor for other factors that accompany diabetes or that may contribute to its onset.)*

This age range close to adulthood was elected to avoid the age-bound difficulties of pubertal adolescents mentioned above. The results found in adolescents 17-19 yr of age can be more easily generalized to broader age-groups. On the basis of this advanced methodological approach, the following questions should be addressed: Do IDDM adolescents have an increased risk for psychiatric disorders compared with somatically healthy peers?

▶ *(Note that the use of a somatically healthy group will answer this question.)*

Can a diabetes-specific behavioral profile be found? Are there sex-specific differences with regard to rates of psychiatric disorders or certain symptom profiles? What roles do metabolic control, real life events, and adverse family environment play in this context?

---

2. What was the purpose of the study?

To determine whether older adolescents with IDDM are at greater risk for psychiatric disorders than healthy (control) counterparts, using controlled conditions (reliable instruments, small age range, control group). The authors attempted to determine whether there is an IDDM behavioral profile; whether sex of the adolescent plays a role in rate of the disorder or profile; and whether metabolic control, life events, or family environment play a role.

Research Design and Methods

Subjects included 93 adolescents with IDDM and 93 somatically healthy adolescents matched for age, sex, and socioeconomic status (control group). The age of the adolescents with IDDM was between 17 and 19 yr of age (mean 18.1 yr of age; control group: mean 18.6 yr of age). Of the subjects, 54 (58%) were boys, and 39 (42%) were girls. The mean duration of diabetes was 8.7 yr (range 1-17 yr of age). Of the participants, 32 (34%) were treated conventionally (rigid diet, 1 or 2 insulin injections a day), and 61 (66%) followed an intensive treatment regimen (more free diet, 3-6 injections a day). Diabetic control as measured by GHB (HbA$_1$) values was good (HbA$_1$ < 7.5%) in 23 (25%) probands, moderate (HbA$_1$ 7.6-9.5%) in 45 (48%) probands, and bad (HbA$_1$ [>] 9.5) in 25 (27%) probands.

---

3. Who served as participants?

A group of 93 adolescent males (58%) and females (mean age = 18.1 years old) with IDDM and 93 somatically healthy individuals matched for age, sex, and socioeconomic status were included. Duration of IDDM was about 8.7 years (mean). Thirty-two percent of the former were treated conventionally, and the rest treated under an intensive program. Twenty-five percent were in good metabolic control, 48% were in moderate control, and 27% were in poor control.

Procedures

. . . Because diabetic patients are not centrally registered in Germany as in most other countries, the effort was made to find all 17- to 19-yr-old adolescents with IDDM living in a certain area. The catchment area consisted of Mannheim and the greater Rhein-Neckar region. . . .

In Germany, diabetic adolescents are primarily treated in diabetic outpatient clinics. Thus, all nine diabetic outpatients clinics within the catchment area were asked to cooperate and all agreed. All 17- to 19-yr-old adolescents living in the catchment area were asked to participate in a study that investigated how diabetic adolescents and their families manage their daily lives. No special information was given that the interview contained questions about psychiatric symptoms or syndromes. Nearly all ($n = 74$, 90.2% of the total patient population [$n = 82$]) agreed to participate. Only a few individuals refused to participate ($n = 8$) and, therefore, did not alter the basis of the available data (socioeconomic status, sex, and metabolic control).

To find diabetic adolescents living in the catchment area and not being treated in the nine diabetic outpatient clinics, two diabetic self-aid organizations wrote letters to their members containing the same information as cited above. An additional 12 adolescents who fulfilled the criteria agreed to participate, and 7 further participants were found by local newspaper advertisements. Altogether, 93 (74 + 12 + 7) adolescents could be investigated. All subjects received a fee sufficient to cover out-of-pocket expenses.

The control group consisted of a random sample of individuals 18 yr of age ($n = 181$) that was longitudinally assessed at 8, 13, and 18 yr of age as part of an epidemiological study. This study was conducted to investigate epidemiology and the course of psychiatric disorders in children and adolescents. The sample of this epidemiological, longitudinal study was randomly drawn at the first stage of the investigation and involved 216 children. . . .

Detailed analyses revealed that no significant refuser effects could be expected to bias the representativity of this sample. . . . No systematic bias caused by the children who had dropped out was indicated. . . . The random subjects at 13 and 18 yr of age, respectively, who remained in the study can probably be regarded as a representative sample of the total population of individuals 13 and 18 yr of age, respectively, living in Mannheim. Consider that the control subjects came from Mannheim, and the diabetic subjects came from the broader catchment area. . . .

A comparison of the two groups (random sample [$n = 181$] vs. diabetic group [$n = 93$]) yielded no significant differences regarding age, sex, IQ, socioeconomic status, and type of school attended. . . . The control group of somatically healthy adolescents ($n = 93$) was chosen out of the 181 adolescents of the random sample by matching age, sex, and socioeconomic status.

▶ *(Note that, except for illness and grade point average [fortunately higher for experimental participants], the two groups were fairly well matched. It would have been even better, however, to match on marital status of the parents as well.)*

---

4. How were the participants recruited?

Diabetic patients were from nine clinics in two regions of Germany (only a small percentage refused to participate) and also recruited via letters and newspaper ads. Control participants were part of a random sample taking part in a longitudinal study, who previously had been interviewed on three occasions.

Both the diabetic and control groups were assessed with the same instruments in the same way. The main instrument was a 3-h, highly structured, psychiatric interview conducted separately with the adolescents and their parents. The interview structure and questions asked in the interviews were identical for both adolescents and their parents. The interviewers knew whether the probands came from the diabetic or the somatic healthy group, but in the diabetic group all assessments were made blindly to diabetes control as measured by GHB (HbA$_1$) values that were taken on the day of the interview. . . .

▶ *(Note additional differences between the two groups. Diabetic participants came from three different sources—clinics, letters, newspaper ads—whereas control participants were randomly selected—we don't know the sources— and were part of a larger study. More important, control participants already had gone through three prior interviews, whereas diabetic participants were being interviewed for the first time. A big flaw in the design—aptly reported—is that interviewers knew whether the interviewee was a control or had diabetes. The fact that he/she was naive regarding level of metabolic control is not nearly as important. Moreover, no mention is made of where [or when] the interviews took place.)*

Measures of analysis

Interviews. The first version of this interview was developed by Rutter and Graham as a semistructured interview for the psychiatric assessment of children. . . . The authors found that the reliability of the overall judgment of psychiatric abnormality was high. . . . This interview was developed into a fully structured interview, adapted to the age of the adolescents by our research group, and published in German. . . . Validity of the applied interview was ascertained in a separate study on 66 outpatients who displayed an extremely high sensitivity (97%). . . . Agreement with an independent clinical evaluation was seen in 81% of the examined patients who received identical diagnoses with both methods.

▶ *(Note that reliability and validity procedures are reported.)*

Diagnostic categories and symptoms. The following symptoms that cover the main areas of clinical importance were assessed, arranged into diagnostic groups, and assigned a rating. . . . Symptoms were grouped into four specific diagnostic categories and added up to four specific symptom scores. These diagnostic categories and the four specific symptom scores, respectively, are a rough categorization of psychiatric disorders found in children and adolescents. . . . Categories encompass . . . introversive (e.g., anxiety disorders, depressive syndromes); antisocial (e.g., conduct disorders, group or solitary aggressive type); hyperkinetic (e.g., attention-deficit hyperactivity disorder); and eating disorder (e.g., anorexia nervosa) syndromes. . . .

If a symptom was elicited, the information was obtained by asking additional questions. . . . Each individual symptom was rated as being absent (0), moderate (1), or severe (2), depending on the information provided at the interview. . . . The recorded combinations of answers were used to generate automated symptom-ratings (absent, moderate, or severe) as is done by other highly structured interviews.

Case definition. After both interviews with the adolescents and their parents, case definition was based on an expert-rating. The ratings were substantially based on the clinical implications of the symptoms; their severity was considered as well as the resulting impairment and the need for psychiatric treatment. The experts were medical doctors and clinical psychologists specially trained in child and adolescent psychiatry. One of these experts had also assessed the random sample; thus, it was guaranteed that both samples used the same procedure.

Diagnostic assessment was based on *DSM-III-R* diagnostic criteria . . . and on ICD-10 diagnostic criteria. . . . Rating the severity of the given disorder on a 4-point scale ranging from 0 (undisturbed) to 3 (severely disturbed) supplemented the diagnostic assessment. A total score of 1 (mild disturbance) was chosen if subjects showed some symptoms, but these only occurred infrequently and did not interfere with the adolescents' performance in everyday life. Adolescents with moderate psychiatric disorders (total score of 2) showed definite symptoms. . . . The highest total score of 3 points was assigned to severely disturbed adolescents whose symptoms caused marked impairments or disrupted their environment, thus making immediate treatment necessary.

The inter-rater reliability for the assessment of severity scores and diagnoses demonstrated a very high level of conformity (between 84.2% and 94.7%; . . . .) In the analyses reported below, severity ratings were dichotomized, yielding two groups of adolescents with (scores of 2 and 3) and without (scores of 0 and 1) psychiatric disorders.

Family adversity. As an overall index of psychosocial and family adversity, the original FAI . . . was used in a slightly modified version. . . . Head of household unskilled worker, overcrowding (> 1.5 people/room), severe marital discord or one-parent family, psychiatric disorder of the mother (any psychiatric disturbance of sufficient severity is covered), delinquency of the head of the household, and institutional care of the child. The presence of each item was scored by 1 point and the total number counted, so that each subject could reach a rating between 0 and 6. A rating of ≥ 2 significantly enhances the risk for child and adolescent psychiatric disorders. . . .

Life events. The measure used consisted of the total of life events within the last 5 yr. The only events that were considered were easy to be seen objectively, such as hospital admissions. . . .

5. What was the general procedure?

Both groups were interviewed (as were parents) in a highly structured manner, each for 3 hours. Questions were designed to measure presence of pathology, which then was classified and ranked by two experts. Questions also measured family adversity and stressful life events.

6. *What were good features of the design?*

Reliability and validity of the interview and symptoms and diagnosis were established; experimental and control participants were well matched, although no mention was made of status of parents.

7. *What were bad features of the design?*

Control participants had been previously interviewed on two occasions and might have been more relaxed than diabetic patients being interviewed for the first time; interviewer knew status of the participant, and this might have unintentionally affected some of the responses (expectancy); no mention was made of where interviews were held, nor when.

Results

The application of case definition (psychiatric disorders of a moderate or severe degree present within the last 6 mo) led to an overall rate of psychiatric disorders of 33.3% ($n = 31$) in the diabetic group, which was more than threefold higher than in the control group (9.7%, $n = 9$; $\chi^2 = 14.0$; $p < 0.001$; Table 2). This result demonstrates the increased risk for psychiatric disorders in IDDM adolescents.

TABLE 2 Severity and Rates of Psychiatric Disorders in Diabetic and Control Groups

	Diabetic Group		Control Group	
	n	*(%)*	*n*	*(%)*
Severity level				
0, undisturbed	34	(36.6)	51	(54.8)
1, mildly disturbed	28	(30.1)	33	(35.5)
2, moderate disturbed	24	(25.8)	6	(6.5)
3, severely disturbed	7	(7.5)	3	(3.2)
Total of severity levels 2 and 3	31	(33.3)	9	(9.7)

The sex-specific ratings of psychiatric disorders in the IDDM adolescents were fairly similar with 35.2% (20 of 54) for males and 28.2% (11 of 39) for females ($\chi^2 = 0.78$; ns)

8. *What was the major result regarding presence or absence of moderate to severe pathology in the two groups?*

   There was a greater incidence (i.e., frequency was higher) among the diabetic than the control participants.

9. *Did this incidence in the diabetic group depend upon sex?*

   No.

Looking only at the severely disturbed adolescents, whose symptoms caused marked impairments that required treatment . . . resulted as follows: in the diabetic group, 7.5% (7 of 93) were severely disturbed, and in the control group, 3.2% (3 of 93; $\chi^2 = 0.95$; ns) were severely disturbed.

10. *The authors report no differences in percent of each group who showed pathology and who required immediate treatment. They based their analysis, however, on the total samples (of 93 each) instead of on the number who showed pathology (31 in the diabetic group and 9 in the control group). Perform the χ^2 test on these ns. Does this change the conclusion?*

	Immediate	Not Immediate	
Diabetes group	7 (7.75)	24 (23.25)	31
Control group	3 (2.25)	6 (6.75)	9
	10	30	40

    $$\chi^2 = [(7 - 7.75)^2/7.75] + \ldots + [(6 - 6.75)^2/6.75] = 0.43$$

    The conclusion is the same.

No significant correlation was observed between the severity of psychiatric disorders as measured by severity ratings between 0 and 3 and metabolic control as measured by GHb (HbA_1) values. . . . A further comparison between the three groups with good . . . moderate . . . and bad . . . metabolic control revealed no significant differences regarding the rate of psychiatric disorders. . . .

11. *Was there any relationship between the adolescents' metabolic control and the severity of a psychiatric disorder?*

No. Overall, there was no correlation between the severity of a disorder and level of glycosylated hemoglobin. Nor was there a difference in frequency of a disorder as a function of good, moderate, and poor control.

12. *Aside from the possibility that there is no correlation between severity of the disorder and metabolic control, what else might account for failure to detect a correlation, if one does, in fact, exist?*

The range of severity scores was 0 to 3, and this may be too restricted a range of scores for a correlation to be detected.

A stepwise discriminant analysis was applied with the four specific diagnostic symptom scores as the independent variables and the group (diabetic or control group) as the dependent variable. (Student's *t* tests led to the same results. A discriminant analysis was applied because this procedure handles multiple dependent variables without the need to adjust the level of significance. Furthermore, only by conducting a discriminant analysis can the best variable set possibly be found.)

▶ *(Note that a multivariate* t *test could have been used if the intent was to see whether the groups differed on the four symptoms. The authors, however, were looking for a profile differentiator, or a difference in clusters of symptoms between the two groups. Furthermore, because there were four predictor variables, a minimum of 80 participants would have been necessary. The numbers in this study far exceeds that minimum n.)*

The results show that the only significant difference between the two groups was the score for introversive symptoms in the diabetic group (mean = 3.71 vs. 2.68; Table 3). However, a significant discriminant function resulted (Wilks $\lambda = 0.9354$; multiple correlation coefficient = 0.254; $p < 0.017$; Table 3) in which all four specific symptoms scores were included and in which the introversive and antisocial symptom scores had more weight than the hyperkinetic and eating disorder symptoms. But discrimination found between the two groups by the independent variables was not good. The result of classification was unsatisfactory because only 53% of the diabetic group subjects and only 66% of the control group subjects were correctly classified. This means that besides a raised score of introversive symptoms in the diabetic group, compared with the control group, no hint was detected of any further diagnostic groups. . . .

TABLE 3 Specific Diagnostic Symptom Scores in Diabetic and Control Groups

Independent Variables	F (Step 0)		P Value	Selection Step	Standardized Coefficient of Discriminant Function
Symptom type					
Introversive	5.60		< 0.02	1	–0.536
Dissocial	2.86	ns	(0.10)	2	0.649
Hyperkinetic	1.25	ns		3	–0.455
Eating disorder	3.28	ns	(0.07)	4	–0.381

▶ *(Note that the data presented could have been more complete. It would have been useful to know means and standard deviations of all four symptoms and to have some indication that they had been tested for normality. Likewise, it would have been useful to report intercorrelations among the four symptoms to estimate whether any unusually high coefficients might have contributed to these results. And, although not necessary with one function, it would have been useful to have the eigenvalue reported.)*

If this stepwise, discriminant analysis (independent variables: the four specific diagnostic symptom scores; dependent variable: diabetic or control group) was calculated separately for boys and girls, in boys the same result would be found. However, girls with IDDM showed (besides the elevated score of introversive symptoms) significantly more eating disorder symptoms (mean = 0.56 vs. 0.18; $p < 0.04$).

---

13. **What was the clearest result of the discriminant analysis?**

The symptom of introversion was the only one that separated diabetic patients from controls; it suggests that adolescents with IDDM show a greater frequency of introversion (as pathology) than do adolescents with no somatic disorder.

14. **What is the basis for concluding that introversion and antisocial behavior were the biggest contributors to the discriminant function?**

Their standardized coefficients (–.536 and .649) were highest.

15. *What is the meaning of the multiple correlation of 0.254?*

Approximately 6.5% ($.254^2 \times 100$) of variability in the occurrence of the four classes of symptoms (mainly introversion) is associated with group membership, participants with or without diabetes.

16. *What other evidence suggests that the groups were not well discriminated?*

Classification verification percentages were relatively low.

What are the possible reasons for the increased rate of psychiatric disorders in the diabetic group? The meaning of life events and adverse familial circumstances as risk factors for child and adolescent psychiatric disorders is well known. . . . If these risk factors play an important role for the increased rate of psychiatric disorders in the diabetic group, an elevated rate of these risk factors should also be present. Therefore, the rates of life events and familial adversities in both groups were tested by Student's *t* tests. . . . The number of life events was significant ($p < 0.01$), and the number of familial adversities tended to decrease ($p = 0.06$) in the diabetic group. The increased rate of psychiatric disorders in the diabetic group was not determined by increased rates of risk factors, such as life events or familial adversities. Therefore, these factors are not responsible for the elevated risk of psychiatric disorders in the diabetic group.

▷ *(At this point, start to think about what factors could account for the increased occurrence of pathology in the diabetic group, if life stress and dysfunctioning families are ruled out.)*

17. *Why was it concluded that life stress and familial adversities do not account for—or contribute to—increased pathology noted in the diabetic group?*

There were significantly fewer life events reported by the adolescents and parents of the diabetic group than the controls and marginally lower occurrences of familial adversities.

Conclusions

In the diabetic group, the rate of psychiatric disorders was, with 33.3%, more than three times higher than in the group of healthy control subjects (9.7%) matched for age, sex, and socioeconomic status. . . . This result lends support to the notion that older IDDM adolescents should also be seen as a high-risk group for psychiatric disorders. According to this, IDDM is weighed with an elevated risk for psychiatric disorders over the whole period from childhood and adolescence to adulthood. (An elevated risk for psychiatric disorders was also found in IDDM adults. . . .) With regard to psychiatric disorders, IDDM children and adolescents are not different from children and adolescents with other chronic diseases, who generally have an increased risk of psychiatric disorders. . . .

No sex-specific differences were observed between the rates of psychiatric disorders in the two groups. . . . The same rate of psychiatric disorders in males and females may be attributable to the older age of the probands in the study, because it is well known that in childhood and early adolescence there is a general preponderance of boys in psychiatric cases . . . , which diminishes with increasing age.

Regarding the severely disturbed cases, no significant difference was found between the diabetic and control groups. This means that the disturbances accompanying IDDM are milder forms of psychiatric disorders. This is an unexpected result because the increased risk in the diabetic group should be the same for psychiatric disorders of a moderate and severe degree. Theoretically, this result could also be caused by the refusal of some severely disturbed IDDM adolescents to participate in the study. However, this is not probable because the analysis of refusers in the control group showed that they did not have any additional behavior problems. . . .

No substantial correlation was detected between severity of psychiatric disorders and metabolic control. Similar results have been found in other studies. . . . Others have found an association between psychiatric problems and decreased metabolic control. . . . Results from more recent studies point to an association between psychiatric problems and good metabolic control. . . . This work suggests that the efforts to maintain good metabolic control may be so demanding that IDDM children and adolescents become more poorly adjusted (i.e., more depressive).

The diabetic adolescents suffered from significantly more introversive symptoms than their healthy counterparts, especially somatic symptoms, sleeping disturbances, compulsions, and depressive moods. . . . This preponderance of introversive symptoms in diabetic children also seems to exist for adults. . . .

The elevated rate of psychiatric disorders in the diabetic group was not accompanied by higher rates of life events and familial adversities. This means that the elevated risk of psychiatric disorders in IDDM adolescents is not mediated by these well-known risk factors for child and adolescent psychiatric disorders. Therefore, this remains an open question—what are the underlying mechanisms for the elevated rate of psychiatric disorders in IDDM adolescents, and how do they operate? Life events and familial adversities have to be excluded from the bulk of possible factors, as demonstrated by these results.

18. **What were the major conclusions reached by the authors?**

    (a) There is a greater frequency of occurrence of psychiatric disorders among adolescents with IDDM than among those who are somatically healthy. (b) There were no sex differences found in the occurrence of psychiatric disorders among adolescents with IDDM, which may be due to older age of these participants. (c) Severity of psychiatric disorder was unrelated to degree of metabolic control of diabetes. (d) Diabetic adolescents showed more introversive symptoms than controls. (e) Psychiatric disorders were unrelated to family harmony and life stress.

19. **Are any of these conclusions justified? Why?**

    Because interviews were based on self-reports of adolescents and parents, and because the interviewer knew the status of the interviewee and might have expected more pathology among adolescents with IDDM, it is possible that differences found between the two groups may be a function of expectancy rather than chronic illness. Another possibility is that behavior required to manage diabetes may have been interpreted as pathology. For example, an introversive symptom includes compulsion. But control of IDDM requires that the patient adhere to a rigid schedule of injections, meals, blood sugar monitoring, and so forth. Too, the diabetic group was interviewed for the first time, whereas the control group had experienced two prior interviews. Therefore, what was in fact nervousness may have been interpreted as pathology (although this is a weak possibility if interviewers were trained).

20. **Does your evaluation mean that IDDM is not accompanied by a greater risk for psychiatric disorder?**

    No. On the basis of the procedures and statistical analysis, we still do not know definitely from this study whether these patients are at greater risk.

21. **What did the results of the discriminant analysis suggest regarding the potential differentiators?**

    Because so little of variance is associated with the one discriminator (introversion), other differentiators may have to be identified, or a more appropriate control (comparison) group may reveal differences.

22. **If the results could be generalized, to what population would they apply?**

    Adolescents in Germany with similar demographic characteristics.

204 ■ EVALUATING RESEARCH ARTICLES FROM START TO FINISH

STUDY EXAMPLE 8.2

This study is from the field of education and deals with an attempt to accelerate the cognitive development of kindergarten children from impoverished environments. Piaget's theory of development guided the research. Accordingly, youngsters at first think very concretely, and their behavior is tied to specific stimuli. As more mature thinking emerges, they are capable of classifying objects such as tools, serializing, and applying principles of conservation (e.g., five pennies are still five pennies regardless of whether they are close to each other or spread over a surface). Whereas many discriminant analysis studies determine characteristics that differentiate groups, this experimental study assigned youngsters to two methods of training and then determined whether the training differentiated the groups on two standardized tests. Although the bulk of results are analyzed by determining discriminant functions, the authors also performed analyses of variance—univariate F tests. One unusual feature of results is that the discriminant functions data are presented in sentences rather than in tables.

The Study

Pasnak, R., Holt, R., Campbell, J. W., & McCutcheon, L. (1991). Cognitive and achievement gains for kindergartners instructed in Piagetian operations. *Journal of Educational Research, 85*(1), 5-13. Reprinted with permission of the Helen Dwight Reid Educational Foundation. Published by Heldref Publications, 1319 Eighteenth St., NW, Washington, DC 20036-1802. Copyright © 1991.

Five-year-old children are highly variable in their cognitive functioning. Some 5-year-olds are still in the preoperational state of cognitive development. Their thinking remains closely tied to perceptual properties of the objects or events that they are considering. Consequently, the children frequently classify items inappropriately, even on simple properties such as form, size, orientation, function, or type. These failures result, at least in part, because the children cannot resist intrusions of irrelevant perceptual characteristics of the items to be classified. Such disorganization often occurs even when the physical objects to be classified can be inspected at length, and it is even more likely when purely mental representations form the basis for classification by similarities and differences.

Likewise, at 5 years the mental operation of seriation—arranging objects sequentially according to some gradation of size, space, number, time, etc.—is often deficient. Children whose thinking is still preoperational may be unable to seriate more than four or five tangible objects that are available for trial-and-error efforts, and their finding the place for a new object within an already formed series is much more difficult. (It is much easier for a child to build a series by sequentially adding to the end of it than it is to interpolate within the series.) Mental seriation of items named is still more demanding. And, preoperational children typically do not understand or apply the operations of addition/subtraction, reversibility, reciprocity, and identity. . . .

Other children, at 5 years, evince more cognitive development. They have progressed to an early form of concrete operational thought and suffer less from perceptual intrusions into their thinking process. . . . Those 5-year-olds have the early concrete operations necessary to classify objects or events along one dimension by singling out the relevant characteristic, and they can easily seriate by one dimension and can conserve number, substance, and some other properties. The progressive development of concrete operational thought throughout the elementary school years involves many other abilities, but classification, seriation, and conservation are probably the key mental *operations* at the outset.

At the beginning of elementary school (kindergarten), performance on classification, seriation, and conservation problems predicts performance on a variety of standard and nonstandard achievement measures . . . and a variety of informal measures contrived by teachers and researchers. Significantly, kindergartners' abilities to classify, seriate, and conserve predict their achievement not only in kindergarten but also subsequently in Grades 1 through 4. . . . The relations of Piagetian operations to achievement suggest that trying to improve kindergartners' concrete operation functioning may be profitable.

Such an intervention seems especially appropriate because it would be intended to benefit children old enough to have need of the thought processes that are normal for their age peers. In many cases, the potential for better cognitive functioning exists, but the children need help in developing it, especially if the children are products of deprived or disadvantaged . . . environments.

Among the most successful methods used to teach concrete operations are the learning set techniques favored by some psychologists and educators. A learning set consists of a large number of problems involving a broad variety of concrete objects. . . . They can all be solved by the same abstract principle. . . . The variety of objects used to construct problems that can be solved via the same principle governs the extent to which the principle is learned and generalized. . . .

The Piacceleration instructional method was developed out of efforts to use learning sets to teach classification, seriation, and number conservation to blind and mildly mentally retarded students. Success with these . . . students . . . led to attempts to use this instructional method to help nonhandicapped children who were slow in developing these three concrete operations and who were not doing well in their kindergarten classrooms.

Preliminary tests of this program with small samples of 5-year-olds who had no identifiable handicaps but who had not been making normal progress indicated that Piacceleration instruction produced significant cognitive gains on a variety of non-Piagetian measures and that the gains persisted for at least a year. There was no evidence for academic achievement gains in the preliminary studies. . . . However, achievement measures were taken . . . just 2 weeks after the intervention was concluded. . . .

Genuine progress in cognitive ability, as defined either by Piaget . . . or by standard psychometric instruments, should eventually be followed by improved academic performance and achievement gains. Hence, we decided to test Piacceleration with a larger sample and more extensive achievement measures taken after more time had elapsed. The target population was children, especially minority children, who were not doing well in their first encounter with a public school system. Because the children were engaged in making both the transition from home to school environment and the transition from preoperational to concrete operational thought, they might represent an especially vulnerable group with great potential to profit from intervention.

Our approach in this study was to offer half of the children instruction on the concrete operations of classification, seriation, and conservation instead of the conventional mathematics instruction that they would otherwise have received for part of the school year. The rationale was that the mastery of the three concrete operations gained from Piacceleration instruction might generalize to improved conceptual functioning and problem solving and . . . subsequently lead to improved achievement not only in mathematics but also in verbal comprehension. . . .

The other half of the children involved in the study served as a control or reference group. They were offered the conventional mathematics instruction from the program of studies used in the cooperating school system. . . . In essence, the comparison provided a test of whether a conventional mathematics curriculum or one that uses hundreds of manipulatives to ensure competence in the key concrete operations would produce the greatest gains in kindergarten mathematics, reasoning ability, and general comprehension for poorly performing kindergartners.

Method

Subjects

Selection. We asked the teachers of all 17 kindergarten classes in six neighboring Northern Virginia schools to select the 5 children in their classes who were lowest in ability, excepting those who had noticeable language difficulties or other special problems. . . . The average ability of the children selected was low, as shown by the Otis-Lennon School Ability Index (SAI) for the untreated children (SAI = 33rd percentile). There were no data on the average ability or intelligence of kindergartners from those schools, but the 56th-percentile average of their fourth graders on the Stanford Achievement Test (SAT) provides a rough estimate. The schools . . . serve a high proportion of low-income and minority families.

Assignment. We assigned the groups of 5 students to experimental or control conditions according to a restricted randomization. The restrictions were to equalize the number of children from each teacher, school, and morning or afternoon kindergarten sessions in the experimental and control groups. This equalization was essentially achieved with one extra afternoon group assigned to the control condition.

Attrition. Two sets of experimental children were lost because of extended illness and eventual resignation of the classroom aides assigned to instruct them. The corresponding sets of control children were also deleted, leaving 30 experimental and 35 control children. Then 2 experimental and 6 more control children were lost because of moves or extended absences. The difference in attrition for the two groups did not approach statistical significance. . . .

Of the children remaining in the experimental group, 17 were White and 11 were minority (7 Black). For the control group, 15 were White and 14 were minority (10 Black). Differences in the ethnic composition of the groups did not approach structural significance. . . . The average age was 6.01 years, (*SD* = .42) for the experimental group, 5.99 years (*SD* = .42) for the control group. No representative socioeconomic measures were available.

Materials

Standardized tests. . . . We selected the Otis-Lennon School Ability Test (O-LSAT) and the Stanford Early School Achievement Test (SESAT) to measure the variables.

The O-LSAT was designed specifically to provide a measure of reasoning especially predictive of success in school. . . . Scores on the Primary I version used in this research correlated with end-of-year course grades in reading (.40) and mathematics (.48). Dyer's . . . review provides additional evidence of validity: correlations with first year Metropolitan Achievement Test scores are .61-.68.

At the 5- to 6-year-old level, this group test has a 15-item Classification scale, a 15-item Analogies scale, and a 30-item Omnibus scale. . . . All the scales consist of multiple-choice questions—one of four drawings to be marked in answer to a question read aloud. The School Ability Index (SAI) is derived from the scales, with all items having equal weights.

The O-LSAT manual indicates that minority students, primarily Blacks, were slightly overrepresented in the 130,000 O-LSAT standardization sample. . . .

Kuder-Richardson (K-R 20) reliabilities of .88 to .90 for the Primary I level are given in the O-LSAT manual, along with a fall-spring test-retest reliability of .84. . . .

The SESAT (Level 2) was especially selected for this research because it measures knowledge of the physical and social environment. . . . Level 2 of the SESAT, for use in kindergarten, also provides measures of achievement in mathematics concepts and skills, verbal comprehension, vocabulary, letters, and phonetics, and has a total of 308 four-item multiple-choice questions. . . .

Median . . . reliabilities of .87 for Level 2 are given in the manual. The split-half reliability coefficient of the SESAT for the present sample [is] $r = .84$. . . . The test has been favorably reviewed by experts, including a minority panel, for content validity. The manual reports median correlations of .62 with the O-LSAT.

Classification instruction. We used 20 problems for each of five types of classification. Texture classification . . . size, form, . . . orientation classification . . . nonverbal . . . [and] verbal discovery of class problems. . . . In each problem, three objects or types of objects were the same and one was different, except for orientation problems. For the latter, all four objects were identical, but one was oriented differently. . . .

Seriation instruction. We used a set of 75 problems, each consisting of three to nine similar objects. The objects within each problem differed in height, length, width, or overall size, so that the children could order them from the largest to the smallest. . . .

Number conservation instruction. This set consisted of 120 problems using 24 types of objects. Each problem had identical items arranged in two rows. . . .

Conventional mathematics instruction. Uniflex cubes, geoboards, pattern blocks, number bingo boards, a large variety of household items kept in "junk" bags, and numerous teacher-prepared work sheets were used for the control instruction.

Procedure

The control children received the standard curriculum throughout the experiment in the normal classroom format. During December through February. . . .

[Activities are described.]

The experimental children received the Piacceleration instruction from their classroom aide during the time ordinarily devoted to mathematics instruction. The aides pulled the group over to a corner of the classroom and worked through the Piacceleration program . . . 15 to 20 min per day, 3 to 4 days per week for 3 months, commencing November 30.

The aides were monitored twice a week by the first author, and they also were provided with lesson plans describing each phase of the instruction.

The children were taught to classify objects according to four primary dimensions: form, size, texture, and orientation. They were also taught to discover the class of an object; . . . to relate it to other objects of similar function, purpose, origin, or identity.

During a session on form classification, a set of four objects that constituted a classification problem was placed in front of each of the children. . . . The children, in turn, were asked which object was different from . . . the other three, and were praised enthusiastically for a correct choice. If the choice was incorrect, the child was coached and encouraged until a correct choice was made. The choices and feedback were seen and heard by all the children. After all the children had made a correct choice, the problems were rotated among them and care was taken to scramble the spatial order or position of the objects in each problem. In addition, the subjects were asked to solve the problem that the neighboring child had solved. This process continued until the children had solved each problem. Effort and attention were always praised, and successful solutions were greeted enthusiastically. . . . When all of the children in a group solved all of the 20 form-classification problems easily, the teachers began instruction on size classification. . . . Problems were rotated among the children, as we had done for form and instruction. The procedure continued until all the subjects could solve all of the problems and had been vigorously applauded for diligence and accuracy.

For orientation problems, all four items were identical, but three were presented upside down and the other right side up (or vice versa), or three were aligned vertically, one horizontally (or vice versa), or three were slanted left and one right (or vice versa). Thus, the relevant dimension was orientation. We used the same procedure as that used for size or form. . . . Again, praise and attention were used to reward the children's continuing efforts.

[Nonverbal and verbal discovery of classes is described in the following sections, along with seriation instruction.]

Children were always congratulated for their diligence, and correct solutions were applauded vigorously.

[Number conservation training is described next.]

The endpoint of instruction varied somewhat depending on the group's rate of progress. Thus, in each group, those children who were the slowest to master the most difficult constructs . . . received more instruction than those who learned quickly. All Piacceleration instruction was finished by February 21.

When the children had mastered all three constructs, they joined their classmates, who were receiving the standard mathematics instruction . . . instead of Piacceleration.

The O-LSAT and the SESAT's Environment, Mathematics, Sounds and Letters, and Words and Stories scales were administered during the third and fourth weeks of May. . . .

Results

The main thrust of our study was to determine whether children who received the Piacceleration curriculum performed differently than did comparable children in the standard mathematics curriculum on the variables measures. Accordingly, the children's summary scores on the O-LSAT and on the SESAT Environment, Mathematics, Sounds and Letters, and Words and Stories scales were first used in a step-wise discriminant function analysis to assess how the variables contribute to group differences. . . .

. . . All of the discriminant analyses reported below used five or fewer predictor variables, and the smallest group was size 28. Thus, the sample size of the smallest group greatly exceeded the number of predictors, as recommended by Tabachnik and Fidell for ensuring stability of the solution. Because we expected that many of the predictor variables would be intercorrelated, we used a stepwise discriminant function analysis to avoid any potential problems with multicollinearity and to ensure that the predictors entered into each discriminant function reached the .05 alpha level.

Accordingly, the discriminant analysis was set to include only variables significant at the .05 level. The O-LSAT sum was included, and the discrimination was significant (chi-square approximation to Wilks's lambda = 8.43, df = 1, $p < .01$). Because the analysis was significant, we analyzed the components of each sum to obtain a more detailed picture of the differences caused by the Piacceleration curriculum. The analyses showed that the components for two O-LSAT scales and the SESAT Mathematics and Words and Stories measures were significantly affected by the difference between the two curricula, whereas the components of Environment and Sounds and Letters were not affected.

Discrimination With O-LSAT Components

The O-LSAT components were more strongly affected by the curricula—the discriminant function was highly significant (chi-square approximation to Wilks's lambda = 10.98, df = 3, $p = .01$). Discriminant function weights showed that Classification was most strongly affected (coefficient = –.74), followed by Analogies (coefficient = -.68) and Omnibus (coefficient = –.35). Univariate F tests confirmed that the Piacceleration curriculum was significantly better than the existing curriculum for the Classification scale . . . $p < .01$, and the Analogies scale . . . $p < .01$, whereas the result for the Omnibus scale was not significant. Means and standard deviations for O-LSAT and SESAT scores for each group are given in Table 1. The direction of the differences favors the Piacceleration curriculum for all scales.

Discrimination With Mathematics Components

The overall effect of the curricula on the Mathematics scale components was significant (chi-square approximation to Wilks's lambda = 11.079, df = 4, $p < .05$). The discriminant weights indicated that Concepts was most affected (1.07), whereas Geometry/Measurement, Addition/Subtraction, and Problem Solving had much smaller coefficients (–.37, –.02, and –.26, respectively). Univariate F tests confirmed that the two curricula produced significantly different performances only on the Concepts part of the Mathematics scale . . . $p < .01$. Piacceleration children averaged 61% correct on this subscale, whereas children in the normal curriculum averaged 47%.

TABLE 1 O-LSAT and SESAT Scores After Normal and Piacceleration Curricula

Test Components	Normal		Piacceleration	
	M	SD	M	SD
O-LSAT				
Full-scale SAI	87.7	15.1	98.0	13.2
Percentile SAI	31.l	27.5	48.3	26.6
Classification	6.5	3.2	9.2	2.8
Analogies	6.3	3.0	8.6	3.0
Omnibus	14.9	5.2	27.2	4.4
SESAT Percentiles				
Environment	22.1	22.2	28.4	21.0
Mathematics	29.2	19.5	38.8	16.3
Letter/Sounds	30.3	16.0	34.4	18.7
Words/Stories	22.9	21.4	32.4	21.3

NOTE: O-LSAT = Otis-Lennon School Ability Test; SAI = School Ability Index; SESAT = Stanford Early School Achievement Test.

Discrimination With Words and Stories Components

The Words and Stories test components were affected by the curricula (chi-square approximation to Wilks's lambda = 8.14, $df = 2$, $p < .05$). The discriminant function weights indicated that the Comprehension component was most affected (coefficient = 1.25), whereas Vocabulary was not affected (coefficient = –.52). Univariate F tests confirmed that the curricula were distinguished by performance on the Comprehension subscale ... $p < .01$. Children in the Piacceleration curriculum averaged 59% correct, whereas those in the normal curriculum averaged 47%.

Summary of Differences

... A range of evidence suggests that the Piacceleration curriculum was significantly superior to the existing curriculum for these low-achieving kindergartners.

[An overall correlation matrix is presented with 90 coefficients.]

. . . The areas of achievement for which the Piacceleraton curriculum was superior (Mathematics Concepts and Verbal Comprehension) are those that correlated most highly with O-LSAT scores. . . .

Discussion

Pasnak . . . previously reported that Piacceleration was a useful instructional program for improving the cognitive functioning of normal kindergarten children who were lagging behind their classmates. Our research confirms that finding for a larger sample from a different locale and with a different measure of ability. . . .

The question remains as to why the Piacceleration instruction would be especially effective, for classification is taught in virtually all school curricula, some form of conservation is taught in many school curricula, and seriation is taught in some curricula. Piaget's . . . answer is that the cognitive structures involved, because they are self-regulating and self-constructing, are remarkably resistant to change, so that ordinary instruction is relatively ineffective. . . . Piacceleration is based on the premise, derived from laboratory research, that the extent to which new cognitive operations can be learned so well that they generalize widely and can be applied to new contexts and situations is directly tied to the number and *variety* of concrete examples used in instruction. Thus, although classification, seriation, or conservation taught with a few excellent materials may fail to generalize broadly and have little impact on a child's cognitive operations, the use of a large variety of ordinary materials seems to ensure generalization. Further, Piacceleration's emphasis is on continuing instruction until the operations are firmly internalized and on involving the children's egos in each operation's expression. Also, all three operations critical to the transition from preoperational to concrete operational thought are taught.

In the absence of a pretest, the conclusion that the Piacceleration group blossomed more than those who received the normal curriculum rests on the assumption that the groups were initially equal. Our use of randomization is usually considered a sufficient guarantee that the groups were virtually equal in all respects at the outset of an experiment. Also, because the attrition that occurred was balanced, it is not likely that either group was favored.

The fact that children in the experimental group received the special attention of the classroom aide is a more important concern. The children were not sophisticated enough to realize that they were participating in research, so that a pure "Hawthorne" effect in the conventional sense was unlikely. However, they had the attention of the aide for 15 min in a small group, while the rest of their class had the attention of their teacher in a large group (16 to

19 students). Control children had to share the attention of the aide and the teacher with all of their classmates during this part of their school day.

This confound would have been more serious if all the children in all classes had not been formed into small groups receiving the undivided attention of either an aide or a teacher at different times during the school day, so that being in a small group with one of these instructors was commonplace. Also . . . the children were accustomed to being formed into small special groups and taught by . . . specialists. Another reason for attributing the effects on the O-LSAT and SESAT to the independent variable . . . is the lawfulness and nature of the effects. Changes were noted primarily on the scales that involved reasoning ability. The less conceptual achievement subscales, on which children who are motivated to extra effort by special attention might be expected to more easily improve their scores, showed only small differences. Presumably, confounds would have had effects on these scales—either primarily on these scales or at least as much on these scales as on the others.

Thus, we concluded that mastery of key concrete operations led to a generalized cognitive gain that led to increased academic achievement in mathematics concepts and verbal comprehension. . . .

. . . The positive outcome of the present experimental intervention is probably best understood as resulting from early remediation of at least some aspects of a developmental lag, to the benefit of a group of children poised to gain from such cognitive opportunities as they became available.

The Piacceleration instructional method, which grew out of research projects with handicapped children, is doubtless only one way to produce cognitive gains for underachieving kindergartners. The distinguishing features of this method are that only three key transitional operations are taught, that they are taught with a wide range of exemplars, and . . . taught under the criterion of full mastery. Because the concrete operations are part of many programs of studies, one should not underestimate the importance of using numerous, widely varying kinds of materials to induce generalization to new examples and materials. . . . Finally, when well done, Piacceleration instruction involves constant efforts to boost children's self-esteem by emphasizing their increasing mastery of cognitive processes that are natural and recurrently useful for their age group. We estimate that any instructional method that incorporates all of these features would be successful, or even more successful, with the population studied.

CRITIQUE OF STUDY EXAMPLE 8.2

1. What was the rationale for the study?

2. What was the purpose of the study?

3. How were participants selected and assigned to the two groups?

4. Can the groups be considered equivalent after attrition?

5. Who were the participants?

6. What measures of reasoning ability and academic achievement were used?

7. Are there questions about reliability or validity of the tests?

8. What was the general procedure for both groups?

9. What were good features of the design?

10. What are questionable aspects of the design?

11. How many sets of discriminant functions were determined?

12. If all five predictor variables were considered in the stepwise analysis, how many discriminant functions would be possible?

13. Is there any justification for conducting two separate analyses?

14. What statistical information is missing from the report of the analyses?

15. Does Table 1 help answer either question?

16. Which subtests of the O-LSAT differentiated the two groups?

17. If you look at means and standard deviations for "Omnibus," you will note very little overlap in scores. For controls, $M \pm 2SD = 4.5$ to 25.3, and for experimental group, $M \pm 2SD = 18.4$ to 38. Yet, this variable was not a differentiator. Can you offer a possible reason for this result?

18. Which aspects of the SESAT differentiated the two groups?

19. Ignoring methodology, what do these results indicate?

20. What was the overall conclusion reached by the authors?

21. On what bases did they rule out the role of the confounds of increased attention and learning in a small group in the experimental participants?

22. How reasonable are these arguments?

23. Overall, is Piacceleration training superior to traditional training?

    For answers to these questions, see page 338.

BIBLIOGRAPHY

Diekhoff, G. (1992). *Statistics for the social and behavioral sciences: Univariate, bivariate, multivariate.* Dubuque, IA: William C. Brown.

Dunteman, G. H. (1984). *Introduction to multivariate analysis.* Beverly Hills, CA: Sage.

Kachigan, S. K. (1986). *Statistical analysis: An interdisciplinary introduction to univariate & multivariate methods.* New York: Radius.

Klecka, W. R. (1980). *Discriminant analysis* (Quantitative Applications in the Social Sciences, Vol. 19). Beverly Hills, CA: Sage.

Stevens, J. (1992). *Applied multivariate statistic for the social sciences* (2nd ed.). Hillsdale, NJ: Lawrence Erlbaum.

Additional Suggested Readings

Grimm, L. G., & Yarnold, P. R. (1995). *Reading and understanding multivariate statistics.* Washington, DC: American Psychological Association.

Huberty, C. J. (1984). Issues in the use and interpretation of discriminant analysis. *Psychological Bulletin, 95*(1), 156-171.

Chapter 9

Two-Condition Experimental Studies

Up to this point the focus of the critiques has been mainly on descriptive studies. We looked at relationships between variables, predicting performance on the basis of several independent variables, describing a performance on the basis of related variables (factors), and differentiating performances on the basis of certain variables. Because no variable was actively manipulated, cause-and-effect conclusions could not be reached, nor were they sought. (There was one exception in Chapter 8: One study manipulated type of training to determine whether groups then would be differentiated.) The remainder of the evaluations focus on experiments: *Independent variables* are introduced and manipulated under the assumption that they will produce some change in behavior or make a difference. These will be the ultimate causes of behavior. The particular response or behavior being measured is the *dependent variable*. This will be the ultimate effect.

Researchers often have to decide whether to test different groups of individuals (between-groups design) or test the same group of individuals (within-groups design). If the focus of a study, the independent variable, is an individual characteristic (males vs. females, young consumers vs. older consumers), there is no choice; different groups of individuals have to be tested. If the focus is on relative distinctions people can make (5 vs. 10 seconds, hot vs. cold pain thresholds), there is no choice; the same group of individuals has to be tested. But in many other instances (effectiveness of different dosages of the same drug or of different drugs, susceptibility to suggestion, effectiveness of speakers in attracting voters), there can be a choice, and the decision almost always is dictated by convenience (number of potential participants available, time to test a single individual, source of participants).

When different groups are tested, it is essential that we have some level of assurance that before the introduction of the independent variable, they are equivalent on whatever response will be measured. This can be accomplished in two ways. One way is to randomly assign the participants to the groups. The other is to first match the participants and then randomly assign them to the various groups. The most popular technique of *random assignment* is through the use of a table of random numbers. After the numerical basis for group assignment has been established (e.g., 1-10 = Group A, 11-20 = Group B), participants are assigned numbers, numbers are read from the table, and participants with corresponding numbers are assigned to the various groups (e.g., a participant whose number is 14 is assigned to Group B). The method assures that no bias is associated with group assignment. Randomization, however, does not guarantee that groups will not differ on an important variable that might just as easily account for results. It just makes it more likely that they will not differ. And the smaller the size of each group, the more likely that even randomization will not control for the extraneous variables that have to be controlled. Thus, even if pretest scores reveal no differences, it could be due to low statistical power rather than to equivalence.

An alternative approach to random assignment is *matching*. This can take several forms but always has the same goal: to ensure that groups are equivalent with respect to the dependent variable before treatment (the independent variable) is introduced. The ideal procedure is to give a test to all participants. Then, one can match participant for participant on the basis of identical scores on the pretest. This procedure, however, involves testing a host of individuals to get enough pairs of identical scores. Or we might devise two groups whose means and variances are alike to yield two matched groups. This is accomplished by ranking all scores, matching on the basis of rank orders, and then randomly assigning to the two groups. Of course, the matching task must be related to the response that will be measured in the study.

If the same group of participants is tested, it is crucial that the levels of the independent variables be introduced in such a way that the results are not due to practice or fatigue. This is accomplished by *counterbalancing* the introductions such that one half of the group receives A followed by B and the other half receives B followed by A; each level appears equally often at each stage of practice.

Two-condition designs are useful for answering one of two questions: Does a particular treatment work? Which of two treatments is relatively more effective? The first question can be answered by testing an experimental group that receives treatment and a control group that receives *placebo treatment,* that is, treatment that contains elements of the independent variable without its crucial characteristic (e.g., a sugar pill that is imbibed, an injection of saline, a sham operative procedure, a group rap session). If there is no carryover effect of treatment, the same group could be tested, but this seldom is the case. The second question can be answered by testing two groups or the same group, depending on the nature of the independent variable.

From a statistical point of view, the precise test used to evaluate effectiveness of the independent variable depends on the dependent variable. If scores are at least part of an interval scale (e.g., scores on a standardized test) and are not terribly skewed, a t test is most appropriate. This involves determining the probability that a means difference of the magnitude obtained would be obtained if treatment were not effective. If that probability is $\leq .05$, the obtained difference is attributed to the treatment. The df is determined by $n_1 + n_2 - 2$. In the event that a t test is inappropriate (e.g., when distributions are very skewed or variances are very different—both of which are likely to wash out any differences that might

**BOX 9.1
Caution Factors
for Two-Condition
Studies**

- There was initial group equivalence by random assignment or matching.

- If groups were matched, the matching task was related to the dependent variable.

- If testing occurred on more than one occasion, there was no selective loss of participants.

- If a pretest-posttest design was used, nothing happened to one group that could affect performance (history).

- If a pretest-posttest design was used, one group did not change more than the other in a way that could affect performance (maturation).

- If a pretest-posttest design was used, the same instruments and testers were used.

- Participants were not selected because they were extreme scorers on a pretest (regression toward the mean).

- Performance on a posttest was not due to prior experience with a pretest (initial testing).

- Control participants could not learn about experimental treatment (diffusion of treatment; compensatory rivalry; resentful demoralization).

- Control treatment did not mimic experimental treatment (compensatory equalization).

- A threat to internal validity did not act selectively on one group (interaction effect).

- Tests used were reliable and valid.

- Testing was performed by someone who was naive with respect to purpose of the study.

- Testing was performed under uniform conditions.

- If a single group was used, conditions were counterbalanced.

xist and lead to a Type II error), a nonparametric test can be used (e.g., Mann-Whitney *U*-test, median test).

When evaluating a two-condition study, there are two important questions to keep in mind. First, is the group equivalence that existed at the beginning of the study maintained? If testing occurs on more than one occasion, there is the possibility that attrition results in a selective loss; that is, remaining participants in each of the conditions may constitute two groups that are no longer equivalent. Second, aside from the independent variable, is there any other variable that can just as easily account for differences in performance between the two conditions? Thus, caution still is required regarding similarity in testing conditions as well as testing by a naive experimenter. If there were pretests and posttests,

then other possible confounds include history, maturation, instrumentation, initial testing, regression toward the mean, diffusion of treatment, compensatory equalization, compensatory rivalry, resentful demoralization, and interaction effects. Finally, unless a study uses subhuman participants, there are ethical considerations that should be reported. (There are strict standards for the humane treatment of animals, as well.) All participants should have signed an informed consent slip, which also gives them the right to withdraw from the study at any time, without penalty. The list of caution factors, which is extensive, is found in Box 9.1.

We will evaluate two studies. I'll evaluate the first one with you, and you will do the second one.

STUDY EXAMPLE 9.1

This study is from the field of nursing and introduces instruction as the independent variable.

The Study

O'Neill, K. L., & Ross-Kerr, J. C. (1999). Impact of an instructional program on nurses' accuracy in capillary blood glucose monitoring. *Clinical Nursing Research, 8*(2), 166-178. Copyright 1999 by Sage.

The increasing level of responsibility assumed by nurses in a variety of practice settings inevitably raises questions of accuracy of performance of techniques. The sheer volume of procedures that nurses are expected to perform competently has risen dramatically over the past two decades, as has the challenge of mastering the full range of nursing techniques for a particular area of practice. . . . Nursing managers responsible for quality assurance must be attuned to the skills required of nurses, because new nursing skills emerge regularly from advances in treatment and care and because new skills are continually being transferred to nursing from other disciplines. Of concern are such issues as how to ensure that new and experienced nurses are competent in the performance of particular techniques and how to assist them to maintain their competence on an ongoing basis. . . .

The importance of practitioner competence in performing nursing procedures has long been recognized in schools of nursing and in staff development, and nursing educators have sought to assist nursing students and registered nurses to gain competence in performing an array of procedures. In nursing departments of hospitals and home care agencies, a process of credentialing using certification for designated procedures has been favored to ensure that nurses have received proper instruction and practice in learning to perform particular techniques. . . .

The inspiration for this research project emerged within the context of quality of practice and professional accountability in clinical nursing practice. The intent was to investigate the impact of an instructional program on the accuracy of performing a common nursing procedure in health agencies, that of visual readings of glucose oxidase strips to monitor capillary blood glucose levels [of patients with diabetes]. Even though the strips may be read accurately by passing them through a reflection meter, the expense of supplying these meters and maintaining their calibration for all areas of an agency where they are used may restrict their use to specialized or intensive care units. As a result, nurses in most agencies are expected to be able to skillfully perform visual readings of glucose oxidase strips.

Background of the Study

In an average 500-bed hospital, nurses can be expected to perform 400 to 500 glucose oxidase . . . procedures per week, the results of which form the basis of critical clinical decisions, including insulin dosage. . . . Although products vary, the procedure is based on the principle of a color change in a reagent strip containing glucose oxidase coupled to a chromosome, in response to the glucose in the capillary blood sample. . . .

Ease of carrying out the procedure, speed of results, and reliability established by comparing strip readings to laboratory findings have led to wide use of this method of capillary glucose monitoring by nurses at the bedside. . . . Studies of measuring capillary blood glucose using glucose oxidase strips have shown remarkable levels of accuracy in the presence of adequate education and frequent performance. . . . Specialized nurses and laboratory workers have shown consistently high correlation coefficients of .92 to .98 compared to reference laboratory values. . . .

The reliability of glucose monitoring by bedside nurses, when measured on a periodic basis, has been less than optimal. Two studies found accurate readings only 50% to 60% of the time when compared with concurrent laboratory findings. . . . Instructional programs have been shown to be associated with increased accuracy, and several studies have documented acceptable levels of accuracy as a result of ongoing educational programs. . . . Despite the frequent use of glucose oxidase strips, there are, however, continuing concerns about the accuracy of monitoring. Although prior to the development of this technology, . . . blood glucose monitory has been a function traditionally performed by laboratory staff. In many cases, nursing departments have assumed this function without the requisite quality control program that has been the hallmark of operating procedures in a laboratory setting.

Research Question

The primary research question in this study was to determine the impact of an instructional program on visual readings of glucose oxidase strips to monitor capillary glucose levels on the accuracy of such measurements by nurses employed on general medical units in a medium-size, urban, community general hospital. Other questions explored accuracy of performing glucose oxidase strip readings by nurses on the four medical units in the study hospital and the effect of the time lapse between the completion of the instructional program and the performance of the procedures on accuracy of performance of the technique.

---

1. What was the rationale for the study?

Nurses today have more responsibilities and require more skills, some of which have come from other disciplines. There is a need for assurance that new and experienced nurses are competent in performing these skills. Some nursing departments in hospitals and home care agencies require that nurses be certified to demonstrate their proficiency.

This study focused on quality of practice of a particular skill, visual reading of glucose oxidase strips to obtain a measure of capillary blood glucose. Meters are available but are limited in availability and require maintenance. Therefore, most readings are visual.

In a 500-bed hospital, nurses typically read 400 to 500 strips per week (for patients with diabetes). Accuracy is important because it determines insulin dosage. Specialized nurses are very accurate; bedside nurses are less accurate. Specialized training is beneficial, but the technique is not always rigorously taught.

> **2. What was the purpose of the study?**
>
> The primary purpose was to evaluate the effectiveness of an instructional program on visual reading of strips by nurses in general medical units of a hospital. Secondarily, accuracy of nurses on four medical units was assessed as well as the effect of time since training on accuracy.

Method

Design

This was an experimental study in which the unit of analysis was glucose oxidase strip readings performed by nurses who consented to participate and were randomly assigned to the experimental or control groups. The instructional program served as the independent variable, and the accuracy of performance as the dependent variable. In exploring the time lapse between instructional input and practice, the time period served as the independent variable, and accuracy of performance the dependent variable.

Sample

Eighty-four nurses employed on four general medical units of the study hospital initially consented to participate in the study and were randomly assigned to experimental and control groups. All patients hospitalized on these units who had an SMA-6 or laboratory blood glucose test ordered by their physician during the data collection period were asked to participate in the study and written consents were obtained from 110 patients, some of whom participated more than once.

▶ *(Note that nurses consented [as did patients] and that the groups were formed by random assignment.)*

Procedure

Each participating nurse was asked to complete two glucose oxidase procedures on patients with laboratory blood glucose or SMA-6 ordered and to notify the laboratory staff in advance that a concurrent glucose oxidase strip reading was to be done. The strip reading was carried out within 1 minute of the time the blood was drawn by the laboratory staff. Data forms with . . . nurse's code number, date, time, and strip reading result were completed by the nurses after each test and placed in a designated box on the unit. . . . The concurrent laboratory blood glucose values were marked on the data forms as soon as the results were obtained. Procedures were the same for nurses in the experimental and control groups, except that the nurses in the control group did not receive the educational program. At the conclusion of the 3-month data collection process, 36 nurses from the experimental group had performed a total of 70 glucose oxidase strip readings, whereas 34 nurses from the control group had performed 68 similar procedures. Six data sheets on procedures had to be discarded because of either incorrect timing or missing information, and four nurses withdrew from the study due to resignation or transfer.

▶ *(Note that the final N is 70 and that only 10 more of the original 84 are accounted for. Also, the instruction program is not described, nor is its length.)*

3. What was the general procedure?

Nurses were randomly assigned to experimental or control groups. When a blood test was required on a patient (who consented to take part in the study), two procedures were conducted. One strip was read by the nurse and the other by a trained technician. Each nurse filled out required forms for each reading and was given a code number. All completed forms were kept in a designated box. Experimental participants received instruction; control participants did not.

4. What was the final sample?

After a 3-month data collection period, 70 of the original 84 nurses completed the study. There were 36 in the experimental group and 34 in the control group; six data sheets had to be discarded, and four nurses withdrew. This leaves four unaccounted for.

5. What information is lacking?

Nothing is presented about the training procedure, number of nurses at each session, length per session, number of meetings, times of meetings, nor what control participants did at the time.

Reliability and Validity

Randomized assignment of nurses to experimental and control groups minimized the effects of history and maturation and such external factors as educational background, work experience, and exposure to previous educational orientation programs were assumed to be distributed equally across the groups. Thus, differences between groups could be attributed to the impact of the intervention.

▶ *(Note that this is not unequivocal because experimental participants may have received more attention during training. We don't know what control participants did. Moreover, although nothing more was said about the loss of participants, it was such a small number that selective loss is unlikely to be a factor.)*

Although 4 participants withdrew from the study, experimental mortality was not a significant factor. . . .

The accuracy and precision of the laboratory glucose test value was assured because of the well-established quality control program in the laboratory. . . .

Data Analysis

Data were analyzed using . . . *t* tests. . . . Results for the experimental and control groups were then compared on the basis of a one-tailed *t* test for independent samples. In analyzing the effect of the time interval between the instructional program and the performance of the test, an arbitrary period of 3 weeks was established. Results for the experimental group were subdivided to those readings that were done within the 3-week period beginning at the time of the instructional program and those performed outside the 3-week time frame. . . . Differences between the groups [were] compared on the basis of a one-tailed *t* test. Significance level for all statistical tests was established at $\alpha = .01$.

▶ *(Presumably, the instruction period lasted 3 weeks. Moreover, half the experimental readings were done during the time of instruction, and half were done after the 3-week period. But we don't know how much later, because data were collected over a 3- month period. Finally, because this was an evaluation study,* t *tests should have been two-tailed. The only saving grace is that alpha was .01, much more stringent than .05.)*

---

6. *Readings by experimental participants were divided into two groups: 35 readings made during the 3-week instructional period by one half the group and 35 made after the instructional period by the other half. What difficulty might this produce for the analysis of results?*

Time since training (recall period) had to be variable for the second group of nurses because the entire data collection period was 3 months. Increased variability could decrease the possibility of finding a significant difference, which in this case would be a favorable finding.

Results and Discussion

Effect of Educational Program on Reading Glucose Oxidase Strips on Accuracy of Performance

The primary research question in this investigation was whether an instructional program offered to nurses would result in more accurate performance of the technique or higher correspondence between visual glucose oxidase strip readings and laboratory blood glucose values. Results indicated that the percentage difference between the glucose oxidase strip and laboratory values in the experimental group was significantly lower than the same percentage difference in the control group. The t test used to compare the mean percentage differences for averaged Test 1 and Test 2 data for each of the experimental and control groups yielded $t(68) = 5.16$, a figure that was far above the critical value of 3.35 for a one-tailed probability of .01 (see Table 1). This confirmed that the experimental group was significantly more accurate than the control group in performing glucose oxidase strip readings using concurrent laboratory values as the standard. Because the groups were randomly assigned and because the only known difference between the groups was their exposure to the intervention, the difference between the groups was attributed to this intervention.

▶ *(Note that the results are significant with a two-tailed test at* p < .02.*)*

---

7. Look at Table 1. Is there any evidence of a practice effect for the control nurses?

Yes. On their first test, they averaged a 71.53% difference in accuracy between their readings and laboratory readings of the strips. By the second test, the average difference was reduced to 41.74%, a difference of 29.79% compared with a difference of 3.33% by the experimental nurses. Put another way, by the second test, the difference in accuracy between both groups was almost half of what it was for the first test.

8. Table 1 also shows that the values of t were virtually the same for both tests. What does this suggest about variability?

Because the difference in means was smaller for the second test (33.63 vs. 60.09), t could only be the same if variability were less. For the first test, 60.09/3.64 = 16.508; for the second test, 33.63/3.68 = 9.139.

TABLE 1 Differences Between Blood Glucose Monitoring Recordings Obtained by Nurses and Corresponding Laboratory Values for Experimental Control Groups

Variable	Number of Cases		Separate Mean	t Value	Degrees of Freedom
PD1	Group 1	36	11.44	3.64[a]	68
	Group 2	34	71.53		
PD2	Group 1	34	8.11	3.68[a]	66
	Group 2	34	41.74		
$PD_{\bar{x}}$ (mean of PD1 & PD2)	Group 1	35	9.87	5.16[a]	67
	Group 2	34	56.63		

NOTE: PD = Percentage difference between chemstrip recording and laboratory blood glucose recordings.
$PD_{\bar{x}}$ = mean of PD1 and PD2 for each of Groups 1 and 2.
a. $p < .01$ for a one-tailed test.

Effect of the Time Interval Following Completion of the Educational Program on Accuracy of Performance of Glucose Oxidase Strip Readings

The experimental group was further subdivided into two groups by the time lapse between the completion of the instructional program and the date of performing the capillary blood glucose strip reading. One subgroup included those who performed strip readings within 3 weeks of the instructional program, whereas the other included those recordings that were performed at a greater than 3-week time interval. The total number of recordings in the experimental group was 70, 35 of which were done within the 3-week time frame and 35 outside this interval. The groups were then compared to determine differences in accuracy of performance.

▷ *(Note that the data were divided into subgroups. No mention is made about the nurses other than that one group made the first 35 readings and the other group made the second 35 readings. If, by chance, the second group had better retentive ability than the first group, their accuracy could well match that of the group tested during training. If the subdivision had been made initially, with one group randomly assigned to test first and the second group to test later, this and other individual characteristics would be ruled out.)*

. . . . The one-tailed *t* test did not yield a significant difference between groups (see Table 2). This finding indicated that the length of the time interval between completion of the instructional program and performance of the test did not have a significant effect on accuracy of performance of the strip reading. Thus, the nurses retained considerable accuracy of their performance on the test when they did not have an opportunity to practice the technique for more than 3 and less than 6 weeks following completion of the instructional program. . . .

▷ *(Note that this time frame includes 9 weeks. If data were collected for 3 months, at least some of the control nurses were tested during this additional 3-week period.)*

---

9. What do the results in Table 2 indicate?

Visual readings were just as accurate within the 3-week training period as they were at least 3 weeks after training.

10. Can any factor other than no loss in retention account for the lack of differences?

Yes. Under the assumption that the two groups were not formed by random assignment, the second group may have been superior in ability to recall. The point is, if this is possible and roles of the nurses were reversed, the "second" group might have shown a loss in retention.

Accuracy of Glucose Oxidase Readings

Another purpose of the study was to determine the accuracy of glucose oxidase readings being done by nurses staffing the medical units of the study hospital. Percentage differences were calculated between the nurses' first and second glucose oxidase strip readings and the corresponding laboratory blood glucose values. For the first set of readings, the percentage difference values ranged from 1.83 to 363.33 ($\bar{X} = 71.53$) . . . $n = 34$. . . . Similar results were found for the second test completed by each of the 34 nurses in the control group. Here, percentage differences between the nurses' strip reading and the laboratory blood glucose value ranged from 1.14 to 236.36 ($\bar{X} = 41.75$). . . . Results indicate that the glucose oxidase strip readings by the nurses were highly unreliable as measured against the standard of the laboratory blood glucose value.

TABLE 2 Differences Between Blood Glucose Monitoring Recordings Obtained by Nurses and Corresponding Laboratory Values According to Time Lapse Between Instructional Program and Test Performance

Variable	Number of Cases		Separate Mean	t Value	Degrees of Freedom
Chemstrip value	Group 1	35	7.08	2.27	34
	Group 2	35	8.90		
Lab value	Group 1	35	7.19	1.98	34
	Group 2	35	9.07		
Difference between chemstrip and lab values	0-3 weeks	35	0.67	0.94	34
	3+ weeks	35	0.97		

NOTE: None of the differences are significant at the .01 level for a one-tailed test.

▶ *(Note that nothing is stated about the basis for selecting the 34 sets of readings. Moreover, the means were virtually identical to those of the control group.)*

Implications of Findings for Practice

Analysis of the control group data confirmed that the initial concerns about accuracy of nurses' performance of the glucose oxidase strip readings without adequate instructional support had been valid. . . .

Although retention of knowledge and skills learned in the educational program was maintained beyond a 3-week time interval in this study, . . . careful examination of study results revealed that there was some decline in accuracy of performance of the procedure in the subgroup when there was a longer time interval between completion of the program and performance of the test. Even though this difference was not a significant one, it does not seem particularly surprising that performance appeared to be enhanced by the presence of a relatively short time interval between theory and practice. . . .

Finally, the powerful impact of a well-designed and implemented instructional program on improving the accuracy of performance by nurses of visual capillary glucose strip readings has been demonstrated in this study.

11. What were the major conclusions reached by the authors?

First, the instructional program had a major impact in improving accuracy in reading glucose oxidase strips. Second, the effects of training were maintained for as long as 3 weeks after the program ended. Third, nurses in medical units cannot read the strips with any reasonable degree of accuracy.

12. Are the conclusions justified?

Despite the lack of crucial information regarding the nature of the training program and treatment of the control group (e.g., sham meetings without training would have been laudable), the first conclusion probably is tenable. Reading strips requires skills that could not be "picked up" even if a Hawthorne effect were operating. Nonetheless, the improvement shown in the control group by the second reading shows that aspects of the skill may be learned without formal training (and, presumably, without feedback).

The second conclusion may or may not be justified. If both experimental groups were equal with respect to their ability to profit from training and to retain the skills, then the conclusion is tenable. There is no basis, however, for assuming this equality, because we don't know why certain nurses were tested first.

Finally, the third conclusion would be justified if the 34 nurses' readings were randomly selected. Given the large ranges in accuracy, the sample does not appear to be biased. The extreme low ends of the ranges, however, also suggest that some nurses were skilled at reading strips.

13. To which population do these results generalize?

The results generalize to nurses in general hospitals in Alberta, Canada, (where the study took place) who have experiences comparable to those of the current sample of nurses.

STUDY EXAMPLE 9.2

This study, also from the field of nursing, is concerned with the effects of a special kind of exercise on various aspects of well-being of elderly individuals.

The Study

Ross, M. C., Bohannon, A. S., Dabis, D. C., & Gurchiek, L. (1999). The effects of a short-term exercise program on movement, pain, and mood in the elderly. *Journal of Holistic Nursing, 17*(2), 139-147. Copyright 1999 by Sage.

As the percentage of the U.S. population grows older, holistic interventions that prevent falls and their debilitating injuries are increasingly important. Many studies verify the age-related changes in the body that impair balance and strength as one grows older and thus place the elderly at an increased risk of falling. . . . Reduction of visual, ankle, and foot inputs results in a loss of balance for up to 50% of the elderly, in contrast to fewer than 10% of younger participants. . . . The elderly also experience a decline in muscle mass and strength. Therefore, it is imperative to identify interventions to lessen these physical changes in the elderly to prevent incidences of falls by them. Tai Chi is one such intervention that has been identified as a safe and appropriate exercise for the elderly.

Tai Chi is not a vigorous type of exercise and can be an excellent choice for the older adult who lacks physical conditioning or the self-confidence required by more traditional exercise programs. . . . It . . . has been used for centuries in China as an exercise among elderly citizens. It is practiced for agility, balance, posture control, and mind-body interactions. . . . Tai Chi consists of a series of slow, purposeful movements that involve turning, shifting one's weight from one leg to the other, bending and unbending the legs, and various arm movements. . . . Tai Chi also has been described as a combination of deep diaphragmatic breathing and relaxation with slow and gentle movements, isometric and isotonic, and maintenance of good posture. . . .

The positive effects of various forms of exercise, especially activities that include body scan techniques or focused breathing, have been thoroughly documented in mind-body studies. Mindfulness activities such as these have positive effects on mental state and physical health. . . .

The physical and psychological therapeutic effects of Tai Chi for the elderly have been the subject of several recent reports. . . . Tai Chi exercise may benefit the elderly, because the exercise incorporates elements of strengthening, balance, postural alignment, and concentration. All four of these factors are essential to prevent fall[s]. . . . Tai Chi focuses on postural alignment, muscle strengthening, and improves the elderly person's perception of body position in space.

Furthermore, inasmuch as the majority of falls occur when the elderly person is walking, turning, or climbing stairs, balance is essential. Tai Chi includes single-stance balance training, which improves coordination and may decrease the elderly individual's risk of falls. . . . For osteoarthritis and rheumatoid arthritis patients, Tai Chi has been shown to have significant effects on lessening pain and tenderness and improving joint flexibility. . . .

. . . Improvements in self-esteem, self-confidence, sleep, and depression have been seen as a result of participation in Tai Chi. . . . In studies . . . Tai Chi students were less anxious and depressed following only 12 weeks of training.

. . . As a safe and enjoyable program, Tai Chi may have timeless implications for the health of today's elderly.

The purpose of this research was to conduct a pilot study to evaluate the effect of a short-term Tai Chi program on flexibility, balance, sway, pain, and mood in the elderly.

Research Questions

The research questions for the study were,

1. Is there a difference in the degree of flexibility in the extremities of elderly persons after participating in a Tai Chi program?
2. Is there a difference in balance and sway in elderly persons after participating in a Tai Chi program?
3. Is there a difference in the amount of pain experienced, with active and passive range of motion of specific extremities of elderly persons, after participating in a Tai Chi program?
4. Is there a difference in the mood of elderly persons after participating in a Tai Chi program?

Method

Sample Characteristics

A convenience sample of 17 volunteers (2 males, 15 females) [aged 68 to 92 years], who were living independently in a public housing facility, participated in the study. Participants were solicited through written flyers and personal invitation delivered to their residences. All participants were screened to determine their physical acceptability for the study. Chronic illnesses, blood pressure, pulse, weight, respirations, medications, previous occupations, and current amount of routine exercise or activity were recorded, as a part of this screening. Those with any conditions, medications, or occupations that may have confounded the findings or may have presented a risk to the participant were eliminated. The participants were ambulatory and English-speaking. The sample included one Black and one Hispanic female. None of the participants reported current use of pain-relieving medication other than NSAIDS or acetaminophen. Those currently in occupational or physical therapy were excluded. Four participants were not included in the final results, because they did not attend at least 90% of the Tai Chi classes.

Procedure

Informed consent was provided verbally and in written form, according to the IRB protocol. The participants were interviewed and pretest baseline measures were taken in the following sequence:

1. A brief pencil-and-paper multifactor instrument, the Multiple Affect Adjective Check List Revised (MAACL-R), was completed by each participant, as a measure of mood. The MAACL-R consists of 132 adjectives describing feelings. . . . The MAACL-R provides valid and reliable data on five affects: anxiety, hostility, depression, positive affect, and sensation seeking. The MAACL-R is written at no higher than the 8th grade reading level. . . . The participants were asked to simply put an "X" by the words that described how they generally felt (trait form). The MAACL-R took approximately 5 minutes for the participants to complete. . . . The MAACL-R was hand-scored to provide a rating on the five scales. Numerous studies have established both validity and reliability of the MAACL-R with adults. . . .

2. A "sit and reach" test of flexibility was performed. The best effort of three attempts was recorded, in centimeters.

3. A single-stance balance test was accomplished. In this test, participants were instructed to lift one foot just off the floor, focus on a point on a nearby wall in front of them, and stand that way for 60 seconds. The test was terminated when the foot touched the ground, rested against the other leg, or the participants raised their arms for balance. Pretest marching in place was used to produce a more natural foot placement, in terms of food abduction and stance width. Research assistants stood on each side of the participants for safety. The single stance was timed by the use of a standard held-held stopwatch.

4. Sway was measured by the tandem walk (heel-to-toe walk). Participants were instructed to walk along a wide line for 15 steps without swaying off the line or grasping an attendant for balance. Each participant was given two trials. The score of his or her best performance on each test was then recorded. If the participant reached the goal of 60 seconds or 15 steps on the first trial, the second trial was not attempted.

5. Active range of motion of upper and lower extremities was performed by each participant, as an additional test of flexibility. A certified athletic trainer used a standard goniometer to measure range of motion, in degrees of flexion and extension of the elbow, shoulder, knee, and

hip. At the end of each range of motion activity, the participant was asked to rate the degree of discomfort, if any, on visual analog (0 to 10) scale.

Identical measures, techniques, and data collections were used at the end of the 8 weeks of the Tai Chi sessions. . . .

Each Tai Chi class was conducted by a certified and highly experienced Tai Chi instructor. The classes took place three times each week and included 10 minutes of preparation and wrap-up administrative time and 50 minutes of actual Tai Chi movements. Registered nurses were in attendance at all classes to observe participants for any distress.

Data Analysis

Pretest-posttest comparisons were made on all measures for the group and individual participants. Demographic data were examined for spurious findings; however, none were observed. Statistical comparisons, including frequencies and *t* tests, were used to determine statistical differences. . . .

Results

Because this was a pilot study with a very small sample, the results must be interpreted conservatively. Statistically significant improvements (*t* tests), at the .05 level, were found in posttest measures of pain (visual analog scale) and mood (MAACL-R). Mean pretest perceived pain was 1.5473 (*SD* = 2.279), and that for posttest was 0.6945 (*SD* = 1.165). The difference was significant, $t(10) = 2.35$, $p = .041$.

Composite scores on the MAACL-R demonstrated improvement, although individual subscale scores did not show a significant change. The mean pretest measure of mood was 1.0909 (*SD* = 1.300), and the mean posttest measure was 0.6364 (*SD* = 1.206). The difference was significant, $t(10) = 2.19$, $p = .053$.

Although not statistically significant, all participants had measurable improvements in flexibility (goniometer measurements), balance (single-leg stance), and sway (length of time walking a line). However, when pre- and posttest scores on each individual were compared, six participants had significant improvement ($p = .05$) in balance, sway, and flexibility.

By nature, a pilot study is used to test research methods that may be improved in a comprehensive study. The research team quickly found that the elderly participants needed frequent reminders and encouragement to attend the beginning classes, until the group developed some cohesiveness and skills in the Tai Chi movements. . . . Testing appointments for elderly partici-pants had to allow time for slow movement between testing areas, privacy for each test, and comfortable seating. Testing appointments prior to 10:00 A.M. were not selected by any of the participants, and food snacks after testing were well received.

Conclusions and Recommendations

This pilot study supports the use of Tai Chi as a safe, viable method of exer-cise for the elderly, that has some statistically significant health results. As such, Tai Chi is a good choice for senior activity centers and senior residential programs.

In this pilot study, positive changes in mood, pain perception, flexibility, balance, and sway were demonstrated with even a limited program of Tai Chi exercise in older adults. . . . Expanded studies should include larger samples of men and women and racial and ethnic diversity. Also recommended are stud-ies with an increase in the number of weeks of the Tai Chi classes. . . .

Tai Chi may be a safe, viable method of exercise for the elderly that has significant positive health results in four dimensions of human life—physical, emotional, mental, and spiritual. . . . Long-term studies of the effect of Tai Chi on the incidence of falls, depression, and analgesic use also may be important.

CRITIQUE OF STUDY EXAMPLE 9.2

1. What was the rationale for the study?

2. What was the purpose of the study?

3. What was the nature of the sample?

4. What demographic information, not given directly, can be surmised about the participants?

5. What was the general procedure?

6. What were some good features of the design?

7. What were some questionable features of the design?

8. How many sets of scores were included in the final analysis of results?

9. What were the findings regarding posttest pain and mood?

10. What were the findings regarding flexibility, sway, and balance?

11. What other reactions to the training sessions were noted?

12. What did the authors conclude on the basis of this pilot study?

13. What other variables could account for the results?

14. What group and design are essential to rule out these confounds?

    For answers to these questions, see page 340.

BIBLIOGRAPHY

Isaac, S., & Michael, W. B. (1995). *Handbook in research and evaluation: A collection of principles, methods, and strategies useful in the planning, design, and evaluation of studies in education and the behavioral sciences* (3rd ed.). San Diego, CA: EdITS.

Lehman, R. S. (1991). *Statistics and research design in the behavioral sciences.* Belmont, CA: Wadsworth.

McMillan, J. H., & Schumacher, S. (1997). *Research in education: A conceptual introduction* (4th ed.). White Plains, NY: Longman.

Neal, J. M., & Liebert, R. M (1986). *Science and behavior: An introduction to methods of research* (3rd ed.). Englewood Cliffs, NJ: Prentice Hall.

Additional Suggested Readings

Ary, D., Jacobs, L. C., & Razavieh, A. (1996). *Introduction to research in education* (5th ed.). Orlando, FL: Harcourt Brace.

Best, J. W., & Kahn, J. V. (1998). *Research in education* (8th ed.). Boston: Allyn & Bacon.

Harris, M. B. (1995). *Basic statistics for behavioral science research.* Boston: Allyn & Bacon.

Chapter 10

Single Classification Studies

The two-groups or two-conditions situations are limited. They inform you about whether or not a qualitative independent variable works or which of two effective treatments is more effective. If more than one level of the independent variable is introduced, then additional questions can be answered about relative effectiveness of each level. Because the treatment is classified in only one way, we call these *single classification* studies. At a minimum, three levels can be studied. They can be two different therapies versus a control condition or two different drugs versus a control, or even three different therapies or drugs. (If effectiveness of each has been established and relative effectiveness is being investigated, a control condition may not be necessary.) If the summary data are means, the type of analysis depends on whether separate groups have been tested at each level or the same group was tested at each level. Keep in mind that we are dealing with qualitative (distinct, noncontinuous) variables. When independent variables are quantitative (continuous, such as levels of anxiety), data are analyzed by multiple regression.

When separate groups are tested, participants are randomly assigned to the different levels of the independent variable. By this procedure, we have some assurance that, before treatment, participants at each level initially are equivalent on the dependent variable and other characteristics related to it. Therefore, differences in performance after treatment can be attributed to the independent variable. If no mention is made about random assignment, nonequivalence among groups looms as a possible confound. (Another procedure, used with small ns, is to match the participants on the dependent variable, or on one related to it, and then assign the conditions to the matched groups.) Likewise, if testing occurs on more than one occasion, you need assurance that any loss of participants is not a selective loss. Furthermore, testing conditions should be uniform, experimenters should be naive regarding the purpose of the experiment, and the measuring instrument should be reliable and valid.

Final performance measures generally are summarized by means and standard deviations (or variances). To detect differences among the groups, an overall test first is performed to determine whether any differences exist among the means. The validity of the test rests on three assumptions. First, all scores within and between groups are independent of each other. This assumption is met if no bias is associated with group assignment. Second, scores within each group are assumed to be normally distributed or at least symmetrically distributed if ns are equal and reasonably large (i.e., at least 12). Third, variances within each group are assumed to be equal. Whereas the normality assumption can be handled by adopting a stringent level of significance (e.g., .01 instead of .05) if it is violated, violation of the last assumption is more serious, because it can lead to a Type I or Type II error. Authors should report whether a test for homogeneity of variance was made (or you can get some idea by looking at the reported values) and whether data were transformed to reduce heterogeneity (if they are not homogeneous) before the statistical test was performed.

The test is *analysis of variance* (ANOVA), and it indicates the extent to which all possible differences among the means (between-group variance) exceed what is expected on the basis of random error or individual variations in performances (within-group variance). If treatment has no effect, between-group variance will reflect random error, within-group variance will reflect random error, and a ratio of between-group variance/within-group variance will be about 1.00. The ratio is F, and it has associated with it $J - 1$ df for the numerator (with J = number of different groups or treatment levels) and $N - J$ df for the denominator (error, with N = total number of participants). If the F ratio is significantly greater than what

is expected if all groups had been drawn from the same population (i.e., treatment had no effect), it indicates that at least the two extreme means differ. Note that calculation of an F ratio is so straightforward (all you need are the group means, standard deviations, and n/group) that any statement about F can be checked.

Specific questions about which means differ (i.e., which treatment is more effective than another) are answered by *post hoc analyses,* analyses performed after a significant F has been found. (Sometimes, on the basis of some theory or special interest, the researcher initially plans to make certain comparisons among the means. That is, the researcher is not conducting an exploratory study; he or she is not interested in establishing whether all possible mean differences are significant. In this case, ANOVA is not performed; *planned comparisons* are performed. In effect, F ratios are formed but only for those means of interest.) The danger in simply performing each comparison between means is an increase in the risk of committing a Type I error: declaring a mean difference to be significant when treatment was not differentially effective. Of concern is the *familywise* Type I error, the probability of making one or more such errors in a set of comparisons between means. The more comparisons (especially with $\alpha = .05$), the greater the probability that at least one difference will be declared significant erroneously. Several methods reduce the overall probability (i.e., familywise error) of committing the Type I error. The most conservative, the *Scheffé test,* allows for as many comparisons between means as the researcher wants. That is, in addition to making comparisons between pairs of means, the researcher might want to compare, say, two treatment means versus a control mean. This type of comparison is not possible with any

([$J - 1$] times the omnibus F tabled value), which makes it more difficult to declare a difference significant. This is why the test is considered conservative. Remaining tests are less conservative (e.g., Tukey, Newman-Kuels, Dunnett). Of these, the *Tukey test* is the most popular, and it is reasonably conservative in guarding against the Type I error. *Newman-Kuels* is very similar but less conservative; *Dunnett* is for treatment versus control mean comparisons. The Tukey test controls for a familywise Type I error by testing each statistic against the most conservative tabled value. The studentized range statistic is computed by dividing the difference between two means by error: $\sqrt{MS_e/n}$, where MS_e is the error term of the original ANOVA. Should the ns in each group be unequal but highly similar, one can use the harmonic n: [J]/[$1/n_1 + 1/n_2 + \ldots + 1/n_J$]. The final statistic is compared with the tabled value for J (number of group means) and df of the error term from the original analysis of variance.

When the same group is tested at all levels of the independent variable, we have a within-group design. Because the same group is tested repeatedly, the levels have to be introduced in a counterbalanced order to rule out, as possible explanations of the results, the effects of practice, fatigue, and carryover. Without counterbalancing, any improvement in performance or increased positive effect with each progressive treatment level could just as easily be attributed to more practice in performing a particular task as to the effect of treatment; any decline in performance could just as easily be attributed to fatigue as to a less effective treatment; and any increase or decrease with each progressive treatment level could just as easily be attributed to positive benefits or an interfering effect of having served in prior conditions as to the positive or negative effect of the treatment per se. The *counterbalancing* procedure requires that each level appears at each stage of practice an equal number of times. Moreover, each level must precede and follow all other levels an equal number of times. By these means, practice, fatigue, and carryover effects are not eliminated; they are neutralized. The means of, say, levels A, B, and C will contain performances when A was presented first, second, and third, and the same is true of means for B and C. If there are still differences, they are not due to practice, fatigue, or carryover effects. That is all that counterbalancing controls, order effects. Please note that any study that uses multiple (standardized) tests must meet the same requirements; the tests, too, must be administered in counterbalanced order.

Data emanating from a within-group design are analyzed by ANOVA for repeated measures. Statistically, this is a much more powerful design—more likely to reveal means differences—because two sources of variance can be isolated from random variability in addition to variability due to the independent variable, namely, variability due to the participants and variability due to the interaction between the effects of treatment and the participants. The latter serves as the error term in the analysis. This results in a smaller error term than would be true if separate groups had been used. However, there is a statistical assumption whose violation can result in a Type I error: *circularity*. If all differences between all possible pairs of scores (e.g., $A - B$, $A - C$, $B - C$) are determined and variances computed of these differences, we have, here, three variances of differences. The circularity assumption is that all variances are the same. If they differ, it indicates that the effect of going from, say, A level to B level is not the same as the effect of going from, say, A level to C level or from

BOX 10.1
Caution Factors for Single Classification Studies

Between-Groups Studies

- Participants were randomly assigned, or matched groups were randomly assigned to the levels.

- Tests were reliable and valid.

- Multiple tests were presented in counterbalanced order.

- Testing conditions were uniform.

- Tester was naive with respect to study's purpose.

- There was no selective loss of participants if testing occurred on more than one occasion.

- If pretested, participants' posttest performance was not due to history, maturation, initial testing, instrumentation, or control group's knowledge of experimental treatment.

- Statistical tests ensured normal distribution of scores and homogeneity of variance.

- Post hoc tests controlled familywise Type I error.

Within-Group Studies

- Participants were randomly selected or no bias was associated with their selection.

- Levels of treatment were presented in counterbalanced order.

- There was no selective loss of participants.

- Tests were reliable and valid.

- Testing conditions were uniform.

- Tester was naive with respect to purpose of study.

- Statistical test ensured that the circularity assumption is tenable or adjusted degrees of freedom were used if it was not tenable.

B level to C level. The net result is that the calculated F ratio may be inflated and result in a Type I error. This is counteracted by reducing the degrees of freedom used to determine whether F is significant. Usually, $df = (J - 1)$ for the numerator and $(J - 1)(S - 1)$ (S = number of participants) for the denominator. If no mention is made about circularity, and especially if F is declared significant at $p < .05$, you can perform a check to determine whether the declaration is valid. Reduce the df to $[1/(J - 1)] \times (J - 1) = 1$ and to $[1/(J - 1)] \times (J - 1)(S - 1) = S - 1$. If F still is significant (check an F table),

then the conclusion is valid. If F is not significant, then the conclusion *may not be* valid. The emphasis is on *may not be* because these reductions in dfs are the maximum. In reality, the adjusted appropriate dfs would be somewhere between $(J - 1)$ and 1 for the numerator and somewhere between $(J - 1)(S - 1)$ and $S - 1$ for error.

A summary of caution factors for single classification studies is found in Box 10.1.

We'll review one study together, with independent groups, and you'll evaluate a study that used the same participants.

STUDY EXAMPLE 10.1: INDEPENDENT GROUPS

This first study involves the use of three independent groups that participated in a study dealing with training to make diabetic patients aware of their blood glucose levels. Terms that might not be familiar to you are hyperglycemia (high blood glucose), hypoglycemia (low blood glucose), and glycosylated hemoglobin. The latter refers to a measure of glucose that becomes attached to hemoglobin in the blood and is an indication of relative blood glucose control over a period of about 2 months. You will be asked to perform F tests on the data as well as post hoc analyses using the Tukey test.

The Study

Cox, D. J., Gonder-Frederick, L., Julian, D. M., & Clarke, W. (1994). **Long-term follow-up evaluation of blood glucose awareness training.** *Diabetes Care, 17*(1), 1-5. Used with permission of the American Diabetes Association.

Blood glucose awareness training (BGAT) is a patient education procedure designed to teach insulin-requiring diabetic patients to more accurately estimate their general blood glucose (BG) levels and specifically detect hypoglycemia. BGAT involves teaching patients how to identify symptoms sensitive and specific to their hypoglycemia and hyperglycemia. Additionally, it teaches patients how to accurately interpret information concerning types, amounts, and timing of insulin, food, and exercise to better anticipate extreme BG levels. BGAT typically requires seven weekly classes, reading the training manual, and daily homework exercises designed to apply and personalize the material presented in a particular chapter of the manual. Numerous studies have now demonstrated, in the short term, that BGAT is effective in improving patients' ability to estimate their BG levels and glycosylated hemoglobin.

Maintenance of such gains is critical in evaluating the cost-effectiveness of BGAT. No studies to date have evaluated the long-term benefits of BGAT. With the growing concern about the increased incidence of hypoglycemia with attempts to normalize BG it is especially important to know whether BGAT leads to greater awareness of hypoglycemia and fewer severe hypoglycemic episodes in the long term.

---

1. What was the rationale for the study?

Blood glucose awareness training sensitizes patients to become aware of shifts in their blood glucose levels, especially hypoglycemia. Although short-term benefits of training have been demonstrated, long-term benefits have not been studied.

This study followed up subjects who had participated in BGAT and control subjects from our previous studies. At follow-up, half ($n = 14$) of the BGAT subjects received a brief booster-training program intended to review BGAT procedures. The general question addressed was: Are BGAT participants better off at long-term follow-up compared with baseline or control subjects? The specific hypotheses tested were 1) at long-term follow-up, BGAT subjects in general would be more accurate at estimating their BG levels and more aware of their hypoglycemia in particular; 2) BGAT subjects would have fewer negative consequences caused by severe hypoglycemic episodes, as defined by lost work days and fewer automobile crashes; 3) BGAT subjects would maintain their improved glycosylated hemoglobin; and 4) a brief booster-training program would enhance overall accuracy of BG estimation and, specifically, sensitivity to hypoglycemia.

---

2. What was the purpose of the study?

To conduct a follow-up study on patients who were trained earlier; half were given booster training, and both groups were compared with a control group. Four hypotheses were tested regarding the benefits of training in estimating blood glucose, detecting hypoglycemia, preventing accidents, and maintaining glucose levels.

	Control Group	BGAT Group	BGAT Plus Booster
TABLE 1 Subject Characteristics for the Three Groups			
Final *n*	13	14	14
Age (years)	41.1 ± 3.1	40.3 ± 3.2	47.2 ± 4.3
Duration of disease (years)	17.6 ± 4.0	14.2 ± 1.8	17.1 ± 2.8
Follow-up (months)	47.0 ± 5.3	51.2 ± 3.6	55.5 ± 4.0

NOTE: Data are means ± *SD*. BGAT = blood glucose awareness training.
(According to the first author [personal communication], what are reported as *SD*s were, in fact, *SE*s [standard errors]. Analyses using *SD*s revealed no differences in participant characteristics, as reported.)

Research Design and Methods

We were able to locate 52 of 64 subjects from two previous studies, 41 of whom were able and willing to participate.

▶ *(Note that 11 refused or were unable to participate. Therefore, a selection factor may be operating—for example, those 41 were most motivated.)*

Twenty-eight of these subjects had undergone BGAT and 13 were past control subjects. Table 1 lists subject characteristics. No significant differences existed between groups on any of these variables. Incentives to participate included a free glycosylated hemoglobin determination and a $75 payment at the conclusion of data collection.

▶ *(The procedure for measuring glycosylated hemoglobin is expensive. Note that the two previous studies were conducted at two different times [probably 1987 and 1990] and that [according to the references] one involved standard versus intensive BGAT. We don't know which training the present participants had received. Moreover, the months since follow-up differ for the three groups. In fact, the F ratio can be calculated from the three means and standard deviations. It is 12.98, p < .01, and a Tukey test reveals that all 3 months since follow-up differ. This suggests that control participants may have been from one study and that the two experimental groups from the two studies may not have been randomly assigned to the two training conditions. Therefore, group nonequivalence should be kept in mind as a potential confound. This is bolstered by the fact that if you calculate F ratios on age and duration, they, too, are significant.)*

3. *Who served as participants?*

They included 41 out of 52 participants located from two previous studies.

4. *The authors' claim that the three groups did not differ significantly on participant characteristics can be checked. Using definitional formulas*

$(MS_b = \Sigma n_j[M_j - M_g]^2/df$ *and* $MS_e = \Sigma[n_j - 1\{SD\}]^2/df),$
calculate F *ratios for age, duration, and follow-up times.*

Age: $M_g = [13(41.1) + 14(40.3) + 14(47.2)]/41 = 42.91$
$MS_b = [13(41.1 - 42.91)^2 + 14(40.3 - 42.91)^2 + 14$
$(47.2 - 42.91)^2 = 395.616/2 = 197.808$
$MS_e = [12(3.1)^2 + 13(3.2)^2 + 13(4.3)^2]/41 - 3 = 488.81/38 =$
12.863
$F = 197.808/12.863 = 15.378, df = 2, 38, p < .01$

Duration: $M_g = [13(17.6) + 14(14.2) + 14(17.1)]/41 = 16.27$
$MS_b = [13(17.6 - 16.27)^2 + \ldots + 14(17.1 - 16.27)^2]/2 =$
46.31
$MS_e = [12(4)^2 + 13(1.8)^2 + 13(2.8)^2]/38 = 8.843$
$F = 46.31/8.843 = 5.237, df = 2, 38, p < .01$

Follow-up: $M_g = [13(47) + 14(51.2) + 14(55.5)]/41 = 51.34$
$MS_b = [13(47 - 51.34)^2 + \ldots + 14(55.5 - 51.34)^2]/2 =$
243.708
$MS_e = [12(5.3)^2 + 13(3.6)^2 + 13(4)^2]/38 = 18.778$
$F = 243.708/18.778 = 12.978, df = 2, 38, p < .01$

5. *Perform the Tukey test on the mean ages. What can you conclude?*

Harmonic $n = 3/[1/13 + 1/14 + 1/14] = 13.65$
Error $= \sqrt{12.863/13.65} = 0.9707$
$[47.2 - 41.1]/0.9707 = 6.284, p < .01$
$[47.2 - 40.3]/0.9707 = 7.108, p < .01$
$[41.1 - 40.3]/0.9707 = 0.824$

The group given booster training was older than the remaining two groups.

6. **Perform the Tukey test on duration means. What can you conclude?**

Error $= \sqrt{8.843/13.65} = 0.8049$

$[17.6 - 17.1]/0.8049 = 0.621$

$[17.6 - 14.2]/0.8049 = 4.224, p < .05$

$[17.1 - 14.2]/0.8049 = 3.603, p < .05$

The BGAT group had diabetes for fewer years than the remaining two groups.

7. **Perform the Tukey test on the time since follow-up. What can you conclude?**

Error $= \sqrt{18.778/13.65} = 1.1729$

$[55.5 - 51.2]/1.1729 = 3.666, p < .05$

$[55.5 - 47.0]/1.1729 = 7.247, p < .01$

$[51.2 - 47.0]/1.1729 = 3.581, p < .05$

The control group was retested after a fewer number of months than the two experimental groups. And the standard training group was retested after a fewer number of months than the group given booster training.

At an introductory meeting, subjects signed an informed consent, completed a questionnaire concerning past experiences with hypoglycemia and driving, and had blood drawn for glycosylated hemoglobin analysis.

Past BGAT subjects were matched on posttreatment BG estimation accuracy and months of follow-up and then randomly assigned to either BGAT or BGAT plus booster training.

▶ *(Note that if matching on follow-up time had been successful, those two times would not have differed. But they do.)*

Before use of the hand-held computer, BGAT plus booster subjects were given a 2-week diary. This diary was similar to those used in BGAT. Each time booster subjects measured their BG, they recorded in the diary any BG-relevant symptoms and relevant information about insulin, food, and/or exercise; estimated and recorded their BG; measured and logged their actual BG; and plotted their estimated-actual BG readings on an error grid. . . . Plotting the actual-estimated BG provided booster subjects feedback on the types of estimation errors being made . . . such as whether they were systematically overestimating their low BGs and/or underestimating their high BGs. After 2 weeks of completing diaries, booster subjects were given hand-held computers to collect follow-up data.

▶ *(Note that nothing is said about the BGAT group's activity during the 2 weeks. Either they were tested during those 2 weeks—so that testing times varied—or waited 2 weeks so that testing for all groups occurred at the same time.)*

All subjects . . . were instructed to use the computer-BG monitoring during routine measurements and whenever they thought their BG was either low or high. Each computer trial required subjects to enter their BG estimates, rate a variety of perceived autonomic and neuroglycopenic symptoms on a 0 = *none* to 6 = *extreme* scale, and measure and enter their actual BG results. Subjects were instructed to make a minimum of 50 such entries or continue until they had at least 10 actual BGs < 3.9 mM to a maximum of 80 entries. This was accomplished during the subjects' daily routine over a 3- to 4-week interval. . . .

The computer tracked date and time of each entry and elapsed time between the computer's prompt to measure BG and the subjects' entry of their actual BG measurement. This allowed a check for compliance by examining whether at least 60 s elapsed between the prompt to measure BG and entry of actual BG. Because it requires at least 1 min to lance the finger, secure a blood sample, and get a BG reading, any BG readings entered in < 60 s were considered unreliable and dropped from analysis. . . . Based on this compliance check, we dropped 5 subjects' hand-held computer data from analysis because they consistently entered actual BG values immediately after instructions to measure BGT. This resulted in the elimination of hand-held computer data from 2 subjects each in the control and BGAT groups and from 1 subject in the booster group.

---

8. What was the general procedure?

Participants first completed questionnaires regarding driving accidents and hypoglycemia occurrences. Experimental participants were matched on posttreatment BG and time since posttreatment and randomly assigned to BGAT or booster BGAT. The latter filled in a diary for 2 weeks regarding shifts in BG, as well as estimated and actual levels and factors related to BG (insulin, exercise, etc.). They plotted actual and estimated BG to detect errors—over- or underestimations. All experimental participants used a handheld computer to record a minimum of 50 or maximum of 80 BG episodes. They entered estimated and actual BG and rated physiological responses. Five participants were eliminated for inaccurate use of the computer (noncompliance).

> **9. What nonexperimental factors may have differentiated the two experimental groups?**
>
> BGAT group may not have been accurately matched with the booster group on time since last participation. And, the BGAT group either started earlier than the booster group or "did nothing" for 2 weeks while booster training occurred.

Data Analysis

The accuracy index is a general index of BG estimation accuracy . . . derived by calculating the percentage of accurate estimates (those within 20% of the measured BG or those estimates and actual BG readings, both < 3.9 mM) and subtracting the number of dangerously erroneous estimates (failure to recognize either hypoglycemia or hyperglycemia).

A univariate analysis of variance (ANOVA) was performed comparing only the three groups' follow-up accuracy index because of the inequity between pre- and posttreatment data and follow-up data. . . .

Because our booster training occurred for only a 2-week period just before data collection, it did not have an impact on long-term variables, such as automobile crashes, lost work days, or glycosylated hemoglobin. Consequently, booster and nonbooster BGAT subjects were collapsed in comparison with control subjects for such variables. Additionally, although subjects whose hand-held computer data were unreliable were not analyzed for accuracy of BG estimation, these subjects were included when analyzing glycosylated hemoglobin and automobile crashes.

Results

Effects of BGAT and Booster Training on BG Estimation Accuracy

A univariate ANOVA on the accuracy indexes for BGAT plus booster, BGAT, and control subjects (39, 30, and 26%, respectively) yielded significant results ($F = 7.02$, $p < .001$). Planned contrasts indicated that BGAT plus booster subjects were superior to both BGAT ($t = 2.49$, $p = .01$) and control ($t = 3.64$, $p = .000$) subjects. BGAT subjects exhibited a trend toward superior estimation of their BG levels compared with control subjects ($t = 1.13$, $p = 0.10$).

▶ *(Note that use of planned comparisons does not require an overall F test. Additional analyses require post hoc tests, which are more conservative. And for the more sophisticated, the comparisons were nonorthogonal, which are more prone to a Type I error if adjustments in alpha are not made.)*

Of specific interest was whether BGAT improves subjects' ability to detect hypoglycemia over the long term. The percentage of low BGs (< 2.8 mM) detected by BGAT plus booster, BGAT, and control subjects was 85, 50, and 43%, respectively. Overall, this was significant ($F = 4.29$, $p < .02$), with BGAT plus booster better than either BGAT ($p < .02$) or control subjects ($p < .01$). . . . This would suggest that, although a trend exists for the original BGAT subjects to be better at estimating their BG levels, subjects who received BGAT with booster training were more accurate in general and specifically more aware of their hypoglycemia.

---

10. What did the significant F = 7.02 indicate?

There was at least one difference in accuracy in estimating BG among the three groups.

11. What were the results of the planned comparisons?

Members of the booster group were more accurate than the remaining two groups in estimating their BG levels. The BGAT group was not more accurate than the controls.

12. What two factors might account for lack of difference in accuracy between the BGAT group and the control group?

First, the control group had diabetes for a longer period of time and may have been more sensitive to BG levels because of experience. Second, the BGAT group had a longer time span between posttreatment and follow-up than the control group and may have forgotten some of the original training.

13. What were the essential results regarding percentage of times that low BG was detected?

The booster group was more successful than the remaining two groups, which did not differ from each other.

Ancillary Long-Term Effects of BGAT

Although BGAT did not lead to fewer self-reported lost work days, BGAT was associated with significantly fewer automobile crashes. Respective crash rates per 1,000,000 miles driven were 6.8 vs. 29.8 ($U = 77.5$, $p = 0.01$).

> *(Note that U is the statistic for a Mann-Whitney test between two groups whose scores are not normally distributed. As such, it is one of the most popular nonparametric tests.)*

Of the control subjects who drove (one subject did not drive), 42% had at least one automobile crash during follow-up. In contrast, only 15% of our BGAT subjects who drove had accidents. One subject in each group had two accidents. The remaining subjects in both groups had only a single accident during follow-up. The mean number of months between the last group treatment session and accidents, for those subjects who had accidents, was 14.0 months for control subjects and 28.3 months for BGAT subjects ($t = 1.02$, $p = 0.13$).

---

14. *What were the general results regarding automobile accidents?*

BGAT groups had fewer accidents—and suggestively after a longer period of time since training—than control participants.

Conclusions

Although BGAT was not originally designed to produce long-term effects, these data indicate that BGAT led to sustained improvement in glycosylated hemoglobin and fewer automobile accidents. BGAT plus a low effort booster training led to greater general accuracy in estimating BG and detecting hypoglycemia in particular. Although improved metabolic control is important, it was not unique to BGAT. Our control subjects, who participated in general diabetes education classes, also showed a sustained metabolic improvement. This would suggest that both group programs were effective in sustaining improved self-care behaviors. However, because we did not have a no-treatment control group, we cannot rule out the possibility that the simple passage of time was responsible for this improvement.

One of the more interesting findings of this study is that BGAT may lead to fewer automobile accidents. . . . Our current data suggest that the effect of BGAT is to increase awareness of when not to drive. The potential of such an effect might be made more robust if periodic booster training were provided.

---

15. *What were the major conclusions?*

BGAT led to long-term improvement in estimating BG and in detecting hypoglycemia—as well as in fewer car accidents.

> **16. Are the conclusions valid? That is, are differences due to training?**
>
> Not necessarily. First, no differences in accuracy or in detecting hypoglycemia were found between BGAT and control groups and can be attributed to more years of experience of the latter and forgetting on the part of the former. Moreover, the booster plus training group was older and had diabetes longer than the BGAT group. These factors could have contributed to superior performance. Finally, because of apparent nonrandom assignment of participants to control and experimental groups, automobile accidents may be unrelated to training (i.e., due to individual factors).
>
> **17. From a practical point of view, if you had to provide advice to newly diagnosed diabetic patients regarding awareness training, what would it be?**
>
> On the basis of the results of this study and because of possible confounds, the best advice would be to undergo BGAT, followed by periodic booster training sessions (i.e., training is probably better than nothing).

▶ *(As a footnote, please note that the author's report of wrong data placed in Table 1 illustrates the value of contacting authors when issues are really important to you and you have some doubts.)*

STUDY EXAMPLE 10.2: WITHIN GROUPS

This experiment represents the simplest instance of a within-subjects design: Three measures of behavior are made on the same group of participants. In this study, the independent variable was the use of music as a potential therapy for reducing anxiety and dyspnea in patients with lung disease. The effects were measured over a period of time. Therefore, the usual confounding variable of order effect did not have to be considered.

Analysis of the data depends on the number of levels of the independent variable. With more than two levels, data can be analyzed by a trend analysis if the independent variable is time, trials, or different magnitudes (e.g., drug dosage, amount of reinforcement, etc.). For other types of independent variables, ANOVA for repeated measures is appropriate. Another alternative, especially when circularity (sphericity) is grossly violated, is to perform a multivariate analysis of variance, which detects whether participants differed in their pattern of responses to the different levels of the independent variable. The study we are about to review did not anticipate a steady decline in anxiety or dyspnea as a function of time; therefore, analysis of variance for repeated measures was appropriate.

The Study

McBride, S., Graydon, J., Sidani, S., & Hall, L. (1999). The therapeutic use of music for dyspnea and anxiety in patients with COPD who live at home. *Journal of Holistic Nursing, 17*(3), 229-250. Copyright 1999 by Sage.

Chronic obstructive pulmonary disease (COPD) is a debilitating disorder that is frequently characterized by dyspnea [difficult or labored breathing]. The mechanisms underlying the experience of dyspnea are not clearly understood. . . . Because there are no medications specifically designed for dyspnea relief . . . other methods for patients to reduce dyspnea need to be examined. . . .

There have been relatively few studies examining interventions aimed directly at the relief of dyspnea. . . . There is, however, evidence of a direct association between dyspnea and anxiety. . . . Music, as an alternate therapy, is hypothesized to provide some relief due to its anxiolytic and relaxation effect. However, most of the studies examining the effect of music have taken place in a controlled setting. The purpose of this article is to report on a pilot study that examined the use of music and its effect on anxiety and dyspnea in patients with COPD who were living at home. . . . Most of the previous studies took place . . . often with a one-time testing period. . . . In addition, the effect of music was examined over time.

Literature Review

Dyspnea

There is evidence of a direct relationship between dyspnea and anxiety . . . that suggests that if one were reduced, the other also might lessen. . . . Studies showing within-participant variation in levels of anxiety directly related to levels of dyspnea, indicate that interventions directed toward reducing anxiety may have an impact on patients' levels of dyspnea.

Music

. . . Music first was used as a therapeutic intervention in the 1800s. . . .
The use of music to promote relaxation, reduce anxiety, and reduce pain is more in keeping with clinical interventions with specific patient

populations. However, it is only fairly recently that attempts have been made to test the effectiveness of music in a clinical setting. . . .

There are obvious discrepancies in the effectiveness of music in reducing anxiety, promoting relaxation, or controlling pain that have been reported in the literature. Some of these differences may be attributed to methodological issues, such as the timing and duration of the intervention. Generally, the sample sizes were small and were not supported by power analysis. This might have contributed to Type II errors. As well, opportunity to select the music and type of music varied with the studies.

Although these studies contributed to the examination and description of the therapeutic effects of music on psychological and physiological outcomes, they were, for the most part, under controlled experimental conditions. Investigations were implemented in laboratory settings or in patients' rooms. Thus, generalization of findings to community or home settings is not possible. In addition, . . . only the short-term effects of listening to music were examined.

Several factors have been identified as important to consider when selecting music as an intervention to promote relaxation, reduce anxiety, or both. These include pitch and tempo . . . type of music . . . personal preference . . . and sensitivity to music in general. . . .

. . . Music with characteristics of slow tempo of 60 to 72 beats per minute . . . and self-selected . . . has been reported to create a sense of relaxation in the individual. In the present study, this type of music has the potential to interrupt the dyspnea-anxiety cycle to promote relaxation and reduced dyspnea.

Objectives of the Study

The specific objectives addressed in this study are

1. To examine the feasibility of using music as a therapeutic intervention for dyspnea and anxiety in patients with COPD who live in their own homes.
2. To examine the effect of music on the perception of anxiety and dyspnea in patients with COPD who live in their own homes.

Method

Design

A mixed quantitative and qualitative design was used in this study. The quantitative aspect of the design consisted of a repeated measures, single-group design that was used to evaluate the effects of music on patients' perceived dyspnea and anxiety. The patients were followed over a period of 5 weeks. Measures of dyspnea and anxiety were taken (a) at baseline, during the first week (Time 1); (b) during the second week, before and after the patients listened to the 20-minute music tape (the scores on dyspnea and anxiety obtained prior to listening to music were considered as second baseline measures within the repeated measures design) (Time 2); and (c) on the fifth week (Time 3). The posttest scores on anxiety and dyspnea from Time 2 and the final individual scores of anxiety and dyspnea on the fifth week (Time 3) represented the posttest measures of the outcomes. This design allows for the examination of the effect of music at a single time period (Time 2) as well as over time. The qualitative aspect of the design involved the completion of two questionnaires that used an open-ended format to identify the participants' use and preference of music as well as their evaluation of the effectiveness of the music during the study.

Setting and Sample

Criteria for inclusion in the study consisted of a diagnosis of chronic bronchitis, emphysema, or both; the ability to read and speak English; and reported experience of dyspnea at least once a week. Persons attending a community support group held in a large Metropolitan area in southern Ontario were recruited until a convenience sample of 25 participants was obtained. Only one participant dropped out of the study following the first week of testing for the reason of lack of interest in the study topic. Of the remaining 24 participants, the majority (79%) were born in Canada and 59% had attained some level of high school education. Fifty-eight percent were female and the mean age was 69 years ($SD = 5.7$). Fifty percent of the sample were married, whereas 58% lived with their families. Fifty-four percent had a diagnosis of emphysema, with an average of 14.3 years since diagnosis. The majority (67%) were not using oxygen. All participants reported use of respiratory drugs, whereas the use of other medications varied.

Instruments and Measures

Visual Analogue Dyspnea Scale (VADS). This was used to measure the level of dyspnea being experienced. The VADS consists of a 10-cm vertical visual analogue scale with anchors of *shortness of breath as bad as can be* on the top and *no shortness of breath* at the bottom. . . . There is considerable evidence to support the concurrent and discriminate validity of visual analogue scales. . . . Test-retest reliability of visual analogue scales also has been reported. . . . The vertical scale was easier for the participants to understand than the horizontal one. The vertical scale was able to discriminate between participants with COPD who had greater airway obstruction, as indicated by a peak expiratory flow rate less than 150 lpm (liters per minute) and those who exhibited lesser airway obstruction, as indicated by a peak expiratory flow rate greater than 150 lpm, thus providing evidence of the construct validity of the VADS. . . .

The participant is asked to mark a point on the line that indicates the amount of dyspnea experienced at that time. The VADS is scored by measuring the distance, in centimeters, from the low end of the scale to the participant's mark. Scores can range from 0 to 10.

Spielberger State Anxiety Scale (STAI, Form X-1). This was used to measure state anxiety, . . . a transitory emotional state that is characterized by subjective, consciously perceived feelings of tension and apprehension and heightened autonomic nervous system activity. . . . The scale consists of 20 statements that ask the individuals to indicate how they feel at a particular point in time. It has been used with patients with COPD. . . . Each item on the scale is rated from 1 (*not at all*) to 4 (*very much*). The higher the score on the scales, the greater the anxiety experienced.

Test-retest correlations have been reported to range from .16 to .54 . . . considered to be consistent with the transitory nature of state anxiety. Internal consistency reliability of the scale ranged from .83 to .92. . . . When used with COPD patients, the internal consistency reliability was reported to be .79. . . . With respect to validity, the scale was found to be sensitive to changes in experimental situations in which the level of stress was manipulated. . . .

When repeated measurements of A-States are desired, scales consisting of four to five STAI A-State items may be used to provide valid measures of A-State. . . . Thus, in this study, all measures of state anxiety consisted of a random selection of four items from the STAI Form X-1. Scores thus could range from a possible low of 4 to a high of 16.

Music Use and Preference Questionnaire. To determine music background and preference, participants were asked how often they listened to music, the circumstances under which they listened, type of music preferred, whether they varied the music on the basis of their mood, why they listened to music, and whether music had an effect on them.

Measures to monitor use and effect of music. Two measures were used to monitor the use and effectiveness of the music—the music diary and the Music Effectiveness Questionnaire.

Music diary. Participants were instructed to use the music whenever they became dyspneic. Each time they used the music, the participants were asked to indicate in the diary their level of dyspnea, on a scale of 0 to 100, immediately prior to and after listening to the music. They also were asked to indicate the length of time they listened to the music as well as the use of a puffer or inhaler.

Music Effectiveness Questionnaire. At Time 3, participants were asked whether they had used the music tapes over the course of the study and the effects they experienced when using the music.

Intervention

. . . Music selections chosen were instrumental and with slow tempo. . . . Participants were able to select the type of music they preferred from a master tape containing classical, easy listening, and new age selections. Sixteen participants chose easy listening, six chose new age, whereas two selected classical music. . . .

Participants were given the following instructions on the use of music:

1. Sit in a comfortable chair.
2. Insert selected tape into the Walkman.
3. Put on headphones.
4. Press the "play" button on the Walkman.
5. Place the Walkman in a convenient location.
6. Focus mind on the music, close eyes if desired.
7. Listen to the music for approximately 20 minutes.
8. When finished with the music, turn off Walkman, remove headphones, and complete the music diary.

Procedure

Patients who expressed interest in participating in the study were contacted to arrange a convenient time for the first home visit. During the first visit, the study was explained to the patients and their informed consents were obtained. A master tape consisting of the selections of three types of music, together with a Walkman tape recorder and earphones, were left with the patients so that they could identify the type of music they preferred. . . . Measures of dyspnea and anxiety were taken at this time (Time 1), and demographic data were collected.

At Time 2, patients were given a tape consisting of 20 minutes of their preferred music. . . . Instructions on the use of the music were provided at this time. Measures of anxiety and dyspnea were taken prior to and following the use of music. Participants were instructed on how to use the music for the remaining study period; they were encouraged to listen to the music as many times during a day as they experienced dyspnea, following the procedure described earlier.

At Time 3, measures of anxiety and dyspnea were taken. The Walkman recorder was collected and the music tape was left with each patient. At all testing times, the measures of anxiety and dyspnea were administered in random order.

Results

Music Background

To examine the history of the person's use of music, music background and preference were assessed at Time 1 by the Music Use and Preference Questionnaire. Thirteen of the 24 participants reported listening to music in the past on a daily basis, whereas 4 reported frequent or every-other-day patterns. The remaining participants did not listen to music on a regular basis. Circumstances under which they listened to music varied from helping to sleep, promoting relaxation, as a background, when alone, for enjoyment, in the car, and when there was nothing else to do. . . .

. . . Most participants indicated that music had an effect on them. . . . Many indicated that they enjoyed music ($n = 14$), it helped them to relax ($n = 8$), it decreased worry ($n = 3$), it provided company when alone ($n = 3$), it gave them a lift ($n = 2$), and made them feel good ($n = 2$).

Use of Music

. . . The findings from the Music Effectiveness Questionnaire indicated that all participants used the music tapes. The majority ($n = 20$) used the tapes whenever dyspneic during the study, whereas the remaining participants ($n = 4$) used them sporadically, claiming they did not have the time.

The music diary provided an ongoing record of the frequency of music use, which ranged from 2 to 71 entries ($M = 18.37$, $SD = 17.39$) over the 5-week period, and the duration, which varied from 7 to 120 minutes ($M = 25.2$, $SD = 13.0$). Out of the total number of reported use of music in the diary ($n = 340$), across all patients over the 5 weeks of the study, use of the inhaler was reported in only 98 instances. That is, approximately 71% of the times that music was used, the inhaler was not used.

. . . Cross tabulations were performed to examine the relationship between previous use of music as reported in the Music Use and Preference Questionnaire and the frequency of music use reported in the diary. No significant relationship was found.

TABLE 2 Comparison of Scores on STAI and VADS Following Use of Music, Time 2 (*n* = 24)

Variable	Mean	SD	t Value	df	2-Tailed Significance
STAI pretest	7.75	3.03	2.62	23	$p < .05$
STAI posttest	6.38	2.32			
VADS pretest	2.83	2.01	3.04	23	$p < .01$
VADS posttest	1.88	1.87			

NOTE: STAI = Spielberger State Anxiety Inventory; VADS = Visual Analogue Dyspnea Scale.

Music Effect

. . . Findings from the Music Effectiveness Questionnaire indicated that participants found the music calmed them and helped them relax (*n* = 18), they enjoyed the music and it made them feel good (*n* = 4), and it helped reduce the shortness of breath (*n* = 3). . . .

The music diary provided a means of monitoring episodes of music use whenever the participant became dyspneic. Participants were instructed to record their level of dyspnea on a scale of 0 to 100, immediately prior to and following the use of music. The diary was analyzed by taking all of the ratings of each participant's pretest and all of those at posttest to yield number of ratings across the participants. The comparison of premusic to postmusic scores showed a significant decrease in the overall dyspnea reported following the use of the music $t(326) = -13.93$, $p < .001$. The reported mean score of dyspnea premusic (*M* = 31.1) tended to be quite low.

To test the effect of music on anxiety and dyspnea at a single time period, a pretest-posttest approach was used to examine the levels of anxiety (STAI) and dyspnea (VADS) following the use of music on the second week of the study. Significant declines in anxiety and dyspnea were found (see Table 2).

To determine whether there was a change in anxiety or dyspnea over time, repeated measures ANOVA was performed. In this design, the measures of anxiety (STAI) and dyspnea (VADS) taken on the first week and second week prior to the use of music represented the baseline measures. Measures of these outcomes following the use of music in Week 2 and the final individual evaluation in Week 5 constituted the posttest measures. There was no significant change in anxiety or dyspnea over time. It is worth noting that the mean scores on the STAI and VADS taken over the course of the study at Times 1, 2, and 3 tended to be quite low (STAI, 6.4-7.8; VADS, 1.9-2.8).

Discussion

The results of this study suggest that people with COPD will use music in conjunction with dyspnea, on their own and in their own homes, and that music may help relieve their dyspnea. There was a significant decline in dyspnea and anxiety following the use of music at Time 2 as well as a significant decline in dyspnea reported in the diary. These findings indicate that music is effective in reducing dyspnea and anxiety at a single time period. . . .

Although music was effective in reducing dyspnea and anxiety at a single time period, there was no significant change over time in either anxiety or dyspnea. There may be several explanations for this inconsistency. Many of the participants reported that at the time of testing their level of dyspnea was not as high as at other times in the day. It is possible that the random one-time testing of dyspnea and anxiety at three consecutive time frames did not capture adequately the dyspnea experience. . . .

Although 20 of the 24 participants reported in the Music Effectiveness Questionnaire that they had used the music regularly over the course of the study, the frequency and duration of reporting in the diary did not support this. . . . This finding suggests a difficulty in the monitoring of the use of music in an uncontrolled setting and, thus, a difficulty in examining effect overtime. . . . Because the use of music was need-based, there was no control over how frequently participants used it. . . .

Limitations

A major limitation of this study was the small sample size, which may have reduced the opportunity to detect differences in anxiety and dyspnea over time. As well, the lack of a control group restricts the interpretation of the findings. No data were collected on the participants' lung function to provide an objective indicator of severity of illness. Although the diary provided some information about use of a bronchodilator during the 5-week period, there was no consistent record of use. Although the participants were instructed to use only the music tape provided, there was no control over the use of other music during the study. Many participants commented on wanting more variety of music.

CRITIQUE OF STUDY EXAMPLE 10.2

1. What was the rationale for the study?

2. What was the purpose of the study?

3. How was the sample obtained?

4. Is the select nature of the participants likely to confound the results?

5. What were the major characteristics of the participants?

6. What measures were used in the study?

7. Are the main tests reliable and valid?

8. What was the general procedure?

9. Could an order effect account for results?

10. Could an experimenter effect account for the results?

11. Could any other participant factor affect results?

12. What were the results regarding music background of the patients?

13. Should the patients' past experience with music affect the results?

14. How well did participants follow instructions regarding the use of music?

15. The authors report that 71% of the time that participants listened to music while dyspneic, they did not use an inhaler. Is this a significant finding?

16. According to diary entries, how effective was the music in reducing levels of dyspnea?

17. The reported t has $df = 326$, based on all ratings. What should have been reported and used in the analysis?

18. How effective was music in reducing state anxiety and dyspnea ratings during the second week?

19. What were the results of the analysis of variance for repeated measures on baseline pretest ratings of anxiety and of dyspnea and follow-up posttest ratings?

20. What did the authors conclude regarding effectiveness of music as a therapeutic intervention?

21. Is the major conclusion justified?

22. What changes in the study might have yielded more clinically significant results?

For answers to these questions, see page 342.

BIBLIOGRAPHY

Girden, E. R. (1992). *ANOVA: Repeated measures.* Newbury Park, CA: Sage.
Howell, D. C. (1992). *Statistical methods for psychology* (3rd ed.). Boston: PWS-Kent.
Iversen, G. R., & Norpoth, H. (1987). *Analysis of variance* (2nd ed.). Newbury Park, CA: Sage.
Keppel, G. (1991). *Design and analysis: A researcher's handbook* (3rd ed.). Englewood Cliffs, NJ: Prentice Hall.
Kirk, R. E. (1982). *Experimental design: Procedures for the behavioral sciences* (2nd ed.). Belmont, CA: Brooks/Cole.
McMillan, J. H., & Schumacher, S. (1997). *Research in education: A conceptual introduction* (4th ed.). White Plains, NY: Longman.
Stevens, J. (1990). *Intermediate statistics: A modern approach.* Hillsdale, NJ: Lawrence Erlbaum.

Additional Suggested Readings

Harris, M. B. (1995). *Basic statistics for behavioral science research.* Boston: Allyn & Bacon.
Keppel, G., & Zedeck, S. (1989). *Data analysis for research designs: Analysis of variance and multiple regression/correlation approaches.* New York: Freeman.
Pedhazur, E. J., & Schmelkin, L. P. (1991). *Measurement, design, and analysis: An integrated approach.* Hillsdale, NJ: Lawrence Erlbaum.

Chapter 11

Factorial Studies

Experiments that introduce more than one qualitative independent variable (factor) are called *factorial studies*. At a minimum, two factors are introduced. You could study the effect of four types of therapy and gender on self-esteem, in the design shown in Box 11.1.

Although factorial studies require many participants, depending on the number of levels of each factor, they are time-savers by virtue of the information they yield in a single experiment. We learn not only whether each separate factor has an effect but also whether the effects differ when both factors are combined. Separate or unique effects of each variable are called *main effects*. These refer to the average effects of each independent variable. When main effects are significant, we generally can make blanket statements about the effectiveness of those variables—statements without qualification. For example, we might be able to conclude that a type of therapy is equally effective for males and females or that males end up with higher levels of self-esteem, regardless of the type of therapy they receive. Combined ef-

fects let us know whether the effects of each variable simply add together, *additive effects,* or whether the effect of one variable depends on the level of the second variable. When the latter occurs, the combined effect is called an *interaction;* this implies that a qualification or stipulation has to be added to the description of effectiveness. For example, suppose we introduce three levels of reinforcements for three tasks of increasing difficulty and measure correct responses. We require three F ratios: one to let us know whether there is an overall effect of magnitude of reinforcement on number of correct responses (main effect), one to let us know if there is an overall effect of task difficulty on number of correct responses (main effect), and one to let us know whether the combined effects of both variables differ from the separate effects (interaction). If interaction is significant, the ultimate conclusion we might reach, after performing multiple comparisons, is that the highest magnitude of reinforcement is most effective—but only for the simplest task.

BOX 11.1
Design of a Two-Factor Study

	Assertive (J1)	Behavioral (J2)	Cognitive (J3)	Rap (J4)
Males (K1)	J1K1	J2K1	J3K1	J4K1
Females (K2)	J1K2	J2K2	J3K2	J4K2

NOTE: There are 4 levels of J (therapy), 2 levels of K (gender), and 8 groups (combined levels of each factor).

The type of analysis performed on the data depends on the design of the study. We have several alternatives, although we will always rely on three F ratios (for a two-factor study) to learn about main and interaction effects. (With more than two factors, the main effects and possible interactions increase in number and complexity.) If participants are independent groups, then a two-way (or three-way, etc.) analysis of variance is appropriate. Most often, each of the independent variables consists of deliberately selected levels (e.g., particular drugs, particular dosages), and a *fixed-effects model* of ANOVA applies to the data. In such studies, each particular level is assumed to have the same (i.e., fixed) effect on all participants exposed to it in the study and all replications of it. But results of the study generalize only for these particular levels. In rare instances, the levels of the independent variables have been randomly selected (e.g., order of presenting Rorschach cards, elementary schools, nursing homes), and a *random-effects model* of ANOVA applies to the data. In this instance, the effect of a randomly selected level is not constant, the levels will vary from study to study (as will their effects), and the dependent variable results can generalize to all possible levels of the variable (e.g., for all orders of Rorschach cards or all personality types of inter-

viewers, if some had been randomly selected). Finally, if the levels of one of the independent variables are deliberately selected (e.g., specific anxiety levels of testers, such as high, medium, and low) and the levels of the other are randomly selected (e.g., ethnic background of testers), then a *mixed-effects model* of ANOVA applies to the data. Here, the dependent variable results will generalize to all ethnic backgrounds, but only for testers with high, medium, and low levels of anxiety. These are critical to know because the model determines the appropriate error term in the F ratio. And if you need to check accuracy of degrees of freedom, for the most popular fixed-effect model, each main effect df (for a two-way ANOVA) equals $J - 1$ (where J = number of columns or levels of one independent variable) and $K - 1$ (where K = number of rows or levels of the other independent variable), whereas that for interaction equals $(J - 1)(K - 1)$. Degrees of freedom for the error term, which is random error, for testing main and interaction effects equals $N - JK$. With a random-effects model, error for testing both main effects is the interaction and its $df = (J - 1)(K - 1)$, whereas interaction is tested by random variability as the error term and df is $N - (J)(K)$. If a mixed-effect model applies, the error term for the fixed-effect variable is interaction and has

BOX 11.2	Model	Component	df	Error
Appropriate Error Terms for Two-Factor Studies	Fixed effect	Main effect(J)	$J-1$	Random error
		Main effect(K)	$K-1$	Random error
		Interaction	$(J-1)(K-1)$	Random error
		Random error	$N-JK$	
	Random effect	Main effect(J)	$J-1$	Interaction
		Main effect(K)	$K-1$	Interaction
		Interaction	$(J-1)(K-1)$	Random error
		Random error	$N-JK$	
	Mixed effect	Fixed main(J)	$J-1$	Interaction
		Random main(K)	$K-1$	Random error
		Interaction	$(J-1)(K-1)$	Random error
		Random error	$N-JK$	

$(J-1)(K-1)$ *df,* that for the random-effect variable is random variability and has $df = N - JK$ for error, and interaction is tested by random variability and has $df = N-JK$. These are summarized in Box 11.2.

In addition, each model has its own statistical assumptions. The assumptions for the fixed-effect model are the same as for one-way classification studies (see Chapter 10). For random-effect studies, because results generalize to the population, the assumption of normal distributions of scores for the different levels of each variable and combined levels is crucial, as is the assumption of homogeneity of variances for each treatment level and their combinations (separate cells). And the same assumptions apply to the mixed-effect studies.

Commonly used statistical packages include tests of each, and results should be reported. Analysis of variance, however, is a fairly robust test, provided that ns are reasonably large and approximately equal within each of the cells (combined levels).

In many instances, factorial studies employ the same participants in more than one condition, and some ANOVA for repeated measures is appropriate for determining main and interaction effects. In rare instances, the same participants serve in all conditions of the study. Most frequently, however, different groups of individuals (one of the independent variables) participate in all levels of the second independent variable (or more for a higher order factorial study). In this instance, a two-way ANOVA with repeated measures on one factor is appropriate. Again, the analysis will let you know whether there is a main effect of the different groups (between-group), a main effect of the different treatments or levels (within-group because all participants take part at each treatment level), and interaction between the two effects. When you want to check on validity of results, degrees of freedom for each effect depend on whether the circularity assumption has been met (see Chapter 10). The assumption does not apply to the variable that consists of separate groups. Here, we assume that variances for the separate groups are homogeneous. Therefore, df = number of groups $(K-1)$, for the group factor, and number of participants $(S)-K$ for the error term. The circularity assumption does apply to the within-group factor, the different levels of treatment to which all participants were exposed. For each separate group, the variances of differences between all pairs of treatment scores are assumed to be equal. And if we were to get average values for each level of treatment by combining the group scores (called pooling), the variances of all possible differences between pairs of the pooled, average values also are assumed to be equal. If the assumptions are met, df for the within-group factor and its error term equals $J-1$ and $(J-1)(S-K)$, and interaction effects of both factors has $df = (J-1)(K-1)$ and $(J-1)(S-K)$ for error. The assumptions, however, seldom are met, and you should be alerted to some statement about adjusting degrees of freedom to guard against a Type I error. With no indication and F ratios declared significant at $p < .05$, you can evaluate the conclusions by comparing the F ratios against tabled values associated with $df = [(1/J-1)] \times (J-1) = 1$ (for the numerator) and $[(1/J-1] \times$

$(J-1)(S-K) = S-K$ (error) for the within-group, repeated measures, factor and $[(1/J-1)] \times (J-1)(K-1) = K-1$ (for the numerator) and $S-K$ (error) for interaction. If F ratios are no longer significant, a Type I error looms as a possibility.

From the point of view of design, you need assurance that participants were randomly assigned to the various groups. Of course, this is not possible if one of the variables is an individual characteristic (e.g., gender, personality disorder, etc.); these individuals should be randomly selected and then randomly assigned to levels of the other variable. Because attrition almost always occurs, especially if testing occurs on more than one occasion, you need assurance that the loss is not selective. And, as with all studies, there should be guards against experimenter effects as well as some assessment of the independent variables; that is, you want assurance that manipulation of the independent variable was perceived by the participant. If tests are used, they should be reliable and valid, and testing conditions should be uniform. If the study uses repeated measures, you also need some assurance that participants were randomly assigned to the various groups or were randomly selected if the group variable is an individual characteristic. Moreover, unless the repeated measures factor is some progressive event, such as trials or time, there should be an indication that levels of that factor were presented in counterbalanced order. Caution factors for a factorial study are presented in Box 11.3.

We begin here by evaluating a separate groups factorial study together, and then we'll do the same for a mixed-design study with repeated measures on one factor.

BOX 11.3
Caution Factors
for Factorial Studies

Between-groups

- Participants were randomly selected or randomly assigned to various groups.

- Administered tests were reliable and valid.

- Multiple tests were presented in counterbalanced order.

- Test administrator was unaware of research hypotheses.

- Attrition did not result in a selective loss.

- Control participants could not learn about experimental treatment.

- Statistical assumptions of ANOVA were met.

- Degrees of freedom are correct.

- Correct error terms were used.

Repeated measures

- All of the above

- Levels of treatment were presented in counterbalanced order.

- Circularity assumption was tested.

- Degrees of freedom were adjusted if necessary.

STUDY EXAMPLE 11.1

This experiment represents the simplest extension of a between-groups design, a 2×2 design. It introduces two levels of each variable. In the present study, participants in a bargaining situation acted either as buyer or seller of an old car. This was the first independent variable. They bargained with confederates who either were truthful with them about their alternatives (price offered by a potential buyer or their need for parts of the car to rebuild another one) or did not disclose their alternatives. This was the second independent variable. The experimenters were interested in the extent to which the participants would bargain honestly in each of the four conditions. A footnote thanks the nine confederates and another individual for coding and entering the data.

The Study

Paese, P. W., & Gilin, D. A. (2000). When an adversary is caught telling the truth: Reciprocal cooperation versus self-interest in distributive bargaining. *Personality and Social Psychology Bulletin, 26*(2), 79-90. Copyright 2000 by Sage.

Consider a hypothetical negotiation between a buyer and a seller, with yourself in the seller role. The year is 1970 and the negotiation involves the possible sale of a 15-year-old car. The only issue to be negotiated is that of price. . . . You and the buyer do not know each other and you do not expect to interact in the future. Both of you have a firm alternative to which you can turn in the event of impasse; in your case, a previous buyer has made you a standing offer of $300 for the car. As luck would have it, you stumbled on some valuable inside information . . . prior to the negotiation. . . . The buyer intends to disassemble your car and use its parts to rebuild another car, and . . . the buyer's only alternative is to purchase these parts elsewhere for $600. . . . There is a $300 surplus between your alternative and that of the buyer. You also happen to know that the buyer (a) has no knowledge of your alternative and (b) is completely unaware of the fact that you have an information advantage.

Under these circumstances, any settlement you negotiate will depend greatly on how you portray your own alternative to the buyer. . . . Honestly portraying your alternative is likely to result in a settlement somewhere in the middle of the $300 to $600 bargaining zone, whereas exaggerating its value (e.g., "I have another buyer who's willing to pay $500") is likely to give you a much more favorable settlement. . . . Assume that you are fully aware of this going into the negotiation.

Given that you already know the buyer's alternative, his or her portrayal of it will have very little effect on the final settlement—you could call the buyer's bluff if he or she tries to exaggerate. Of course, the buyer does not realize this so you suspect that he or she might try this strategy. Suppose, however, that instead of exaggerating, the buyer truthfully discloses his or her alternative. You must now decide how to portray your own alternative, knowing full well that the buyer has done so honestly. What would you do under these circumstances? . . . You could safely exaggerate and claim most of the surplus or you could portray honestly and give much of the surplus away; either way, the buyer won't know the difference. . . . On the other hand, the buyer has clearly made an honest disclosure, undoubtedly in the hope that you will do the same. Perhaps you should reciprocate this cooperative gesture. Note that if you do reciprocate, your cooperation will benefit the buyer at a cost to yourself. Not only would you be giving him or her a portion of the surplus, the buyer would not even realize, much less appreciate, that you have made a concession on his or her behalf. . . .

To what extent will bargainers cooperate under these circumstances? . . . We conducted an experiment in which participants were put in the exact situation described above (actually, half of our participants were put in this exact situation; the other half were put in a mirror-image situation in which the participant's role was changed from seller to buyer). . . .

Reciprocity and Self-Interest

The reciprocity rule is a social norm that pervades human culture. . . . In its simplest form, the reciprocity rule merely states that "we should try to repay, in kind, what another person has provided us." . . . One consequence of this rule in bargaining contexts is that a concession by one party will usually cause the other party to concede in return. . . .

. . . Results suggest that a discernibly cooperative move by one's opponent . . . is likely to be reciprocated to at least some degree. (Note that a cooperative move . . . is clearly discernible only when one knows the limit of one's opponent.)

. . . The opponent in our study was ignorant of the participant's limit, and participants knew this. . . . Because of the information asymmetry in our experiment, participants could give the appearance of reciprocating without really doing so. For example, by revealing their own alternative and exaggerating its value, our participants could lead the buyer to believe that they had made a reciprocal disclosure when in fact they had not. Thus . . . one might expect self-interest to override any reciprocal motive to cooperate in the present experiment.

Indeed, recent evidence would seem to support this latter expectation. . . .

. . . The key finding in . . . research [involving the prisoner's dilemma] is that, in comparison to conditions in which the opponent's choice was unknown, the frequency of cooperation did not increase when participants knew their opponent had already cooperated. In fact, just the opposite occurred. . . . Results suggest that bargainers in the seller role are unlikely to reciprocate the buyer's cooperation.

Additional . . . experimenters led participants to believe they were playing a one-shot prisoner's dilemma with an anonymous opponent and varied . . . whether participants knew their opponent's choice prior to making their own decision to cooperate or defect. . . . The frequency of cooperation did not increase when participants knew the other party had already cooperated. These results cast further doubt on the possibility that bargainers will cooperate under the circumstances of interest here.

At this point, it should be noted that the experimental contexts . . . were distinctly nonsocial. . . . The opponent was not physically present and there was no communication between players. . . . Under these conditions, the social norm of reciprocity may be unlikely to be activated.

In contract, participants in the present research negotiated face-to-face with a scripted opponent (a confederate) posing as a participant. In half of these negotiations, the confederate initiated the discussion by making an honest disclosure about his or her alternative (in the other half, the confederate initiated the discussion but did not make an honest disclosure). . . . Our participants actually observed the other party cooperating and then proceeded to bargain with him or her. Under these conditions, the reciprocity rule may be more likely to be activated.

. . . We expected that our confederate's unsolicited cooperation would create at least some feeling among participants that they should cooperate in return. However, given that our participants could give the appearance of cooperating, we were particularly interested in the extent to which they would cooperate genuinely versus merely pretend to do so.

. . . Each participant also was given an incentive to maximize his or her individual outcome. Consequently, our participants could not cooperate genuinely without potentially endangering their own self-interest. Under these circumstances, we expected that participants might attempt to resolve this conflict (between their own self-interest and the obligation to reciprocate) by feigning cooperation. . . . Thus, we attempted to measure both genuine and feigned cooperation in the present study.

---

1. What was the rationale for the study?

In bargaining situations, sellers and buyers have alternatives. If the seller is aware of the buyer's alternative, but the buyer is unaware of the seller's knowledge, the seller can cooperate with the buyer by presenting an honest alternative and thereby lose money, or the seller can present an exaggerated (dishonest) alternative and lose nothing. In that case, the seller would be acting out of self-interest.

In prior research, it was found that knowledgeable participants (akin to sellers) are not likely to cooperate with an opponent (akin to buyers). The situations, however, were nonsocial; bargainers did not have face-to-face contact, leading to less likelihood of cooperation. In the present study, participants, in the role of buyer or seller, bargained with confederates who disclosed or did not disclose their alternatives. It was anticipated that because participants observed confederates cooperating (disclosing alternatives), they would feel obligated to reciprocate cooperation. But they also had incentives to maximize their outcome (increased self-interest) and could feign cooperation to resolve the conflict between reciprocity and self-interest.

Hypotheses

The preceding considerations give rise to two hypotheses. . . . We expected to find support for either or both of these hypotheses. The first of these is formalized as follows:

Hypothesis 1: An unambiguously cooperative move at the outset of a distributive negotiation will cause the opposing bargainer to truthfully reveal more information, exaggerate his or her alternative less, and make a less demanding offer than he or she would in the absence of such a move.

We refer to this as the genuine reciprocation hypothesis. . . .

The second hypothesis, referred to here as the feigned cooperation hypothesis, has the following form:

Hypothesis 2: An unambiguously cooperative move at the outset of a distributive negotiation will cause the opposing negotiator to disingenuously reveal more information while exaggerating just as much and making offers just as demanding as he or she otherwise would.

. . . To the extent that our confederate's disclosure activates a secondary motive to cooperate in return, it seems likely that bargainers will want to appear cooperative while pursuing their self-interest.

---

2. *What was the purpose of the study?*

On the basis of past research, two hypotheses were tested. The first hypothesis stated that genuine cooperation would be evident when the opponent cooperated at the outset of bargaining. The second hypothesis stated that feigned cooperation, because of self-interest, would be evident when the opponent cooperated at the outset.

Method

Design

Participants assumed the role of either buyer or seller in a negotiation simulation involving the sale of a used car. The roles were written such that participants had a clear alternative of their own as well as accurate information about the other party's no-agreement alternative. A confederate posing as a participant assumed the opposite role and followed a detailed script. The script was varied such that the confederate either did or did not disclose his or her no-agreement alternative at the outset of the negotiation. Thus, the design was a 2 (no disclosure vs. disclosure) × 2(buyer vs. seller) between-participants factorial.

Participants

Seventy-seven undergraduates (44 females and 33 males) from courses in business and psychology participated in the experiment for course credit and the chance to earn some money. The mean age of participants was 26.4 years ($SD = 7.6$). Of the participants, 86% were working either full- or part-time. There were 18 to 21 participants in each of the four conditions.

▶ *(Note that research participation is a common requirement in many universities, provided that students can choose the experiment[s] of their choice. Also, the fact that 86% work full- or part-time explains the large mean age of these undergraduates and also suggests that they would have little chance to talk to one another about the experiment. Finally, although we know that the four cell sizes ranged from 18 to 21, it would have been helpful to know exact numbers and numbers of males and females in each condition. We know that two of the cells had 18 and 21. The remaining 38 participants could have been divided evenly, or there could have been 18 in one and 20 in the other. But nothing is said about attempts to equalize males and females in the cells. If there was an even split of females—11 in each—this could have resulted in a range of 7 to 10 males in the cells, which may or may not make a difference. We need to be on the lookout for a test to assure no differences between the sexes in the results.)*

Confederates

Five female and four male undergraduates served as confederates . . . required to learn four scripts, one for each cell of the design. In training the confederates, great emphasis was placed on delivering the scripted lines the same way in the no-disclosure versus disclosure conditions. That is, they were instructed to use the same tone and inflection in both conditions, even though some of the words and phrases differed. They were also told that (a) the research was exploratory, (b) there were no specific research hypotheses, and (c) they should avoid forming any hypotheses of their own and instead concentrate on delivering the scripted lines the same way each time.

▶ *(This aspect of instructions to confederates is very sticky. On one hand, the random assignment of them to all conditions rules out differential effects of the confederates. On the other hand, having each serve in all conditions makes it more likely that, contrary to their instructions, some hypothesis might be formed about the purpose of the study. And the more sessions each takes part it in, the more likely it becomes.)*

Prior to any actual data collection, the confederates rehearsed each script by playing the role of participant for one another. Live practice sessions also were conducted. . . .

---

3. Describe the participants and confederates.

Forty-four female and 33 male undergraduates participated for course credit and a chance to earn extra money. They were about 26.4 years old, and 86% worked full- or part-time. Confederates, also undergraduates, were told that the study was exploratory with no particular hypotheses being tested. They were instructed to focus on their scripts and not try to formulate their own hypotheses. All were thoroughly trained to deliver their script lines in the same tone of voice and participated in live practice sessions.

Participant Roles

. . . Participants in both roles were told to assume that the time was 1970 so that the negotiation would not be influenced by current car prices.

Buyer role. The buyer description put participants in the role of an amateur mechanic who is interested in buying a 1955 Street Streaker for purposes of removing some of its parts to rebuild another car. The buyer is told that he or she could buy these parts new for $600 and that this is his or her only alternative to settlement. Inside information about the seller's no-agreement alternative was written into the buyer role. . . .

[Precise instructions inform the buyer via a friend that someone, the seller, was offered $300 for just such a car.]

Seller role. The seller description put participants in the role of a parent who is interested in selling a 1955 Street Streaker that belongs to his or her son who is overseas in the military. The seller is told that a local used car dealer has offered him or her $300 for the car and that this is his or her only alternative to settlement. Inside information as to the buyer's no-agreement alternative was written into the seller's role. . . .

[Written instructions inform the seller, via a friend, that an expected caller, the buyer, just wants the parts of the car, which can be purchased new for $600.]

Confederate Scripts

. . . There was one script for each of the four conditions. Each script contained an opening remark followed by seven blocks of lines. The confederate delivered the first block of lines at the very outset of the negotiation, before any offers were made; this block was varied such that the confederate either did or did not disclose his or her alternative. Each subsequent block was contingent in the sense that the script had two tracks, one for responding to stingy offers from the participant and the other for responding to generous offers. . . . It should be noted that the confederate tried to elicit a monetary offer from the participant after each block. That is, if the participant's response to a given block did not include a monetary offer, the confederate asked the participant to suggest a price before proceeding to the next block.

---

4. *What were the buyer and seller roles of the participants?*

All participants assumed that they were negotiating the price of a car in 1970. Buyers acted as mechanics trying to buy the car for its parts. If negotiations failed, they could buy new parts for $600. The buyer also knew that the seller had been offered $300 for the car. Sellers acted as a parent trying to sell a son's car. If negotiations failed, they could get $300 for the car. The sellers also knew that the buyer wanted to buy the car for its parts, which would cost $600 new.

5. *What were the confederate roles?*

If paired with a buyer, the confederate was a seller; if paired with a seller, the confederate was a buyer. In the disclosure condition, the "seller" revealed the offer of $300 for the car, whereas the "buyer" revealed that the cost of new parts would be $600. In the nondisclosure situations, they revealed nothing.

Procedure

Two to four participants were run in each experimental session, and each session was randomly assigned to one of the four conditions. At the outset of each session, participants were told that they would be required to assume the role of either buyer or seller and that they would attempt to negotiate the sale of a used car with another participant in the opposite role.

▶ *(Note that with four participants per session, there would have been a minimum of 19 sessions and probably more because the range was two to four. The variations are likely due to a population of working students who are not readily available for testing. It would have been useful to know when sessions were conducted and over how long a period of time. Random assignment will tend to reduce the effects of different times, but the different times could increase variability and account for unexpected nonsignificant results.)*

Participants were told that two $5 prizes would be awarded, one for the buyer who negotiated the lowest price and one for the seller who negotiated the highest price. . . . Participants always competed against either two or three others for a $5 prize. Informal observation indicated that this was a strong incentive. Not only did participants want to earn the money, they also sought the distinction of being the "best."
. . . A single sheet containing the role description was handed to each participant while a written copy of the script was given to each confederate for reference. The two sheets were identically formatted so as not to arouse suspicion.

▶ *(Note that this is a good feature of the design. Presumably, one of the authors greeted the participants and could have unintentionally influenced them if instructions were verbal. Using written descriptions greatly reduced this risk.)*

Prior to assigning negotiation pairs, the experimenter grouped the participants by role and directed each group to its own private room. She entered the participants' room and verified that they knew their own alternative and that of the other party by quizzing them and restating these values aloud. . . . In addition to this knowledge, it was necessary that participants believe the other party was ignorant of the participant's alternative. . . .

▶ *(She gave a brief speech assuring the participants that the other party did not know their alternatives. Note that questions to the participants and her speech served as manipulation checks. If the participants did not fully understand their alternative and were not convinced that the opponents did not know their alternatives, effectively, there would be no independent variables operating.)*

The experimenter then went into the confederates' room to give the appearance that she was instructing them as well. After returning from this room, she called everyone back into the main room where she paired each participant with a confederate and assigned each pair to a room.

Participants were given up to 20 minutes to complete the negotiation. They were told that they should keep a running record of every monetary offer given and received during the negotiation as well as comments made by each party. Separate sheets were given to the buyer and seller. . . .

Immediately after the last negotiation was finished, everyone was called back into the main room and a postexperimental questionnaire was administered. . . . After all questionnaires were completed, the experimenter determined which buyer and seller negotiated the lowest and highest price, respectively, and paid each $5. The confederates walked away from the room . . . but returned discretely and completed another questionnaire regarding the participant's responses in the negotiation.

6. What was the general procedure?

Two to four participants were run per session and were informed that they would act as buyer or seller of a used car and that $5 would be awarded to the best negotiators. Roles were randomly assigned to each session. Participants and confederates initially were in separate rooms, after each had been handed written descriptions of the role or script (confederate). After participants were assured, by the experimenter, that the opponent did not know their alternative, the pairs were assigned to separate rooms to negotiate for up to 20 minutes. Participants and confederates were reassembled, each filled out questionnaires, and awards were given to lowest buyer and highest seller prices.

7. What were good aspects of the design?

Each session's participants were randomly assigned to one of the four conditions; confederates were trained and served in all conditions; the experimenter had minimal contact with participants.

8. What were questionable aspects of the design?

Because confederates served in all conditions, they may have caught on to the purpose of the study. And, there is no description of distribution of the participants in all conditions by gender. If there is a gender difference in negotiating, it could affect results.

Measures

Demandingness. Of particular interest here were the price offers made by participants in response to each block of the script as well as the final settlement price. Given that the buyer and seller limits were $300 and $600, respectively, a buyer's offer of, say, $250 for the car would be numerically equivalent to a seller's offer of $650 (i.e., these offers are equidistant from $450, the midpoint of the bargaining zone). . . . Each offer was converted to an index of demandingness (D) . . . by subtracting each buyer offer (B) from $450 (D = 450 − B) and subtracting $450 from each seller offer (S) (D = S − 450). . . . The larger the index, the more demanding the participant's offer.

Exaggeration. In every negotiation, the confederate asked the participant to disclose the value of his or her alternative (i.e., "How much were they asking?" or "How much did they offer you?"). . . . If the participant gave a numerical response to this question, an index of exaggeration (E) was computed for that participant. Specifically, each buyer's response (B) was subtracted from the true value of the buyer's alternative (E = 600 − B), whereas the true value of the seller's alternative was subtracted from the seller's response (S) (E = S − 300). . . . The more a participant exaggerates, the larger the E index.

Participant questionnaire. . . . One item [asked] them to rate how well they thought they had negotiated compared to others in the same role and one item [asked] them to indicate whether their counterpart had negotiated effectively and why they thought so. . . . And two items [pertained] to the participant's previous negotiation experience. Of these latter items, one asked them to describe any on-the-job bargaining experience and the other asked them to describe their negotiation experience in contexts other than work.

Confederate Questionnaire 1. . . . asked them to record demographic information about the participant, the duration of the negotiation, and ratings of the extent to which (a) they were able to follow the script without needing to ad lib, (b) the participant appeared to suspect their confederate status, and (c) the participant said things during the negotiation that deviate[d] from his or her role description. . . .

Confederate Questionnaire 2. . . . This questionnaire required them to refer to, and elaborate on, . . . the concurrent record they had kept of the participant's responses. . . .

Truthfulness ratings. We were interested in the extent to which participants made truthful statements, particularly about their alternative, as well as the overall amount of lying they exhibited. Therefore, the second author and an assistant independently read the participants' statements (as transcribed by the confederates) and rated the extent to which they (a) disclosed truthful information about their alternative and (b) told lies in general (both 7-point scales where 1 = *not at all* and 7 = *to a great extent*). Raters were blind to condition. Interrater reliabilities were .86 and .81 for items a and b, respectively. A composite rating was formed for each item . . . referred to as the truth and lie composites.

Experience ratings. The two raters also read each participant's description of his or her bargaining experience and rated the participant accordingly (on a 7-point scale where 1 = *no experience* and 7 = *great deal of experience*). The interrater reliability for this item was .93, and a composite rating, referred to here as experience, was formed for this item as well.

---

9. What measures (dependent and other variables) were used?

Demandingness was an index of the difference between $450 and the buyer's offer (450 – B) and the seller's price and $450 (S – 450). The higher the index, the more demanding the participant. Exaggeration was an index of the difference between a buyer's quoted alternative and the actual quoted price ($600 – B) and between the seller's quoted offer and the actual offer (S – $300). The larger the index, the greater the exaggeration.

Participants' questionnaire contained several questions, including their past experience in negotiating on-the-job and in other situations. There were two questionnaires filled out by the confederate. One focused on the extent to which the participant appeared to believe the role played by the confederate. The second focused on elaborating notes they made about the participant response during the session.

Truthfulness ratings on a 7-point scale of participant's statements (noted by confederate) were made independently by the experimenter and a "naive" assistant and combined into a composite truth and lie score. Experience ratings were made (also independently) of the amount of prior experience in negotiating had by each participant.

10. What additional measure might have been made?

Each confederate might have been asked, at the end of the study, to state the probable hypothesis being tested, to ensure that each had not caught on to the purpose of the study.

Results

Demandingness

Our first set of results concerns the price offers made by participants in response to each scripted block as well as the final settlement price. A 2 (no disclosure vs. disclosure) × 2 (buyer vs. seller role) ANOVA was conducted on each D index. . . . Each D index was plotted and found to be normally distributed, with the exception of one outlier on indexes D1 to D4. This participant, assigned to the seller role, demanded an extremely high price in each of the first four bargaining rounds. . . . Each of these prices resulted in a D index that was more than twice as large as the next largest D index in that round. This participant was therefore excluded from the analyses of D1 to D4 (this participant was in the no-disclosure condition . . .).

▶ *(Note that a check for at least one of the assumptions of ANOVA was made. It is assumed that variances probably were homogeneous among the four cells. Again, the test is fairly robust with respect to homogeneity provided that cell numbers are reasonably large, which they are in this case, and are relatively alike, which they are. Finally, there is good justification for eliminating the outlier from the analyses.)*

One participant refused to state a price in the first round of bargaining, leaving a total of 75 participants for the analysis of D1. By the second round, this participant no longer refused to state a price. However, two participants settled immediately after the first round, leaving 74 participants for the analysis of D2. Ten additional participants settled right after the second round, so there were only 51 participants for the D4 analysis. Last, 5 participants failed to reach a settlement, leaving 72 participants for the analysis of Dfinal.

The ANOVAs on D1, D2, and D3 each revealed a main effect for the disclosure manipulation (see Table 1). . . . Participants in the disclosure condition made less demanding offers than participants in the no-disclosure condition in Rounds 1 through 4. This effect was largest in Round 1 and decreased over rounds. By the fourth round, the difference was smaller and nonsignificant. . . . This lack of effect in Round 4 . . . was probably nonrandom attrition; that is, most of the participants who settled early were in the disclosure condition. . . . The disclosure manipulation also had a significant effect on the final settlement price. Again, participants in the disclosure condition made lesser demands than those in the no-disclosure condition. . . . Thus, it appears that the confederate's disclosure elicited genuine, as opposed to feigned, cooperation in the form of less demanding offers and settlement terms.

TABLE 1 ANOVA Summary Table for Dependent Variables

Variable	Source of Variation	df	F	η^2
D1	Disclosure	1	13.02**	.16
	Role	1	1.06	.02
	Disclosure × Role	1	2.39	.03
	Error	71		
D2	Disclosure	1	9.91**	.12
	Role	1	.75	.01
	Disclosure × Role	1	1.18	.02
	Error	70		
D3	Disclosure	1	5.41*	.08
	Role	1	2.25	.04
	Disclosure × Role	1	2.97	.05
	Error	60		
D4	Disclosure	1	2.43	.05
	Role	1	1.12	.02
	Disclosure × Role	1	1.96	.04
	Error	47		
Dfinal	Disclosure	1	9.04**	.12
	Role	1	14.76**	.18
	Disclosure × Role	1	2.53	.04
	Error	68		
E index	Disclosure	1	11.74**	.23
	Role	1	.01	.00
	Disclosure × Role	1	7.70**	.16
	Error	40		
Truth	Disclosure	1	9.65**	.12
	Role	1	.41	.01
	Disclosure × Role	1	2.28	.03
	Error	68		

NOTE: D1 = the index of demandingness for the participant's first offer, D2 = the index of demandingness for the participant's second offer, D3 = the index of demandingness for the participant's third offer, D4 = the index of demandingness for the participant's fourth offer, Dfinal = the index for the final settlement price, and E index = the exaggeration index.
*$p < .05$; **$p < .01$.

▶ *(Note that the report of loss of participants from each round explains why the df for the error terms change in each consecutive round and lets you determine that they all are correct. But F ratios cannot be checked because means are not reported in the table [they are shown in a figure but were hard to read]. Also note that if there had been no loss of participants from one round to the other, the data could have been analyzed by a 2 × 2 × 5 ANOVA with repeated measures on the last factor, representing the rounds and final price. But the analysis would have been more complex, with unequal ns in the cells, and the status of the circularity assumption would be questionable.)*

There was no role effect in Rounds 1 to 4, and there was not a Disclosure × Role interaction on any of the D indexes (see Table 1). There was, however, a significant role effect on the final price; participants in the role of buyer (*M* = 66.5) demanded more than those in the seller role (*M* = 31.4). Although un-anticipated, this finding is consistent with previous laboratory experiments in which buyers have been found to outperform sellers. . . . Indeed, there was a role main effect on the duration of the negotiation, $F(1, 72) = 5.63$, $p < .05$, $\eta^2 = .07$, [η^2 is equivalent to a coefficient of determination and indicates the percentage of variability in, in this case, duration of negotiations associated with role of the participants] with participants in the buyer role (*M* = 10.3) ne-gotiating longer than those in the seller role (*M* = 8.0 minutes). This suggests that buyers may indeed have held out longer near the end of the negotia-tions. There was no effect for disclosure or the Disclosure × Role interaction on duration.

11. *What model was assumed in performing the ANOVA (i.e., what type of independent variables were introduced?*

Both variables were deliberately manipulated; therefore, a fixed-effect model would be appropriate.

12. *Analyses were performed to determine whether disclosure of alternatives by confederates had any effect on subsequent offers. Degrees of freedom for each bidding round successively decreased. Did these represent selective losses of participants?*

In a way, yes. Those situations in which the confederate disclosed his or her alternative (offer of $300 for the car or $600 to buy the parts new) were more likely to reach an early settlement on the sale or purchase of the car.

13. *What were the major findings regarding demandingness?*

For rounds 1 to 3, there was a significant main effect due to disclosure: Those participants paired with a confederate who disclosed a selling offer or cost of new parts were less demanding; that is, they were more likely to offer to sell the car at a price well below $600 or to buy the car well below $300 than were participants paired with a confederate who did not disclose their alter-native.

14. *Did the role of the participant make any difference with respect to disclosure by the confederate?*

No, none of the Disclosure × Role interactions were significant.

15. *Did the role of the participant make any overall difference?*

Yes, only in terms of final bid. Those who were sellers demanded less (offered to sell at prices closer to the midpoint bargaining range of $450) than did buyers (offered to buy at prices further from the midpoint range of $450). If we use the demand formulas with rounded-off means, buyers offered (demanded) $450 − $66 = $384 for the car, which resulted in a profit for the seller of only $84. But sellers offered to sell their cars for $31 + $450 = $481, which saved the buyer $600 − $481 = $119.

16. *What other evidence suggested that buyers were more demanding?*

They spent a longer time negotiating than did sellers.

Exaggeration/Truthfulness

Participants' responses to the confederate's question, "How much were they asking?" or "How much did they offer you?" were analyzed for evidence of feigned cooperation. Recall that prior to asking this question, confederates in the disclosure condition had already revealed their alternative truthfully. Thus, if participants in this condition wanted to feign cooperation, they could easily do so by describing their own alternative in monetary terms (thereby returning the confederate's favor) while still exaggerating its true value.

Six participants refused to answer this question (4 of these were in the no-disclosure condition). Of those who did answer, 44 described their alternative in monetary terms. The majority (27 or 61%) of these participants were in the disclosure condition, but this difference was not significant. . . .

A 2 (no disclosure vs. disclosure) × 2 (buyer vs. seller) ANOVA on the E index revealed a main effect for disclosure (see Table 1). Participants in the disclosure condition did exaggerate the value of their alternative ($M = 163.9$) but not nearly as much as did participants in the no-disclosure condition ($M = 337.6$) . . . there was a significant Disclosure × Role interaction. . . . Further analysis indicated that the disclosure main effect was much larger for sellers than for buyers and that this was the source of the interaction. Specifically, the mean E index for sellers was 94.2 in the disclosure condition and 405.5 in the no-disclosure condition, whereas for buyers these means were 228.6 and 261.3.

▶ *(Note the meaning of this interaction. Buyers in the disclosure position claimed to have been quoted $600 – $229 = $371 for new parts, whereas those in the no-disclosure position claimed to have been quoted $600 – $261 = $339 for new parts. Sellers in the disclosure position claimed to have been offered $300 + $94 = $394 and in the no-disclosure position to have been offered $300 + $405 = $706. These results are rather interesting because in the end, the buyers, not the sellers, were more demanding.)*

. . . . eight participants disclosed the true value of their alternative . . . and all 8 of these participants were in the disclosure condition. Moreover, even when these 8 participants were removed, there was still a main effect for disclosure on the E index. . . .

In view of the fact that some participants in the disclosure condition co-operated by answering the confederate's question about other options yet still exaggerated the true value of their alternative, we can infer that these participants feigned cooperation to some extent. . . . However, these participants were significantly more truthful than those in the no-disclosure condition. . . . None were completely truthful in the no-disclosure condition. Thus, the present data indicate that . . . in general the confederate's disclosure caused participants to be more genuinely cooperative than they would have otherwise been.

To further examine the truthfulness of participants' responses, 2×2 ANOVAs were conducted on the truth and lie composite ratings as well as on the questionnaire item in which confederates rated the extent to which the participants said things during the negotiation that deviated from their role description. Only one significant effect emerged in these analyses: a main effect for disclosure on the truth composite (see Table 1; there was missing data for 5 participants in this analysis . . .). Participants in the disclosure condition ($M = 2.89$) revealed more truthful information about their alternative than did those in the no-disclosure condition ($M = 1.97$) . . . (the correlation between the truth composite and the E index was $-.61$, $n = 44$, $p < .001$).

---

17. **What were the major findings regarding exaggeration and truthfulness of participants?**

Participants who were asked about asking price for new parts (of buyers) or offers for the car (of sellers) either refused to answer, gave truthful answers, or feigned cooperation by exaggerating the quotes (majority). Of the exaggerators, those in the disclosure condition were more truthful (exaggerated less) than those in the no-disclosure condition. Moreover, the interaction term was significant:

	Disclosure	No-Disclosure
Sellers	94.2	405.5
Buyers	228.6	261.3
	163.9	337.6

The summary table indicates that the difference between means of sellers and buyers in the disclosure condition (228.6 – 94.2 = 134.4) was not much lower than that for the no-disclosure condition (405.5 – 261.3 = 144.2). But the difference between means for sellers (405.5 – 94.2 = 311.3) was much higher than that for buyers (261.3 – 228.6 = 32.7). Therefore, the sellers in the no-disclosure condition exaggerated an offered price much more than did the remaining groups. Further analyses revealed that participants in the disclosure group were more truthful about their alternatives than were those in the no-disclosure group.

Further Analyses

We suspected that participants with the least negotiation experience may have been the most susceptible to the disclosure effects reported above. Therefore, we conducted 2 × 2 ANCOVAs on the D, E, and truth measures, with the experience composite ($M = 2.75$, $SD = 1.69$) serving as the covariate.

▶ *(In such an analysis, the effect of the unwanted variable is partialed out and the analysis effectively is on participants as if all had equal experience.)*

The covariate accounted for little or no variation, and the analyses otherwise revealed the same effects as before. Thus, negotiation experience did not moderate the effects observed here. We also tested for possible gender and/or confederate effects, and there were no such effects on any of the dependent measures.

▶ *(Note that this is very useful information and answers points brought up earlier with respect to gender differences and the confederates. But we still need to look for any possibility that confederates caught on to the hypotheses being tested.)*

When asked if they thought their counterpart had negotiated effectively, 88.3% of the participants responded affirmatively, and this percentage did not differ by condition. In explaining why they thought so, none of the participants gave any indication that the confederate had acted [in a manner that was] unusual, suspicious, or odd in any way. . . . The confederates also indicated that, for the most part, they were able to follow the script without having to ad lib.

▶ *(Note that the question about confederates is answered. On the basis of participant reports, it is unlikely that the confederates caught on to the real purpose of the study.)*

---

18. What did the remaining analyses reveal?

These were very important in removing additional variables as possible explanations of the results. There was no effect of experience of participants in past negotiations on their performance here. Moreover, gender differences were investigated, and no effect was found. Finally, there was no unwanted effect due to the confederates.

Discussion

In the present research, we examined a distributive bargaining situation in which the participant's counterpart either did or did not make an unambiguously cooperative move at the outset of the negotiation. . . . Given the strength of the reciprocity rule in face-to-face interaction, . . . we expected that participants would feel as though they should cooperate in return, at least to some extent. . . . Because (a) cooperation ran counter to self-interest and (b) participants could get away with pretending to cooperate while still pursuing their own interests, we anticipated only that they would display more seeming cooperation that could in reality be genuine, feigned, or some combination of both.

One possibility we envisioned was that participants in the disclosure condition would reveal a monetary limit significantly more often than those in the no-disclosure condition, yet would exaggerate this limit to the point of making equally small concessions. As it turned out, . . . those in the no-disclosure condition gave a monetary response almost as often as did those in the disclosure condition, and although the latter exaggerated somewhat, they did so to a much lesser extent than did those in the no-disclosure condition. Moreover, participants in the disclosure condition made less demanding offers and settled for significantly less profit. Thus, it appears as though the confederate's unsolicited cooperation caused participants to cooperate genuinely in return.

We contend that these effects occurred because, at some level, the reciprocity rule was activated. This is only an inference, however, because reciprocal impulses were not measured here. . . .

Alternative Explanations

. . . It is important to consider other explanations. One possibility . . . concerns participants' awareness that the experimenter knew they had an informational advantage. . . . Some participants in the disclosure condition who would have used the inside information to its fullest advantage held back because they did not want to be viewed by the experimenter as someone who would use this advantage to exploit an honest opponent. However, . . . any effect of this wariness should have been the same across conditions because the experimenter presumably did not know what was being said behind closed doors. . . . For this reason, it is very unlikely that the effects observed here are due to participants' knowledge of what the experimenter knew.

A second possibility concerns participants' certainty about the value of their opponent's alternative. . . . Going into the negotiation, all participants were fully aware of this information. . . . If . . . uncertainty did arise, it would not have remained equivalent across conditions. This is because once the negotiation began, the value of the other party's alternative was verified in the disclosure condition. . . . Consequently, those in the former condition would have become more certain about this value, whereas those in the latter condition would have remained less certain. To the extent that they were less certain, participants in the no-disclosure condition might have thought there was an outside chance that their opponent's alternative was actually weaker than what they had been told and that more extreme offers were therefore warranted. . . . This could explain why participants' offers and settlement terms were more demanding in the no-disclosure condition . . . [and] could explain why they were less truthful when the confederate inquired about their alternative.

. . . It should be noted that none of the participants gave any indication—to the experimenter, [to] the confederate, or on the postexperimental questionnaire—that they questioned the veracity of information provided. . . . In fact, most participants appeared to be so caught up in the competition for the money prize that they never thought to question the validity of the information provided. For these reasons, it seems unlikely that differential certainty could have produced the sizable effects observed here.

Yet another alternative explanation is that our confederate's disclosure, rather than activating a reciprocal motive, created an expectation on the participant's part that the confederate would continue to cooperate in the negotiation. . . . As a result of this expectation, participants in the disclosure condition may have been less concerned about making a demanding first offer that would guard against any demanding counteroffers the other party might subsequently make. In other words, these participants may have become less defensive, and this reduced defensiveness may have resulted in less demanding offers and a greater willingness to disclose information truthfully. . . . Of the three alternative explanations considered here, this latter possibility is probably the most plausible.

Conclusions and Future Directions

. . . Bargainers in the present experiment became more cooperative, even though there were no incentives for cooperation, when their opponent made an unambiguously cooperative move at the outset of the negotiation. . . . None of our participants knew their opponent. . . . The negotiation was purely distributive and bargainers were given an incentive to maximize their individual outcomes. Under these conditions, reciprocal cooperation ran counter to participants' economic self-interest. Nevertheless, they reciprocated by making less demanding offers, disclosing more truthful information about their own alternative, and settling for less profit. Thus, it appears as though our confederate's cooperative move may have activated the reciprocity rule (or perhaps an expectation that the confederate would continue to cooperate, as suggested by the alternative explanation discussed earlier).

To the extent that the reciprocity rule was indeed responsible for the effects here . . . self-interest does not appear to dominate bargaining behavior as much as previous research would suggest. Moreover, these results suggest that, in distributive negotiations, an unsolicited cooperative move may invite less exploitation than one would expect.

---

19. *What conclusions did the authors reach?*

In this face-to-face negotiating situation, participants who were bargaining with cooperative confederates (disclosure condition) reciprocated by being cooperative: They did not exaggerate their alternatives as much as those in the no-disclosure situation, and they made less demanding offers; they settled for smaller profits even when self-interest ($5 award and title of best negotiator) was at stake. Their cooperation was due to the confederates' cooperation (reciprocity). Another less preferred explanation is that participants in the disclosure situation became less defensive and cooperated because they expected the confederates to continue to be cooperative.

20. *Are the conclusions justified?*

Yes. This was a well-designed study, and all potential confounds were controlled or shown to be ineffective.

21. *To what population do these results generalize?*

Results generalize to undergraduate college students, about 26 years old, who are enrolled in psychology and business courses and who work full- or part-time.

STUDY EXAMPLE 11.2

We will review this study together because the design differs from that of the first one, although both are two-factor experiments. The study reviewed previously employed independent groups of participants who were randomly assigned to the four conditions. The study we are about to review included male and female students who wrote essays on their perceptions of teasing when they were the perpetrators and the victims (within-group factor). Therefore, some of the data were analyzed by 2×2 ANOVAs with repeated measures on the second factor.

The Study

Kowalski, R. M. (2000). "I was only kidding!": Victims' and perpetrators' perceptions of teasing. *Personality and Social Psychology Bulletin, 26*(2), 231-241. Copyright 2000 by Sage.

▶ *(The author includes a footnote thanking five individuals for helping in data collection.)*

In the course of everyday life, people do a lot of mean and unpleasant things to one another. They embarrass each other, betray one another, complain and nag, hurt each other's feelings, make each other feel guilty, and inflict many other sorts of psychological distress. Collectively, behaviors such as these have been termed "aversive interpersonal behaviors.". . . One of the more enigmatic of these aversive interpersonal behaviors is teasing. . . . Ironically, no matter how threatening a tease is to the recipient, the teaser can always claim that he or she was "only kidding" and, by doing so, seemingly disavow . . . any responsibility for harmful effects resulting from the tease. If, indeed, people are just kidding, then why do high school students list as their primary fear the fear of being teased? . . .

Teasing is difficult to define and study because it is a multifaceted phenomenon—some aspects of which have very positive connotations and some aspects of which have very negative connotations. . . . Because of its positive and negative connotations, teasing can include benign attempts to joke with others and poke good-natured fun or it can be used aggressively to hurt another person's feelings or to ostracize an individual from the group. . . . Depending on the target's current mood and the reactions of others who hear the tease, a particular taunt may be perceived as enjoyable on one occasion but unpleasant on another. . . .

... Part of the ambiguity underlying teasing arises from the target's difficulty in understanding the motives of the person initiating the tease. Is the teaser just joking around or is he or she attempting to ridicule or humiliate? ...

Teasing can have both positive and negative effects on the instigators and the targets of the tease. On the positive side, teasing may be used to demonstrate camaraderie and to strengthen social bonds with the target of the tease. ... On the negative side, teasing may be a means of strengthening social bonds with people other than the target by ostracizing the target. ...

So, when does teasing become aversive? When are teases labeled "good" or "acceptable" teases and when are they labeled "bad" or "unacceptable" teases? ... Teasing appears to become aversive when it is perceived to indicate relational devaluation. ... The relational devaluation may be unintentional on the part of the teaser but the feelings of embarrassment, identity challenge, and in some instances, exclusion are enough to suggest its presence to the target of the tease. Thus, teasing that implies interpersonal rejection and social exclusion (i.e., bad teasing) is perceived very differently from teasing that promotes camaraderie and social inclusion (i.e., good teasing).

Victims' and Perpetrators' Perceptions of Teasing

If there were no ambiguity in the perceived motives behind teasing, and if teasing never involved relational devaluation, perpetrators and targets of teasing might not be expected to differ in their perceptions of a teasing interaction. However, research on other aversive interactions ... suggests that victims and perpetrators frequently form very different perceptions of the interaction. Relative to victims, perpetrators minimize the negative impact of their behavior, view their behaviors more benignly, perceive the behavior as motivated by rational motives, and see the consequences of their behavior as more limited in scope. ...

The frequency with which people tease and their reactions when teased may depend on the person's early experiences with teasing. ... People who have had favorable experiences with teasing in the past will likely respond positively to other teasing encounters. On the other hand, people who have been mercilessly teased or who have been adversely affected by teases in the past will respond more negatively.

Personality variables also moderate perceptions of teasing behavior. ...

In addition, because of differences in the ways in which men and women are socialized, gender differences in perceptions of teasing behavior would be suspected. ... Women's teasing tends to be more playful and relationship-enhancing, whereas men's teasing is harsher and more likely to be relationship-demeaning. ...

. . . Because of . . . differential patterns of socialization, men's and women's feelings about teasing someone else or about being the victim of teasing would be expected to differ.

The present study was designed to examine differences in victims' and perpetrators' accounts of teasing episodes. Because of the ethical considerations involved with teasing participants in a laboratory setting, we relied on the use of autobiographical narratives. The efficacy of this methodology has been demonstrated. . . .

In the present study, each participant was assigned to write two autobiographical narratives, one that described an incident in which they were teased by someone else and another in which they perpetrated the tease. . . . It is important to note that each participant assumed both a victim and a perpetrator role. . . . Relative to victims, perpetrators were expected to downplay the adverse effects of their teasing and to see the situation as more humorous. Furthermore, the long-term effects of teasing were hypothesized to be more serious for victims than for perpetrators.

▷ *(Note that there were several ways in which the study could have been performed. Teasing could have been introduced as a variable, with one group as perpetrators and another as victims. However, ethics prevents introducing any variable that might be potentially harmful. The author could have shown films of teasing and being teased and asked participants to describe feelings of the actors or actresses. But the same potential for harm exists. Therefore, the author did the next-best thing by having participants describe their feelings when they actually were in both roles.)*

1. What was the rationale for the study?

Teasing is among aversive interpersonal behaviors. It can be seen as a joke, a way to establish camaraderie to strengthen a social bond; or it can be seen as aversive, an attempt to ridicule someone to devalue a relationship. The way in which teasing is perceived depends on the motive of the perpetrator.

Perceptions and frequency of teasing depend on past experiences with teasing. Those with positive experiences will respond positively, whereas those with negative experiences will respond unfavorably. Males and females also react differently. Female teases are playful and relationship-enhancing. Male teases are harsher and relationship-demeaning. Thus, feelings about being teased and about teasing are expected to differ.

2. What was the purpose of the study?

This study investigated the perception of teasing by individuals who wrote autobiographic descriptions of themselves both as perpetrators of a tease and as victims of a tease. Perceptions were predicted to be more negative and longer lasting for victims.

Method

Participants

Fifty female and 22 male undergraduate students participated in partial fulfillment of a course research requirement. The mean age of the participants was 22.4 (range 18-44), and more than 96% of the individuals taking part were Caucasian. Students participated in groups ranging in size from 10 to 30. To assure privacy, participants did not interact with one another at any time during the session.

▶ *(Note that there were more than twice as many females as males. The author has a note indicating that males refused to take part in the study because it would be embarrassing to report on teasing occasions. One then has to wonder whether the males who consented to serve differed from those who did not. For this reason, it is fortunate that each participant served as his or her own control. Moreover, we don't know about where the study took place [e.g., a large room with tables and chairs, an auditorium], especially with as many as 30 participants at a time. Furthermore, noninteraction does not ensure privacy. Unless participants were out of each other's view, there is potential eye contact or mere looking at someone. Finally, number of sessions could have been a minimum of three or a maximum of five.)*

---

3. Who were the participants?

Seventy-two mainly Caucasian undergraduates (50 males and 22 females) took part to fulfill a course requirement. They were about 22 years old but ranged in age from 18 to 44 years. Testing was in groups of 10 to 30.

Procedure

After signing a consent form, each participant was instructed to write two narratives. The order in which the narratives were written was counterbalanced. In one narrative, participants wrote about an event when they were teased by someone else. The instructions were as follows:

Please write a true story from your life about a time that you were teased. Nearly everyone has experienced being teased on more than one occasion; please choose an especially powerful and memorable experience of being teased. Be as thorough and complete as you can and tell the full story about the instance in which you were teased.

The other narrative focused on an incident in which they teased another individual. The instructions for this narrative resembled those for the victim narrative in every respect except that instead of writing about being teased, they wrote about a time when they were the teaser. Thus, in one story, participants were the victims of a tease, and in the other, the participants were the perpetrators.

▶ *(Note that nothing is said about how instructions were given, verbally or in writing, and, therefore, how counterbalancing was effected.)*

After writing each narrative, participants completed a questionnaire examining their perceptions of the experience. To examine participants' views of the positive features of the teasing situation, they were asked to rate how humorous they perceived the situation to be and the degree to which they thought their self-esteem was raised as a function of the teasing event. These questions were answered using 12-point scales with five scale labels (*not at all, slightly, moderately, very,* and *extremely*). Participants also indicated how positively they viewed the other individual and how positively they perceived they were viewed by the other person. Responses were again made using 12-point scales with five scale labels (*not at all positively, somewhat positively, moderately positively, very positively,* and *extremely positively*).

Because of the negative features that some people assign to teasing incidents, a second set of questions examined participants' perceptions of the negative features of the incident recounted. Specifically, participants indicated how negatively they felt about the experience, how negatively they perceived the other person to feel, the degree to which their self-esteem was lowered by the teasing encounter, how annoyed they felt, and how guilty they felt. Participants responded to each of these items using 12-point scales with five scale labels (*not at all* to *extremely*).

A third set of questions examined participants' prior experience with teasing. They also were asked how frequently they were teased by others and how frequently they teased other people. Twelve-point scales with five scale labels (*not at all* to *extremely*) were again used.

▶ *(Note that the questionnaire started with a measure of positive reactions and then negative reactions, which might or might not make a difference on the next autobiography. Half the time, they were followed by the essay of a victim [which might exaggerate the negative reactions], and half the time they were followed by the essay of a perpetrator [which might temper the positive reactions because of possible guilt]. Or they might make no difference at all. Although presumably, they were filled out twice, we know nothing about time intervening between the end of the first questionnaire and the second essay, during which time some forgetting might occur to lessen any potential carryover effect.)*

---

4. What was the procedure?

Participants met in groups of 10 to 30 per session and did not interact. Half wrote an autobiographical account of a powerful teasing incident when they were victims and then another essay about an incident when they were teasers. The other half had the reverse procedure. Each account was followed by a questionnaire that measured positive and then negative effects in both roles and the prior teasing history of participants.

5. What were good features of the design?

Good features included counterbalancing of autobiographies, instructions of noninteraction among participants, and use of independent assistants to gather the data.

6. What were questionable aspects of the procedure?

We don't know how much privacy each participant had when writing; we don't know how instructions were delivered; we don't know time limits for writing and for filling out questionnaires, nor the interval of time before beginning the next autobiography; and the positive and negative questionnaires were not counterbalanced.

Results

Content Analyses of Narratives

All narratives, both victim and perpetrator, were content analyzed along two dimensions: content of the tease and the relationship between the victim and perpetrator. . . . Two raters independently coded the narratives. Interrater reliability for both content and relationship exceeded .80.

▶ *(This was a good feature of the study.)*

. . . Seven categories were derived to classify the content of all of the teases: relationships . . . body parts/appearance, behavior . . . intelligence, medical conditions, stereotyping/social group . . . and other. . . . Each narrative was coded as belonging to only one content category.

> **7. What did preliminary analysis involve?**
>
> Scripts of victims and perpetrators were coded for relationship between the teased and teaser and for content of the tease.
>
> **8. What were the results?**
>
> After ensuring high interrater reliability between coders of the scripts, the author analyzed content into seven categories, including relationships, body parts, behavior, and so on.

Victims. . . . More than 45% of the victim narratives focused on physical appearance . . . followed by relationships (11.2%) and behavior (11.2%). . . .

. . . A chi-square analysis by gender conducted on the content areas revealed a significant gender difference, $\chi^2(6) = 15.01$, $p < .02$. For women, by far the largest percentage of teases dealt with body parts/appearance (52%). Men also were teased frequently about their appearance (27.3%) but were teased equally often about their relationships (27.3%).

The relationship between the teasing victim and perpetrator was coded as falling within one of four categories: romantic partners, friends, schoolmates, and relatives. . . . In more than half of the teasing episodes recounted by victims, the victim and perpetrator were schoolmates (55.7%). The teasing episodes recounted by male and female victims did not differ significantly in the relationship between victim and perpetrator, $\chi^2(3) = 1.77$, $p > .62$. Both male and female victims were teased more frequently by schoolmates.

▷ *(Note that except for romantic partners, presumably of the opposite sex, the remaining categories [friends, schoolmates, and relatives] could be of the same or opposite sex and that impact of a tease may be a function of this factor as well as the relationship per se.)*

> **9. What were the major sources of teasing for recipients?**
>
> Most females were teased about their appearance, whereas most males were teased about their appearance (27.3%) and their relationships (27.3%). Moreover, most of the teasers were schoolmates, followed by friends, and these results applied equally to male and female victims.

Perpetrators. The seven categories used to content analyze the victim narratives also were used for the perpetrator narratives. . . . The largest percentage of teases dealt with behavior (30.6%), followed closely by body parts/appearance (23.6%). The teasing episodes of male and female perpetrators did not differ significantly in the type of tease instigated, $\chi^2(3) = 9.53$, $p > .14$.

▶ *(Note that degrees of freedom are reported to be 3 instead of 6 [(7 – 1) (2 – 1)]. If you check the 9.53 in a chi-square table, you'll see that it has a p of about .14 with 6 df but would be significant for df = 3. Therefore, the reported 3 is a typographical error.)*

In general, the narratives in which participants reported teasing another individual involved people with whom the individual was either a friend (34.3%) or a relative (26.9%). When examined by gender, however, this overall pattern changes, $\chi^2(3) = 13.53$, $p < .003$. For men, the relationship between the victim and perpetrator was usually a friendship (65.0%), followed by schoolmates (20.0%). Women, on the other hand, were more likely to tease relatives (36.2%) than schoolmates (25.5%) or friends (31.9%).

---

10. What were the results regarding the content of teasing by perpetrators and their relationship to the victims?

For male and female perpetrators, most teases were about behavior and appearance (body parts). Males, however, were more likely to tease a friend, whereas females were more likely to tease relatives.

Linguistic Analysis

A text analysis was conducted on each of the participants' teasing narratives using the Linguistic Inquiry and Word Count strategy (LIWC). . . . This computer software analyzes the affective, cognitive, and structural elements of written text on a word-by-word basis. Sixty-one output variables are produced. . . . We were interested in this study in the composite variables of negative emotionality, positive emotionality, self-references, and other references.

The negative emotionality profile is calculated based on words such as *angry, ashamed,* and *worthless.* Positive emotionality, on the other hand, reflects words such as *excitement, peace,* and *security.* Split-plot analyses of variance with sex (male/female) as the between-participants factor and role (victim/perpetrator) as the within-participants factor were conducted on these composite variables. A main effect of role was obtained on the negative emotionality variable, $F(1, 70) = 5.34$, $p < .02$. Interestingly, participants' narratives reflected more negative emotionality when they wrote about teasing another person as opposed to being teased. Part of this may reflect the remorse and guilt that many participants reported when they wrote about teasing others. No significant effects were obtained with the positive emotionality variable (see Table 3).

TABLE 3 Main Effects of Role (Victim/Perpetrator)

Item	Victim		Perpetrator	
How negatively did you feel about the experience?	9.1	(3.3)	4.9	(3.5)
How negatively do you think the other person felt?	2.9	(2.8)	8.3	(4.0)
To what degree was your self-esteem raised?	2.1$_a$	(2.3)	3.3$_a$	(3.1)
To what degree was your self-esteem lowered?	7.5	(4.1)	3.1	(2.8)
How annoyed were you by the experience?	10.0	(3.1)	3.6	(3.3)
How guilty did you feel about the experience?	2.6	(2.8)	5.5	(3.8)
How humorous did you perceive the experience to be?	2.8	(3.2)	7.2	(3.7)
How positively do you view the other individual involved?	4.8	(3.6)	7.4	(3.9)
How positively do you think the individual views you?	5.8	(3.5)	7.1	(3.7)
Negative emotionality (LIWC)	3.5	(2.5)	4.5	(3.4)
Positive emotionality (LIWC)	2.2$_a$	(1.7)	2.1$_a$	(1.8)
References to self (LIWC)	11.3	(2.6)	8.8	(3.9)
References to other (LIWC)	3.3	(3.4)	8.3	(3.7)
Total word count (LIWC)	103.7	(57.5)	87.6	(42.5)
Exclamation marks (LIWC)	.41	(1.3)	.12	(.47)

NOTE: LIWC = Linguistic Inquiry and Word Count. Means in a single row sharing a common subscript do not differ significantly, $p > .05$. Standard deviations are reported in parentheses.

. . . Participants used more self-references when they wrote about being teased compared to teasing another, $F(1, 70) = 15.28$, $p < .001$. Conversely, more references to others were used when writing about teasing another than when writing about being teased, $F(1, 70) = 47.72$, $p < .001$. (Means are reported in Table 3). However, this effect was moderated by the gender of the participant, $F(1, 70) = 12.22$, $p < .001$ . . . men ($M = 5.1$, $SD = 4.6$) used significantly more other references than did women ($M = 2.4$, $SD = 2.5$). In addition, women used more other references when their narratives concerned teasing others ($M = 8.8$, $SD = 3.9$) than when they focused on being teased ($M = 2.4$, $SD = 2.5$), $ps < .05$.

▶ *(Note that circularity is not an issue in split-plot studies. Degrees of freedom, too, are as low as they can be. Furthermore, the results can be seen in a table to clarify them. Marginal means are in Table 3, and three cell means are given. Only the mean for male perpetrators is missing, but we can calculate it by knowing ns in each group, the corresponding cell mean for females, and the overall marginal. We set up an equation, $22(X) + 50(8.8) = 72(8.3)$; $22(X) = 597.6 - 440$; $X = 7.1$. Therefore, the table and all means are as follows:*

	Males (22)		Females (50)
Victims	5.1	2.4	3.3
Perpetrators	7.1	8.8	8.3)

From a structural perspective, participants used significantly more words when writing about being teased than about teasing, $F(1, 70) = 6.90, p < .01$. The proportion of exclamation marks used also was greater in narratives dealing with being teased than when teasing, $F(1, 70) = 4.40, p < .04$.

---

11. Scripts were analyzed for their structure, affect, self-references, and other references. What were the major findings?

Perpetrators used more negative words than did victims, but there were no differences between the two in the use of positive words. Victims used more self-references than did perpetrators, whereas the teasers used more references to others. Male victims, however, used more "other" references than did female victims. But the main effect of use of other references was due to females: Female perpetrators used more other references than did female victims. Finally, victims used more words and more exclamation points in their narratives than did perpetrators.

Postnarrative Questions

Two-by-two split-plot analyses of variance with sex as the between-participants factor and role as the within-participants factor were conducted on the remaining dependent variable measures. Overall, participants felt more negatively about the experience when they were the victim of a tease than when they perpetrated the tease, $F(1, 69) = 47.63, p < .001$. (Means for the role main effect are reported in Table 3.)

▶ *(Notice that apparently, one participant did not complete this part of the questionnaire. The* df *went from 70 to 69.)*

A main effect of gender obtained on negativity ratings revealed that men ($M = 5.8, SD = 3.6$) felt less negatively about the experience than did women ($M = 7.6, SD = 3.3$), $F(1, 69) = 7.20, p < .01$.

The analysis of the question that asked how participants perceived the other person felt as a result of the teasing incident revealed a main effect of role, $F(1, 68) = 77.04, p < .001$. Relative to victims, who perceived that the perpetrators felt mildly negative about the teasing event, perpetrators rated victims as feeling very negative about the experience.

. . . Analysis of the self-esteem enhancing effects of the experience revealed an interaction of sex and role, $F(1, 69) = 6.03$, $p < .02$. When recounting an event in which they were teased, men ($M = 3.3$, $SD = 3.1$) reported that their self-esteem was raised more than was reported by women ($M = 1.6$, $SD = 1.6$). However, women reported that their self-esteem was raised more when they perpetrated a tease ($M = 3.5$, $SD = 3.2$) than when they were teased ($M = 1.6$, $SD = 1.6$), $ps < .05$. . . . Overall, participants reported their self-esteem to be only slightly affected in the positive direction by the experience.

The negative effects of teasing on self-esteem were more pronounced. First, women's ($M = 5.8$, $SD = 3.4$) self-esteem was lowered more than men's ($M = 4.4$, $SD = 3.5$), $F(1, 69) = 4.32$, $p < .04$. . . . Victims of teasing reported more detrimental effects on their self-esteem than were reported by perpetrators, $F(1, 69) = 38.07$, $p < .001$.

Main effects of role also were obtained on questions examining how annoyed participants were by the experience, . . . how much guilt they felt, . . . and how humorous they found the experience to be. . . . Participants were more annoyed when they were the victims as opposed to the perpetrator. On the other hand, although participants not surprisingly reported finding the experience more humorous when they perpetrated the tease than when they were teased, they also experienced more guilt as the perpetrator than as the victim (see Table 3).

. . . Whereas men's reports of the amount of guilt experienced did not differ as a function of whether they were the victim ($M = 3.5$, $SD = 4.0$) or perpetrator of the tease ($M = 4.0$, $SD = 3,7$), women reported significantly more guilt when they initiated the tease ($M = 6.0$, $SD = 3.7$) than when they were the victim ($M = 2.2$, $SD = 2,1$), $ps < .05$.

Main effects of role also were obtained on ratings of how positively participants viewed the other individual, $F(1, 69) = 12.95$, $p < .001$, and how positively they thought the other individual viewed them, $F(1, 69) = 4.94$, $p < .03$. . . . Perpetrators viewed the targets more favorably than victims viewed perpetrators. On the other hand, perpetrators perceived that they were viewed more favorably by victims than victims thought they were viewed by perpetrators (see Table 3).

---

12. *What were the results regarding the questionnaire responses?*

Victims felt more negative than did perpetrators, but this was more true for females than males. Victims, however, rated perpetrators as feeling mildly negative about teasing, whereas perpetrators rated victims as feeling very negative. Positive self-esteem was slightly affected by either experience, but males reported higher self-esteem after being teased than did females, whereas females reported higher levels after teasing than after being teased. In contrast, females felt lower self-esteem than males (or at least were more willing to admit it) after being teased, and both sexes felt lower self-esteem after being teased than after teasing. Victims also found teasing more annoying, whereas perpetrators found the situation more humorous, although they experienced more guilt about teasing. The experience of guilt, however, depended on gender. Males felt equally guilty as victim and perpetrator; females felt guiltier after teasing than after being teased. Finally, victims viewed perpetrators less favorably than teasers viewed victims, whereas teasers felt that they were viewed more favorably by their victims than victims felt about how they were viewed by the teaser.

Discussion

Consistent with predictions and with previous research, victims and perpetrators perceived teasing episodes differently. Relative to victims, perpetrators not surprisingly perceived the incident to be more humorous. In addition, whereas perpetrators did not perceive the teasing encounters to be particularly annoying, victims reported being very annoyed by them. Perpetrators also reported higher feelings of guilt relative to victims. Perhaps reflecting these feelings of guilt, recollections of episodes in which the participant perpetrated the tease contained more negative emotionality than did victim accounts.

. . . Victims perceived that they were viewed less positively than perpetrators said they viewed them. Perpetrators, on the other hand, thought they were viewed more favorably than victims actually perceived them. Four explanations may account for this. First, victims may have misinterpreted the motives of the perpetrator and viewed the tease as more malevolent than was the case. . . . In other words, they perceived the perpetrator's behavior to indicate relational devaluation. . . . Second, perpetrators may have teased because they disliked some aspect of the target but were unwilling to admit so in the experiment. Third, even if perpetrators actually viewed the target negatively at the time of the incident, the passage of time and personal feelings of guilt may have led them to regard the target more favorably. Fourth, victims' negative evaluations of perpetrators may have become more negative with the passage of time. The content of some of the narratives, particularly those written by victims, suggested that many of the victims had ruminated about the teasing incident since its initial occurrence. These ruminations might have magnified the event in the victim's mind, thereby enhancing negative feelings that he or she had about the incident and the individual who perpetrated it. . . .

. . . Victims reported more negative effects on their self-esteem than did perpetrators. Teasing may be aversive because it is threatening to the self. . . . Teasers characterize the victim in negative ways and often impose an identity on the victim that is inconsistent with his or her self-perception. If the tease is perceived by the victim as an indication that the perpetrator does not adequately value his or her relationship with the victim, then the victim's self-esteem is likely to be affected. . . .

Also of note is the finding that perpetrators were well aware of the negative effects of their teasing. . . . Victims rated perpetrators as feeling mildly negative about the incident, whereas perpetrators rated victims as feeling very negatively about being teased. Perpetrators' knowledge of the negative feelings induced by the teasing may have facilitated the feelings of guilt that perpetrators reported.

▶ *(Note the inconsistency in reports by perpetrators. They perceived negative effects of teasing and felt guilty. That is consistent. But they also viewed the situation as more humorous than did victims and believed that victims perceived them favorably.)*

Content of Teases

The overwhelming majority of the victim narratives and a notable percentage of the perpetrator narratives focused on body parts and physical appearance. . . . Because physical appearance represents a readily observable feature, it is an easy target for teasing. Physical appearance is also a primary factor influencing perceptions of social approval and acceptance. . . . Because people who are physically attractive are perceived as more sociable, intelligent, psychologically adjusted, and skilled . . . teases about appearance perhaps more than any other type of tease may be used by perpetrators to convey dislike, relational devaluation, and social exclusion.

▶ *(Keep in mind that victims were teased mainly by schoolmates and then friends, whereas perpetrators teased mainly friends and then schoolmates. Moreover, it doesn't seem plausible that a teaser would view a victim positively and yet want to convey dislike or devalue a relationship.)*

Gender differences that were observed in relation to the content categories . . . although consistent with what one might expect, should be interpreted cautiously. These differences may reflect discrepancies between men and women in the salience of particular types of teases rather than the frequency with which those teases are actually perpetrated. . . . When being asked to retrospectively recall episodes of teasing, those related to appearance may be more salient to women than to men, in large part because of society's emphasis on women's physical appearance. . . .

. . . Relative to relationships, about which men were teased most frequently, people have less control over their body parts and their physical appearance, about which women were teased most frequently. Because of the less changeable nature of the content of the tease, women may be more adversely affected by teasing than are men. . . . Women's self-ratings of attractiveness and self-esteem are highly correlated, which suggests that they may be particularly susceptible to negative evaluations of appearance. . . .

Relationship Between Victim and Perpetrator

All of the teasing incidents involved victims and perpetrators who were acquainted with one another. One reason for this is that teases, whether motivated by benevolent or malevolent concerns, miss their mark with strangers. . . .

Consequences of Teasing

The long-term, primarily negative impact of the teasing incident on the victims was clear in victims' ratings as well as in the narratives themselves. Many of the victims wrote about the teasing incident as being something that they will never forget or as an event that they "vividly remember." . . . Statements . . . convey victims' feelings that teasers do not value them or their relationship. . . .

Perhaps more surprising than the long-term effects of teasing on the victims were the negative effects recounted by perpetrators. After thinking back on the instances in which they teased someone else, many perpetrators reported feeling guilty or wondering what happened to the person that they teased. . . .

Many of the victim/perpetrator findings from this study parallel those of other studies in finding that victims not surprisingly view the experience more negatively than do perpetrators. . . . Rarely did perpetrators in the present study deny that their teasing had any negative effects. . . . Many of the episodes recounted occurred during middle and high school. Thus, maturation alone may account for some awareness on the part of perpetrators regarding the negative effects of their teasing. In addition, . . . teasing is almost never justified. The victim of teasing rarely if ever deserves to be teased. . . .

Limitations

. . . Certain limitations need to be acknowledged. The methodology relies on narrative accounts of teasing episodes that were "especially powerful and memorable." . . . Thus, we cannot be sure that the results presented here will generalize to recollections of more mundane teasing episodes.

. . . The narratives in which an individual teased and those in which they were teased reflect different events. This leaves open the possibility that the victim and perpetrator narratives are qualitatively different from one another, thereby undermining any conclusions that might be drawn. . . . We believe that the events recounted in the victim and perpetrator narratives are qualitatively similar.

In addition, the unwillingness of some men to participate in the study leads to the question of whether those who did participate represent a different group of individuals from those who chose not to be included. Descriptive statistics showing approximately equal variances for the male and female participants suggested that this was not the case.

▶ *(Not necessarily so; these statistics show that males and females who volunteered for the study were similar in the statistical descriptions. They do not show that the males who refused to volunteer were the same or different. That is, their descriptive statistics might well differ from the males and females who volunteered.)*

The gender effects examined in this study were based solely on the gender of the participants. Thus, we do not have information related to the frequency with which men and women were teased by members of each gender.

---

13. What were the major conclusions?

Perpetrators and victims perceived a teasing situation differently. Perpetrators perceived it as more humorous and with less annoyance but with more guilt. And their narratives contained more negative words, perhaps a reflection of the guilt. Perpetrators viewed victims more positively than victims felt they were perceived. But they also felt that they were perceived more favorably than victims perceived them. Perpetrators also rated victims as feeling more negative about the tease than victims rated themselves.

Because physical appearance was the biggest source of teasing, particularly for female victims, and social acceptability is correlated with physical attractiveness, teasing may be used to convey dislike and relational devaluation.

Negative impacts of teasing are greater on victims than perpetrators; however, many perpetrators feel guilty about having teased the victim.

14. Are the conclusions justified?

Because the narratives were written by the same individuals who had been victimized by powerful teases and, likewise, had victimized others in the same way, the conclusions about the findings per se probably are justified. Order of narratives was counterbalanced, and narratives were of events that took place at about the same time.

Although testing conditions may have been less than ideal, they should have had equal effects on both narratives. The major stipulation relates to the postnarrative questionnaire, in which sets of questions were not counterbalanced. These questionnaires focused on positive aspects of teasing, negative aspects, then prior teasing history. A reminder of negative aspects could have affected a victim report by emphasizing them and could have had the opposite effect on perpetrator reports. Or the questionnaire could have had no effect. Moreover, there were inconsistencies in narratives of perpetrators, but these temper the explanations of the findings, which may be open to debate (e.g., relational devaluation as an explanation of teasing). Moreover, we might be missing some valuable information from males who refused to participate. Nonetheless, their biggest loss is on external and not internal validity.

15. To what population can these results generalize?

Results can generalize to college undergraduates willing to write about powerful teasing episodes that took place in middle school, high school, or both and involved mainly schoolmates or friends.

BIBLIOGRAPHY

Girden, E. R. (1992). *ANOVA: Repeated measures.* Newbury Park, CA: Sage.

Hays, W. L. (1988). *Statistics* (4th ed.). New York: Holt, Rinehart & Winston.

Howell, D. C. (1992). *Statistical methods for psychology.* Boston: PWS-Kent.

Iversen, G. R., & Norpoth, H. (1987). *Analysis of variance* (2nd ed.). Newbury Park, CA: Sage.

Stevens, J. (1990). *Intermediate statistics: A modern approach.* Hillsdale, NJ: Lawrence Erlbaum.

Additional Suggested Readings

Jaccard, J. (1998). *Interaction effects in factorial analysis of variance.* Thousand Oaks, CA: Sage.

Keppel, G. (1991). *Design and analysis: A researcher's handbook* (3rd ed.). Englewood Cliffs, NJ: Prentice Hall.

Pedhazur, E. J., & Schmelkin, L. P. (1991). *Measurement, design, and analysis: An integrated approach.* Hillsdale, NJ: Lawrence Erlbaum.

Chapter 12

Quasi-Experimental Studies

The major characteristics of a true experimental design, like those considered in the preceding chapters, include random assignment of participants to the various experimental and control conditions of the study. This procedure makes it more likely that groups initially are equivalent and therefore eliminates alternate explanations of results. In many instances, random assignment is not possible or not permitted by an administrator when, for example, special programs in institutions, medical settings, or mental health clinics need to be evaluated. Participants, such as those being treated after attempting suicide, abused children, drug addicts, and so forth, would not be amenable to random assignment. For these reasons, experimenters sometimes are forced to work with intact groups. The net effect is that the various groups cannot be assumed to be equivalent before treatment. Therefore, the studies are not considered to be true experiments but instead are referred to as seemingly experimental or *quasi-experimental* designs. A variety of such designs are available. Keep in mind that we are dealing with intact groups, not groups that have been randomly assigned to different conditions. Therefore, the important issue is to work with these possibly nonequivalent groups in such a way that we may still be able to draw cause-and-effect conclusions.

There are two basic categories of these designs. Repeated measures types obtain a number of measures of the dependent variable before and after the intervention (independent variable) on the same group of participants. Any change in behavior after intervention is less likely to be contaminated by the usual confounds. This is the rationale behind the *interrupted time-series* study. It is suitable for behaviors that can stabilize but still have room for improvement or change in trend. These might include changes in accidents involving a driver who was under the influence of alcohol or drugs before and after legislation was introduced regarding drunk drivers, changes in rate of recovery for certain surgeries before and after hospital policy changed, or changes in some aspect of scholastic achievement before and after a critical curriculum change was introduced. To minimize some of the threats to internal validity (history, maturation, selectivity, pretest sensitization), a control group is added, if feasible. This group will not receive the treatment, but it is another intact group, not one that was formed by random assignment. The design is known as *multiple time-series*.

Separate groups quasi-experimental designs include experimental and control groups. Participants in each condition, however, are not randomly assigned; they are intact groups (e.g., separate classes of students, patients in different mental health clinics, workers in different parts of a factory). Therefore, groups cannot be assumed to be equivalent with respect to variables that might affect performance, and the designs are known as *nonequivalent control group* designs. First, there is the *posttest-only nonequivalent control group* design. In this case, posttreatment scores of an experimental group are compared with an untreated control group. We are talking about intact groups, so there is no basis for assuming group equivalency or for assuming that posttest differences might have occurred anyway, even without treatment. Another alternative is the *nonequivalent pretest-posttest control group* design, which is used so frequently in medical research and involves between-groups comparisons. It resembles the pre-posttest design, which includes a control group that only gets the tests but differs from it in that the groups come from two different sources and hence are not considered equivalent at the beginning. They are preexisting rather than random groups. A third type of nonequivalent control group employs *cohorts*, groups of individuals who are similar in age, group membership, or both and, presumably, experience. Thus, second-year students in a Psy.D. program are considered to be cohorts.

Performance in an Intermediate Statistics course might be compared before and after the introduction of a computer program, using the new group of students compared with those second-year students of 1 or 2 years ago. Should there be an improvement, it would be difficult to interpret. Admission policies may have become more stringent and resulted in brighter students in the new group, the faculty member may have improved teaching skills, the textbook may have been changed to a clearer one, and the experimental students may not be as phobic about statistics!

Although the factor of initial nonequivalence on the dependent variable cannot be controlled experimentally, it is sometimes possible to achieve some degree of equivalence statistically, by means of *analysis of covariance* (ANCOVA). With this technique, an initial measure (pretest) of the dependent variable, or a variable that is linearly correlated with it, is made. This is the covariate or concomitant variable. Then, that part of variability of the posttreatment dependent variable associated with the covariate (r^2 for the entire set of posttreatment and covariate scores) is removed. The final analysis of variance is performed on the remaining part of variability to determine how much is due to treatment and how much to experimental or random error. And the group means that are compared have been adjusted linearly.

As in any statistical procedure, there are certain assumptions made before the final analysis is performed. First, the relationship between the covariate and dependent variable is assumed to be linear, because this is the assumption underlying regression analysis, the basis for the adjustment. Second, the most glaring assumption is that the relationship between the covariate and dependent variable is about the same in all groups (i.e., all within-

BOX 12.1
Caution Factors
With Quasi-
Experimental
Studies

■ History did not produce posttreatment performance.

■ Maturation did not produce posttreatment performance.

■ Pretest experience did not produce posttreatment performance.

■ Changes in the measuring instrument did not produce posttreatment performance.

■ A group was not specifically selected because it would react to treatment.

■ Posttest performance is not due to regression toward the mean.

■ Posttest performance is not due to interaction between select group and history or maturation.

■ Posttreatment performance is not due to selective loss of participants.

■ Nonequivalent control group is carefully matched with experimental group.

■ Covariate and other test measures are reliable and valid.

■ Testing conditions are uniform.

■ Experimenter is blind with regard to purpose of the study.

■ Statistical assumptions of ANCOVA are met.

group slopes are equal). Therefore, there should be some indication that a test of "homogeneity of regression slopes" has been performed. If they are not equal, analysis of covariance is inappropriate, and another statistical test would be performed. A final as-sumption relates to measures of the covariate. If these are other than standardized test scores, they are subject to errors of measurement, can affect treatment mean differences, and can produce misleading results. In checking for accuracy of the statistical test, $df =$

number of groups – 1 for the numerator and total N – number of groups – 1 for the error term.

It is worth noting that there is considerable controversy concerning the use of ANCOVA as a statistical control procedure when experimental control is not possible. First, unless the covariate is measured before treatment is introduced, you cannot be certain that it was not affected by treatment (unless it is something like age, level of education, etc.). Therefore, removing its effect from total variance may also remove some of the treatment effect. Second, the intent of ANCOVA is to equalize groups on that variable by removing its effect. But such equalization may not be realistic. It would be similar to using initial weight as a covariate to compare weight gain by fathers and young sons after a special diet. Realistically, they are not equal in weight.

There are other arguments, but the most potent is that ANCOVA does not produce equivalent groups from intact groups. Although these groups will be equivalent with respect to the covariate(s), there will always be other variables that differentiate intact groups, which otherwise would be distributed by random assignment. The researcher can only hope that critical ones that can just as easily account for the results have been isolated. Caution factors associated with quasi-experimental designs are found in Box 12.1.

We will evaluate two studies, the first together and the second by you alone. Each introduces nonequivalent groups, but they are introduced for different reasons: one uses the group as an experimental group, and the second uses it as a control group.

STUDY EXAMPLE 12.1

The present study compares moral development in early adolescents from two countries, Norway and Canada. The Norway data are contemporary; the Canadian data were gathered at an earlier time. Both sets of data are compared with gender as a second factor.

The Study

Skoe, E. E. A., Hansen, K. L., Mørch, W-T., Bakke, I., Hoffmann, T., Larsen, B., & Aasheim, M. (1999). Care-based moral reasoning in Norwegian and Canadian early adolescents: A cross- national comparison. *Journal of Early Adolescence, 19*(2), 280-291. Copyright 1999 by Sage.

The theoretical and empirical foundations of psychology are rooted deeply in Western culture, especially that of the United States. . . . The area of moral reasoning is no exception. Most theories and research have been North American. However, development always occurs in a cultural context . . . and socialization varies both across cultures and across countries within cultures. Although prominent theories of moral development . . . stress social experience, little research has examined cultural variation, especially in the case of the Gilligan . . . theory.

Gilligan . . . has proposed that an "ethic of justice" characterizes the moral voice of men, and "ethic of care" characterizes women. . . . However, whereas some studies . . . have found gender differences in moral orientation (care/justice), others have not. . . . Both genders resort more to the care orientation than to justice when discussing relational real-life dilemmas, and both tend to use justice more than care when discussing nonrelational dilemmas. . . . Women's tendency to report more relational conflicts results in their showing more care responses than do men. . . .

Extensive research on gender differences . . . has tended to obscure a second important implication of the Gilligan . . . work: the concept that care reasoning, like justice reasoning, follows specific developmental pathways and varies individually. The Skoe and Marcia . . . Ethic of Care Interview (ECI) measures the following five hierarchical levels of development in the care ethic, in accordance with the Gilligan . . . theory: exclusive self-concern, questioning of self-concern as a sole criterion, primarily other-concern, questioning of other-concern as a sole criterion, and balanced self-and-other concern. The ECI uses a real-life dilemma in addition to standardized dilemmas involving care issues. Recent research . . . validates a care-based approach to moral development. . . . The ECI has been found to be related positively to age, ego development, the Kohlberg justice stages, androgyny, empathy, and prosocial behavior. . . .

No gender differences have been observed on the ECI among late adolescents and young adults in North America or in Norway. . . . However, in a study of Canadian early adolescents . . . girls scored higher than did boys on the ECI, and more girls scored at ECI Level 2 (conventions of goodness, caring for others). These gender differences, occurring in early adolescence but not in young adulthood, are consistent with North American research in related areas such as justice-based moral development . . . ego development . . . and prosocial moral reasoning. . . . To date, no research has investigated levels of care in Norwegian children.

. . . The early adolescent gender differences commonly reported in North America are not universal necessarily. . . . To the extent that national social contexts vary, developmental patterns also might differ. . . . Values vary cross-nationally, reflecting different mental programs that are developed in the family and reinforced in schools, organizations, and the media. One such program concerns gender role expectations.

The present study compared care-based moral reasoning and real-life moral dilemma content in Norwegian male and female early adolescents with data obtained previously from Canadians of the same age (Skoe & Gooden, 1993). There is reason to believe that gender role socialization differs in Scandinavian and North American contexts . . . American gender concepts traditionally [are] more stereotyped than were those of Sweden. Swedish women were assigned more instrumental traits (e.g., ambitious, hardworking, willing to take a stand); American women were ascribed more expressive ones (e.g., compassionate, caring, eager to soothe hurt feelings). Only the Swedish women were described as liberated.

▶ *(Note that many American woman, myself included, would look at these findings and wonder which American country was surveyed. The study was conducted in 1988, but the title of the book refers to American youths.)*

. . . Recent research has shown that Scandinavian girls and boys alike value self-sufficiency and independence. . . . Therefore, fewer gender differences in care-based moral reasoning would be expected [in] Norway than in Canada.

. . . In Norway, as compared to North America, boys and girls both tend to demonstrate traditionally masculine instrumental traits of self-reliance and independence. . . . Unlike Americans . . . Norwegian adolescent girls and boys have been found not to differ significantly on masculinity measures. . . . Thus, Norwegian norms for feminine behavior might emphasize individuation more, and interpersonal connection less, than might Canadian norms. . . .

. . . In the present study, fewer gender differences were predicted in Norway than in Canada and stronger national differences for girls than for boys. Biological and social changes focus early adolescents' attention on gender role behavior in new ways. Norway and Canada might differ even more in gender expectations for females than for males. If so, Canadian and Norwegian girls might differ more dramatically than might boys from both countries in the gender role content that is important in early adolescence. Thus, it was expected that Norwegian and Canadian girls would differ on care-reasoning level and on self-reported real-life dilemma content, whereas no such differences would be found for boys. Specifically, because female role expectations and socialization practices traditionally stress interpersonal connection, it was predicted that more Canadian than Norwegian girls would score at ECI Level 2 (caring for others) and generate relational real-life dilemmas.

▶ *(Keep in mind that data from Canada were collected about 7 years earlier than data in Norway.)*

1. What was the rationale for the study?

Research on moral reasoning has been conducted mainly in North America. But development occurs within a culture, and socialization varies between cultures and in countries within cultures. Its development in different cultures hardly has been studied, particularly regarding Gilligan's theory. Gilligan proposed that male moral orientation is dominated by justice ethics, whereas a female's orientation is dominated by care ethics. Research support is ambiguous, but orientation may depend on the type of conflict generating the orientation. Relational dilemmas generate a care orientation; nonrelational dilemmas generate a justice orientation.

An implication of Gilligan's theory that has not received much attention is variations in the development of care reasoning. The Ethics of Care Interview (ECI) measures five levels of its development, from self-concern to a balance between concern for the self and concern for others. A study of North American and Norwegian late adolescents revealed no gender differences in ECI. But in a study of Canadian early adolescents, girls scored higher than boys on the interview, and more girls scored at the second level of development. No study investigated Norwegian children.

2. What was the purpose of the study?

This study compared moral reasoning and real-life moral dilemma content of Norwegian early adolescents with data obtained earlier on Canadian early adolescents. Because of differences in gender role expectations between countries, fewer gender differences in moral reasoning were expected among Norwegian than Canadian children. But because gender expectations are emphasized more for females, greater between-country differences were predicted for females. In particular, more Canadian than Norwegian females were predicted to score at the second level of development (caring for others) and to generate more relational real-life dilemmas.

Method

Participants

The Norwegian sample consisted of 79 (45 girls and 34 boys) fifth- and sixth-grade early adolescents, with a median age of 12.0 years, from a small coastal city in northern Norway. The Canadian sample, also used in a previous study . . . consisted of 46 sixth-grade students (23 girls and 23 boys), with a median age of 11.8 years, from a Canadian East Coast town. All participants were Caucasian and volunteered to participate. The Canadians, who started school 1 year earlier, had more education ($X = 6.0$, $SD = 0.0$) than did the Norwegians ($\overline{X} = 5.4$, $SD = 0.50$), $F(1, 123) = 63.10$, $p < .001$, indicating a need to control for grade level in analyses.

▶ *(Note that the Norwegian location is described as a "city," whereas the Canadian location is described as a "town," a unit that is generally smaller. Moreover, median ages are reported, and this is usually the statistic of choice with the presence of extreme scores. Median for Norwegian children is 12 years, and they were from fifth and sixth grades. Canadian children's age is 11.8, and they were from sixth grade. In addition, a standard deviation of 0.00 is highly unusual but in this case indicates that all the Canadian children had attended school for exactly 6 years, whereas the Norwegian children had attended school for 5 or 6 years, with more attending for 5 years because the mean is below 5.5. What is important is that if Canadian children had more education, they may have had extra gender-role training as well, if this is conducted in the school. If this is true, grade level per se is not an appropriate covariate. Finally, nothing is reported about economic level of the children nor their family status, for example, marital status of the parents.)*

---

3. Who were the participants?

The Norwegian sample included 45 girls and 34 boys, all volunteers and all Caucasian, from fifth and sixth grade, who lived in a small coastal city. The Canadian sample, tested in 1993, included 23 girls and 23 boys, also Caucasians, who volunteered, from sixth grade, who lived in a coastal town. Median ages were 12 and 11.8 years, and Canadian children had more education than the Norwegian children.

4. What are some questions regarding group equivalence, except for country of origin?

The Norwegian children were exposed to social and cultural practices that occurred 7 years later than those to which Canadian children were exposed in their country. Also there may have been bigger differences in ages between the two groups than are reflected in the medians. Moreover, Canadian children may have experienced more training in gender role expectations because of their extra year of education. Finally, economic levels may not have been equivalent, and this might affect the training the children received.

Procedure

Permission to conduct the study was obtained from the school administration. Subsequently, consent was obtained both from the children and their parents. A female researcher first individually administered the real-life dilemma and then an interpersonal dilemma from the children's version of the ECI . . . chosen for its cross-national appropriateness: "Siri/Per has been invited by her/his friend, Kari/Jon, for dinner on Friday. The next day, another friend, Vigdis/Nils, invites Siri/Per to a big birthday party on the same Friday. What do you think Siri/Per should do?" The real-life dilemma was elicited first to avoid biasing real-life dilemma choice by providing an example beforehand. Participants described a personal moral conflict and then standard probes were used, such as "What were the conflicts for you in that situation?" and "Did you think it was the right thing to do?" The standardized dilemma was read aloud to the participants while they read along. Probes such as "What do you think Siri/Per should do?" and "What would you do if you were in the same situation? Why?" were used to examine dilemma reasoning.

▶ *(Note that noncounterbalancing was deliberate, but justification would have been stronger with experimental support of the assumption that the self-report would have been influenced by the presented dilemma. Note, too, that a female tested both males and females.)*

The audiotaped interviews were scored according to the *Ethics of Care Interview Manual.* . . . Level 1 is survival (caring for self). The aim is basically to protect self; there is little care for others. Level 1.5 is transition from survival to responsibility. Although aware of the needs of others, the person still will favor self-interest in relationships. Level 2 involves conventions of goodness (caring for others), characterized by a concept of responsibility. *Good* is equated with self-sacrificial care for others, and *right* is externally defined, often at the expense of self-assertion. Level 2.5 concerns transition from a conventional to a reflective care perspective, and from goodness to truth and honesty in relationships. Commitment to others still is important, but there is more flexibility, thoughtfulness, and struggle with the dilemmas than at the earlier levels. Level 3 fully realizes the ethic of care (caring both for self and others). This perspective focuses on the dynamics of relationships and dispels the tension between selfishness and responsibility through a harmonization of the needs of self and others. . . .

Level scores for each of the two dilemmas were added, yielding a total score ranging from 2.0 through 6.0. Overall level scores then were halved and rounded to the nearest .5 level (e.g., 1.88 = Level 2, 1.13 = Level 1). The correlations of care reasoning levels across the two dilemmas for the Norwegian and Canadian samples were .66 and .67, respectively (both $ps < .0001$). Two independent judges rated a random sample of 50 ECI tapes (25 girls and 25 boys). Interscorer agreements for the real-life and Siri/Per dilemmas were 94% and 96%, respectively (Cohen's kappas were .91 and .94). . . . The real-life dilemmas also were scored as either relational (involves an ongoing significant relationship) or nonrelational (involves a person whom the participant does not know well or an issue primarily intrinsic to self). Two raters classified independently all dilemmas with 100% agreement.

▶ *(Note that no mention is made of where interviews took place, nor the time of day, nor the length of time it took to be interviewed. Moreover, the scoring range is narrow, and no justification is given for halving overall scores. Nor is it clear who the scorer was.)*

5. What was the procedure?

Participants were tested by a female research assistant. Each first described a real-life dilemma and its resolution. Then each was read an interpersonal dilemma and was asked to resolve it. Order of the two deliberately was not counterbalanced to control the effect of the standard dilemma on the one elicited. Each audiotaped interview was scored for level on the ECI. Two judges rated a random sample of tapes of 25 girls and 25 boys. Interscorer agreements for each were 94% and 96%. Finally, each real-life dilemma was classified as relational or nonrelational.

6. What are some questionable aspects of the procedure?

Only a female assistant interviewed the children, and assistants had to differ for the Canadian and Norwegian children. Testing conditions are not described at all. Standardization procedures for the interview are not reported, nor are validity or reliability coefficients reported (except for the 50 random interviews). Moreover, scoring procedure is not clear and appears to result in a very narrow range of scores.

Results

A 2 (Gender) × 2 (Norway/Canada) analysis of covariance, with ECI total score as the dependent variable and grade as a covariate, revealed a significant interaction, $F(1, 120) = 8.05$, $p < 01$. Follow-up one-way analyses showed that Canadian girls scored significantly higher than did Canadian boys, $F(1, 44) = 8.94$, $p < .005$. There were no significant gender differences in Norway, $F(1, 77) = .33$, n.s. Also, whereas Canadian girls scored significantly higher on the ECI ($X = 3.53$, $SD = 0.53$) than did Norwegian girls ($X = 2.95$, $SD = 0.51$), $F(1, 66) = 19.22$, $p < .0001$, Canadian ($X = 3.02$, $SD = 0.63$) and Norwegian ($X = 3.02$, $SD = 0.60$) boys did not differ significantly, $F(1, 55) = 1.00$, n.s. There was no significant effect for the covariate.

▶ *(We have enough information to set up a table. We can do minimal checking because the adjustments for the covariate are made on between-group and interaction mean squares as well as error. But because we are unsure about the appropriateness of the covariate [including its relationship with ECI, which is supposed to be linear and the same for both countries], we can calculate an unadjusted F ratio and see how it compares with the obtained F.*

	Norway	Canada	
Male	3.02 (0.60;34)	3.02 (0.63;23)	3.02 (57)
Female	2.95 (0.51;45)	3.53 (0.53;23)	3.15 (68)
	2.98 (79)	3.28 (46)	3.09 (125)

$MS_{int} = 34(3.02 - 3.02 - 2.98 + 3.09)^2 + \ldots + 23(3.53 - 3.15 - 3.28 + 3.09)^2 = 2.4365\ (df = 1).$

$MS_e = [33(.60)^2 + \ldots + 22(.53)^2]/121 = 0.316.$

$F = 2.4365/0.316 = 7.710.$

▶ *Interaction is significant at* p < .01, *so the covariate added some power to the test. Note, however, that the post hoc tests were inappropriate. Usual F tests were performed, which were wrong on two counts: The error term should have been the adjusted one from the original analysis, and the means should have been adjusted for the covariate. Nonetheless, the findings are accurate; the difference between the means for the Canadian males and females is significant.)*

A 2 (Norway/Canada) × 3 (ECI level) chi-square analysis was conducted on the participant frequencies for each ECI level (see Table 1). More Canadian than Norwegian girls scored at ECI Level 2, and more Norwegian than Canadian girls scored at the two lowest levels (phi = .47), $\chi^2(2, N = 68) = 15.12, p < .001$. In contrast, there were no significant differences among the boys.

▶ *(Note that these statements can be checked by performing chi-square tests on the data for females and males. The test for females indeed yields 15.12, as the authors report. Now, each cell can be examined to determine the extent to which observed frequency differs from its expected frequency. In fact, only one difference is significant: For Canadian girls who responded with Level 2 responses, the observed frequency is 14 and the expected frequency is [21(row total) × 23(column total)]/68 (total girls)] = 7.103. Then, Z = observed frequency − expected frequency / $\sqrt{\text{expected frequency}}$ = (14 − 7.103) / $\sqrt{7.103}$ = 2.2588, p = .0048. No other difference is significant. Therefore, we can conclude only that more Canadian girls than Norwegian girls responded with Level 2 responses.)*

TABLE 1 Frequencies of Participants in the Ethic of Care Interview (ECI) Levels				
	Norway		Canada	
ECI Level	%	n	%	n
Girls				
1	20.0	9	4.3	1
1.5	64.4	29	30.4	8
2	15.6	7	60.9	14
Boys				
1	20.6	7	21.7	5
1.5	50.0	17	52.2	12
2	29.4	10	26.1	6

Table 2 presents participant frequencies for the relational and non-relational real-life dilemma categories. A 2 (gender) × 2 (Relational/nonrelational) chi-square analyses showed no significant gender differences for the Norwegians (phi = .07), $\chi^2(2, N = 46) = 8.26$, $p < .005$. Also, significantly more Canadian than Norwegian girls generated relational dilemmas, and more Norwegian than Canadian girls generated nonrelational ones, $\chi^2(1, N = 68) = 4.63$, $p < .05$. For boys, there were no significant national differences.

▶ *(Here, too, statements can be checked by looking at individual cells. Note that four chi squares were calculated: for Norwegians, Canadians, females, and males. No differences are found for Norwegians. Two differences are found for Canadians: females gave fewer nonrelational responses than expected, $[0 - 3.5]/\sqrt{3.5} = -1.871$, and males gave more nonrelational responses than expected, $[7 - 3.5]/\sqrt{3.5} = 1.871$. This means that males gave more nonrelational responses than females, but no differences were found regarding relational responses. For females, one difference is found: Canadian females gave fewer nonrelational responses than expected. Although all Canadian females gave more relational responses, the number did not differ from what is expected by chance.)*

---

7. What were the results regarding use of caring solutions to the dilemmas facing boys and girls of the two countries?

First, Canadian females responded at a higher level of caring than did Norwegian females, but a similar difference was not found among males.

Second, more Canadian females responded at Level 2 of the ECI than did Norwegian females. Although the authors report that more Norwegian than Canadian females responded at the lower levels, none of these frequencies were significantly different from what was expected by chance. Third, the authors reported that Canadian females generated more relational real-life dilemmas than did Canadian males, and Norwegian females generated more nonrelational real-life dilemmas than did Canadian females (who generated none). Analysis of the data reveals that, in fact, Canadian males generated more nonrelational responses than females and that Canadian females made fewer nonrelational responses than Norwegian females.

TABLE 2 Content Analysis of the Nature of the Relationship in Real-Life Dilemmas

	Norway		Canada	
Nature	%	n	%	n
Girls				
Relational	82.2	37	100.0	23
Nonrelational	17.8	8	0.0	0
Boys				
Relational	76.5	26	69.6	16
Nonrelational	23.5	8	30.4	7

Discussion

. . . Canada and Norway are urbanized, industrial Western countries with similar characteristics and values, but their social norms for gender behavior differ. This likely influences how young people reason morally about the needs of self and others. The present study casts doubt on the universality of developmental gender differences in care-based moral reasoning. . . . As predicted, early adolescent Canadian girls scored higher than boys on the ECI and generated more relational real-life dilemmas. In contrast, Norwegian boys and girls scored similarly on these measures. The Canadian results are consistent with the North American theory and research. . . . However, the Norwegian results do not follow that pattern. As predicted, there were significantly fewer girls at ECI Level 2 (conventions of goodness, caring for others) in Norway (15.6%) than in Canada (60.9%). Also, as predicted, significantly more Canadian girls reported relational real-life dilemmas (100%) than did Norwegian girls (82.2%). These results are congruent with the . . . finding that American adolescents were more gender stereotyped than were Swedish adolescents and . . . observations that in Norway, unlike in North America, girls and boys both tend to focus on self and independence.

. . . Gender stereotyping, which traditionally has encouraged females toward care for others . . . seems to remain stronger in North America than in Norway, where the current cohort of young adolescents [has] available stronger social models of female independence and participation in public life, and an environment of greater gender equality. Thus, girls in North America and Scandinavia likely perceive somewhat differing sets of characteristics as gender appropriate. The stronger Norwegian tendency to encourage girls toward self-assertion and achievement probably focuses them on their own interests, rather than on primary concern for others.

. . . Canadian girls simply might acquire Level 2 reasoning early (compared to Norwegian girls and to boys in both countries) because early adolescent sensitivity to gender expectations differentially orients them toward such reasoning at a younger age. . . .

The gender differences of early adolescence are sometimes attributed to biological factors, such as a growth spurt for girls in physical and cerebral cortical maturation . . . or to social experiences. . . . The present findings support the latter explanation. Surely, there are many major life experiences behind gender . . . and several are determined culturally. Longitudinal cross-cultural research that addresses both the ethics of justice and care is necessary to assess further developmental issues in morality and to delineate the roots of individual as well as cultural differences.

---

8. What did the authors conclude?

Because social norms for gender behavior differ in Norway and Canada, these differences likely influence moral reasoning about needs for the self and for others. Canadian females scored higher on the ethics scale and generated more relationship real-life dilemmas than males. Norwegian males and females scored alike. Fewer Norwegian than Canadian females responded to the dilemmas at Level 2, and more Canadian than Norwegian females responded to the real-life dilemma with relational responses. These findings support the notion that North American adolescents are more gender stereotyped than are Scandinavian females and that Norwegian males and females are more focused on independence and the self. Stereotyping of the feminine role to care more for others seems stronger in North America than in Scandinavia. Thus, gender-appropriate responses are perceived differently by adolescents of both cultures. Canadian females may respond more at Level 2 because this orientation is taught at a younger age.

9. Are these conclusions justified?

On the basis of some statistical tests, two conclusions appear justified. Canadian females scored at a higher level than their male counterparts on the ECI, and more Canadian than Norwegian females responded to a real-life dilemma with relational examples. The remaining conclusions are negated by inappropriate interpretations of significant overall chi-squares. More important, the selection of a group that was assessed 7 years earlier makes the conclusions not justified. First, the critical factor of history cannot be ruled out as a confound. Social changes had to have occurred during this period of time, which might have put the Norwegian adolescents at an advantage and might have changed the results from what they would be, had the Canadians been measured at the same time. Second, Canadians had more education than the Norwegians, and the use of grade as a covariate (which may or may not be linearly related to ECI) did not adequately control for its effect. If training goes on at school, as it probably does, it would have been a better design to test both groups at equal grade levels and use age (which is related to ECI) as a covariate. Third, testers had to differ, and each may have had different effects on the adolescents (especially if gender affects responses). Fourth, the test itself may not fully measure level of development of moral reasoning.

STUDY EXAMPLE 12.2

This is a second example of a quasi-experimental design. Here, too, data of an experimental group are compared with data gathered earlier, but the latter serve as control data, and the experimenter made sure that both groups were matched on important variables. The study attempted to isolate important variables in rating pain in infants. This study is more advanced than ones we've come across. It is a three-factor study with repeated measures on one factor. So we'll simplify things by looking at the design and then appropriate degrees of freedom for the analysis in Box 12.2.

A final point to note about this and similar studies using repeated measures is that when the circularity assumption is not met and *df*s are adjusted, that adjustment comes into play only when the calculated *F* is evaluated; it is *not used* in the calculation.

The Study

Fuller, B. F., Neu, M., & Smith, M. (1999). The influence of background clinical data on infant pain assessments. *Clinical Nursing Research, 8*(2), 179-187. Copyright 1999 by Sage.

BOX 12.2
Experimental
Setup for Study
Example 12.2

Age (K)	Video+ None	Mild	Moderate	Severe	Video (J) None	Mild	Moderate	Severe (L)
0-3	$n_{jk} = 6$				$n_{jk} = 10$			
4-6								
7-9								
10-12								

Source	df	
Between	$(S - 1) =$	$(64 - 1) = 63$
Video	$(J - 1) =$	$(2 - 1) = 1$
Age	$(K - 1) =$	$(4 - 1) = 3$
Video × Age	$(J - 1)(K - 1) =$	$(2 - 1)(4 - 1) = 3$
Error (within$_{gp}$)	$\Sigma(n_{jk} - 1) =$	$4(6 - 1) + 4(10 - 1) = 56$
Within	$K(L - 1)(n_{jk}) =$	$4(4 - 1)(6) + 4(4 - 1)(10) = 192$
Pain	$(L - 1) =$	$(4 - 1) = 3$
Pain × Video	$(L - 1)(J - 1) =$	$(4 - 1)(2 - 1) = 3$
Pain × Age	$(L - 1)(K - 1) =$	$(4-1)(4-1) = 9$
Pain × Age × Video	$(L-1)(K-1)(J-1) =$	$(4 - 1)(4 - 1)(2 - 1) = 9$
Error (pain × within$_{gp}$)	$(L - 1)(\Sigma n_{jk} - 1) =$	$(3)(56) = 168$

This study evaluated the influence of clinical background data on infant pain assessment performed by nurses in a clinical setting. Pain assessments of videotaped infants by nurse participants who were not provided with infant background information [were] compared with the assessments of nurse participants who viewed identical videotapes that were accompanied by written clinical background data.

Problem

In earlier studies, nurse participants assessed infant pain by viewing 3-minute infant videotapes and reading clinical background data about each infant. The background data described the infant's birth history; age; diagnosis, type of surgery, or both; time since admission or surgery; parent comments about the infant's usual behavior; and all medications, nutrition, and fluids given to the infant during the 48 hours prior to videotaping. The nurse participants in these studies reported using, as assessment cues, many details provided in this background information. . . . The importance of clinical background information in assessing pain is underscored by another study that showed that nurses who viewed only videotaped snippets (without any background knowledge of the infant) could not agree on infant pain assessment. . . . These disagreements may have occurred because the snippets were very brief, showed the infant alone, and did not include the infant's response to comfort measures or other interventions. A model of nursing assessment of infant pain . . . suggests that these assessments are based, in part, on the infant's response to comfort measures and clinical background data that inform the nurse about the likelihood of pain.

Infant age influences pain-related behaviors. Pain responses of older infants are more goal directed than are those of younger infants. . . . Pain-induced facial expressions differ between younger and older infants. . . . Such age-related differences may affect nursing assessments. Pediatric nurses report that it is easier to evaluate pain in older infants because they exhibit more behavioral cues than do younger infants. . . . If so, then younger infants may be assessed as having less pain than older infants. . . . In pain assessments based solely on videotapes, infant age differences in the richness of behavioral cues that indicate pain may have more influence on these assessments than they would were the videotapes accompanied by clinical background data.

The purpose of this study was to determine the importance of knowledge of clinical background data in nursing assessments of infant pain. Three questions related to this purpose are:

1. What is the difference in levels of assessed infant pain between pediatric nurses who view infant videotapes and read infant background data and pediatric nurses who only view infant videotapes?
2. What is the influence of level of infant pain on any differences found for Question 1?
3. What is the influence of infant age on the assessment results for Question 1?

Method

Design

A quasi-experimental design compared the infant pain assessment of 24 pediatric nurses in an early study . . . who viewed videotapes of infants that were accompanied by written background information about each infant (video-information group), to the assessments of 40 pediatric nurses, recruited in 1997, who viewed the same videotaped infants without written background information (video-only group).

Variables

The dependent variable was level of infant pain as assessed by the 64 nurse participants. The three independent variables were the presence or absence of written clinical background data about each videotaped infant, age of the infant, and level of infant pain as assessed by a panel of five expert pediatric nurses. The clinical background data described the infant's birth history, age, number of previous hospitalizations and reasons for each admission; diagnosis, type of surgery, or both; time since this admission; time since surgery (if applicable); parent comments about the infant's usual behavior; and all medications, nutrition, and fluids given to the infant during the 48 hours prior to videotaping.

Participants

A convenience sample of 64 pediatric nurses with 5 or more years of pediatric nursing experience and a bachelor of science in nursing degree was used. The video-information group consisted of 24 White female nurse participants recruited in 1993 for a previous study. The video-only group consisted of 40 nurse participants recruited in 1997. One participant was male. . . . Of these participants, 36 were White, 2 were Black, 1 was East Indian, and 1 was Asian. No differences existed between the two groups in years of pediatric experience or level of education. Mean length of pediatric experience of the entire sample ($N = 64$) was 11.7 years. This experience included . . . general pediatrics to neonatal, pediatric intensive care, or both. Twenty-three percent had a master of science in nursing.

Videotaped Infants

To ensure that the assessments covered a broad spectrum of pain and infant ages, a 16-cell matrix of four ages (0-3 months, 4-6 months, 7-9 months, and 10-12 months) and four levels of pain (none, mild, moderate, severe) was filled with videotaped infants, based on the independent determinations of an "expert panel" composed of five R.N. clinical nurse specialists with a B.S.N. and M.S.N and ≤ 13 years current pediatric experience. . . . The expert panel members, working independently, viewed 150 videotapes that were accompanied by notes concerning the infant's history, diagnosis, medication, and nutritional and fluid status. The experts rated the pain of each videotaped infant on a 4-point scale: *no pain, mild pain, moderate pain,* and *severe pain.* Infant videotapes were included in the matrix only when at least four of the five expert nurses agreed on the level of assessed pain (EAP). Each of the 16 matrix cells was filled with five infant videotapes. . . . Each infant was represented by a single videotape. Forty-three of the 80 infants were surgical patients. . . . Medical diagnoses included severe respiratory disorders, severe dermatitis, gastroenteritis, otitis media, and seizures. Twenty-nine infants received analgesic medication within 0 to 2 hours prior to videotaping. Parents were present during videotaping for 52 infants. Twenty-three infants were girls, 57 were boys. The videotapes showed the infant during periods of quiet and crying, the infant's behavior during a routine nursing intervention (e.g., bathing or vital signs), and the infant's response to routine comfort measures.

Procedure

All 64 participants designated which age categories of infants (i.e., 0 to 3, 4 to 6, 7 to 9, and 10 to 12 months old) were most familiar to them and were then assigned to assess the pain of 20 infants belonging to one of those age categories. Five of the 20 infants of each age category represented four pain subsets . . . : no pain, mild pain, moderate pain, and severe pain. The participants of both groups assessed infant pain on a 4-point scale in which $0 = no$ *pain* and $3 = severe$ *pain.* Six participants in the video-information group and 10 participants in the video-only group viewed the videotapes for infants of one age category. The participants of the video-information group also read written background information about each infant; the participants of the video-only group did not.

Data Analysis

For each of the 64 pediatric nurses, four mean values of the assessed pain levels were obtained. Each mean represented the level of assessed pain for the five infants that represented one of the four subsets of expert-panel-assessed pain (EAP) per age category. These means were compared using a three-level repeated measures analysis of variance. The within-participants factor was EAP. The between-participants factors were infant age category and group type (video-information, video-only). For comparisons involving EAP, the results of Mauchly's Test of Sphericity indicated a rejection of the null hypothesis (i.e., the assumption of compound symmetry or equal variances and covariances among levels of the repeated measures factor); therefore, the degrees of freedom used to determine the F value were first adjusted by the

TABLE 1 Means of Assessed Pain by the Video-Information and Video-Only Groups of Pediatric Nurses for the Five Infants Belonging to Each of the Four Groups of Expert-Levels of Assessed Pain (EAP)[a]

Age	Group	Expert Levels of Assessed Infant Pain			
		None	Mild	Moderate	Severe
0-3 months	Video-information	0.56	1.63	1.67	1.90
	Video only	0.24	0.65	0.72	1.12
4-6 months	Video-information	0.63	1.40	1.83	2.23
	Video only	0.36	0.72	1.13	1.67
7-9 months	Video-information	0.63	1.43	1.80	2.50
	Video only	0.29	0.73	1.00	1.25
10-12 months	Video-information	0.60	1.1	1.93	2.30
	Video only	0.43	0.65	1.50	1.7

a. Data for infants of all age categories are combined.

Greenhouse-Geisser epsilon for these comparisons. The assumption of homogeneity of variance was supported . . . so no adjustments were necessary.

Results

Mean values of pain assessed by the pediatric nurse participants for group, age, and EAP are shown in Table 1. The video-only group of nurses had lower levels of assessed pain (mean = 0.89) than did the video-information group (mean = 1.52), $F(1, 55) = 53.00$, $p = .000$. There were no differences in the levels of assessed pain across the four age categories of infants, $F(3, 55) = 1.23$, $p = 0.31$, and no Video Group × Infant Age interaction, $F(3, 55) = 1.03$, $p = 0.31$. Mean levels of pain assessed by the pediatric nurse participants did differ across EAP, $F(2.57, 45.4) = 221.18$, $p = .000$. Individual contrasts showed that mean levels of pain differed among each of the four levels of EAP. Mean levels of assessed pain by the nurse participants were greatest for the EAP = severe category, next greatest for the EAP = moderate category, next greatest for the EAP = mild category, and lowest for the EAP = no pain category.

The only significant interactions were between EAP and infant age, $F(7.7, 141) = 4.1$, $p = .000$, and between EAP and group, $F(2.57, 45.4) = 8.9$, $p = .000$. The mean levels of pain assessed by the pediatric nurse participants of the video-information and video-only groups were lowest for the 10- to 12-month-old infants belonging to the EAP = mild category but highest for the 10- to 12-month-old infants belonging to the EAP = moderate category, in comparison to assessed levels of pain for the younger age groups. Nurse participants in the video-only group rated the 0- to 3-month-old infants as having lower levels of pain in all EAP categories than they rated older infants. This differs from the nurses in the video-information group who rated 0- to 3-month-old infants in the EAP = mild category as having a higher level of assessed pain than infants in other age groups.

Discussion

Nurses in this study assessed lower levels of pain when they assessed the infant without additional clinical data than they did when they viewed the infant and had access to clinical information about the infant. These findings underscore the importance of clinical data and clinical context in making infant pain assessments and the risk of underestimating pain when such data and context are not considered. Infant behavior by itself, however, did signal pain to nurses of this study, as indicated by the increase in levels of pain ratings in the video-only group that paralleled the increase in EAP assessments. The lower pain ratings for the 0- to 3-month-old infants compared to the older infants in the video-only group suggest that nurses may have more difficulty interpreting the pain-related behaviors of the 0- to 3-month-old infants. The 10- to 12-month-old-infants, on the other hand, seem to express their pain more effectively than younger infants, as indicated by pain ratings that were higher than those of younger infants in the moderate and severe categories of both groups. . . .

A potential limitation of this study was that the assessments of the two groups of nurses were separated by several years, posing the risk that hospital practice or medical advances might influence scoring. This seems unlikely, however, because the video scenes used in this study were identical for both groups and involved activities that have been common practice for many years. Nurses in both groups had similar pediatric experience and educational level. The only difference in the assessment situation was access to clinical information about the infants.

It is possible that parents and nurses who care for an infant for several days are able to interpret and use an individual infant's behavioral cues that indicate pain better than did the nurse participants of this study who only watched a relatively brief video scene of each infant. The video scenes viewed by the nurses also did not include "hands-on" assessment or testing of comfort measures that would be done in the clinical area. Comparisons of assessments of nurses caring for infants in the clinical setting with and without access to clinical data may be less divergent than what was found in this study and is an area for future research. . . .

CRITIQUE OF STUDY EXAMPLE 12.2

1. What was the rationale for the study?

2. What was the purpose of the study?

3. What variables were measured or manipulated?

4. Who were the participants?

5. Can the two groups be considered equivalent at the start of the study?

6. Are groups nonequivalent for all aspects of the study?

7. How were videotapes selected?

8. What was the general procedure?

9. What information is missing?

10. How were the data analyzed?

11. What steps were taken to remedy any failure to meet assumptions of the test?

12. What were the results regarding main effects of each variable?

13. What were the results regarding interactions? Are all statements accurate regarding significant interactions?

14. If you look at degrees of freedom for the error term in the F ratio for pain level (45.4), you'll see that it is too far removed from 168, even for an adjusted value. This suggests that the wrong error term was used (55 in the other two also are wrong; they should have been 56, but the 1 df won't make a difference). But you can estimate the correct error term by using an interaction that is reported significant and uses the appropriate error term, the interaction between EAP and age. The means are summarized below. Each is the weighted mean of (video+ $\times$ 6 + video $\times$ 10)/16.

	None	Mild	Moderate	Severe	
0-3	0.36	1.02	1.08	1.41	0.97
4-6	0.46	0.98	1.39	1.88	1.18
7-9	0.42	0.99	1.30	1.72	1.11
10-12	0.49	0.82	1.66	1.92	1.22
	0.43	0.95	1.36	1.73	1.12

Each cell mean has $n = 16$. The $SS = \Sigma 16$ (cell mean − row mean − column mean + grand mean)^2. Calculate MS_{int} and, by means of $F = MS_{int}/MS_e$ and $MS_e = MS_{int}/F$, determine the error term.

Now go back and reevaluate the F ratio for the main effect of pain level. The $SS_{pain} = \Sigma 16$ (Mean$_{level}$ − Mean$_{grand}$)^2. Does the conclusion change?

15. The group × pain level interaction also used the wrong error term. The table is presented below.

	Video+	Video	
None	0.61	0.33	0.43
Mild	1.39	0.69	0.95
Moderate	1.81	1.09	1.36
Severe	<u>2.23</u>	<u>1.43</u>	<u>1.73</u>
	1.51	0.88	1.12

Calculate the SS_{gxp}, keeping in mind that there are 6 scores in each cell of the video+background group and 10 scores in the video-only group. Then, recalculate the F ratio with MS_e arrived at in Question 14. Does the conclusion change?

16. What did the authors conclude?

17. Are the conclusions justified?

For answers to these questions, see page 344.

BIBLIOGRAPHY

Cook, T. D., & Campbell, D. T. (1979). *Quasi- experimentation: Design & analysis issues for field settings*. Chicago: Rand McNally.

Kazdin, A. E. (1992). *Research design in clinical psychology* (2nd ed.). Boston: Allyn & Bacon.

Kirk, R. E. (1982). *Experimental design: Procedures for the behavioral sciences* (2nd ed.). Belmont, CA: Brooks/Cole.

Neale, J. M., & Liebert, R. M. (1986). *Science and behavior: An introduction to methods of research* (3rd ed.). Englewood Cliffs, NJ: Prentice Hall.

Additional Suggested Readings

Best, J. W., & Kahn, J. V. (1998). *Research in education* (8th ed.). Boston: Allyn & Bacon.

Mason, E. J., & Bramble, W. J. (1997). *Research in education and the behavioral sciences: Concepts and methods.* Dubuque, IA: William C. Brown.

Pedhazur, E. J., & Schmelkin, L. P. (1991). *Measurement, design, and analysis: An integrated approach.* Hillsdale, NJ: Lawrence Erlbaum.

Vockell, E. L., & Asher, J. W. (1995). *Educational research* (2nd ed.). Englewood Cliffs, NJ: Prentice Hall.

Wiersma, W. (1995). *Research methods in education: An introduction* (2nd ed.). Boston: Allyn & Bacon.

Answers to Study Example Critiques

CHAPTER 2

1. There is a need to racially diversify faculty in universities and lower educational institutions, but this need has not been met. In addition to a lack of supply (because of the small number of Black scholars in academia), there is also evidence of a racist perception that restricts access to higher education institutions and stifles the professional growth of those in the institutions. Although some faculty believe that there is diversity, others do not. A relevant question might be, What do students of color believe? Diversification includes recruiting, training, and understanding students of color.

2. This longitudinal study intended to further our understanding of university students of color, in terms of the complex problems they face, in the hopes of improving the recruitment and retention of these underrepresented students.

3. Participants included 11 graduate students in the Department of Educational Leadership, including 1 working on the dissertation and 10 engaged in course work. There were 7 males and 4 females. Of the 11, 7 were African American, 1 was Asian American, 1 was Hispanic American, 1 was from Jamaica, and 1 was from China.

4. The researchers were two European American faculty members, both of whom left the university (one for a position elsewhere and one to retire).

5. Three semistructured interviews were conducted. The initial one was least structured, and the next two took place within a span of 1½ years. The researchers looked for themes.

6. Member checks allowed the participants to study the themes to check for accuracy, and the researchers' nonaffiliation with the university freed them from constraints in their interpretations.

7. Multicultural perspectives, and the feeling that the program did not offer multicultural perspectives. Issues of gender, especially for some females, in terms of expectations of them, as well as gender issues in subject matter. Impact of the program on individuals and self-efficacy, the feeling that the program had a positive impact on the participants and increased their self-efficacy. Others felt that their self-efficacy diminished when they left important positions to become graduate students. Dissertation experience, which was viewed as challenging but rewarding. Impact of the students on the program, which was felt to be positive in some ways but not profound.

8. Support from family and nonfamily members was mentioned by almost all participants, although sources differed for each. Support from special situations were available to at least three participants (advice, secretarial help, access to special libraries). Participants recognized their minority-group status but did not believe that they were representative of their group. Particular conditions in the participants' lives led them to pursue graduate studies when they did. These were financial support, encouragement by an employer, the participants' ages, growth of their children, spousal relationships. Some reported that the doctorate made them unique individuals among family, friends, social acquaintances. Some reported being criticized for getting the degree. All participants reported being motivated for the degree, mainly for self-efficacy. All participants reported that doctoral work was difficult, although not unexpectedly so. Some participants were in cohort groups and were enthusiastic about membership for all doctoral students. Some participants received help from a mentor, but only two reported mentoring as a special factor in their success as students.

9. Nothing is reported about its development or testing prior to administration.

10. A control group was composed of students at similar stages in the doctoral program (their ages, sex, and n are not reported).

11. Method of selection and testing are not reported.

12. The authors reported that substantial differences (significance not tested) occurred with respect to multicultural perspectives: Participants thought a dominant cultural perspective was evident; counterparts thought a multicultural perspective was evident.

13. First, faculty in doctoral programs need to be more culturally sensitive, need to include more minority members, and need to read important works from authors of other cultures. Second, female minority participants considered gender issues more important than racial and ethnic issues when the two were separated. Third, self-image was positive at entry into the program, followed by apprehension. With academic success, participants experienced greater self-esteem, but the doctorate was not its major source. Fourth, minority students were similar to European American counterparts in their attitudes and perspectives about the doctoral program except in the area of multicultural diversity. Fifth, participants felt that their presence influenced other students but did not have a great impact on the program or depart-

ment. Sixth, faculty and administrators need to consider higher education from the perspectives of minority students when they are trying to recruit. Their perspectives are more complex than were suspected.

14. The most glaringly weak conclusion regards the need for multicultural perspectives and diversity. Only this doctoral program was studied, and conclusions may not apply to other programs (e.g., mathematics, sciences, etc.). Importance of gender issues may apply to all female students rather than just minority female students. Apprehension and increased self-efficacy may not be unique to minority students. The conclusion that minority views were similar to those of their majority counterparts was based on a semantic differential instrument that may not have been valid, whose results were not analyzed statistically, and whose measurements may have included a comparison group that differed from the participants in age. Finally, aside from the need for multicultural diversity and perspectives, many of the concerns were those expressed by graduate students in general (e.g., difficulty of program, experience of the dissertation, etc.).

15. The researchers were European Americans no longer associated with the university, and they conducted a member check on their interpretations.

16. Judging from the reasons given for entering the program when they did, these students may not have been in financial need as are so many graduate students, and they may have been older than the typical graduate student. Therefore, the concerns they expressed may not be con-

fined to the particular graduate program but may be a carryover from their previous experiences (prior education, employment) and from previous readings. Moreover, although a member check was performed, it was performed at least 1½ years after the first interview, so memory may have played some role.

17. Although the need for multicultural perspectives is tacitly recognized, it was not demonstrated in this study. Members of diverse minority groups may have been interviewed, but they may not be representative members of their groups who go on to graduate school, in terms of financial standing, experiences they bring with them, and age. Moreover, such diversity may be required in doctoral programs that train individuals to work with diverse populations but may not be required in other programs.

(THERE ARE NO ANSWERS FOR CHAPTER 3)

CHAPTER 4

1. Whereas rape on campuses was considered to be a serious problem in the 1980s, a backlash view subsequently emerged that undermined its occurrence by attributing it to regret by the victim that a consensual encounter had taken place. Furthermore, women who supposedly were raped when drunk blame themselves for losing control and letting things go too far. There is question about whether such women became emotionally upset after such an experience,

whom they blamed, and whether they considered themselves raped.

2. This survey compared differences between women who were assaulted when drunk and those who were forcibly assaulted. Three hypotheses were tested: First, the women who were raped due to intoxication were significantly less affected by the event than the women who were raped due to physical force. Second, the women raped because of alcohol or drugs blame themselves for the event more than do the women raped by physical force. Third, the women who have been raped because of force will be more likely to label their experiences as rape than will women who had unwanted sex because they were too intoxicated to resist.

3. On the first day of classes, questionnaires were administered to 25 out of 36 senior classes. Participation was voluntary, and only 5 females did not complete the forms. Questions were taken from a previously used survey, but some were tightened to remove ambiguity. Moreover, several questions were added to measure rapetype: while the victim was intoxicated or by force. There was a question to measure self-blame and another to measure the extent to which victims were psychologically affected by the experience.

4. First, as recognized by the authors, the use of seniors may not include those who quit college or transferred to another college because they were raped. These would most likely include victims of forcible rape who were afraid and would not be as likely to experience self-blame. Second, as also mentioned by the authors, 11 instructors refused to participate be-

cause they could not afford the class time—and this is on the first day of classes. Although they may not have been from a particular area of study, they probably teach more intensive courses than those who consented. Seniors can select teachers when more than one teaches the same course, and whatever was related to seniors choosing these particular instructors may set them apart from the seniors who took part in the survey. Third, because this was a one-time-only survey, we have no way of knowing about absentees who missed the first day of classes.

5. Nothing is said about reliability or validity of the adapted scale. Presumably, because an established scale was used, reliability and validity were established for it. But new questions were added, and nothing is mentioned about procedures leading up to their final inclusion in the survey.

6. As is true of all self-reports, not everyone answers honestly and accurately. We have no way of knowing how many of the females deliberately lied (because they felt ashamed, or they might be in denial). Moreover, someone experiencing self-blame might not be willing to admit being victimized. Nor is there any mention of obtaining information regarding the time between the assault and the survey. If the interval was long enough, there may be some forgetting, a shift from self-blame, or a lessening of the emotional impact because the victim sought psychological help. Finally, some emotional scars show up much later as posttraumatic stress disorder.

7. There were no differences as a function of type of rape. Most women reported be-

ing affected whether rape occurred while intoxicated or by force.

8. Yes. There are four degrees of affect and two types of rape: $(4 - 1)(2 - 1) = 3 \, df.$

9. There are 35 women who reported being raped while intoxicated: $35/65 = 53.8\%$; 30 reported being forcibly raped: $30/65 = 46.2\%$.

10. Both types of rape victims reported blaming themselves for the assault. This was true for 79.3% of victims who were intoxicated and 50% of the victims who were forcibly raped. However, chi-square was not significant, so self-blame did not differ as a function of type of rape.

11. Table 2 has to be based on fewer than 65 cases. This means that some of the women did not respond to the self-blame question. This is seen immediately by looking at total N for the alcohol group: $.569 \times 65 = 37$, but only 35 had reported being assaulted while intoxicated. (The authors later reported that only 43 women answered the question, but a recalculation of percentages did not match their figures in Table 3.)

12. Although the 51 women who answered this question had admitted to the assault, either while intoxicated or through use or threat of force, only one woman in the alcohol group and 5 women in the physical force group openly answered yes. The remainder said no. These women did not define their assault as rape.

13. The question may have been too painful. These may have been women who might have answered yes.

14. $\chi^2 = 1,167 + 1.668 + 0.156 + 0.222 = 3.84$. The chi-square is not significant, but barely, and there is no evidence that

a yes or no response depends on type of rape.

15. Women who were raped while intoxicated were just as affected as women who were forcibly raped. Assuming no selective loss (physically, by lying in response to that question, by memory) of those forcibly raped—those who would have been affected or deeply affected—then the conclusion is justified. The authors, however, admit that some may have lied and that some may have left campus, so the conclusion is tentatively justified.

16. About one fourth of the victims tended to blame themselves for the rape, regardless of whether they were intoxicated or forcibly raped. This lack of difference leads to rejection of the hypothesis that self-blame would be more evident among victims who were intoxicated. If there was no selective loss of those forcibly raped, who would have blamed the man, then the conclusion is justified. There is no reason to believe that individuals who left campus out of fear would blame themselves, so statements about equal tendencies toward self-blame seem justified. (It is interesting that, if this question was answered by 43 women, 56.9% of 43 = 24 of the alcohol group and 43.1% of 43 = 19 of the physical force group responded. This means that 11 women in each of the groups chose not to respond to this question. A selective factor might predict more nonresponders among those forcibly raped.)

17. The authors concluded that more women who were forcibly raped would admit to being raped, but the conclusion was only technically correct because chi-

square was significant. The technical conclusion is not justified; the corrected and more accurate chi-square is not significant.

CHAPTER 5

1. Service learning (the integration of community service with academic outcome) or community service often is required for graduation from public school. Whereas the value of community service is recognized, its connection to the public school system is not. Community service bridges the gap between theory and reality. Service learning allows for learning from direct experience. Data indicate, however, that most programs focus on interpersonal and personal knowledge instead of on subject matter learning.

   Students have derived a number of benefits from service learning programs: enhanced self-esteem, civic responsibility, clarification of values, personal and social development, better academic performance. The programs are a way of getting the students to connect with their community and become good citizens. But this requires focusing on the meaning of volunteering, good citizenship, multicultural societies, and the broad meaning of community. Not all student participants experience positive changes in attitudes and school performance. Researchers need to expand their knowledge of student experiences and features of programs that make them successful.

2. It examined the strengths and weaknesses of 10 service learning programs on the basis of data from a 3-year evaluation of programs to determine critical elements of a successful program.

3. They were introduced in an economically poor urban district in southern California, where one third of the population consisted of teenagers who were involved in gang-related activities, were parents, and who failed to be graduated from high school. The service learning programs were intended to change these trends. A program was introduced in one school during the first year, in two additional high schools by the second year, and in all six high schools by the third year.

4. There were 172 students, half of them male, who were mainly Hispanic (60%) or Caucasian (20%), with the remainder being African American or Asian American. Nothing is reported about the participants' usual school attendance, performance in school, and attitude before the program was introduced, their gang membership, and so forth. Therefore, if a positive attitude is associated with the program, you might not know if it was there before the program and continued to be manifest or whether it is associated specifically with the program.

5. Interested teachers may have used other means to motivate their students or may have been talented enough to motivate their students to learn and develop positive attitudes without the programs.

6. Programs ranged in duration from 1 week to 1 year. They took place in class, at schools, at home, or in the community. They involved minimum interactions with others or interactions with school

visitors, peers, or elementary school children.

7. The variables were general academic success (achievement, grades, participation in class discussion, teacher's efficiency), school socialization (relationship with other students, multicultural attitude, participation in school activities, general high school experience), future plans (future educational goals, role of altruism in life goals), self-perception (appearance, happiness, respect, achievements), and community pride (perception of neighborhood with respect to safety, desirability, and pride).

8. Nothing is reported about standardization of the questionnaire, especially important because 60% of the responders were Hispanic.

9. The aspects were duration, location, personal contact, and focus of the project. The authors determined each of these to be important characteristics differentiating successful and unsuccessful programs after evaluating programs for 3 years. Each variable was rated, by the authors, for each program.

10. There is potentially one weakness: The authors' ratings may be based on expectations of "importance" and unintentionally might affect the correlations.

11. Whereas there are quantifiable bases for ratings of duration, location, and personal contact, there are no definitions of *some, moderate, significant,* and *extensive* focus of the project.

12. Some of the projects may have been underrated by the authors. For example, Stereotypes Presentation involved a workshop on tolerance, presented to peers. Duration is rated 1 because it took place in less than 4 weeks; it was con-

ducted on campus, so location received a 2. But personal contact was rated 1, meaning that there was no personal contact with the beneficiaries of the service. Yet, workshops do include personal contact, and the possible beneficiaries of the service should include peers. Also, the program received a 1 for focus, presumably because it involved little or no focus on a service to the community. Yet, if the peers begin to practice tolerance in the community, this can be considered a big service. Thus, ratings reflect beliefs of the authors about what is personal contact, who are the beneficiaries of the service, and what is community service.

13. There is no description of which came first, but half the participants should have had the essay first, and half should have had the questionnaire first to guard against carryover effects.

14. There is little way of knowing when the questionnaires were answered and the essays were answered. Presumably, these activities took place at the end of the project, and if this was the case, they took place at different times for the different classes (and the time could very well affect responses) and presumably occurred in the classrooms (and therefore under different conditions). These differences could very well effect variability in responses and have the effect of lowering potential correlation coefficients.

15. For $r = .39$, alpha $= .0025$; $r = .38$, alpha $= .05/19 = .0026$; $r = .34$, alpha $= .05/18 = .0028$; $r = .32$, alpha $= .05/16.5 = .003$; $r = .29$, alpha $= .05/15 = .0033$; $r = .27$, alpha $= .05/14 = .0036$; $r = .25$, alpha $= .05/13 = .0038$; $r = .24$, alpha $= .05/12 = .0042$; $r = .21$, alpha $= .05/11 = .0045$.

All coefficients up to and including $r = .24$ are significant. However, for $r = .21$, alpha $= .0045$, it is reported significant at $p < .005$, which is not significant. None of the remaining coefficients are significant. On this basis, none of the criterion variables is correlated with attitude toward academic achievement; focus of the project is not correlated with plans for the future; self-esteem is not correlated with duration or extent of personal contact (marginally); and none of the criterion variables is correlated with attitudes toward the community.

16. $(.39)^2 = .1521$: 15.21% of the variability in attitudes toward plans for the future is associated with extent of personal contact in the project. $(.24)^2 = .0576$: 5.76% of variability in attitude toward school socialization is associated with focus of the project.

17. Yes, the correlations between duration and plans for the future and school socialization were significant.

18. Yes, the correlations between location and plans for the future, self-esteem, and school socialization were significant.

19. No. This variable correlated only with plans for future and school socialization. When adjustments in alpha levels were made, correlations with academic achievement and self-esteem no longer were significant. Therefore, extent of personal contact is not the most significant criterion.

20. No. Focus was correlated only with self-esteem and school socialization. When alpha levels were adjusted, the correlation with future plans no longer was significant.

21. The highest attitudinal scores were associated with projects of the longest duration and greatest personal contact, projects conducted away from school, and projects that provided the greatest community service. The higher scores can lead to academic achievement and citizenship. Increased personal contact is associated with increased attitudes toward academic achievement. Projects that took place off campus were associated with increased self-esteem.

22. Because the study was correlational, any implication of cause-and-effect is unwarranted. The first statement is justified. Some of the higher attitudinal scores were associated with off-campus projects that provided the most community service and the most personal contact with service beneficiaries, that went on for the longest period of time. The statement that high scores can lead to academic achievement and citizenship is not justified. Scores only can be associated with other scores; they lead to nothing. Moreover, positive attitudes toward academic achievement were not associated with any of the criteria. This, too, makes the next statement unjustified. Even if $r = .16$ were significant, $r^2 = .0256$, which would say that 2.56% of variability in attitudes toward academic achievement is associated with personal contact in the project. Off-campus projects, however, were associated with increased self-esteem.

23. First, service and learning must be delicately balanced to have meaning for students. Projects with emphasis on direct service seemed to fare better than those that used service as an adjunct. Second, crucial aspects of the project are long du-

ration, off-campus sites, and personal contact with the beneficiaries. Third, the effects of service learning may not be evident in short-term academic achievement, but they are evident in student attitudes: the longer the duration of the project, the greater the positive attitudes scores, especially citizenship and academic performance.

24. They are, with one exception. Benefits do not include an increase in citizenship and academic performance. A demonstration of increase requires a measure of performance before the project as well as after. And, again, attitudes toward academic achievement did not correlate with any criterion variable.

25. They are based on two sets of scores from two scales. The questionnaire may not be a reliable and valid instrument, or it may not provide a wide enough range of ratings. The rating scale may have to be revised to provide more clear-cut criteria for each rating (e.g., some, moderate, etc.). That, too, may not provide a wide enough range of ratings. Moreover, the areas tapped for attitudes may have to be redefined. For example, academic achievement referred to all academic performance. Perhaps there was a benefit only in the course that required the project but not in other courses. Overall ratings might be lower than if they were for the specific course. Finally, the relationships may not have been linear. This possibility could have been ruled out if a scatter plot had been presented.

26. First, without a more complete description of students taking part in the various projects, their attitudes before the experience have to be considered one of the factors. Second, the teacher of the

class (and leader of the project) also has to be considered a potential source of positive attitudes. Third, the length of time between the end of the project and the measurements, as well as whether the scale followed or preceded the essay, also must be considered a source of positive attitude because of what might have been going on at that time to enhance (or lower) attitudes. Fourth, the nature of the scales (discussed in answer 25) also might have contributed to the quality of the attitudes, which were measured by one of the scales.

CHAPTER 6

1. The population of older adults is predicted to increase from 12% to 20% within the next several years. Along with aging, there is an increase in chronic illness, which may affect dependency of these people. Some become more dependent; others continue to remain independent and can carry out their daily activities. Reasons for these different outcomes are not clear.

   When aging is considered a developmental process, self-transcendence is seen as an aid to maturing. Self-transcendence, the capacity to extend oneself to others as well as to integrate the past and future with the present, may be one factor that differentiates dependent and independent older individuals. It may enable the individual to extend beyond his or her self and orient toward activities, such as daily living, even though there are health problems. But research revealed only one study that found a (positive) relationship between self-transcendence, health status, and functioning.

2. This study examined the relationship between self-transcendence, health status, and activities of daily living in noninstitutionalized older adults.

3. Eighty-eight men and women who were 65 years old or older, were independent, were part of senior-citizen or community-center organizations, were not senile, and could read and write English.

4. No. The author specifically selected individuals who were independent, literate, and active in the community.

5. The investigator appeared at center meetings, explained the study, and distributed consent forms and the questionnaires.

6. We don't know how many different centers were used; where participants were when they filled out the questionnaires; hour of the meetings (morning, afternoon, early evening); where the investigator was when questionnaires were filled out; and whether the questionnaires were counterbalanced or in the same order for all.

7. Nothing. You don't know whether sporadic items were not answered or whether a specific scale was omitted.

8. None. All are established to be reliable and valid.

9. Most were non-Hispanic White women, younger than 75, widowed, with some education beyond high school, and with a monthly income of less than $2,000.

10. Self-transcendence scores had a mean of 52 and standard deviation of 5.1. Therefore, the bulk of the scores ranged between 46.9 and 57.1, which correspond to scale ratings between 3 and 4. Like-

wise, health scores had a mean of 9.9 and standard deviation of 1.8. Therefore, the bulk of scores ranged between 8.1 and 11.7, which correspond to scale ratings between 2 and 3 (4 questions with ratings of 2 equals 8, and 4 questions with ratings of 3 equals 12). Thus, this group viewed their health as fairly good. The range also shows the highest score to be 13, not the maximum 16. Finally, the independence of the group is shown by the high scores on the daily activities scale.

11. The $r = .47$ indicates that $.47^2 = .2209$ or 22.09% of variability in ability to carry out daily activities is associated with health status. The $r = .39$ indicates that $.39^2 = .1521$ or 15.21% of variability in ability to carry out daily activities is associated with ability to extend oneself to activities and perspectives beyond the self. These, however, are zero-order correlations.

12. Stepwise multiple regression was performed in which the variable with the highest correlation with the criterion is entered first.

13. No. With the knowledge that R^2 is the sum of squared semi-partial correlations between the criterion and the predictor variables, the same information could have been obtained by the sum of $.47^2$ and the squared .39 with the effects of SHS partialled out from it.

14. Health status and self-transcendence contribute to daily living functioning. Whereas health status is a logical predictor of independence, self-transcendence may contribute to it by adding a sense of well-being.

15. Tentatively, yes. Although testing may have occurred under varied conditions, standard deviations for two of the scales

were small. If scale orders were not counterbalanced, however, then responses on one scale may have had a positive carryover effect on responses on the next scale. Moreover, as the author notes, other potential predictor variables may have mediated the effects of the two that were tested. Furthermore, the select nature of the group ensured that participants were not only active but probably experienced self-transcendence. Individuals who experience little self-transcendence but are in good health may be just as capable of caring for themselves.

16. These results generalize only to a similar population of non-Hispanic White, mainly widowed female older adults who are basically healthy, active in a community center, literate, with sufficient income to meet their monthly expenses.

CHAPTER 7

1. Socioeconomic development and better medical care led to the growth of the elderly population in Korea, requiring more focus on factors affecting their health and well-being. Research on the relationships between aging, depression, and related affective disorders most often has emphasized the elderly's happiness and satisfaction with life. Studies using a variety of scales have found a correlation between well-being and health, socioeconomic status, and social activities for adults of 60 years of age or older.

   Currently, little is known about the relationship between mood variations and affect in this older population. Mood states are considered critical factors in psychological health. But mood states have been measured with scales developed in young adult populations. Of the comprehensive scales available, the most comprehensive is the Profiles of Mood States (POMS). This 65-item test, however, is too long for the elderly. Moreover, the elderly, particularly Koreans, are conservative in expressing negative moods. Scales that are valid and reliable for the elderly population can be used in gerontological research. But Korean elderly can be studied with such scales only if they are first psychometrically evaluated with this population.

2. This study intended to evaluate the POMS for use with the Korean elderly and to use the revised scale to measure their mood states.

3. The 370 original participants were asked to take part in the study, all from personal contact or senior centers in five cities of Korea. With the exclusion of 51 incomplete questionnaires, 319 were usable. More than half the sample were between 60 and 69 years of age, the oldest being older than 80 years. More than half were women; most did not work, were married, and had no formal education. The remainder had attended elementary school, but almost one fourth had attended a university. All participants were able to read and write Korean. Only one fourth listed their income level as middle-low; the rest were in middle-high or high income brackets. Most depended on themselves or their spouses for income.

4. Yes. Those who did not volunteer or agree to participate may have experi-

enced negative mood states, which were measured at the final phase of the study. Most of the sample had no financial concerns and were married. We don't know how these figures compare with the general elderly population of Korea.

5. The original POMS scale of 65 items was translated to Korean in 1993. Factor-analytic studies had identified factors that reflected six mood states, whereas there was a suggestion of a seventh. Prior studies scored on six factors. This study scored all seven. The main study was conducted after face validity had been established, which resulted in word changes to facilitate understanding.

6. The POMS is a well-known, much-used test whose reliability and validity have been established.

7. Probably not. Because these are not described, we have to assume that testing took place at the senior centers or homes of those personally contacted.

8. Following item analysis and face validity procedures, 31 items were deleted from the original 65-item scale, leaving 34 items deemed adequate to measure mood states of elderly Koreans.

9. This was not an exploratory study. Seven (or six) factors already had been established for the test. This analysis focused on variance common to all 34 items in an attempt to determine whether the same seven factors would emerge.

10. Thirty-one items, almost half the test, were eliminated. The bulk of these were from Depression-Dejection, Tension-Anxiety, Anger-Hostility, and Friendly. Finally, the sample was different from

those previously studied; they were older, and they were Korean.

11. There is some basis. Angry (V1) and peeved (V8) fit with spiteful (V13), ready to fight (V24), and deceived (V28). But they also fit in with bitter (V21) of Factor 1.

12. Item V21 (bitter) is not consistent with the name of this factor. This suggests that the translation, despite face validity of the scale, does not fully convey the American meaning of the term. If it did, it would have loaded more heavily on Factor 3 or Factor 5 (along with angry and peeved).

13. The highest mean score was on the Vigor factor (Factor 2), which indicated low levels of this factor (because of reverse scoring). When scores were analyzed by demographic characteristics, results were as expected: More positive mood states were measured in males and in those elderly who were younger, employed, and married; who had more education; and who relied on themselves for income.

14. Standard deviations were relatively low, which indicates low variability in scores despite the varied testing conditions.

15. No differences were found for this factor. Either the scale items do not differentiate levels of anger for different demographic variables or the Korean elderly do not express (or admit?) anger.

16. The revised POMS scale is reliable for Korean elderly, reduced to the measurement of three clearly defined factors, (a) a combination of four previously identified negative mood states, (b) positive mood states, and (c) negative mood states that differed from those of Factor

1. The reduction of the scale in part was justified by overlap seen in the original scale and Korean people's training to restrain their reports of moods and emotions.

These elderly reported relatively low levels of negative mood states, which is consistent with their demographic characteristics. Moreover, the report of low levels of Vigor is consistent with older age.

These conclusions are tentatively justified but only for the population of Korean elderly sampled in this study, which may be more affluent and better educated than the general Korean elderly population. Although the analysis was appropriate, a lot depends on the face validity criteria for eliminating items (based on judgments) and the meaning of the translated items. As the authors noted, further studies are warranted.

CHAPTER 8

1. Cognitive functioning of 5-year-old children varies. Some think at what Piaget called a preoperational level. They cannot sort objects by form, size, and so forth, or serially in graded fashion. Others have attained a level that lets them understand such concepts as conservation of numbers. Performance of kindergarten children on problems involving classification, seriation, and conservation predict later performance on standardized achievement tests. If preoperational children can be identified

and given special training at this age, their later achievement performances might improve. Learning set methods have been most favored as ways of teaching deficient children to classify objects, seriate, and understand the principle of conservation. Many problems are presented with various objects, all of which can be solved by the same principle. It is believed that if these concepts are grasped, they will generalize to conceptual functioning and problem solving, which should lead to improvements in mathematics and verbal achievements. The Piacceleration method has been tested in preliminary studies with handicapped and nonhandicapped children, but data are limited because measures of achievement were made just 2 weeks after training ended. No study has used a large sample and tests of achievement after more time has elapsed.

2. To evaluate the effectiveness of the Piacceleration method in improving academic achievement and performance of young children who are likely to profit from such training. Their achievement was to be compared with that of a comparable group taught traditional mathematical concepts in kindergarten.

3. Each of 17 kindergarten teachers selected 5 children who were likely to be the lowest achievers in their classes. These were from six schools that serviced low-income children. Each group of 5 children was randomly assigned to experimental or control conditions, with the restriction that there would be equal numbers from morning and afternoon classes of the same school and same teacher.

4. Yes. The assignment was random and attrition was due to illness of the children.

5. After attrition, there were 17 White and 11 minority children in the experimental group (average age was 6.01 years) and 15 White and 14 minority children in the control group (average age was 5.99 years).

6. The Otis-Lennon School Ability Test was used to measure reasoning ability, and the Stanford Early School Achievement Test was used to measure knowledge of the social and physical environment as well as mathematical and verbal achievements.

7. No. Reliability and validity have been established for both tests.

8. Control children remained in the class and were taught mathematical concepts by their teachers, from December through February. Experimental children were brought to a corner of the room at the time that mathematical concepts were taught. Instruction occurred from November through January, except for slower children, who learned by February. Experimental children were taught by two aides, who praised each success and gave positive or negative feedback for all to hear. When a child successfully learned, he or she joined the class and received further lessons on mathematical concepts. Tests were administered 3 months later.

9. The methods for selecting participants and assigning them to the two groups, the use of reliable and valid tests, the use of two (presumably somewhat naive) independent aides to teach the experimental children.

10. Experimental children were taught in the same room while class was in session and might have known that they were receiving extra attention and praise; children who learned and could solve all problems joined their classmates and potentially had as much as a month of extra lessons; and the two tests may not have been given in counterbalanced order.

11. Two: one for subtests on the Otis-Lennon School Ability Test and one for subtests on the Stanford Early School Achievement Test.

12. There were two groups and five predictor variables; therefore, one discriminant function would be possible.

13. There are two possible justifications: The authors conducted one analysis on summary scores to determine if any differentiation occurred. Then, they looked for differentiators in ability and achievement subtests. And although they believed that they had a sufficient number of participants, an overall analysis would have required a total n of $5 \times 20 = 100$; they had only 57 children.

14. The authors did not report whether scores were normally distributed in each group nor whether correlation matrixes were similar for both groups.

15. Standard deviations were fairly similar for both groups and suggest similar distributions of scores.

16. Classification and analogies tests.

17. Omnibus scores may be correlated with those of classification and analogies.

18. Mathematical concepts and comprehension of words and stories.

19. Piacceleration led to greater ability to classify objects, identify analogies, understand mathematical concepts, and understand the meaning of words and of stories than did traditional training.

20. Piacceleration training improved the cognitive abilities of kindergarten children from impoverished environments.
21. First, that the children were used to working in small, special groups and, second, that the increased attention they received would have facilitated performance on achievement scales in which children should respond to extra attention, but differences here were small. Instead, differences in conceptual scales were evident.
22. Somewhat. Small-group format may not have made the children feel special, but special training is confounded by attention and lots of reinforcement for correct answers, and those parts of the subtests on which the children excelled were directly related to the special training. Moreover, the authors' explanation does not take into account the possibility that some of the children received additional training when they joined the rest of their class. (The fact that the tests may not have been administered in counterbalanced order would not be a big problem in this case because if there was an order effect, it would affect experimental and control children alike.) Finally, the children achieved mastery before moving to another level, which may not have been true in the traditional learning situation. This, too, may have been a beneficial factor rather than the skills taught per se. Although the authors note that mastery is crucial for Piacceleration training, if mastery were to be found for traditional training as well, then the advantage of Piacceleration training would be lost.
23. This study does not show this conclusively.

CHAPTER 9

1. The elderly are more prone to falling because of reduced input from visual, ankle, and foot cues. Exercise that includes strengthening, postural adjustment, balance, and concentration should be beneficial in reducing falls. Tai Chi is one set of exercises that incorporates these elements. It includes focus, deep breathing, balance training, and movements. It improves coordination and may reduce falls, which generally occur while the elderly are walking, climbing stairs, or turning. Because of movement exercises, Tai Chi also has reduced arthritic pain. And Tai Chi has been found to affect psychological well-being by increasing self-confidence and self-esteem and by reducing anxiety, depression, stress, and fatigue to the same extent as does moderate exercise.
2. This pilot study evaluated the effects of a short-term Tai Chi program on balance, flexibility, sway, pain, and mood of the elderly.
3. The sample of 2 males and 15 females, age 68 to 92 years, who lived in a public housing facility, volunteered to take part in the study. Aside from one Black and one Hispanic female, all were Caucasian; all were English-speaking. None were chronically ill, were in occupational or physical therapy, or took pain medication stronger than aspirin. A record was made of current amount of routine exercise.
4. Because they are in a public housing facility, they are likely to be poor and probably are not educated beyond high school. Because they volunteered, they

had the time to participate or may have been bored or lonely.

5. All participants were interviewed; took a reliable and valid paper-and-pencil mood test; were measured for flexibility, balance, sway, and range of motion. This part was done on an individual basis with two research assistants on hand.

   Tai Chi training took place in group format. Participants attended 60-minute sessions three times per week for 8 weeks. At the end of the 8 weeks, all participants (except 4, who missed 90% of the sessions) were posttested.

6. Individuals whose occupation or routine exercise schedule would have confounded the results were eliminated. Moreover, the paper-and-pencil test was reliable and valid. Finally, range of motion was measured by an expert, and Tai Chi training was conducted by an expert.

7. Only one group of participants was pre- and posttested. Pilot studies, as well as quasi-experimental studies, include at least one control group. Second, because of the volunteer status of these participants, motivation to take part probably was high, and any treatment might have been beneficial. Along with this, a Hawthorne effect might operate. Third, pre- and posttest measures were not counterbalanced. Aside from possible carryover effects, fatigue probably played a role in the final measures. This would tend to decrease those scores and leave more room for improvement on the posttests or leave those scores unchanged, again because of fatigue. Fourth, measurements were made by individuals who knew the purpose of the study, and this knowledge may have unintentionally affected their recordings.

8. The t test for matched samples has $n - 1$ degrees of freedom, so the $df = 10$ for these tests; therefore, 11 sets of scores out of the original 17 were included, or 64.71% of the original group.

9. Both measures showed a significant reduction in mean ratings. The pain scale, however, ranged from 0 to 10, and the pretest mean rating was only 1.5473. Moreover, although the MAACL-R scores were lower, subscale scores did not change, and it is difficult to know whether the decline in mood state was a reflection of reduced anxiety, hostility, depression, positive affect (increase), or sensation seeking.

10. No significant declines were found for the group as a whole, although 6 out of the 11 participants did show improvements on the posttest.

11. The group became more cohesive and enjoyed food snacks that were supplied after each session.

12. Tai Chi is effective in producing some health changes in the elderly, notably pain perception reduction; positive affect; and improvements in flexibility, sway, and balance.

13. The typical variables that may operate in pretest-posttest situations, which include any event in the lives of the participants during the 8-week period (history), changes in their perception of their lives (maturation), benefits derived from the pretest experience that might have led them to react to the posttest in a more relaxed manner (initial testing), increased ability to test and measure on the part of the testers (instrumentation). (Regression toward the mean is not a factor because pretest scores were low to begin with and be-

cause participants were not specifically chosen on the basis of this pretest scores.) Furthermore, there may have been a Hawthorne effect because the participants knew they were taking part in a study, as well as an experimenter effect because testers knew the purpose of the test and data were recorded by hand. In addition, these participants may have derived physical benefit from simply attending the sessions; that is, they may ordinarily spend their days watching television and now were walking to the training facility and moving more during training. Moreover, increased group cohesiveness itself may have been beneficial. Without self-focus, they could have had less opportunity to focus on minor aches and pains and/or to feel lonely. Finally, after-training snacks may have provided added social benefit beyond what may have been provided by training.

14. Volunteer participants had to be randomly assigned (or first matched on pretest scores and then assigned) to experimental and control groups. The control group must meet, as would experimental participants, the same number of times at the same times and engage in some neutral activity that does not include the elements of Tai Chi.

CHAPTER 10

1. Dyspnea often accompanies chronic obstructive pulmonary disease, but no medication is available specifically to relieve the condition. Moreover, dyspnea and anxiety are associated. Music is a possible alternate treatment; it is known to reduce anxiety. Earlier studies, however, have tested the effects of music in controlled settings and with a one-time test.

2. The study sought to determine whether music is a feasible intervention for patients living at home who experience anxiety and dyspnea. It also attempted to determine the effects of music intervention on dyspnea and anxiety for such patients.

3. They were volunteers who were part of a support group. Of the 25, 1 dropped out because of lack of interest.

4. Possibly. Although each participant serves as his or her own control, if something was learned in the support group that affects relaxation, it could pose as an alternate explanation of results.

5. They were approximately 69 years old, English-speaking, and with some high school education. More than half were female and lived with their families. Although most did not use oxygen, more than half had suffered from emphysema for about 14 years, and all had weekly bouts of dyspnea. All used some respiratory drug.

6. Extent of dyspnea was measured by the Visual Analogue Dyspnea Scale (vertical), a rating scale from 0 (*no shortness of breath*) to 10. State anxiety was measured by four randomly selected items from the Spielberger State Anxiety Scale. Each item is scored from 1 (*not at all*) to 4. A Music Use and Preference Questionnaire determined the participants' use of music and whether it had an effect on them. A music diary was used to record the participants' use of music whenever they had difficulty

breathing, to rate the dyspnea before and after listening to the music, to record length of time they listened, and to specify whether they had used a puffer or inhaler. Finally, a Music Effectiveness Questionnaire determined whether participants used the music tapes and their effects.

7. Yes, the dyspnea and state anxiety tests are well-established tests.

8. During the initial home visit, the participant signed a consent form, was measured for dyspnea and anxiety, and was left with a master tape of three types of music. Demographic information also was collected. At Time 2 (1 week later), dyspnea and anxiety were measured before the participants listened to the preferred music tape (with earphones, while seated), which lasted 20 minutes, and then were posttested. They were instructed on how to listen to the music and encouraged to do so whenever they experienced dyspnea. At Time 3 (3 weeks later), participants were posttested again and allowed to keep the tape.

9. No, both tests were presented in random order.

10. Yes. Nothing is said about the home visitor being a research assistant. The visitor probably was one of the authors, all of whom (as described in their brief biographies) are interested in music as a therapeutic intervention. Unintentional cues could shift results in the anticipated direction. On the other hand, the visitor probably established rapport with the participant. This could have the opposite effect of reducing anxiety and dyspnea and reduce pretest-posttest differences.

11. Participants were part of a support group, and any anxiety-reducing technique they learned could reduce pretest anxiety.

12. Most reported listening to music daily or every other day for relaxation; to help them sleep; or when they were alone, driving, or had nothing else to do.

13. No. None reported having listened to music when dyspneic.

14. According to diary entries, 20 of the 24 participants reported listening to music when they were dyspneic. On the average, this was 18.37 times for 25.2 minutes during the 5-week period.

15. We don't know, because typical use of an inhaler was not reported.

16. Although level of dyspnea was relatively low before the use of music (mean rating was 31.1 on a scale of 0 to 100), there was a significant reduction in ratings after the use of music.

17. Mean ratings before and after music should have been established for each participant, especially because number of entries probably varied, and the t test should have been conducted on these mean ratings.

18. There were significant declines in both measures on the posttest, but pretest ratings were rather low for anxiety (mean of 7.75 out of 16), and posttest ratings were a bit lower (mean of 6.38). Likewise, pretest VADS ratings yielded a mean of 2.83 (mild shortness of breath), and posttest ratings yielded a mean of 1.88.

19. No significant declines over time were found for either measure.

20. Music reduced anxiety and dyspnea on a one-time basis but not over time. More significant results were not obtained because tests occurred when dyspnea was relatively low to begin with. Moreover, participants did not use the music as regularly or frequently as they had reported in their diaries.

21. Yes and no. Differences were found when anxiety and dyspnea ratings were low to begin with, and the authors noted some factors that prevented more significant results from emerging. The authors' expectancy, however, might have reduced both measures by their attempts to put the participants at ease. Moreover, participants also were sitting comfortably, and this alone could have produced the difference. Without a control group or a control condition, the factor is hard to rule out. By the same token, one doesn't stand to hear music to relax, and sitting comfortably may be a component of the music's effect.

22. First, participants were part of a support group and might have learned some other techniques to help reduce anxiety or even dyspnea. Ideally, the participants could have been randomly selected from various patient lists of lung specialists. Second, they should have been measured on trait as well as state anxiety. People whose trait anxiety is low are not as likely to have highly elevated state anxiety levels when dyspneic (we still don't know which comes first). Third, the tester should be naive with respect to the hypothesis. Because testers can catch on to the purpose of a study conducted over time, different, equally competent testers should be used. Fourth, the same dyspnea rating scale should be used throughout. Participants might learn to make more subtle distinctions than they would when they are switched from a rating scale of 0 to 10 to one that is an arbitrary 0 to 100. Fifth, participants could be monitored by regular telephone calls to encourage them to follow instructions. Along with this, fill-in charts might be easier to keep than the diary. Sixth, the study time could be ex-

tended. This might increase attrition, but demographic information will assess whether the loss is selective. Seventh, control conditions should be interspersed with experimental conditions to determine the extent to which just sitting quietly reduces anxiety and dypsnea. Finally, more music tapes could be made available to reduce the chances that the participants will listen to other music. This is not necessary, however; the intent to see whether any kind of music is beneficial.

(THERE ARE NO ANSWERS FOR CHAPTER 11)

CHAPTER 12

1. Earlier studies on assessment of infant pain revealed that nurses who were provided with background information of the infant in the videotape used that information in assessing the infant's pain. Nurses who viewed only restricted videotapes, without information, could not agree on their assessments. This disagreement may have been due to the brevity of the videotape, the fact that the infant was shown alone, lack of background information, lack of a view of the infant's response to comfort. Important factors in assessment are presumed to be background information and a view of the infant's response to comfort. Infant age may be another important factor for pain assessment. Older infants in pain behave differently from younger infants, and nurses have found it easier to assess pain in older infants, whereas pain in younger infants may be underrated. It appears that age would be a more important factor in assessing pain of a videotaped infant than would be back-

ground information accompanying the videotape.

2. The study attempted to answer three questions regarding superiority of a videotape plus background information versus the videotape alone in assessing infant pain, the added effect of degree of pain on the differences in assessment, and the influence of age of the infant on assessment.

3. Level of infant pain assessed by the participant nurses was the dependent variable. Three manipulated variables were introduced: presence or absence of background information, age of the infant, and the level of pain as rated by experts.

4. Twenty-four White female nurses who viewed the video with background information were part of a previous study that took place in 1993. Forty mainly White female nurses were measured in 1997 and only viewed the video. Both groups were equivalent in years of education and pediatric nursing experience.

5. No. They are equivalent with respect to two important variables that might affect assessment, but they differ with respect to the 4 years of advances in medication and treatment that the 40 nurses might have been exposed to as well as personality and other differences that usually are neutralized by random assignment.

6. No. They are equivalent with respect to use of background information with the other two variables within their group but not across groups, because they were not randomly assigned to the background versus no-background conditions.

7. A panel of five experts rated 150 tapes of infants in four age ranges for levels of pain, using a 4-point scale. Videotapes were selected if four out of five experts agreed on the ratings. In the end, there were five videotapes in each combination of age and level of pain. They included infants who had received a medical diagnosis with or without subsequent surgery. Infants were videotaped while quiet, crying, receiving routine nursing care, and being comforted.

8. Nurses who claimed to be experts with infants of a particular age group rated videotapes for that age group. The remaining nurses presumably were randomly assigned to the remaining age levels (they were, I learned by personal communication). Each nurse rated infants on 20 videotapes, 5 at each pain level. Presumably these were randomized (they were; personal communication). Twenty-four nurses (six at each level) had background information available, and 40 nurses (10 at each age level) did not have this information available.

9. Although it is stated that the same videotapes were used for both groups, there is no such clarity about the medical facility from which the nurses came. (They came from the same hospital; personal communication.) Moreover, conditions under which testing took place is not described, so there is no way to assess its effect. (Through personal communication, I learned that *all* testing was conducted in the same room of the same facility.)

10. Data on mean ratings for each level of pain were analyzed by a 2 (video+background/no video) × 4 (age levels) × 4 (pain

levels) analysis of variance with repeated measures on the last factor.

11. The test for circularity revealed that this assumption was not met, and the degrees of freedom for factors involving repeated measures were adjusted. Variances were homogeneous, and no correction was necessary.

12. Pain assessment differed as a function of background information, with lower pain ratings by nurses without that information; pain ratings did not vary with age of infants; but pain ratings did vary with amount of pain level as rated by the experts: lowest with the lowest rating, then significantly higher with mild, then moderate, and then severe pain.

13. Rated level of pain for levels of expert pain assessment (EAP) depended on age of the infants. Infants in the mild-level category who were 10 to 12 months old were rated as being in the lowest levels of pain, whereas infants of the same age in the moderate-level category were rated as being in the most pain when compared to younger infants. Rated level of pain also was dependent on the group to which the nurses belonged. These statements are in accord with the interactions.

    Nurses in the video-only group rated infants 0 to 3 months of age as having lower pain at all pain levels, compared with older infants, and nurses in the video + background group rated 0- to 3-month-old infants in the mild pain category as being in more pain than other age groups. These statements refer to a triple interaction, which was not significant.

14. $SS_{int} = 16(0.219) = 3.504; MS_{int} = 3.504/(4-1)(4-1) = 0.3893$
    $F = 4.1 = 0.3893/MS_e; MS_e = 0.3893/4.1 = 0.095$
    $SS_{pain} = 16(0.9357) = 14.955; MS_{pain} = 14.955/4 - 1 = 4.985$
    $F = MS_{pain}/MS_e = 4.985/0.095 = 52.474, p < .001$, which was expected because df for the error term is higher.

15. $SS_{gxp} = 6(0.623) + 10(0.0245) = 3.983; MS_{gxp} = 3.983/(4-1)(2-1) = 1.328; F = 1.328/.0950 = 13.975, p < .001.$

16. Ratings of pain by nurses who viewed only a video were lower than by nurses who had additional background information about the infants. The video-only group's lower ratings of the 0- to 3-month-old infants suggest more difficulty in assessing pain of such young infants. There was less difficulty in assessing pain of older infants. The differences in years of data collection are unlikely due to differences in clinical practice 4 years later. Both groups viewed the same tapes, were equivalent in experience and education, and engaged in practices that have not changed.

17. The conclusions are justified with one exception: There was no basis for concluding that the video-only group had more difficulty rating pain of the 0- to 3-month-old infants. The group by age and triple interactions were not significant. But one could conclude that this group received the lowest ratings by all nurses; the age by pain level was significant, and the 0- to 3-month-old group did receive the lowest overall ratings. Furthermore, if the 4-year time span of the study made a difference, it would have favored the video-only group, and they were less ac-

curate in their assessments. Moreover, it was learned (personal communication) that nurses came from the same facility, were randomly assigned to the age levels when they expressed no specialty, viewed the videos in random order, and were tested in the same facility and same room. Finally, years of experience and education were the most important contributory variables, and groups were equivalent on these.

Glossary

Additive effects: The combined effects of independent variables in a factorial study in which the effect of one variable increases (or decreases) the effect of the second variable to the same extent at each level of the second variable.

Analysis of covariance: A statistical procedure to effect statistical control for nonequivalence by partialling out a potentially contaminating variable and perform an analysis of variance on remaining variability due to treatment and random error.

Analysis of variance: A statistical test that partitions total variability of all scores around the grand mean into at least two components, between groups (which reflects treatment effects) and within groups (which reflects random error). To the extent that treatment was effective, the ratio between the two sources will be significantly greater than 1.00.

Backward elimination: A stepwise multiple regression analysis in which all variables are added to the equation and those least correlated with the criterion are progressively removed until only the remaining variables are correlated with the criterion.

Beta weight: Standardized regression coefficient, β, in multiple regression that is based on Z-scores rather than raw scores. This conversion allows all beta weights to be directly compared for relative contribution of their independent variables in prediction of the criterion variable.

Case study: An intensive qualitative investigation of a single individual or group of individuals.

Chi-square test: A statistical test that estimates the probability that obtained frequencies of occurrence in various categories differ to the extent that they do from those expected by chance.

Circularity: A statistical assumption in within-group designs that variances of all possible treatment-level differences are the same. Violation increases the probability of a Type I error.

Coefficient of determination: A measure, r^2, of the percentage of shared ("explained") variance by two variables or percentage of variability in one that is accounted for by the other variable.

Cohorts: Groups of individuals who are similar in age or group membership and, presumably, experiences.

Compensatory equalization: A threat to internal validity in which some treatment is administered to a control group and reduces the treatment effects between experimental and control groups.

Compensatory rivalry: A threat to internal validity in which a control group rivals in performance with the experimental group, which reduces treatment effects between experimental and control groups.

Communality: The sum of squared factor loadings for a variable. It indicates percentage of variability of that variable's scores accounted for by all the factors.

Confound: A variable or variables in an experiment whose effects are tied to an independent variable in such a way that they can just as easily account for the results.

Construct validity: The extent to which a test measures the unobservable characteristic that it was intended to measure.

Content validity: The extent to which test items measure the intended characteristics.

Contingency test: A chi-square test that compares obtained and expected frequencies for two or more different categories to determine whether the categories are independent or related to each other.

Controlled observation: Experimental situations in which data are gathered under precise conditions that minimize, eliminate, or counteract the effects of extraneous variables.

Convenience sample: A nonrepresentative sample whose members were chosen because they were available and accessible.

Correlation coefficient: A numerical value ranging from 0 to ±1.00 that describes the direction and extent of relationship between two variables.

Counterbalancing: A method of presenting the various levels of an independent variable to the same participants in such a way that each level appears at each stage of practice an equal number of times to neutralize the effects of practice and fatigue.

Criterion validity: The extent to which test scores correlate with (concurrent) or predict (predictive) a behavior measured by a test.

Criterion variable: The dependent variable in a regression analysis that is predicted.

Cronbach's alpha: A method of measuring reliability by determining the extent to which there is consistency in responding among testees to test items whose responses are a range of numbers that might reflect degree of agreement.

Dependent variable: In an experiment, this is the aspect of behavior measured after the introduction of the independent variable. This is the ultimate effect of that introduction.

Diffusion of treatment: A threat to internal validity in which treatment effects unintentionally spread to a control group and reduce the treatment effects between the experimental and control groups.

Discriminant analysis: A method of differentiating groups on the basis of a linear combination of continuous predictor variables. It functions to determine the variables that differentiate the groups, how well they differentiate, and which variables are the most powerful differentiators. Or the net result of analysis can serve to place unknown cases into their most likely groups.

Discriminant function: In discriminant analysis, this is the weighted sum of independent predictor scores, such that each function maximizes group differences.

Dummy code: The assignment of a numerical value to a categorical variable included in a regression analysis.

Dunnett test: A post hoc test for testing the significance of differences between experimental and control means.

Eigenvalue: The sum of squared factor loadings for a factor, whose value when divided by the number of variables indicates the percentage of total variability accounted for by a factor and whose value indicates the average number of variables accounted for by that factor.

Ethnographic analysis: A description of a social unit that re-creates shared feelings, beliefs, actions, and knowledge of some experience or event to arrive at the perception and meaning of that event to the group.

Equivalence reliability: A method of establishing reliability by administering alternate or equivalent forms of a test to the same group of individuals.

Experimenter expectancy: A threat to internal validity in which the research expectations of an experimenter unintentionally affect performance of participants in the direction of the expectancy.

Factor analysis: The analysis of correlated variables that reduces them to a smaller number of independent (or correlated) hypothetical characteristics underlying the correlation.

Factor loading: The correlation coefficient of the relationship between a factor score and a variable's Z-score. The higher the correlation, the more that factor accounts for or underlies that variable.

Factorial study: An experiment that introduces at least two different qualitative independent variables.

Familywise Type I error: The probability of mistakenly declaring a means difference to be significant when a set of comparisons is made.

Fixed-effect model: An analysis of variance statistical model that applies to independent variables whose levels were deliberately selected and whose major assumption is that each level has the same effect on all participants exposed to it now and in replicated studies but whose effects only generalize for these levels.

Goodness of fit: A chi-square test that compares obtained and expected frequencies for categories that vary on a single dimension.

Hawthorne effect: A threat to internal validity in which participants' performance improves (usually) because of their participation in an experiment rather than because of treatment.

Hierarchical analysis: A multiple regression analysis in which each variable is entered in the regression equation on some a priori basis.

History: A threat to internal validity, mainly in pretest-posttest situations, in which some intervening event may account for posttest performance.

Homoscedasticity: A description of the relationship between two variables such that the extent of relationship is equally strong for all values of the independent (X) variable.

Independent variable: In an experiment, this is the variable specifically introduced or manipulated (presented at one or two levels) with the intention of producing a change in performance. It is the intended ultimate cause of the behavior.

Initial testing: A threat to internal validity in pretest-posttest studies in which experience with the pretest can just as easily account for posttest performance.

Instrumentation: A threat to internal validity, mainly in pretest-posttest studies, in which a change in the measuring instrument or assessor from pre- to posttest can just as easily account for the results.

Interaction effects: The combined effects of independent variables in a factorial study such that the effect of one variable depends on the level of the second variable.

Internal consistency: The extent to which items within a test measure some characteristic consistently.

Internal validity: The extent to which justifiable conclusions can be drawn from the results of a study.

Interrater agreement: A measure of the percentage of agreement between two or more observers of the same behavior.

Interrater reliability: The correlation between ratings on the same behavior made by two or more independent observers.

Interrupted times-series study: A form of quasi-experimental study in which the same group of participants is repeatedly measured before and after an intervention.

Kaiser criterion: A basis for deciding which factors should be retained in the final factor analysis. This criterion retains those factors with eigenvalues of at least 1.00.

Kendall's tau: A statistic that describes extent of agreement between pairs of ranks, the number of times pairs of ranks agree and disagree relative to the number of ranks.

Kuder-Richardson: A method of establishing reliability for tests whose items can be scored on a dichotomy (right or wrong, pass or fail). It is a measure of the extent to which the participants responded appropriately to each item.

Main effect: Unique, average effect of the different independent variables in a factorial study.

Matching: A method of pairing individuals with identical pretest scores (or other scores correlated with the dependent variables) or arriving at groups with similar means and variances for some pretest measure to ensure that groups are initially equivalent with respect to the dependent variable.

Maturation: A threat to internal validity, mainly in pretest-posttest situations, in which a change within the participants following the pretest can just as easily account for the results.

Mixed-effect model: An analysis of variance statistical model that applies to independent variables, some of which have levels that are specifically selected and others that have levels that are a random sample of all possible levels.

Multicollinearity: In multiple regression analysis, this is the high correlation between two predictors or between a predictor and some linear combination of other predictors.

Multiple *R*: The correlation between a criterion variable and independent predictor variables. Its squared value is the percentage of shared variance between the criterion and predictors.

Multiple regression analysis: The statistical procedure that leads to prediction of a criterion variable on the basis of more than one predictor independent variable.

Multiple time-series study: A quasi-experimental study in which two intact groups are repeatedly measured, one with an intervention at some point in the series and another without the intervention.

Narrative analysis: A qualitative method of understanding a life event by the experiencer that includes the impact of the event on the individual, events leading up to it, and its actual or potential effect on the narrator, determined in part by how the story is told in the way that it is.

Negative relationship: A relationship between variables that covary in opposite directions.

Newman-Keuls test: One of the least conservative post hoc tests, it determines the significance of differences between all possible pairs of means.

Nonequivalent control group design: A quasi-experimental study that uses intact experimental and control groups.

Nonequivalent pretest-posttest control group study: A quasi-experimental study in which intact experimental and control groups are pretested and then posttested after the experimental intervention.

Nonprobability sample: A sample that is not representative of the population.

Oblique rotation: A mathematical procedure in factor analysis of rotating one axis (representing one factor) at a time, to maximize factor loadings of variables, which results in correlated factors.

Partial correlation: The correlation between two variables with the effects of a third variable removed from both, also called a first-order correlation.

Pearson's *r*: A correlation coefficient that describes the direction and strength of a linear, straight-line relationship between two variables.

Placebo treatment: A control procedure in an experiment that consists of all nonessential elements of treatment (the independent variable).

Planned comparisons: The statistical analysis of experimental data in which mean comparisons were planned prior to the experiment because they were of particular interest to the experimenter.

Positive relationship: A relationship between two variables that covary in the same direction.

Post hoc tests: Statistical tests to determine which means differ after a significant *F* ratio has been found.

Posttest-only nonequivalent control group study: A quasi-experimental study with intact experimental and control groups, both of which are only

posttested after the experimental intervention.

Predictor variable: The independent variable in a regression analysis that predicts the dependent variable.

Principal axis factor analysis: Factor analysis that concentrates on extracting factors that account for the greatest percentage of common variance (excludes unique variance) of all data.

Principal components: A method of factor analysis that yields a number of factors that account for the largest percentage of variability of all the data.

Probability sample: A representative sample from a population in which all members had a certain probability of being selected.

Quasi-experimental studies: Studies that use intact groups of participants instead of groups formed by random assignment of participants.

Quota sample: A nonrepresentative sample with a particular characteristic whose members were selected from a particular location in the same proportion that exists in the population.

Random assignment: A method of assigning participants to different groups without bias so that groups can be considered initially equivalent with respect to the dependent variable and all extraneous variables that could affect performance.

Random-effects model: An analysis of variance statistical model that applies to independent variables whose levels represent a random sample of all possible levels, whose effects vary from one occasion to the next but generalize to the whole population of levels.

Regression analysis: The prediction of a continuous characteristic on the basis of a continuous or noncontinuous, categorical independent variable, or a description of the role of the independent variable in the dependent variable.

Regression coefficient: In multiple regression, this statistic, designated *b*, reflects the average amount of change in the criterion variable for each unit of change in an independent variable when the effects of remaining independent variables are statistically controlled (partialled out).

Regression toward the mean: A threat to internal validity, mainly in pretest-posttest studies, in which extreme performance on a pretest is followed by a predicted shift in posttest performance, and this can just as easily account for results.

Reliability: A state of consistency or repeatability that applies to empirical research and to its measuring instruments, including standardized tests. Reliable instruments yield accurate measures. Reliable tests yield scores that are repeatable and are in the same relative standing on more than one occasion.

Resentful demoralization: A threat to internal validity in which control group performance declines because of its known lack of treatment. This increases treatment effects between experimental and control groups.

Sample frame: The population that has a chance of being selected and from which members are chosen.

Scheffé test: The most conservative post hoc test, which guards against a Type I error by increasing the critical *F* value.

Scree test: A graphical method of deciding which factors to retain in the final factor analysis. In a plot of eigenvalues with their ordinal positions, the cutoff is the point at which the curve levels off because eigenvalues in later positions are of about the same value.

Selection bias: A threat to internal validity in which particular individuals are selected for a study, whose particular characteristics can just as easily account for the results.

Selective loss: Also known as mortality or attrition, this is a threat to internal validity because of the loss of participants with particular characteristics, leaving remaining participants with a characteristic that can just as easily account for results.

Single classification study: An experiment in which only a single kind of independent variable is introduced that is varied along the one dimension.

Spearman rank correlation coefficient: A statistic that describes the direction and extent of relationship, correlation, or agreement between pairs of actual or imposed ranks.

Split-half reliability: Also known as inter-item reliability, this is a method of establishing reliability by comparing scores on the first half of a test with those of the second half or comparing scores on even-numbered items with those of odd-numbered items.

Spurious correlations: Under- or over-estimation of relationships between two variables due to a small range of X values (attenuation, underestimation), effects of a common third uncontrolled variable (overestimation), or use of a more heterogeneous group of participants than exists in the population (overestimation).

Stepwise multiple regression: The progressive addition of predictor variables most highly correlated with the criterion to the regression equation until the last addition does not appreciably increase the value of R^2.

Stratified sample: A representative sample chosen from various segments of the population in the same proportion as exists in each segment.

Surveys: Methods of gathering data from a representative sample to assess likes or dislikes (attitude survey) or test specific hypotheses (research survey) in such a way that results generalize to the population.

Test-retest reliability: A method of establishing reliability by administering a test to the same group of individuals on two occasions. Scores should be highly correlated with each other if the test is reliable.

Tukey test: A moderately conservative post hoc test for testing the significance of differences between all possible pairs of means.

Type I error: A wrong statistical conclusion in which the null hypothesis is rejected and a difference is called significant when the null hypothesis of no difference was true.

Type II error: A wrong statistical conclusion in which the null hypothesis of no difference is retained when the null hypothesis was false and a difference does exist.

Validity: A state of appropriateness that applies to the conclusions reached, based on the procedures used to arrive at them, as well as procedures themselves, based on a manipulation or test.

Varimax rotation: A mathematical procedure in factor analysis of rotating factor axes together that results in a redistribution of factor loadings of variables such that variance of each factor is maximized. Some variables now have higher loadings on one factor, and others have higher loadings on another factor, and the factors are uncorrelated.

Zero-order correlation: A correlation coefficient between two variables that does not control for effects of any other variable.

Author Index

Subject Index

About the Author

Ellen R. Girden received her bachelor's degree from Brooklyn College (1956), with a major in biology and minors in education and psychology. She earned her master's degree in general psychology (1958), also from Brooklyn College, and studied at Northwestern University for the doctorate in physiological psychology (1962). For 2 years, she taught at Hobart and William Smith Colleges in Geneva, New York, where she completed her dissertation. In 1963, she joined the faculty of Yeshiva University in Manhattan, New York. After a joint appointment with the graduate and undergraduate schools (Stern College for Women), she was able to confine her teaching to the female undergraduates and reached the professional rank of Associate Professor. During these years, she conducted studies related to the physiological basis of fear-motivated behavior of rats, time estimation by students, and a series on the effects of crowding and litter size on various behaviors of rats.

In 1977, she married and moved to Florida. A year later, she was one of the original faculty of the School of Professional Psychology of Florida, teaching courses in research design, statistics, learning, and the history of psychology. In 1981, the School merged with Nova University. Within a few years, she was promoted to Professor and focused on research design and intermediate and advanced statistics. She remained in that position until 1993, when she retired. She now devotes her time to writing.

Besides research, she supervised dissertation projects, coauthored a chapter with her husband, and wrote a monograph for Sage on repeated measures analysis of variance.